COUNTRY
BRANCH LINE

DEDICATION
In memory of
A. E. SMITH

Photo: H. C. Casserley

COUNTRY BRANCH LINE

An Intimate Portrait of the Watlington Branch

VOLUME ONE

THE STORY OF THE LINE
from 1872 to 1961

PAUL KARAU & CHRIS TURNER

ISBN 1 874103 43 7

Designed by Paul Karau
Printed by Amadeus Press Ltd., Huddersfield

Published by
WILD SWAN PUBLICATIONS LTD.
1-3 Hagbourne Road, Didcot, Oxon,
OX11 8DP

CONTENTS

APPENDICES

Photo: H. C. Casserley

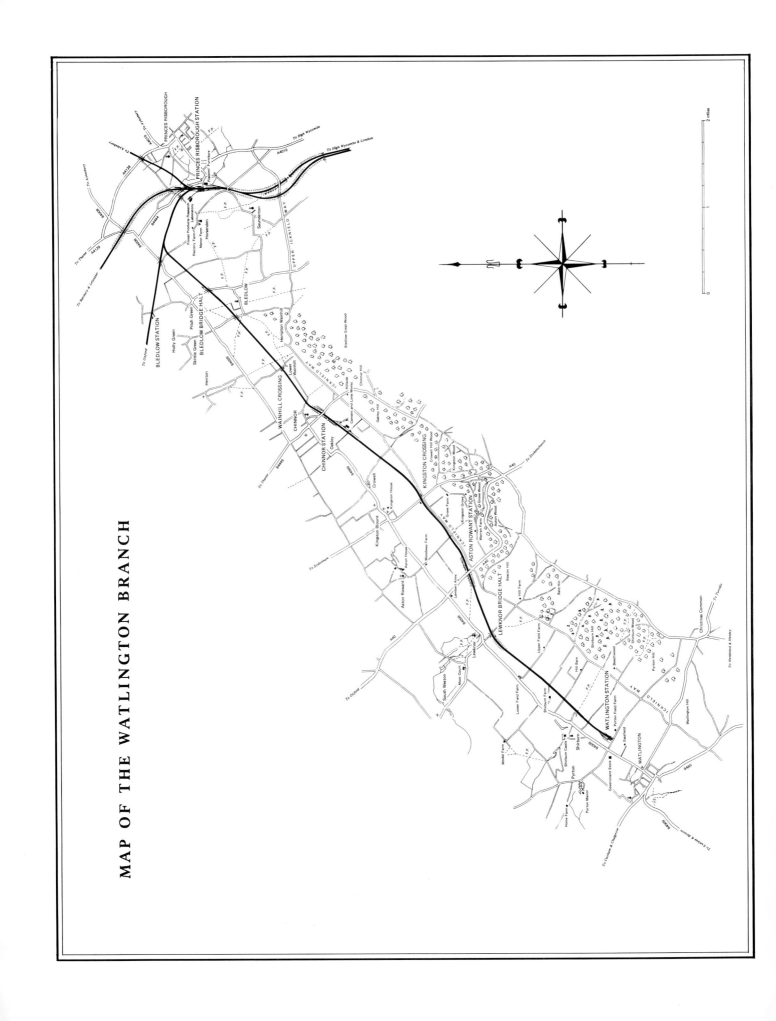

MAP OF THE WATLINGTON BRANCH

INTRODUCTION

WHEN I first started cycling out to Watlington to visit the remains of the station over thirty years ago, I was still in my early teens. Steam had already disappeared from my home station at Henley and the familiar worn streets of my 1950s childhood were changing fast or being razed to the ground in the 1960s mania for modernisation. It was all very disturbing.

For the time being at least, the quiet town of Watlington seemed overlooked, and the almost magical network of country lanes I used to reach it were timeless. As I explored the abandoned station, I examined every inch of the site, trying to picture what it had all been like in happier times when it was still needed by the community.

The derelict buildings all looked so sad and, as the broken glass crunched under my feet, I felt despondent – I had been born too late to see it in all its glory but I wanted to find out more. I had no idea that in time I would find the photographs I was looking for and track down many of the people who knew it, let alone realise how kind and helpful they would be. Of course, some of the characters had died before I set foot in Watlington, but they live on in people's memories and consequently have become so familiar to me that I now almost feel that I knew them.

Reg Pocock, who served as station master at Watlington from 1924 to 1946, is one of the more prominent characters in the story which follows. In addition to his position on the railway, he was a family man and a prominent member of the local community and the church. His many activities are detailed elsewhere in these pages, but, at a time when life is changing more rapidly than ever before, I like to reflect on the simpler past and think of him taking part in the traditions of pre-war life. At that time, Reg went to church twice every Sunday, and I can easily imagine him looking smart in a dark suit and the wing collars he always wore, standing with his fellow townsmen in the softly lit hallowed interior of St Leonard's with his son Cecil and daughter Gwen at his side. His wife Beatrice only accompanied him to Evensong because on Sunday mornings she stayed behind at their home in Gorwell preparing the Sunday lunch. Towards the end of the service Reg would step into the aisle and work his way down the church, passing the collection bag along each of the pews while the congregation sang a traditional hymn.

While all this was going on, another Sunday morning ritual was taking place amidst the fields across the other side of town where, at the station, the two porters, Frank Saunders and Joe Nicholson, were cleaning the auto-trailer. They went in for a couple of hours every Sunday to wash down the bodywork and sweep out the interior. They were not necessarily the only ones there, because the firemen, Peter Robinson, George Nicholson and Maldwyn Jones, often took it in turns to earn overtime, loading ashes into an empty coal wagon or unloading stock coal, usually working in pairs and enjoying each other's company.

Although I never met Reg Pocock, he is one of those figures who has become so familiar through our researches that I had no difficulty in visualising the scene described when, with the sound of the church organ in my head, I stood at the foot of his grave in Watlington, where a marble memorial records him simply as 'Church Warden of this Parish and Secretary of the Church Council for 25 years'.

It was a beautiful summer's morning, and while I searched for inscriptions, stepping carefully through the long shadowy grass concealing even the narrow paths between the graves, a quiet and unassuming old gentleman had asked if he could help. When I told him I was searching for Reg Pocock's grave, he replied quite spontaneously "The station master?", then pointed to the area I wanted. This simple gesture somehow encapsulated my experience of the intimate community. Reg had retired from his position as station master in 1946, died in 1953, and the railway closed to passengers in 1957, yet in the summer of 1998 the first person to speak to me that day not only knew him, but instantly recalled him as station master. It was heartwarming to find that although the churchyard looked so sadly neglected, for the time being at least, its inhabitants are certainly not forgotten.

This book sets out not only to record the modest history of this insignificant railway backwater, but to convey something of everyday life along a country branch line. This study would certainly never have been so comprehensive had I not enlisted the help of Chris Turner some 12 years ago. He not only caught on to the essential need to track down more former staff and townspeople, but became completely engrossed in the spirit of the Watlington branch. Never hesitant to follow the most unlikely lead, Chris managed to find some of our most valuable interviewees and, as time went by, we continually kept each other going with discoveries and conclusions. I couldn't have wished for a better, more willing and dedicated co-author.

We have been privileged to get very close to a small corner of a lost age, and it is our sincerest wish that something of the fellowship, warmth and general good nature amongst the community we have studied lives on in these pages.

Paul Karau

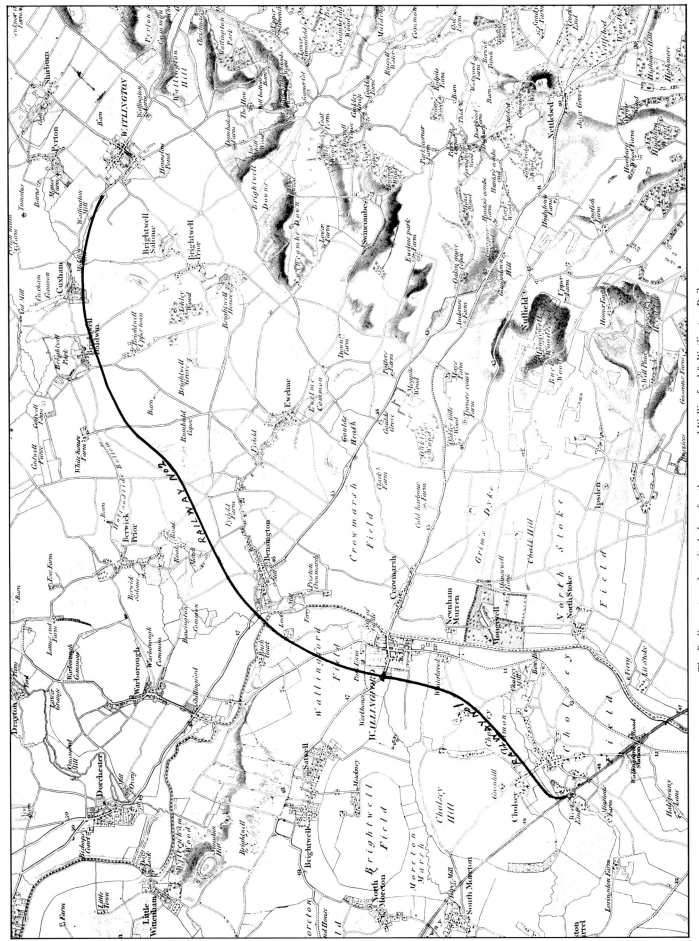

The Parliamentary deposited plans for the proposed Wallingford & Watlington Railway.

CHAPTER ONE
FALSE HOPES

THE entry for Watlington in the *Parliamentary Gazeteer* for 1843–4 says:

'The town is situated about half a mile from the Icknield Street, and between the lines of the two roads from London to Oxford. It is large but irregularly built; the streets are narrow and the houses are rather mean. There is a curious market house in the centre, at the junction of four ways (Carfax), built, in 1644, by Thomas Stonor Esq., who founded the Grammar School. A market has been held here since the reign of Richard I, on Saturday. Fairs for cattle are held on April 5th and the Saturday before October 10th; on the latter day there is also a statute fair for the hiring of servants . . . The seat of Col. Tilson contains about 300 acres, in which all the various features of the Chiltern Heights are blended; the woods contain some of the finest beech trees in the county.'

The Victoria County History points out that compared with the markets of Henley, High Wycombe or Thame, Watlington's market was 'unimportant'. It suggests 'lack of good communications more than anything else probably prevented Watlington from keeping up with its rivals, particularly after the development of new routes to London through Stokenchurch and Henley'. The nearest navigable water was 6 miles away at Benson, and *Paterson's Roads*, published in 1822, describes the roads around Watlington as 'probably the worst in the country'. Whilst this is by no means a unique claim, it was undeniably 'a circumstance fatally adverse to the prosperity of the place'. Although Watlington was not on a through route to London, by 1830 a post coach was advertised as leaving the Red Lion at 8.0 a.m. and midday on alternate weekdays and running to Stokenchurch Hill where, presumably, passengers and mail were transferred to other coaches for the onward journey to London.

The Victoria history says Watlington flourished mainly as a local centre, the 1851 census recording shopkeepers, butchers, victuallers, two saddlers, a builder and wheelwright, a millwright, cooper, thatcher, three blacksmiths, an iron founder, a tinman and brazier, five master shoe and boot makers, and about 200 agricultural labourers. Farming was mixed, with good crops of wheat and barley. The total population was 1,884.

Against this background, it is hardly surprising that many of the local people felt it would be of great benefit to link the town to the growing railway system which was spreading tentacles all over the country. The main roads to London might have missed Watlington but a railway might bring the industry and prosperity hitherto lacking in this quiet backwater.

The first scheme to link Watlington with the GWR main line came about in 1861. The proposed railway was to stem from a junction with the GWR at Cholsey and run through Wallingford, Benson, Watlington, Shirburn, Chinnor and Bledlow to join the 'Wycombe Extension to Aylesbury' at Princes Risborough. Although this proposal was apparently soon dropped, local interest was aroused the following June by the circulation of a plan of the scheme and it was thought that half the capital required to build the line would be raised in Wallingford. Little difficulty was anticipated in obtaining the land and the *Reading Mercury* was of the opinion that the line would soon be commenced and that some 'principal landed proprietors' had expressed their willingness to aid the project.

Application was made to the 1863 session of Parliament for authorisation to construct the line as far as Wallingford, but by

February the scheme had been withdrawn to enable what was described as 'a more extended one' to be introduced 'with the view of accommodating the whole of the district'.

The *Thame Gazette* of 3rd November 1863 carried the following report:

THE PROPOSED WALLINGFORD AND WATLINGTON RAILWAY — The surveys of this line, proposed to be constructed with the view of accommodating Wallingford, Watlington, Benson, Ewelme, Berrick, Newington, Chalgrove, Shillingford, Warborough, Dorchester, Brightwell, Cuxham and the adjacent district, are being proceeded with, to enable an application to be made to Parliament in the ensuing Session. It is pretty certain that the project will receive a fair amount of support in Wallingford, and we hope that the landowners, through whose property the line will be carried, will lend the movement their best support. We believe the solicitors, Messrs. Walker and Manning and Walker, Westminster, are prepared to explain the details of the matter and that a public meeting will shortly be held for that purpose. We trust that the public will take the matter up in earnest. If the new line be constructed (and the fact of a mail-cart being driven over the ground twice a day, shows that the route could be used to advantage), we believe the share-holders would receive a good percentage on their outlay. It would increase the market. It would improve the trade of the town, by bringing into it people who would have easy access from the neighbourhood of the line; whilst tradesmen, by getting their goods delivered quicker, and at a cheaper rate, would be enabled to do business on the same terms that rule the Reading and Oxford markets. Householders would find the advantage by getting their coals at least 3s. per ton cheaper, and we should all, when travelling, be saved the tedious ride to and from Wallingford Road Station.

Revised plans were ready by the end of 1863 and submitted for the following session of Parliament. The proposed railway was described as two lines, Railway No. 1 commencing from a junction with the main line at Cholsey, some 48½ miles from Paddington, heading north-eastwards across open countryside to Wallingford and terminating at the turnpike road leading out of the town towards Wantage about 130 yards to the west of the Cross Keys public house.

Railway No. 2 was a continuation across the turnpike, over the Thames and on through Benson, terminating on the outskirts of Watlington in Upper Moor Meadow, alongside the Oxford Road.

The Engineer of both schemes, James Burke, attended public meetings held at Watlington on Wednesday, 13th January, and Wallingford on Friday, 15th January, 1864, to 'consider the desirability' of the railway. The following account of the Watlington meeting appeared in the *Thame Gazette* for 19th January:

PROPOSED WALLINGFORD AND
WATLINGTON RAILWAY

A public meeting was held at the Hare and Hounds Inn, Watlington, on Wednesday last, to consider the desirability of supporting the proposed branch line from the Great Western Railway to Wallingford and Watlington. Hugh Hammersley, Esq., Chairman of Quarter Sessions, presided, and among those present were F. E. S. Viret, Esq., – Jones, Esq., Rev. G. Day, Messrs. A. Cooper, Cliffe, W. Hine, M. and R. Wiggins, Elliott, Costar, J. and W. Barnes, J. Spyer, W. G. Spyer, C. Lovelock, J. Dimmock, T. W. Hicks, &c., &c. Mr. Walker (of the firm of Manning and Walker, parliamentary agents, London),

Mr J. B. Burke, engineer, and Mr. E. Neighbour, of Wallingford, attended on behalf of the promoters.

The CHAIRMAN, in opening the meeting, remarked that it was needless now, unlike twenty or thirty years ago, to persuade people that a railway was a very useful thing. This was universally admitted, and it must be a very exceptional case where a railway was not beneficial. This neighbourhood, being so remote from such accommodation, was certainly in greater need of it than any other part of the district. (Applause.) If a person wished to go to London, the expense of a conveyance to the nearest station was greater than the whole railway fare, and the same was the case with getting a parcel, and with obtaining fuel and everything else. The only question therefore was, how they were to get a line, and he was sure the meeting would be glad to hear from the deputation present the fullest information with regard to the project. (Applause.)

Mr. BURKE observed that having been for several years connected with this district, and resided at Abingdon while making the branch to that town, he had been communicated with by several gentlemen of Wallingford on the desirability of a railway to that place, and an extension to Watlington. At their request he consulted with Mr. Furness, the contractor, and found that he was willing to construct the line if the country would subscribe one-third of the capital. It was evidently useless to make the line if it was not wanted, and while nowadays capital could always be raised for such an undertaking, it was important that a portion of it should be subscribed by the country, because it would give them an interest in throwing as much traffic on it as they could. Local support was therefore a very material element (Hear, hear) In reply to the Chairman and others, Mr. Burke explained that the cost of the line was estimated at 80,000*l.*, and that the country was asked to raise about 27,000*l.*, but if they could get some of the land at a rent-charge instead of purchase, the amount would be proportionately less. The distance from the Great Western to Wallingford would be 2½ miles, and there was no question that a sufficient sum being subscribed for this, so that it might be deemed an accomplished fact. From Wallingford to Watlington would be 6½ miles, and this part of the line would be rather more expensive than the former, so that the cost might be put down at 60,000*l.* He had stated 27,000*l.* as the proportion asked from the country, because they thought they ought to subscribe as much as this, but if the sum only fell a little short of this, the undertaking would of course be carried out. The contractor would take debentures for one-third of the capital, and the usual borrowing powers would be taken for another third, while the country was asked to subscribe the remainder.

The CHAIRMAN remarked that as to the purchase of the land, 200*l.* an acre was paid on the Thame and Oxford line.

Mr. BURKE said he presumed the sum varied very much in different places, and he did not think they ought to pay 200*l.* here.

Mr. VIRET remarked that in one case he knew 250*l.* had been paid by the Thame Company for land by no means as good as this.

Mr. BURKE observed that landowners must not expect as much as they could get elsewhere, but must act as they did in many other parts. He had bargained for land in Somersetshire on the Great Western, where the rent for grass land was £5 per acre, and the owners sold it for 60*l.*, because they wanted the railway.

Mr. VIRET said the depreciation of what was not sold must be taken into account, and some of his, for instance, would be very much injured.

Mr. BURKE remarked that if he, a stranger, were to negotiate, a landowner would probably say, "I must have a pretty good price for this;" but it was for them to get the land, and they must use their personal influence, and persuade gentlemen whose property was cut up, that it was not so. (Laughter.) If they represented that they wanted the railway, that the land formed part of their subscription, and that they were all interested in getting it as cheap as possible, they would no doubt be met in a liberal spirit by the landowners.

The CHAIRMAN – If a railway is desirable, it may be worth the whole of large proprietors to offer facilities.

Mr. W. BARNES asked if it was intended to stop at Watlington, or to carry on the line to Princes Risborough.

Mr. BURKE said their present intention was to terminate here, but if the country would find a third of the capital for an extension to Risborough, it could no doubt be effected in the same way.

Mr. BARNES expressed his opinion that Watlington would be a bad finish, and pointed out that a route to London by Risborough would be shorter and cheaper than by Wallingford.

Mr. BURKE replied that if it proved desirable hereafter, the extension would be made, but it formed no part of the present scheme. He might mention that he had been in communication with the Great Western, and that Company considered the project a very legitimate and proper extension of the railway system, and that if it was required by the country and was carried out, they would be willing to work the line with their own engines and carriages at a percentage of the receipts. Upon this arrangement, no matter whether the company was absolutely a paying one *per se* or not, the shareholders would be sure of some return. If, for instance, they worked and maintained it at 50 per cent. of the receipts, which was somewhere near the mark, half of what was earned on the line would be divided among the shareholders, so that they ran no risk. In reply to the Chairman, Mr. Burke added that the Abingdon branch, being but two miles in length, was worked by the Great Western at 60 per cent., as they could not do it in the same ratio of expense as a longer line; but the Thame, which was under circumstances very similar to the one proposed, was worked on more favourable terms than 50 per cent., and promoters had proposed to the Great Western that, it being a similar class of country, there should be the same terms.

The CHAIRMAN said he thought they would have a better country than the Thame line. (Hear, hear.) One of the most important considerations was the question of fuel. By the broad gauge they would get coal from South Wales, Somersetshire, and indeed all the west country, but not from the midland counties. In certain parts of the Great Western system the narrow gauge was laid down as well, but he observed that Mr. Saunder's letter assumed that the broad gauge would be used – "Assuming the scheme to be one which is supported by the district it is intended to accommodate, and that it will be made on the broad gauge, and laid out in a manner satisfactory to the company, we shall be prepared to recommend the trustees to enter into an arrangement for the working of the line." He would ask Mr. Burke if there was any probability of getting a mixed gauge, so as to procure midland counties coals. He did not know what the policy of the Great Western might be with regard to the narrow gauge.

Mr. BURKE said they were extending it voluntarily. Mr. Saunders had, he knew, written in haste, and he did not think the company would make the broad gauge a condition. His own opinion was that the narrow gauge would be more advisable, and that the Great Western would offer no objection, as they had it laid down on that portion which this branch would touch. All the Welsh communication *via* Worcester was by the narrow gauge.

Mr. COOPER, Mr. M. WIGGINS, and Mr. CLIFFE urged the propriety of a broad gauge as well as, to secure communication with the west.

Mr. BURKE said they had not yet gone into details with the Great Western, as they were waiting to see how the project was taken up.

The CHAIRMAN thought it would materially further the undertaking if an assurance could be given that the narrow gauge would be laid down. It would greatly influence the decision of the country.

Mr. BURKE said it was only a question of £7000 or £8000 more to lay down the mixed gauge, but he thought the line should be narrow gauge exclusively. There was no doubt the mixed was the best, but the question was whether they were in a position to get the best. If the country, however, would subscribe a third of the extra cost, the promoters were ready to lay down the mixed gauge.

The CHAIRMAN – That is very satisfactory. What is the extra cost per mile?

Mr. BURKE – £800 and £1600 more, so that if you find £3000 in addition to the £27,000, we will lay down the mixed.

The CHAIRMAN said he understood the Board of Trade considered £10,000 per mile sufficient, unless there were unusual engineering difficulties.

Mr. BURKE, in reply to questions, said it would be a single line, and there would be stations at Watlington, Brightwell or Cuxham, Bensington, and Wallingford.

The CHAIRMAN – There is a good line of villages all the way.

Mr. BURKE – Yes, it is a rich agricultural district, and my impression is that it will be a good paying line. We have been in communication with Mr. Morrison, and he is willing to take a rent-charge for his portion, which extends from the Great Western to the Wallingford and Oxford turnpike, being one-fourth of the whole distance. The proper course would be that you undertake to find the land, and the contractor guarantee to do everything else for a given sum. That would prevent any increase of capital or anything else.

Mr. NEIGHBOUR, in reply to the CHAIRMAN, said that nine-tenths of the owners and occupiers affected had given their assent.

Mr. VIRET – I have given a very qualified assent to mine.

After a little further conversation on the propriety of a mixed gauge, to secure coal from both directions

Mr. NEIGHBOUR stated that the area affected by the railway was 40,000 acres, of which 8,000, he estimated, were villages, homesteads, and meadow land, and 32,000 arable. Half the latter would be cropped with corn yearly, and taking the average produce at 2½ qrs. per acre, and the proportion consumed at home at one third, there would remain 40,000 qrs. Estimating the saving of carriage at 1s per qr. it would come to £2,000 per annum, which would represent a capital of £50,000 at 4 per cent.

The CHAIRMAN, Mr. VIRET, and other gentlemen expressed an opinion that the average produce was more than Mr. Neighbour estimated, but that the proportion of two thirds being sent to a distance was excessive.

Mr. NEIGHBOUR was proceeding to refer to artificial manures, but it was remarked by the Chairman that the consumption was very small in this district. As to coal, he estimated the consumption of the Watlington district at £10,000 tons a year, and that the saving would be 3s. in the carriage and 2s. in the price, which would amount to £2,500 per annum, representing a capital of £62,000 at 4 per cent.

The CHAIRMAN remarked that he obtained his coals from Mr. Round, of Oxford, and that the carriage was 7s. per ton in the winter and 6s. in the summer.

Mr. BURKE – When the Abingdon branch was opened, although they were only three miles from a station before and had canal and river supply, the price fell 7s.

No further questions being put to Mr. Burke,

Mr VIRET observed that there could be no difference of opinion on the desirability of a railway, as they must all be convinced, it would afford great facilities in various ways. The feasibility was another question. As to the corn, Mr. Neighbour had made a very fair statement, and had indeed under-estimated the produce of the district; while as to coals, his calculation was very sound, and they must all be agreed that the present mode of supply involved a considerable extra outlay. He concurred with Mr. Neighbour in the desirability of extending the line if they should get it but that was not before them now, for they must get it here before they could carry it on. (Laughter.) He moved:- "That, in the opinion of this meeting, the making of a line on the mixed gauge, from the Great Western Railway to Wallingford and Watlington, would be of great benefit to the town of Watlington and the surrounding district of country." (Applause.)

The Rev. G. DAY seconded the resolution remarking that his only objection was that the line would come a little too near Britwell Lodge, to be ornamental, but the public interests were of more importance and he did not think the railway could have been better planned. (Applause.) He trusted they would work together for the public benefit, and if those interested would put their shoulder to the wheel, he did not doubt they would accomplish it. (Applause.)

The resolution having been unanimously adopted, it was agreed, on the motion of Mr. CLIFFE, seconded by Mr. R. WIGGINS, to request the Members for the County to give their sanction and support to the proposed line.

The CHAIRMAN then thanked the deputation for the clear and straightforward way in which they had answered every inquiry, and hoped the scheme would prove successful.

On the motion of Mr. WALKER, seconded by the Rev. G. DAY, a cordial vote of thanks was accorded to the Chairman, who, in reply, expressed his readiness to assist whatever was beneficial to the neighbourhood. The people of this district liked to see their way clear before they threw themselves heartily into any undertaking; but when they did this, he was sure they would do all they could to bring it to a successful issue. One important point had not been referred to – the benefit to the poor from the cheapening of fuel, which was one of their largest expenses. (Hear, hear.) He hoped they would secure a mixed gauge.

The proceedings then terminated. – *Oxford Journal*

The line was sanctioned on 25th July 1864, the authorised capital for the project being £80,000 in £10 shares with borrowing powers for a further £26,000 after the shares were fully taken up. The original directors of the Wallingford & Watlington Railway Company appear to have been speculators with no local connections. They were William Hawes, chairman, Edward Poole and James Childs, all of whom were in the legal profession and presumably acquainted. Hawes, who was also a merchant, had strong links with the City of London and the company's office at 4 Skinner's Place, Sise Lane, London, was also used in part by him. This was also the venue for most of the meetings. Childs and Hawes were also on the Board of other railway schemes, as was G. W. Hastings, who also became a director of the company.

Burke seems to have had the only real ties with the district, having been Engineer of the Abingdon Railway and lived in that town at least during the 1860s. He had also engineered the Calne branch and, by the time the Wallingford Railway opened, was able to boast an office in Westminster.

The first directors meeting was held on 28th July 1864 when it was resolved to approve the contract dated 5th May 1864, for the construction of Railway No. 1 awarded by the promoters to a Mr. Thomas White.

The Act authorised the construction of the line to either broad or narrow gauge; however, the main line through Wallingford Road had been converted to mixed gauge by this time and it was decided to construct the line to the narrow gauge, thus becoming the first narrow gauge branch off the original GWR main line.

The turning of the first sod does not appear to have been recorded, but on Monday, 9th May 1864, Burke and a staff of assistants had commenced setting out the line from Cholsey to Wallingford, and at the time it was contemplated that the first turf would be turned 'in about a month hence'. With great optimism it was also estimated that the line would be completed by the end of the year!

By the end of 1864 the original contract, which excluded Wallingford station, was superseded by another to cover the continuation of the line from the intended junction to Wallingford Road station, an estimated additional cost of £7,832. This figure, which still excluded the station, included the maintenance of the line for a period of twelve months after it was opened for public traffic. In January 1865 White undertook to complete the line by 1st October 'under a penalty of £100 per week for every week's delay after that date'. (This is not referred to again and may have been dropped later.) The contract also provided for 'deduction by the company from the payments to which the contractor will become entitled of 10 per cent as a guarantee fund to be retained in hand for 12 months.'

Another well attended public meeting was held at Wallingford Town Hall on Friday, 12th August 1864. T. E. Field was again in the chair and the directors of the Wallingford and Watlington Railway were present. The object of the meeting was to enable the directors to explain their intentions and 'any gentleman present would be at liberty to put questions, and no information would be kept from them'.

Hawes spoke at length in his quest for support, he could foresee no financial problems and had every reason to believe that 'they would have a larger dividend than was paid on other railways [!]. They would not only have a good communication by rail, but a sure dividend of five or six per cent'. Savings in the movement of goods were anticipated with a possible reduction of six or seven shillings per ton on coal alone.

After further discussion it was resolved that 'having heard the explanation of the Directors of the Wallingford & Watlington Railway, this meeting is satisfied that the line will be of great benefit to the Borough and neighbourhood, and is prepared to give the undertaking its cordial support'.

Although the matter of the extension of the line beyond Wallingford had previously been deferred, it was resolved at a board meeting on 21st March 1865, to obtain a tender from White for the continuation to Benson. Incidentally, this was more frequently referred to by the Board by the older name of Bensington.

In May James Childs undertook to purchase an additional 400 shares and to use his influence with his friends to complete the line to Benson on condition that he became Chairman of the company. In response Hawes expressed his willingness to resign and subsequently became Deputy Chairman under Childs.

The following month, in a letter of reply to a conversation with a Mr. Peel from Watlington about the extension, Childs stated that if not less than 1000 shares were taken in the neighbourhood and if the land required was given at an average price not exceeding £150 per acre (partly paid in shares) the directors would continue the line from Benson to Watlington forthwith.

At this stage the company seem to have been quite committed to the continuation as far as Benson, and Burke was instructed to prepare plans and surveys for that portion. His estimate for the construction of Railway No. 2 was presented in two divisions, viz:

Wallingford to Benson which included a 3 arch viaduct over the Thames	1 m 60 ch	£15,452
Benson to Watlington	4 m 60 ch	£16,148
	Total	£31,600

These figures were presented at a meeting on 20th June when it was resolved that a letter be sent to Mr. Peel urging an immediate decision and reply to the Chairman's letter regarding the Benson to Watlington extension.

In the meantime the construction to Wallingford had proceeded well, several excavations having been made in the

Cholsey area by February 1865. The engineer certified the first payment to the contractor in June. The station at Wallingford was now under consideration.

As already mentioned, the junction with the main line was made at the existing station at Wallingford Road, the branch running alongside the GWR double track from there to the point of divergence, a distance of some three quarters of a mile. The new junction was to be built by the GWR at an estimated cost of £900 made up as follows:

9 crossings at £17		£153
Additional Signals		£100
Locking gear		£280
	Total	£533

the balance of £367 'being charged to Mr. White's contract'. The Wallingford Company approved the expenditure but urged the GW to carry out the work as rapidly as possible. The GWR had announced their intention to charge a rent of £150 per annum apart from any charge for the use of Wallingford Road station or any duty performed by the GWR for the Wallingford Co. However, after subsequent meetings between the two companies, a letter from James Grierson, General Manager of the GWR, dated 9th April 1866, stated that he would recommend that the directors of the GWR accept the Wallingford Co.'s proposal of £120 per annum as 'easement over the land occupied by the Wallingford Co. and for the use of the arches and excavations belonging to the Great Western'. He would also recommend Burke's suggestion that the charge for working the line should be reduced to 50% when the receipts amounted to £15 per mile per week, a minimum sum being paid to the Great Western until the line is completed to Watlington'.

The Wallingford company's solicitors then set about negotiations with the GWR over the working agreement which was finally secured and dated 30th June. Briefly, the GWR worked the line exclusively and paid a rental of 40% of gross receipts after deductions. The GWR provided all the rolling stock, staff, stores, etc. and, after the first twelve months, they were also to take over the maintenance of the line. In the absence of any evidence to the contrary, it must surely have appeared that the line actually belonged to the Great Western.

The *Reading Mercury* for 7th October 1865 reported that the construction of the line was progressing rapidly. The 60ft deep cutting described as nearly perpendicular, in Cholsey Field near Wallingford Road station, was nearing completion and the rails were laid for a considerable distance near Wallingford. The same journal also tentatively mentions 'The Cholsey Station (it is said) will be near the Church, which will be a most convenient spot, not only for the inhabitants of Cholsey, but for Aston, Blewbury, and the adjoining villages to the west.' This is the only mention of such a station and presumably arose from local speculation.

The Board of Trade inspection was carried out on Thursday, 26th June, and the line was opened on Monday, 7th July 1866, but the opening ceremony was without any particular demonstration because the public announcement had only been made on Saturday the 5th!

According to the *Reading Mercury* the scene was as follows:

The first train started at 7.50 on Monday morning, by which time a considerable number of persons had assembled at the station to witness the departure of the train. The engine was gaily decorated with flags, and about 60 persons took their places for the first trip. The train proceeded at a good rate of speed over the new line, and all expressed their satisfaction of the train and the comfortable arrangement of the carriages. There seems to be a distinction evinced by the GWR, who are working the line, to afford every facility possible to travellers as there are nine trains out and the same number in, during the day. The late train, viz. the 9.4 p.m. from Wallingford Road, arriving at Wallingford at 9.14, will be a great boon to many visitors to the Metropolis either for business or pleasure.

It appears that initially only passenger traffic was dealt with as it was brought to the notice of the board on 17th July that goods could not be conveyed over the line as the Great Western had not supplied any details of the rates to be charged! The secretary was instructed to write to the GWR on the subject.

With the excitement of the new railway now over and the prospects for its continuation in doubt, Childs resigned as Chairman because of his 'numerous engagements at the time'. He was succeeded by G. W. Hastings who, in taking the chair, also inherited the company's financial problems.

At a Board meeting on the day of opening, it had been pointed out that the powers of compulsory purchase of land were about to expire. This brought about a discussion over the continuation to Benson, but the matter was deferred. A special meeting was held on 14th July 'to consider the propriety of giving notice to landowners for the purchase of the land between Wallingford and Bensington' but it was not until the following February that the Board considered an estimate from White for the extension to Benson. This had now risen to £16,218, a quarter of which he was willing to accept in shares. He also proposed 'to construct the station similar to that at Wallingford with the exception of Engine House and Water Arrangements for the sum of £2,645 all to be paid in cash'.

In January 1867 Hastings contacted the GWR Board and requested that the agreed sum of £500 a year, to be taken out of the gross receipts on completion of the line to Benson, should be effective at once provided the GWR were satisfied that the capital necessary to complete the line had been provided. The matter was deferred until the GWR had further information.

The GW directors subsequently met the Wallingford Board on 18th July 1867 to arrange the guarantee of interest on £10,000 to be applied in continuing the line to Benson. The Great Western agreed to grant every facility to complete the arrangement for guaranteeing interest to the extent of £500. Further money was not, however, forthcoming and the company's financial status was not improving. Money was owing to the GWR and by the end of the year the contractor was still pressing for payment of the outstanding amount due to him. In an effort to improve their position, the GW, at the request of the company, raised 1st and 2nd class fares from 1st January 1868, and the company secretary accepted a reduction in salary from £80 to £60 per annum. Meanwhile, in desperation, White assigned the debt of £2,200 due to him to another party, namely Peter & Forster Graham, and later, at the end of the year, the W&WR company's solicitors were given 'a mortgage of surplus land at Wallingford' as a security for the amount due to them.

At a meeting on 15th December 1868 a letter from the company's solicitor was read, pointing out that a notice had appeared in the *London Gazette* of an application for a Bill to authorise the construction of a railway from Watlington to Princes Risborough. Certainly from this point in time hopes for the intended extension seem to have been abandoned.

Inevitably, Hawes and Bristow, one of the company's solicitors, approached Grierson with a view to selling out to the GWR, the meeting being held on 10th August 1870. In his official reply dated 17th August, Grierson declined, stating, 'The chairman and I have both come to the conclusion that the balance being small we could not make you an offer which you would be likely to accept and besides at present we have a number of schemes on hand which have to be brought before the shareholders and therefore we think that for the present at all events the matter had better stand over and as the traffic is somewhat improving we may be able to make you a more satisfactory proposal than we can do just now.'

Another approach was made to the GWR in the summer of 1871 with regard to vesting the line in the larger company. It was explained that the Watlington portion had not been constructed and that there was difficulty with the capital for the existing line. The terms proposed by the GWR involved an increased payment based on the present earnings of Railway No. 1 and authority was given for the negotiations to continue on that basis.

The company was in difficulty over the capital for the existing line, only £17,575 having been paid up. They were anxious to obtain powers to abandon Railway No. 2 and rearrange and reduce their capital. This was made clear during further negotiations the following year and in a letter of 5th June 1871 the GWR offered £3,515 of 5% GW preference stock to be paid for the ordinary stock of the Wallingford Co. They were also to pay £16,750 in cash or preference stock. The offer was accepted and the Wallingford company requested the cash for the payment of their outstanding debts.

The line was vested in the GWR on 2nd December 1872 and the shareholders later received GW 5% preference stock in proportion to their holding.

The Wallingford & Watlington Railway never did reach Watlington, but presumably travellers from the Watlington area must have travelled to London via the Wallingford Railway. This seems to have rendered redundant what had become a thrice-weekly coach service which latterly left the Red Lion, Watlington, at 8.30 a.m. for Wycombe instead of just Stokenchurch Hill. According to local directories, this ceased to run after the opening of the railway to Wallingford in 1866 and, of the once numerous carriers to London, only John Hatton offered a waggon to London, from the Hare & Hounds Hotel, Watlington, every Wednesday and Sunday, and this service ceased before 1872.

Bell Street, Princes Risborough, c.1895.

CHAPTER TWO
TAYLOR'S RAILWAY

WHEN hopes of the Wallingford and Watlington Railway actually reaching Watlington were fading fast, the announcement of an alternative scheme in the *Thame Gazette* for 12th May 1868 must have heartened many:

RAILWAY — We understand that an eminent firm in London has lately in conjunction with Mr. Jones, the solicitor of this town, organised a scheme for a line of railway, so as to bring us within easy reach of the metropolis. The proposal is to run a branch from Watlington, which will join the Thame and Wycombe railway at Princes Risborough; the engineering difficulties would by no means be numerous, as it would as nearly as possible, pursue the course of the old Roman road called the 'Icknield Way'. The projected line appears to meet with general approval, and the land owners along the contemplated line are one and all desirous to help the scheme in every way possible. Watlington has much cause to rejoice at the proposal, as it has often been threatened by an attack from the iron king, but as yet it has been only "a rumour of war", and the place has been completely isolated since the days of coaches. There now seems some probability of success, and we trust ere long to hear the snort of the "fiery horse" which will so speedily convey us hither and thither wherever we may wish. The scheme seems to be the most suitable of any that has been talked of, and the town will be placed in more direct communication with London and the North West than it would have been by any of the former proposals. There is no doubt there will be a good traffic both as to passengers, coal, timber, and corn, and it will tend ultimately to much increase the revenue and importance of the Aylesbury, Thame, and Wycombe Railway, and it may be the commencement of a much greater extension, and open up a country not as yet favoured with railways.

Furthermore, progress was not tardy, the same journal reporting less than a month later:

THE PROJECTED RAILWAY — We alluded a few weeks back to the probability of a line of railway to unite this town with Princes Risborough. We are happy to say that the probability now seems likely to prove a reality. We have noticed in all the conspicuous places the following bill:- "Watlington and Risborough Railway. Notice is hereby given, that a meeting will be held at the Hare and Hounds Inn, on Wednesday, June 3rd, at one o'clock p.m., with reference to the above proposed railway. Messrs. Lucas and Wilkinson, engineers, Duke Street, Westminster, will attend. (Signed), A. Jones, solicitor." This really appears to be business, and a step in the right direction. We not only wish the movers a good attendance, but a speculative one and such that measures may be at once taken to obtain the necessary sanction of Parliament. From all we can gather in the neighbourhood, the matter is most warmly taken up by the leading owners of property.

Unfortunately, as we shall see, it seems doubtful that the minute books of the Watlington and Princes Risborough Railway survive. Therefore, instead of the privileged insight into the affairs of the company normally afforded by such records, we are largely dependent on published accounts of shareholders meetings which appeared in the local press, and snippets of what was happening in surviving correspondence. The first report of a shareholders meeting appeared on 9th November 1868 in the *Thame Gazette* and is quoted in full:

WATLINGTON & RISBOROUGH RAILWAY

A meeting of the shareholders of this proposed railway was held on Saturday, the 30th ult., at the Hare and Hounds Inn, Watlington, in reference to carrying out the project. The Directors, T. Taylor, Esq., F. E. S. Viret, Esq., T. A. Allnutt, Esq., and J. H. Peel, Esq., were present

(the Rev. W. H. Davey having resigned); and the following shareholders were present:- The Earl of Macclesfield, Messrs. A. H. C. Brown, A. Cooper, Watson, Eustace, M. Wiggins, W. J. Wiggins, Smith, J. Hill, Humphries, Spyer, Stopes, Charlton, A. Jones (secretary, pro. tem.), and Mr. Wilkinson (the engineer). Mr Taylor occupied the chair.

The Chairman opened the meeting by remarks on the balance sheet and state of the finances and share list, implying some doubts as to the ultimate success of the project, which were met by Mr. Peel, who said that he did not take so gloomy a view of the matter as the Chairman; he (Mr. Peel) had made a calculation, based on the income of other railways, and the probable income of the Watlington and Risborough Railway, which bespoke much success in a financial point of view to the shareholders as a profitable investment; the estimated cost of making the line, including the cost of land, was £37,000 (and this was founded on contractors' offers, and not a visionary calculation), to meet which the following sums were now available:- Debentures, £12,000; shares to contractors, £11,500; cash from shareholders, £8,500, so that only £4000 to £5000 more was required. As to income, he had been informed by the officers of several railways that their earnings were £14 per week per mile, which, after allowing for the working expenses by the Great Western Railway, would give for the Watlington and Risborough Railway a profit of 5 per cent on the debentures and 9¼ per cent on the ordinary shares; but if only £10 per mile, which was below the average of other railways, was earned, that would leave, after paying the percentage on the debentures, something like 6 per cent to the shareholders. Mr. Peel concluded his remarks by offering 50 per cent additional on his shares already taken.

Mr. Viret then rose and said that the figures, the financial part of the concern, had been so clearly put before the meeting by the Chairman, Mr. Taylor, and by his co-Director, Mr. Peel, that, on such portion of the proceedings, he would refrain from troubling the shareholders present. There were, however, one or two points upon which he would like to say a few words. In the first place, it had to be observed, that this portion of the county, the parish of Watlington, with its surrounding villages, was deprived of any direct railway communication. The Noble Lord present (the Earl of Macclesfield) had made it known that a telegraphic line was about to be extended to Watlington, and thus Mr. Viret remarked that if a railroad followed, this rural and remote community would, so to say, be brought within the pale of 'civilization'! Mr. Viret went on to remark, in the second place, that the prospect and probability of railway communication had proceeded further than it had ever done before — a Bill had been obtained without opposition, the concurrence of the Great Western Railway had been secured, and, if the present occasion were allowed to fail or to fall to the ground, what hope could there be for the future? True it was that no very large number of shares had been subscribed for at Watlington, but that proceeded rather from want of means than from disinclination; because it was manifest to all that the proposed line to Risborough would be of great advantage to this retired and rural parish. At present coals had to be brought from a distance at an enlarged cost, and that expensive inconvenience applied likewise, in all its force, to the means, of personal locomotion, and to the other disadvantages inseparable from the absence of a railway station. To a greater or less extent, all this was felt by the neighbourhood, and it was therefore most earnestly hoped that the present opportunity of securing so much good would not fall to the ground for want of the small sum, not exceeding £4,000, which was yet wanted to enable the company to break ground. The line presents no engineering difficulties, and an assurance was given by the Engineer that it might be completed within nine months. The whole matter, however, was now before the Shareholders and the public, and Mr. Viret concluded by expressing a sanguine hope that the rich and

The original 1862 station at Risborough seen here with the broad gauge of the Wycombe Railway in the foreground and a standard gauge wagon in the Aylesbury bay behind. This picture was taken sometime between October 1867, when the Aylesbury branch was converted to standard gauge, and August 1870, when the Wycombe Railway was converted. Although the nameboard carried the abbreviated 'Risborough', timetables gave the full name. The wooden building in the background was the Railway Hotel which survived until 1962.   *Henry Taunt, cty. Beatrice Wallen*

Thomas Taylor made his fortune in Lancashire cotton mills and bought Aston House when he moved south. He lived there from 1858-91, and became something of an art collector. Some idea of the calibre of his acquisitions can be gained from a snippet in the *Thame Gazette* for 9th April 1878 when an accident occurred to a painting 'Applicants for admission to a casual ward', by Luke Fildes. "It was being conveyed from the Gallery at Aston House to the Railway, for transmission to the Paris Exhibition, in a large furniture van, and soon after passing through Watlington, while going up Howe Hill the van overpowered the horses, ran back, and overturned. The frame of the picture was smashed and a small rent made in the painting itself, but it is hoped it may be restored. We understand the value of this picture to be about three thousand guineas." It would appear that the picture was being taken to Reading station rather than via the Watlington and Princes Risborough Railway!   *National Monuments Record*

wealthy of the neighbourhood would assist the far poorer town of Watlington in completing a work which, from its acknowledged want and undoubted utility, would not only benefit the town, but the adjacent neighbourhood also.

After some few remarks by other shareholders, Mr. Taylor agreed to take 100 shares; Lord Macclesfield, 20 shares; Mr. Peel, 25 shares; Mr. Viret, 10 shares; and Mr. Allnutt, 10 shares, in addition to their former engagements, which, with a few smaller sums, represented nearly £1,700, towards the required sum. The following officers were appointed:- Messrs. Taylor, Viret, Peel, and Allnutt, directors; Messrs. W. G. Spyer and Walter J. Wiggins, auditors; Messrs. Lucas and Wilkinson, engineers; and Mr. A. Jones, secretary. A letter was read from Mr. Grierson, general manager of the Great Western Railway, as to the working of the proposed line, which was considered satisfactory. A new prospectus and a renewed canvass for shares was determined on, to which it was hoped the neighbouring gentry and land-owners would respond, so that the works may be commenced immediately. The meeting was then adjourned.

The Watlington and Princes Risborough Railway Act received Royal Assent on 26th July 1869 and incorporated the Watlington and Princes Risborough Railway Co. which was empowered to construct a standard gauge line from Princes Risborough, on the Wycombe section of the Great Western Railway in the county of Buckingham, 8½ miles to Watlington in Oxfordshire. The estimated cost of the line was £33,889, the Act authorising a capital of £36,000 in £10 shares, with powers to raise a further

£12,000 by borrowing, and allowing the company five years in which to build the line.

The first directors were Thomas Taylor, JP, Lord of the Manor, Aston House, Aston Rowant; Francis Edward Stephens Viret, JP, of Hill House, Watlington; John Henry Westcar Peel, Brewer of Brook Street, Watlington; William Harrison Davey and Thomas Alexander Allnut of Watlington Farm, one of the landowners. The Secretary (*pro tem*) was Augustus Jones, Solicitor, Clerk to the Magistrates for Watlington Division, Clerk to the Commissioners of Taxes and District Highway Board, Commissioner to administer oaths in chancery and common law court. The engineers were Lucas and Wilkinson of Duke Street, Westminster, and auditors W. G. Spyer and Walter J. Wiggins. W. G. Spyer & Son were listed as chemists & druggists, stationers, printers and booksellers, of Market Place, Watlington, whilst Walter Wiggins of Watcombe Manor, was a magistrate and landowner.

The Chairman, Thomas Taylor, one-time High Sheriff of Oxfordshire, came from Wigan, where his father was a tanner. Thomas and his brothers erected cotton mills in Wallgate. The reporter for the *Thame Gazette* was accurate when he wrote "True it was that no very large number of shares had been subscribed for at Watlington", for it appears that only £8,000 was raised towards the cost of the W&PR and that Taylor put up all the rest. Financing the line turned out to be a very bad investment, but were it not for this wealthy mill owner adopting Aston Rowant as his new home, the line would probably never have been built.

In April 1870 the *Thame Gazette* reported:

We are informed that the Directors of the proposed railway from Watlington to Risborough have come to terms with an eminent contractor for the construction of the line, and that the works will be commenced with the least possible delay, with every prospect of it being finished and opened for traffic within a twelve month.

In view of the paucity of original documentation, we are fortunate that the agreement made with the contractor, Henry Jackson, survives and is reproduced here in full, not least because it provides some idea of the appearance of the line as built:

THE WATLINGTON & PRINCES RISBOROUGH RAILWAY
Heads of an Agreement made the 18th day of April 1870 between the Watlington & Princes Risborough Railway Company incorporated by the Watlington and Princes Risborough Railway Act 1869 of the one part and Henry Jackson of Charlton Lodge, Surbiton in the County of Surrey, Contractor for Public Works of the other part.

Whereby the said Henry Jackson agrees to accept and take a Contract and the said Watlington and Princes Risborough Railway Company agrees to enter into a Contract with the said Henry Jackson for the construction of the authorised line of the said Watlington and Princes Risborough Railway as and for a single line of Railway and based upon the centre line of the Parliamentary Plans with the alterations contained in the Act upon the following terms:-

Permanent Way & Ballasting — For a single line of Railway narrow gauge for a total length of about eight miles and four chains, the rails to be sixty pounds to the yard lineal and fished. The rails to be properly fastened to the sleepers with wood screws and fang bolts. The sleepers to be half round nine feet long by nine inches by four and a half inches of good sound Larch or other approved fir. The ballasting of Chalk shall be not less than 10 feet wide at the upper surface of the sleepers by 18 inches deep. The Contractor to have the use of the permanent rails during the construction of the line. The embankments to be 15 feet 6 inches wide at formation level, and the cuttings to be 15 feet 6 inches wide at formation level. The slopes of embankments and cuttings to be such as the Engineers may direct.

Fencing and rails. To be of good Larch or other fir. The posts to be 9 feet apart from centre to centre, 7 feet long by 7 inches by 3½ inches. The portion underground of the posts to be charred or tarred, intermediate posts to be provided at least 5 feet 6 inches long by 4 inches by 2 inches to be likewise charred or tarred. The rails to be 3 inches by 1½ inches and properly morticed to the main posts and nailed to the intermediate.

Earthwork. The main line and all approaches for crossing main line including public road crossings and occupation crossings to be complete.

Stations. Three small stations to be erected complete including small Station house containing Booking Office and Waiting Room; Platform, small Goods Shed, Cattle Pen, Carriage Dock, Waggon Weighing machine and proper road approaches. At Watlington Station a small Engine house to be erected, a Water Tank, Coal Stage, a Well to be sunk and proper pump to be provided. Proper Signals to be erected at each Station with conveniences.

Sidings. The sidings in the three Stations not to exceed one mile in length with all necessary points and crossings.

Bridges. The necessary Public & Turnpike Road bridges to be built as per the plans, to be furnished by the Engineers.

Accommodation Level Crossings to be placed where necessary and provided with proper approaches, gates &c.

Public Road Level Crossings to be placed where necessary and provided with a small gatekeeper's house containing two rooms and closet; the necessary gates across the Railway to be erected.

Culverts. The necessary culverts to be built in brickwork or drain pipes as the Engineers may direct.

The whole of the work to be carried out in accordance with the plans to be furnished by the Company's Engineers Messrs. Wilkinson & Smith of 31 Duke Street, Westminster and the whole of the work and materials to be to their satisfaction, and so as to meet the requirements of the Board of Trade.

Commencement and Completion. The line to be commenced forthwith (sufficient land being provided by the Company for the purpose) and finished complete in every respect within nine months from the date hereof, provided that the Company finds as and when reasonably required by the Contractor all necessary land for the purposes of the line.

Payments. The Contract price shall be £30,000 of which sum £6,500 shall be Cash, £12,000 nominal in Debentures bearing 5 per cent interest, which interest is guaranteed by the Directors for 3 years, and the balance in Ordinary Shares. The Contractor shall be paid monthly from the date of commencing the works on the Certificates of the Engineers for work done and materials delivered pro rata Cash, Debentures issued when the Company can lawfully do so and Shares.

All plants which may be placed on the works to be the property of the Company until the completion of the line but no allowance shall be made for the same in the Certificates.

In the event of difference between the Company and the Contractor as to any of the provisions herein contained, the same to be referred to Charles Hutton Gregory Esquire whose decision shall be final.

Witness the common Seal of the said Watlington and Princes Risborough Railway Company and the hand and seal of the said Henry Jackson the day and year first above written.
(Signed) Tho. Taylor
Henry Jackson

The earthworks and engineering features were minimal, the line being laid almost directly across farmland. In the authorised plans, there was only one underbridge and that was at Lewknor, where the line passed over a minor public road, otherwise the company was authorised to cross the remaining public roads on the level, including the important Stokenchurch Turnpike to Oxford (later the A40) at Aston Rowant. However, as each of the level crossings would have required the employment of a gatekeeper, and presumably the provision of a house, the W&PRR Co. evidently and very sensibly decided to alter the gradients in order to bridge the two roads at Bledlow, and although incurring two not insubstantial cuttings, excavate for the line to pass beneath the roads at Chinnor and Aston Rowant, leaving level crossings only at Wainhill and Kingston.

By the end of 1870, work on the line had evidently reached the stage where supplies needed to be brought in by rail, a letter of 20th December 1870 from the W&PRR Co. indemnifying the Great Western from any accident which might arise from the construction of a temporary junction, where the branch joined the Wycombe line ¾ mile to the west of Risborough. Incidentally, the Watlington Act provided for mixed gauge from this junction to Risborough station, but by early September 1870 the Wycombe line had been converted from broad to standard gauge.

The next evidence of progress comes from the GWR Board minutes for 6th July 1871 which record that Mr. Grierson, the general manager, was authorised to negotiate with the Watlington & Princes Risborough Railway Co. 'an arrangement for working that line on the basis of terms which were discussed by the Board'.

It had been intended to site the junction for the Watlington Railway some three-quarters of a mile outside the station at Princes Risborough, the temporary junction for the contractors presumably being established on the same spot. However, by

As first planned, the line was to cross the road to Chinnor Hill on the level, but, in the event, a cutting, apparent on the left of the picture, was excavated to help take it below the level of the road. Embankments were also built to raise the road approaches to the necessary height for the bridge, which is just off the left-hand side of this view. The road to Thame can be seen in the centre of the picture, above the sturdy Norman tower of Chinnor church. This view, looking north-west over Chinnor, also features Donkey Lane level crossing on the right.

CHINNOR

March 1872 the GWR decided to extend the line to run independently alongside the Thame branch the rest of the way to the GWR station. The cost of doubling the line on the approach to Risborough was estimated at £2,500 and an additional £1061 13s 4d was authorised for 'Platform and sidings required by the Board of Trade at the Princes Risborough station in connection with the junction with the Watlington and Princes Risborough Railway'.

The details behind these decisions are unknown but the 'platform and sidings' were evidently not originally anticipated by either company. The new arrangements avoided the need for a signal box at the remote junction, and, despite the extra works, the Watlington and Princes Risborough Railway were still only expected to contribute £1,352 9s 6d, the formerly agreed cost of the aborted junction, together with the £75★ per annum agreed for working and maintaining the junction.

The agreement between the two companies for the revised junction arrangements dated 7th May 1872 stipulates:

> The Great Western Company shall work and accommodate in a proper manner the Watlington Company's traffic at the Princes Risborough station as provided for in Section 47 of the Watlington & Princes Risborough Railway Act of 1869 and the Watlington Company shall pay such a proportion of the interest on the cost of the station such cost up to the date hereof to be taken to the sum of £4000 and of the working and maintenance thereof as their traffic bears to the whole of the traffic booked to and from the same station provided that no charge shall be made by the Great Western Company for interest on the cost of the said station or for the use thereof or for any services rendered to the Watlington Company in such station during the period of 3 years from the opening of the Watlington Company's railway.

The W&PRR seems to have made good progress, but at the half-yearly meeting of shareholders on Saturday, 30th March 1872, the extra work now required was viewed with pessimism:

> As the Board of Trade requires an additional station at Risborough there is little prospect of the line being opened for general traffic for some weeks if not months.

Without waiting for the independent extension into Risborough and the extra platform, etc, to accommodate their trains, the W&PRR sent a letter to the Board of Trade on 15th April 1872 advising them that the line was ready for inspection, and another on 29th May giving notice of their intention to open. When their inspecting officer eventually visited the line on 11th June 1872, it cannot have been a surprise that he would not sanction the opening.

RAILWAY DEPARTMENT
BOARD OF TRADE
11th June 1872

Sir,

I have the honor to report, for the information of the Board of Trade, that in compliance with the instructions contained in your Minute of the 29th ultimo I have inspected the Watlington and Princes Risborough Railway.

The New Line commences at a point about ¾ of a mile to the North of Princes Risboro' Station on the Wycombe Branch of the Great Western Railway and extends thence to Watlington.

It is a single line about 8 miles long. The intermediate stations are Chinnor and Aston Rowant.

The permanent way consists of a Vignoles pattern rail, that weighs 58lbs per yard linear. It is laid in lengths of 23 feet. The rail is fished and fixed with fang bolts (6 to each length of rail) and dog spikes to

★ Formal agreements between the two companies state £75 per annum. However, at the GWR board meeting of 21st March 1872, a reference is made to £70 or £90 (the first figure is indistinct).

sleepers laid transversely at an average distance of 3 feet apart. The line is ballasted with chalk. The gauge is 4ft 8½in. There are three under bridges and two over bridges that have masonry abutments and wt. iron girders. These works are of sufficient strength. The steepest gradient is 1 in 68 and the sharpest curve has a radius of 13 chains.

There are two authorised level crossings of public roads. The gates close across the roads and railway and there are houses for the gatekeepers. The following works are required.

That the line should be continued from the point ¾ of a mile north of Princes Risborough station to the station. At present there is no terminus at the station to deposit the passengers at.

The locking gear at Chinnor requires adjusting and the station East Distant Signal requires clearing of trees. The locking gear at Watlington Stn. also requires adjusting and a baulk about 10ft thick is required at the back of the buffer stops to prevent engine or coaches running on to the public road.

Distant signals are required at Kingston level crossing and cross bar signals and lamps on the gates.

Mile Posts are required on the Railway and clocks at the stations.

The platforms of under bridges require to be protected from fire and the station platforms require gravelling.

The occupation gates should be protected with padlocks and notices painted on them that they must be left locked.

There are no turntables. The rails are very light and the station platforms very short, all tending to show that the traffic is expected to be very light. The railway is a surface line with continual changes of gradient. It should be worked at very moderate speed. The Company should be requested to send in a description of the class of engine with which they propose to work the line as well as an undertaking as to the proposed mode of working.

I submit that the Watlington & Princes Risboro' Railway cannot be opened for passenger traffic without danger to the public using the same, in consequence of the incomplete state of the works.

I have the honor to remain your obedient servant.

(Signed) F. H. Rich

In reply to the Board of Trade on 13th June, the W&PRR confirmed that they would at once proceed to comply with the report.

We have not discovered any recollections of the contractor or navvies employed on the construction of the line proper, but those engaged on the short section of line between the original intended junction and Risborough station made quite an impression as we can see from the *Bucks Herald* for 15th June:

PRINCES RISBOROUGH AND WATLINGTON RAILWAY — The Rev. W. E. Partridge, on the 7th inst., gave seventy-six of the navvies employed in making the road from Princes Risborough to the junction of the Watlington line, for the purpose of laying in another line of rails (as a token of his opinion of their general good conduct and behaviour during the time they have been employed on the work), a substantial dinner, consisting of 144lbs of beef, with something more than the usual quantity of vegetables and bread, and an allowance of three pints of beer and a screw of tobacco to each man. The repast was provided by Mr. Dover, of the Railway Tavern, Risborough Station, in the large coach-house belonging to his premises, tastefully fitted up for the occasion, the arrangements being, as usual, when he caters, first-class. After dinner, the health of the rev. gentleman was proposed by Mr. Dover, and the hearty response it met with from the throats of the recipients of his bounty was distinctly heard in the town, a distance of three quarters of a mile, and clearly proved that the navvy is not ungrateful for any act of kindness shown him. During the evening several other toasts were given and heartily responded to, the remainder of the evening being spent in singing. — On Tuesday last, the 11th inst., the Government Inspector, Colonel Rich, R.E., went over the Watlington branch of this railway and proved all the chief works. The only requirements which he made were such as involve merely a question of labour, as that the line will be practically finished in fourteen days. The opening of the line, however, for traffic, depends upon the completion of the parallel line from Bledlow to the Princes Risborough station, the works of which the Great Western Company are busily pushing forward. It is expected that the line will be opened about the middle of July. We understand that the line for Watlington to Risborough has been the cheapest yet constructed in the kingdom, the cost exceeding very little over £5,000 a mile. The line will be under the management of Mr. J. G. Rowe, manager of the Aylesbury and Buckingham Railway.

Not long after the Colonel's inspection, the engine shed at Watlington caught fire, on Sunday, 16th June, the *Bucks Herald* reporting:

The new fire engine lately purchased by this Parish was brought into use for the first time on Sunday last, at the terminus of the Watlington and Princes Risborough railway, and rendered effectual service in extinguishing a fire in the engine shed, occasioned by boiling gas tar, on that morning. The building was constructed of wood, and would have been soon destroyed had not the engine promptly arrived, as many of the boards were burnt quite through, and the quartering much injured.

This was unfortunate in view of the company's impending responsibility to the Great Western for housing the locomotive they were about to hire under an agreement of 20th June. Although we would not expect the locomotive type to be specified in such an agreement, the weight diagram accompany-

ing the Board of Trade inspector's report, is for a 517 class 0–4–2ST. Under the agreement, the GWR were to provide tank engines not exceeding laden weight of 28 tons, engineman, stoker, fuel, waste and oil and sufficient rolling stock for 3 trains each way per weekday. The engine crew were subject to approval by the W&PRR and considered servants of that company. For this the W&PRR were charged £1,100 per annum, any extra trains or shunting being subject to additional charges. The W&PRR had to provide an engine shed, coal stage and water tank.

In Colonel Rich's second inspection on 11th July, he still complained that the works were incomplete:

Sir,
I have the honor to report, for the information of the Board of Trade, that in compliance with the instructions contained in your Minute of the 29th Ultimo, I have inspected the Watlington and Princes Risboro' Railway.
The Works reported incomplete in my letter of the 11th ultimo have been executed except the connecting line, of ¾ of a mile long, from the New Line to Princes Risboro Station, which is to be laid down by the Great Western Railway Co.
The Clocks are ready, but have not been put up at the stations for fear they should be damaged before the Railway is opened.

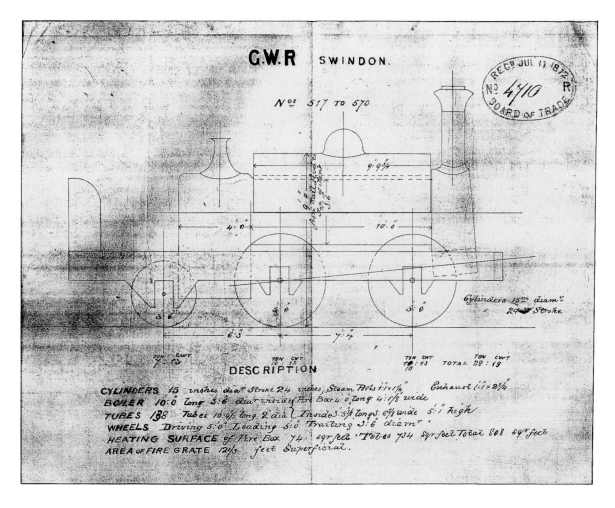

This official diagram of a '517' class engine was attached to Colonel Rich's report.

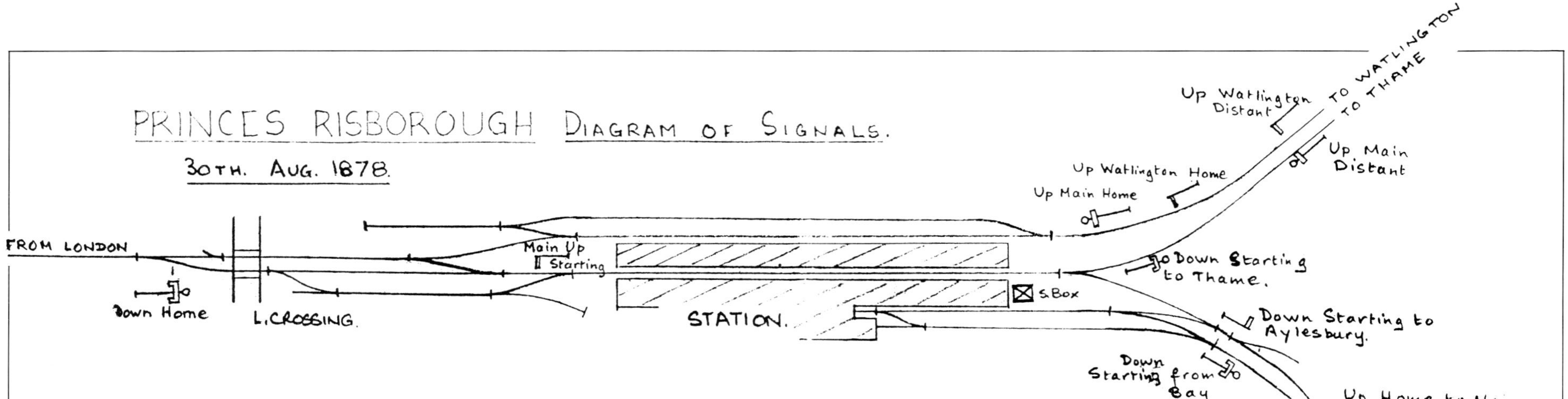

PRINCES RISBOROUGH DIAGRAM OF SIGNALS.

30TH. AUG. 1878.

TO WATLINGTON

TO THAME

Up Watlington Distant

Up Main Distant

Up Watlington Home

Up Main Home

Down Starting to Thame.

Down Starting to Aylesbury.

Up Home to main

TO AYLESBURY

Down Starting from Bay

Up Home to Bay.

Up Aylesbury Distant.

S.Box

STATION.

Main Up Starting

Up Main Home

L. CROSSING.

Down Home

FROM LONDON

This diagram of the signalling arrangements at Risborough in 1878 provides an idea of the additional 'platform and sidings' required by the Board of Trade which evidently comprised a run-round loop at the end of the new independent single line, a very narrow island platform and a crossover connecting the W&PRR to the Wycombe Railway. Whilst signals protected the junction station from the approach of W&PRR trains, there does not appear to have been any starting signal. Col. Rich's report stated that the junction between the two railways was 'not completed for passenger traffic', hence the absence of signals for such movements.

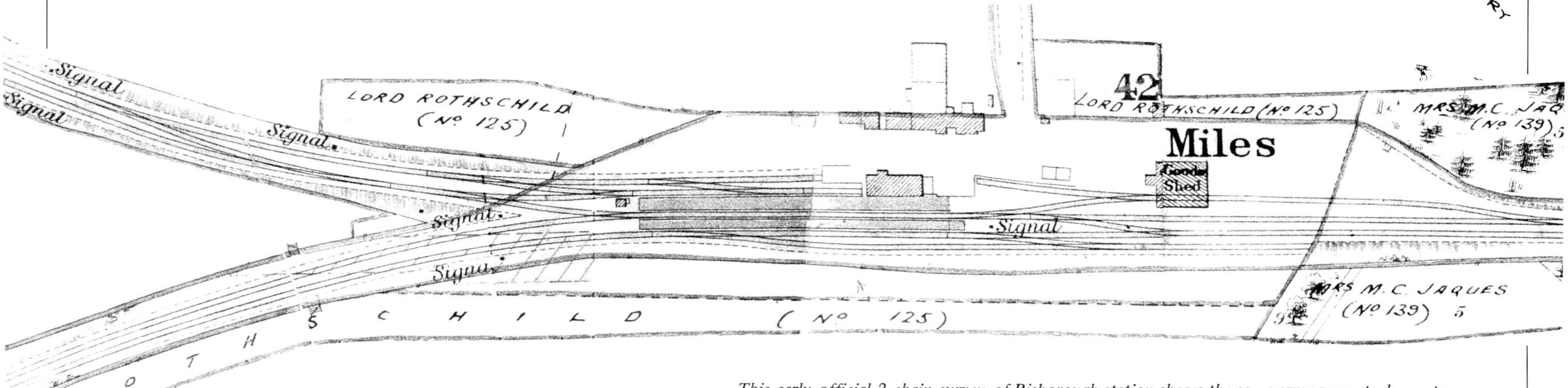

M.C. JAQ (No. 139) 5

MRS M.C. JAQUES (No. 139) 5

LORD ROTHSCHILD (No. 125)

Miles

42

Engine Shed

Signal.

LORD ROTHSCHILD (No. 125) 1

Signal.

Signal.

Signal

Signal.

ROTHSCHILD (No. 125)

This early official 2 chain survey of Risborough station shows the same arrangements drawn to scale. Apart from the additional platform, the general appearance of the station would have hardly changed from the picture on page 8/9.

I enclose a drawing of the Class of Engine which the Great Western Railway Co. propose to use, in working the New Line. I consider that the weights of 10ton 13cwt on the leading and driving wheels are very great for the 58lbs Rail, that the wheel base is short and the saddle tank not conducive to easy, steady and smooth running, on a surface line with heavy gradients such as the Watlington & Princes Risborough Railway.

The difference of weight on the leading and trailing wheels is not conducive to safe running when the engine is run with the trailing wheels in front.

I can not report that it is positively dangerous to use such engines on the Watlington & Princes Risboro' Railway but the engine will probably knock the light permanent way about and test severely the soft inferior chalk ballast that is used on the line. The safety will depend on the line being well maintained and these heavy, short based, top heavy engines being run at moderate speed — I have received no undertaking as to the proposed mode of working the railway.

I submit that the Watlington & Princes Risborough Railway cannot be opened for passenger traffic in consequence of the incomplete state of the works, in that there is no terminal station at which to take up and deposit the passengers on the Railway.

I have the honor to be your obedient servant
(Signed) F. H. Rich

It seems likely that despite the Colonel's comments, 517s were nevertheless used on the line, but subject to an appropriate speed restriction. His third inspection was more satisfactory, but there is no indication as to why the W&PRR were so reluctant to commit themselves to the method of working the line, unless it was a simple communication problem between the two companies. The Colonel's report of 9th August was as follows:

Sir,
I have the honor to report, for the information of the Board of Trade, that in compliance with the instructions contained in your Minute of the 29th Ultimo, I have inspected the Watlington & Princes Risborough Railway.

The Line which connects this Railway with the Princes Risboro' station of the Great Western Railway has now been completed, and I submit that the Board of Trade may sanction the opening of the above named Railway, so soon as a satisfactory undertaking as to the proposed mode of working is sent in.

No notice has been forwarded to me to inspect the ¼ of a mile of new Railway which has been laid by the Great Western Railway Co. from the termination of the Watlington & Princes Risboro' Railway up to Princes Risboro' Station. The only works on this new section of Railway are one under bridge of small span & one large culvert. These appear to be good. The permanent way is satisfactory and in a fit state for running on.

If it is necessary for the Great Western Railway Co. to give notice of opening I presume that they will do so when the Co. decides to open the Railway.

I have the honor to be your obedient servant
(Signed) R. H. Rich

P.S. The junction between the new line and the old line at Princes Risborough Station is not completed for passenger traffic.

Following the eagerly awaited inspection, the Secretary of the W&PRR wrote to the Board of Trade on 12th August:

As this company have complied with all the requirements of Col. Rich and been running goods trains over the line for the past week the Directors are at a loss to know why I do not open it for passenger traffic.

May I therefore ask when I am likely to receive the necessary permission from your office as the delay is not only of inconvenience to the district but tends to create a feeling of doubt in the minds of the people as to the safety of the line.

The Board of Trade replied the following day:

I am in receipt of your letter of 12th instant relating to the proposed opening of the Watlington and Princes Risborough Railway for passenger traffic.

In reply I am to inform you that as soon as the undertaking as to the proposed mode of working the Railway, referred to in the letter from this Department to the Secretary of the Company of the 10th instant has been received the BoT will sanction the opening of the Watlington and Princes Risborough Railway for public traffic.

On the 14th August the W&PRR sent an undertaking to the Board of Trade dated 6th August that the line would be worked by 'Train staff and ticket according to the mode in use on the Maidenhead and Princes Risborough Branch of the Great Western Railway.'

The line was opened for passenger traffic on Thursday, 15th August 1872, but the local press directed its attention to unrest among farm labourers. The only record we can find of any festivities is a belated account in the *Thame Gazette* for 27th August:

THE WATLINGTON AND PRINCES RISBOROUGH RAILWAY — The above line of railway was opened for passenger traffic on the 5th (sic) inst., and will, no doubt, prove a great convenience to the residents, of the district through which it passes, viz., Chinnor, Oakley, Crowell, Kingston Blount, Aston Rowant, Lewknor, South Weston, Shirburn, Pyrton and Watlington. On the opening day the manager of the line, Mr. Rowe, kindly gave the Watlington School children (a train load of them) a free ride to Risborough and back, which was greatly enjoyed by the juveniles, and will no doubt prove a red letter day in their history. The scenery through which the line passes is of the prettiest character, and passengers can obtain capital views of West Down, Crowell Hill, Beacon Hill, Watlington Hill, and other prominent features of a very interesting tract of country. Branching out of the Great Western Railway at Risborough, the new line skirts the end of Bledlow, and passes along at the foot of the Chiltern range to Chinnor, Aston Rowant, and Watlington. For a considerable distance the line runs nearly parallel with the old Icknield Road of the Romans. The villages on some of the high grounds are frequently resorted to by invalids for the sake of the salubrity of the air, and now that new facilities of access are afforded will no doubt be more generally visited.

From the outset, working expenses nearly always exceeded receipts, expenditure to 31st December 1872 totalling £789 1s 4d against receipts of £665 18s 11d. The report in Bradshaw's Shareholders Manual, however, tended towards optimism:

Since opening receipts have been sufficient to cover working expenses within the sum of £123 2s 5d and so far been able to discharge the GW account for loco power and hire of stock to 31st December 1872. In the accounts for this half year balances due on account of works mentioned in the last report have been included together with £3000 which had been retained for the due performance of the Contract, and also £1000 which had been treated as a loan to the contractor for the half year ending December 1870. With a view to developing traffic, directors have obtained a supply of wagons and sheets on hire from the Wagon Co. of Birmingham having experienced great difficulty in getting a proper supply from the Great Western for the purpose.

The same source records that against the authorised £36,000 in shares, they had received £35,972 whilst the £12,000 loan had been raised by 31st December 1872.

Although traffic increased during 1873, receipts still failed to match the running expenses, the directors explaining to the shareholders at the half-yearly meeting at the Hare and Hounds Hotel on 20th October, 'We are sorry to add that the balance on the half year is on the wrong side, the expenditure exceeding the income by a considerable sum'. To attract more traffic, they considered lowering the rates for 'heavy and large quantities of goods, especially corn'. In the circumstances, it must have been particularly annoying to find the Chinnor station master, Silas Finch, was stealing coal from the company. He was evidently dismissed and charged at the Watlington Petty Sessions on 2nd December.

At Princes Risborough the increased traffic brought by the opening of the W&PRR Co. seems to have prompted the request for an extra lad porter, and, although this was not immediately approved by the GWR Board, it prompted a report which subsequently revealed:

> Since the opening of the Watlington line the work of the station has been considerably increased as it frequently happens that three trains are at the station at the same time, viz, trains from the Watlington, Aylesbury & Wycombe Branches, and the staff, consisting of a man and a boy, are quite insufficient to attend to these properly.
>
> The traffic has also increased as will be seen from the subjoined statement:

	Goods		Passengers
4 months ending	tons	£	£
Dec. 31st 1872	4,642	1227	866
Dec. 31st 1871	3,480	1067	683

> and as the Superintendent of the Division has again strongly urged that an extra man be authorised, the Board are recommended to comply with the request.

The GWR also sanctioned £125 for office accommodation at Princes Risborough.

The W&PRR directors might have been able to report an increase in passenger traffic at the shareholders meeting in April 1874, but the undertaking continued to sink further into debt and there was no balance 'to justify the delivery of a dividend'. Great Western Board minutes in February 1874 record a balance of £565 9s 5d outstanding against the W&PRR in addition to the toll payable for the use of the GWR line at Risborough 'the minimum payment in respect of which is £150 p.a. Repeated applications have been made for the money without effect. Steps are being taken to enforce the payment.'

In March, James Grierson, the GWR's General Manager, reported that the W&PRR 'now owe this company a sum of about £340 upon Traffic Account and that repeated applications have been made for payment without effect and further that the Watlington Company have set up a counter claim against this company for loss through alleged delay in carrying out the works of the junction with their line'. This interesting tactic to delay payment did not stop the GWR from resolving to take steps to 'enforce the payment'.

In the absence of W&PRR minute books, we can only speculate over details, but it is possible that the GWR threatened the withdrawal of their locomotive, carriages and enginemen if the account was not settled and that the W&PRR in desperation to maintain services, hastily sought a locomotive and stock from an alternative source. On the other hand, the W&PRR might have felt that if it could not increase receipts, then apart from the immediate debt, it needed to reduce the working expenses, much of which was being paid to the Great Western for the hire of locos, stock, engine crew, etc. Either way, rather than a well-thought-out decision, this was a desperate attempt to reduce continually excessive running costs, and, by September 1875 the

These two engines, a 2–2–2WT owned by the Weston Clevedon & Portishead Railway and a 2–4–0T owned by the LBSCR, provide examples of Sharp Stewart designs of similar vintage and therefore probably of similar appearance to those purchased by the W&PRR.
Collection Jack Braithwaite

W&PRR had taken delivery of a second-hand Sharp Stewart 2–2–2WT for £900. They also had three carriages which must have been second-hand and pretty poor specimens at that because, by the beginning of 1878 they had to be replaced.

The purchase of a 17-year-old 2–2–2WT was surely a stopgap because a 5ft 6in single-wheeler would hardly have been the most ideal choice for hauling mixed trains up Chinnor bank. It seems likely that it just happened to be the only engine available at a time of crisis because more sensibly, just five months later, the W&PRR appears to have taken delivery of another Sharp Stewart engine, this time a far more suitable 2–4–0T with 4ft diameter driving wheels, purchased new for £1,475. It seems logical to suspect that this was ordered at the time the 2–2–2 was purchased. This all points to the change in operation policy being made in extreme haste, and a snippet from the *Thame Gazette* for 15th December 1874 makes it clear that the railway was under imminent threat of closure, though it does not mention that services ever actually lapsed:

> RAILWAY MEETING — A meeting of the shareholders of the Watlington and Risborough Railway was held on Saturday the 5th inst, the Earl of Macclesfield presiding. We especially notice it on account of a report prevailing that the line would probably soon be closed, whereas we are glad to say that those present, who represented nearly nine-tenths of the capital subscribed, agreed unanimously to assist in removing the present supposed difficulties, and in working the line on a more advantageous plan, so as to prevent any embarrassments that might otherwise arise.

As referred to in the locomotive and rolling stock agreement, the regular train service had consisted of three return trains each day, leaving Watlington at 9.15 a.m., 2.15 p.m. and 6.15 p.m. and returning from Risborough at 10.5 a.m., 3.35 p.m. and 6.43 p.m.

They were run mixed, i.e. passenger and goods. However, with the purchase of its own locomotive and stock, the W&PRR, taking advantage of its new freedom and seeking to increase receipts, introduced extra train services. From the beginning of 1875, the existing service was augmented by an early train leaving at 7.20 a.m. to connect with the first train to London, returning from Risborough at 8.0 a.m. and an evening train leaving Watlington at 7.15 p.m. to connect with the last train from Oxford to London, returning at 7.55.

Two return trains were also run on Sundays, leaving Watlington at 10.5 a.m. and 6.10 p.m., returning at 10.46 a.m. and 6.52 p.m. to connect with trains to and from London and Oxford.

Despite the fact that the *Thame Gazette* said the need for the trains 'had long been felt in the district', they did not receive sufficient support and were withdrawn that summer.

Although the W&PRR were no longer hiring locomotives and stock from the GWR, they appear to have continued to hire GWR engine crews, at least to start with. The first fireman, William Thurston, served on the branch from July 1872 before it was opened to passengers, until November 1874, significantly when the W&PRR first acquired their own inferior engine. However, his place was taken by John Cooke who served from November 1874 until September 1877. Both men were passenger firemen transferred from Oxford, Thurston having joined the GWR at New Milford. The first driver we have discovered was Thomas Belcher who served on the branch from August 1872 until August 1873. He was a 'goods engineman' who also transferred from Oxford, but we did not discover the name of his successor while trawling through copious GWR staff records.

Whilst these men were clearly GWR employees, this policy may have changed as the list of W&PRR staff inherited by the GWR in 1883 intimates that engine driver J. Almond and 'fireman and cleaner' F. Robinson were W&PRR staff who joined the company in September 1882 and May 1883 respectively. In support of this, the first entry on the staff record of fireman Robert Eugene Holloway unusually shows him as simply 'W&PRR Co.' before his transfer to Aylesbury in October 1883.

Before moving on, it is timely to point out that a steam locomotive needs constant attention and maintenance, not least to the boiler, from skilled and experienced fitters and boilersmiths. The GWR locomotives would undoubtedly have been changed periodically to allow attention at the parent shed or works, but the independent and impoverished W&PRR must have relied on hiring expertise (from the GWR?) and even then they had no workshop facilities or machinery for repairs. We have no details, but in these circumstances it seems likely that a 'make do and mend' situation prevailed, and this is borne out by the dreadful condition of the locomotives revealed in the 1883 reports (see page 28).

Meanwhile, writing from his London address, 19 Hyde Park Gardens, Thomas Taylor sent the following letter dated 24th April 1875 to the Chairman of the Great Western Railway, Sir Daniel Gooch:

I shall be much obliged if you can let me have an early answer to my proposition to lease to your Company the Watlington and Princes Risborough Railway. I am prepared to grant to the Great Western Company a lease of our line for three years at the low rent of £600 p.a. which is only about 1% on the cost of the line.

If you deduct from our expenses the cost of management you will find that the line is now about paying its way, and as the traffic is steadily increasing I have no doubt under your management it would be profitable to the GWR Co.

The rent to be paid to go in liquidation of the amount now owing by our Company.

Yours truly,
(Signed) Thos. Taylor

At a GWR Board meeting on 1st July 1875 the Chairman reported that the company had been asked to take over the W&PRR Co. 'After discussion the Board authorised Mr. Grierson to negotiate with the view of acquiring the undertaking and to report further to the Board.'

Thomas Taylor's claim that the line was 'now about paying its way' does not accord with the figures for the half year ending 30th June 1875, with expenditure at £1,405 0s 8d against receipts of £850 9s 0d, and there was still a substantial amount owed to the Great Western.

This was also a time of change, for Viret died, Peel, who was also secretary, retired, Allnutt resigned from the Board, and Rowe resigned from his position of manager (see below). The number of directors was reduced from five to three, the Earl of Macclesfield and Edward Robinson (a railway contractor based at Canon's Marsh, Bristol), were elected onto the Board and Richard Wileman Lemmon was appointed manager and secretary, Taylor remaining as Chairman. Lemmon was employed by the W&PRR from September 1875.

The locomotives and stock being purchased were held under the independent Watlington Rolling Stock Co. whose subscribers were the Earl of Macclesfield, Thomas Taylor, Albert Sandeman (wine merchant of Britwell Park), J. Allnut, E. Robinson, J. H. W. Peel (brewer), John Smith (of Britwell House), Hugh Hamersley, JP (of Pyrton Manor), A. H. C. Brown, Robert Palmer, Henry Reynardson (of Adwell House), and secretary R. W. Lemmon. The shareholders of the W&PRR were told that the directors had made arrangements with the Watlington Rolling Stock Co. for the use of their locos and carriages 'which they confidently hope will conduce to the more economical working of the line'.

The period around 1874/5 was understandably a time of great worry and uncertainty, and this climate took its toll on the board. The resignation of Rowe seems to have come about because of his unpopularity (for whatever reason), but it is tempting to believe that at least to some extent he was a scapegoat. Some of the circumstances surrounding his departure are revealed in the following extract from the *Thame Gazette* for 29th June 1875.

Mr. Robinson referred to the rolling stock account, and Mr. Rowe explained how and why the rolling stock project broke down, entering somewhat fully into matters affecting himself personally, the gist of which was that with a view to help the Company to provide a second or reserve engine, he himself took the responsibility, and bought coaches, which were accepted on hire at a meeting held 14 days afterwards. From Mr. Rowe's statement it appeared that a further meeting was held the same day, in another room, which he was not asked to attend, when it was decided, amongst other reorganisation nostrums, to obtain a cheaper man as manager, and on this coming to Mr. Rowe's knowledge he appears to have taken the Directors at their word and refused to act beyond the close of the year — hence the present state of affairs. The Earl of Macclesfield contradicted Mr. Rowe's version of the purchase of the coaches, but the matter seems to turn on a question of dates, and we shall probably hear more of it.

church, beer, spirits, and wine. Granted.

SHIRBURN.

ACCIDENT.—The train from Princes Risborough arriving in Watlington at 11.20 on Wednesday, came into collision, near the village of Shirburn, with a waggon drawn by two horses, the property of Mr. Joseph Burton, which was crossing the line in charge of a boy. It struck the shaft horse and, breaking the shafts, threw it off the line. The boy, who had dismounted from it and ran to the leader, had a narrow escape, as he hardly perceived the train till it was upon him, and as the accident occurred a short distance from the Watlington Station the train was proceeding at a slow rate. The horse, which was a valuable one, was so injured that it had to be destroyed.

Leyton, Essex.

PRINCES RISBOROUGH.

BAPTIST CHAPEL.—On Sunday evening the Rev Dr. Hillier, who has been pastor for three years and a half, announced that he should close his labours in Risborough with the present month, in consequence of having received an unanimous invitation to become the pastor of the Union Chapel, Wingrave.

THE RAILWAY.—Under date June 10th "A Traveller" writes to a contemporary as follows:—"There can be no excuse for persons taking third class tickets and occupying second class carriages. I know how this is brought about. Friends meet unexpectedly at the carriage doors and enter into some interesting topic of business or conversation, and upon the supposition that it is of "no odds," the third class ticket is made use of for a second class accommodation   Is the fault altogether with travellers? or does not a laxity in general management bring about such irregularities? He would be a bold man who would attempt such a trick on the London and North-Western Railway, because he would know that on a first attempt he would probably be detected. The railway authorities are perfectly justified in taking steps to avoid any imposition, but these steps should be take to prevent the occurrence and not to punish afterwards. Whilst guarding their own interests it is also the duty of the company to secure the comfort of their travellers. I think the company sin as much as they are sinned against. Take for instance the great nuisance of smoking. I have seen officials on the Risborough railway show smoking passengers with dirty pipes full on in their mouths, into non-smoking carriages, to the annoyance of other travellers. Again, look at the miserable accommodation afforded at Risborough station, which may be termed a junction, and at which it is the misfortune at times to have to wait a long time for some trains. Here there is an open shed, a ticket office, and a den labelled "Ladies' Waiting Room." This waiting room is a place which no lady would care to spend a quarter of an hour in. The ticket office is the only place where there is a fire. In having to spend an hour here short time ago, a man (I cannot call him a gentleman) took possession of the fire-place, lit up his pipe, and filled the whole place with his filthy smoke. No officials interfered, although they could not fail to observe the annoyance caused; the waiting-room had more the appearance of a pot-house than a railway station. Those who did not approve of the smoke might certainly adjourn to the open shed or open air, which, although excessively cold, were either preferable to stale tobacco smoke."

SCHOOLS.

TOWERSEY.

Extracts from Thame Gazette for 10th September 1878 and 17th June 1879.

The Chairman stated that the Great Western Company were in treaty for the line, but had made no definite offer for it.

A little more about Rowe, who, it will be remembered, was also manager of the Aylesbury and Buckingham Railway, is revealed in the *Thame Gazette* for 17th August 1875. The report mentions chalk traffic being despatched to Slough from Aston Rowant station at 4/6d per ton, 1/9d of which was received by the W&PRR '1/- as paid on' and 9d as their proportion of the through route to Slough. 'The company did not collect the money for the chalk, as that was paid by consignees to the Great Western Company. Mr. J. H. W. Peel stated that the consignees had been applied to, and, as they refused to give any information, no more chalk was sent.'

In Rowe's time, 2,084 tons of chalk had been sent, creating a balance of net revenue of £2,926 8s 6d, of which Rowe was entitled to £34 18s 0d commission. 'It was not his intention to have claimed a penny of it, but that he had been left to pay the balance of an account for repairing the road to the Watlington station, by which transaction he lost over £11. They would now be about level. Lord Macclesfield said Mr. Rowe need say no more about that, as the £34 18s 0d was his due.'

In the figures for the half year ending 31st December 1875, expenditure again exceeded receipts by £176. 0s 4d, this time attributed to £202 spent on the purchase of sleepers, fastenings and fencing. Whereas there was a £20 balance in favour of receipts against expenditure for the half year ending 31st December 1876, there was a £572 loss after the next 6 months end, by which time incidentally the auditors were W. J. Bloomfield. This loss might have been caused by payment of £1,173 15s 11d to the GWR 'in full settlement of all annual payments due from them to the Great Western Company . . . up to the 30th of June 1876' for use of the approach line and station at Princes Risborough. According to an agreement dated 11th October 1877, the W&PRR thereafter had to pay a fixed annual sum of £250 by twelve equal monthly payments.

The Watlington Rolling Stock Co. Ltd is particularly poorly documented, but one of its meetings, held on 27th January 1877 at the Hare & Hounds, was reported by the *Thame Gazette*. It comes as no surprise to learn that the meeting was chaired by the Earl of Macclesfield. According to the report, £115 was due from the W&PRR to the rolling stock company on account of working the traffic, but it is interesting that 'an order of the Court of Chancery had been obtained directing the payment of this amount by the receiver of the Railway Company's receipts. This order as yet has not been complied with'.

In the midst of all the W&PRR financial concerns, the *Bucks Herald* for 19th January 1878 was able to include a light-hearted note about the railway in its columns, although the directors may not have shared in the humour:

PRINCES RISBOROUGH

The Watlington Branch Line — A very amusing incident occurred here to the Watlington train due out at 6.30, on Wednesday, the 2nd inst. Passengers were duly booked, and having taken their seats, the usual signal "all right behind" was made, and the final signal from the station master having been given, they steamed off, not observing the consternation on the platform nor regarding the shouts to stay for the carriages, which were left behind. Strange to say, it was not till Jones and his stoker pulled up at Chinnor that they discovered to their astonishment there were no carriages with them. Retracing their steps they met the Guard on foot, danger light in hand, who explained that the carriages had not been coupled to the engine at Risborough.

Shirburn Castle, the seat of the Earl of Macclesfield.   *GWR*

That the three second-hand carriages purchased in 1874 were not a good investment is evidenced by the apparent approach to the Lancaster Wagon Co. which in June 1878 submitted a specification for three new carriages for delivery in four months. However, other than this, local newspapers reveal little of note during the next few years, although we can gather that the economic performance of the railway continued much as it always had. The occasions on which the half-yearly figures showed a balance in favour of four or five pounds, were offset by subsequent periods where expenditure exceeded receipts by over £200, attributed to 'the purchase of iron fencing £233 10s 0d' which was 'absolutely necessary to prevent losses which might arise from cattle straying on the line' or 'rebuilding wagons which have become the property of the company'. Rails, sleepers and fastenings had also been purchased because they were 'absolutely required to maintain the line in good working order'.

In 1880, E. Robinson's place was taken by Henry Clerke Brown, JP, of Kingston Blount, whilst the auditor was now given as Donald Kennedy. The following year, by 30th June, the Earl of Macclesfield resigned from the Board. He was replaced by Peel, and later, when Brown resigned, his place was taken by

Robinson who was 'now living in Weston Super Mare'. The shareholders were told of 'improvements and renovations' made to the permanent way and maintenance of the line generally during the half-year ending June 1881.

From the beginning of April 1882 another Sunday service was provided, perhaps with slightly more success since it was not 'discontinued for the Winter months' until the end of October.

At a Great Western Board meeting of 9th February 1882, the General Manager reported that the agreement between their company and the W&PRR for the use of Risborough station had expired on 31st December last and that the W&PRR had asked for renewal for a further five years on the same terms. 'After some discussion the General Manager was authorised to negotiate an agreement'.

While in communication with the Great Western, Taylor once more offered the W&PRR to them, Grierson, the GWR General Manager, reporting to the GWR Board on 2nd November that the W&PRR 'is desirous of coming to an arrangement with this company either for the working or for the purchase of the line, and he submitted a statement of the position of the company and a report from Mr. Owen upon the present condition of the line'.

'He also stated that Mr. Toogood is desirous of obtaining the cooperation of this company in an application to Parliament for powers to construct a railway from Watlington to Didcot, Wallingford or Reading'.

The Board declined Toogood's suggestion but authorised the General Manager 'to negotiate for the acquisition of the Watlington Railway'.

The minutes of the GWR Board meeting on 16th November record the following statement 'proposed by Mr. Taylor'.

1.   Great Western to pay the Watlington and Princes Risborough Company £1,500 on 1st July 1883, for the purpose of paying all outstanding debts.

2.   At the same time to give bonds at 4% for £12,000 — interest on which to be payable as from 1st January 1885.

3.   At the same time Great Western to give bonds at 4% for £9,500. Interest thereon not to be payable until 1st January 1890.

4.   Rolling stock to be purchased at a valuation.

5.   Watlington line to be properly maintained until handed over to the Great Western Co.

The matter was left in Grierson's hands, but the Directors 'declined to sanction the issue of a bond for £3,000 suggested by Mr. Taylor'.

Great Western Board minutes for 30th November record that a letter was read from the W&PRR 'accepting on behalf of that company the terms mentioned in that minute [16th November] for the transfer to this company of the undertaking of the Watlington Company. An agreement is to be prepared to give effect to the intended arrangement'.

The decision to offer the Watlington Railway for sale to the Great Western does not, however, as might be expected, seem to have been made jointly by the Board. It appears to have simply been Thomas Taylor's personal wish. He had evidently had enough of the venture, which, as far as he was concerned, had only ever been a drain on his resources. It will be remembered that the *Thame Gazette* for 9th November 1868 reported his 'doubts as to the ultimate success of the project' at the outset, and now, understandably, he was keen to cut his losses and be rid of it at almost any cost, in spite of the objections of his fellow Board members and investors. Unfortunately for them, Taylor's controlling stake was so large as to make them virtually powerless to do anything about it.

The *Thame Gazette* for 19th June 1883 takes the story further:

RAILWAY MEETING — A half-yearly meeting of the shareholders of the Watlington and Princes Risborough Railway Company was held at the Hare and Hounds Hotel on the forenoon of Saturday week. Thomas Taylor, Esq., was in the chair, and there were also present the Earl of Macclesfield, Messrs. J. H. W. Peel, E. Robinson, directors; A. A. Allnutt, A. H. C. Brown, Jones, Carter, G. Hatton, Viret*, Palmer, Hicks, Smith, Hill, H. Hamp, Webb, Rowe, Richards, Watson, Stevens, and R. W. Lemmon, secretary. The accounts were read and passed, and showed the total receipts for the half-year ending the 31st of December, 1882, to be £1,258 12s 8d, and the expenditure £1,248 16s 11d, leaving a balance of profit of £9 15s 9d. The Chairman then apologised to the meeting for the impossibility of their considering, according to notice and expectation, the proposal of a sale of the line to the Great Western Company. The meeting had, as usual, been advertised in the County papers, but he had only the day before been made aware that by a standing order (64) of the House of Lords it must also be advertised in two London papers, and the omission to do this would render their proceedings in respect of the contemplated transfer invalid.

As, however, so many had attended he would say in reference to the matter which it had been intended to vote upon, that the line had been for years a source of trouble and anxiety to him. For ten years not only had there been no profit, but their indebtedness was increasing at the rate of about £550 a year, and now stood at £23,269, in addition to that against them at the commencement of

* Presumably a relative of F. E. S. Viret who died in 1874.

ASTON ROWANT.

TEMPERANCE FÊTE.—The annual excursion of the Aylesbury Church of England Temperance Society took place on Thursday, the *rendezvous* being Aston Rowant Park, the seat of Mr. T. Taylor. The members of the Society, strengthened by contingents from Lower Winchendon and Stone, were conveyed to their destination by special train on the Great Western Railway *via* Princes Risborough, and arrived at Aston Rowant about two o'clock. A somewhat ludicrous incident occurred on the Watlington Railway. Just before the special reached Chinnor, the occupants were surprised by the train gradually coming to a standstill. After a while, those seated in the rear of the train were still more astonished to find that the engine had gone off with only half of them, leaving the remaining carriages stationary on the metals. Those left behind were in some fear that they were forgotten, but their fears were soon pacified, when it was explained that the poor engine was "dead beat" and could not drag its unusually heavy burden any farther, but that it would return for them presently —a promise which was duly fulfilled. Arrived at Aston Rowant the excellent Band of the No. 4 Company 1st Bucks Volunteers placed itself at the head of the large party, and played a selection of music during the walk to the park, which is situated about a mile from the station. The Temperance Drum and Fife Band was also in attendance, and played a number of airs at intervals. Upon entering the park the member dispersed about the grounds to amuse themselves in various ways. The principal attraction, however, proved a very nice picture gallery, which was thrown open to the Society by the kindness of Mr. Taylor. Some athletic sports had also been organised, including a 100 yards handicap, 120 yards hurdle race, quarter-mile handicap, one mile handicap, Siamese throwing at the wicket, and tug of war. The Rev. C. S. B. Riddell kindly officiated as judge, and Mr. R. Muyne as starter. An excellent tea was supplied by Mr. Evett, of Watlington. After tea had been partaken of, dancing was indulged in by those of the party who were so inclined, for the space of two hours. The Vicar then intimated that it was time to think of returning home, and moved a vote of thanks to Mr. Taylor for allowing them to spend their holiday in his beautiful grounds. Mr. Madder also moved a vote of thanks to Mr. Gibson (the steward). It need scarcely be said that these votes were given with all heartiness. After the evening hymn had been sung, the members retraced their steps to Aston Rowant station, the bands again playing selections alternately on the road. Arrived at the station the special was soon in attendance, and without any mishap or stoppage Princes Risborough was reached in safety. A special engine was here in waiting, and another move for home was made, Aylesbury being reached by about ten o'clock. With the exception of a few showers in the afternoon, which caused some slight inconvenience whilst they lasted, the weather was fairly favourable. A word of praise is due to the hon. secs., Mr. J. Ivatts and Miss Clift, especially to the former, who had the organization of the whole arrangements, and who will doubtless feel himself fully repaid by seeing his labours brought to a successful issue.

Thame Gazette 11th July 1882

The Hare and Hounds Hotel, in the centre of Watlington, where the meetings of the W&PRR were held.
Cty. Mrs. D. Hobbs

its working. He had resolved, for himself, not to go on but to bring the matter to a close. Mr. Peel (director) was unable to concur in the pessimist view of the situation taken by the Chairman, and deprecated the suicide he would commit. He disclaimed for himself and his co-director (Mr. E. Robinson) all responsibility for the proposed sale to the Great Western Railway, or approval of the amount offered. This he understood was £23,000, £1,500 to be paid on ratification of agreement, and the remainder in bonds for the amounts of £12,000, and £9,500 bearing interest at 4 per cent per annum, the interest on the first sum to be payable from 1886, and on the 2nd from 1890, such sums to be paid to the chairman, whose receipt should be sufficient discharge. Of this £23,000 it appeared £21,500 was to be retained by the Chairman, and of the remaining £1,500 the receiver was to get £600, and a firm of solicitors £365. But the railway had debts outstanding of about £700, a claim on them by one party of £100, and by another solicitor of £150, or £1,915, to be paid with £1,500. The Earl of Macclesfield held Lloyd's bonds for £550. The line had been made with the money of the original directors, and the proposal would 'shunt' them the Chairman expected; they had received no interest on £12,000 debenture bonds, but the Chairman had received £1,800 a year by way of interest on his (Mr. Taylor: "Not since 1875"). Why was not some alternative scheme offered them? Things could not be financially worse than they were, and they might gain by holding on — Mr. Robinson (director) took the same view. They had been in much worse case; the permanent way was in good order; if they went to the expense of some £1,250 now for sleepers and fencing they would find the Great Western Railway offering in the future £30,000 or perhaps £40,000 instead of £23,000. The Great Western Railway had taken over as unprofitable lines and paid 10 and even 24 per cent to the ordinary shareholders for their shares. If the Rolling Stock Company would for a couple of years forego their interest he saw his way to working the line and selling the line at a far advanced price to that which the Chairman would get for them in a bargain, which he inveighed against in an attack on that gentleman. He also complained that he had received no notice of the proposed sale. — The Chairman would not notice Mr. Robinson's attack on himself, but asked him how he supposed the line had been worked if not by himself, with the Earl of Macclesfield's assistance. The line now was, he might mention, indebted to him in the sum of £50,672 15s 7d — thus accruing,

debentures £18,800, Lloyds' bonds £9,516, and interest £10,356 16s 7d. Matters had been brought to a crisis by the refusal of the Great Western Railway to continue to allow the Company to run over their line at Risborough at the reduced rate paid for the last five years, of £250 per annum, they being empowered to charge £600 a year for the running powers. After some questions from Mr. Watson and some remarks from Mr. Rowe, the meeting stood adjourned to the 29th of the present month (Friday), as did a meeting of the Watlington Rolling Stock Company (Limited).

GWR Board minutes reveal that following the shareholders meeting, Taylor had written to the Great Western on 12th June:

At the meeting of the shareholders of the Watlington and Princes Risborough Railway Company there had been unanimous opposition to the Agreement for the acquisition by the G.W. Co. of that undertaking as it was considered that the sum to be paid for the line is much below its value, and that objection was also made to the Bonds for 5 years only. Mr Taylor further stated that he would agree to accept £20,000 in cash or in GW Debenture Stock instead of the bonds for £21,500 named in the Agreement.

The Board declined to sanction any increase in the sums named in the Agreement, but would not be indisposed to pay in cash the present value of the Bonds to be given under the Agreement, the present value of which is estimated at about £18,000.

Taylor evidently persuaded the *Thame Gazette* to include the following note in their 26th June edition:

THE WATLINGTON AND PRINCES RISBOROUGH RAILWAY COMPANY — We have been requested to publish the following letter, which has been forwarded by the Chairman (T. Taylor, Esq.), to all the Shareholders of the above Company:

Aston Rowant,
June 22nd, 1883

Dear Sir, — As a report of the half-yearly meeting of the Watlington and Princes Risborough Railway Company, held on June 9th, has appeared in some of the local newspapers, which is likely to prejudice shareholders against the agreement which, on behalf of that company, I have entered into with the G.W.R. Co., I think it due to you and to myself to put you in possession of the facts relating to the proposed

Dated   1883.

THE WATLINGTON AND PRINCES RISBOROUGH RAILWAY.

THE GREAT WESTERN RAILWAY COMPANY
TO
THOMAS TAYLOR, JOHN HENRY WEST-CAR PEEL AND EDWARD ROBINSON, ESQUIRES.

Bond

FOR PAYMENT OF PART OF THE PURCHASE MONEY FOR THE UNDERTAKING OF THE WATLINGTON & PRINCES RISBOROUGH RAILWAY.

Payable 1st July, 1895.

No.

Amount £100.

Waterlow & Sons, Limited, Printers, London Wall, London.

transfer. Some months since, finding the G.W.R. Co. was less indisposed to treat with our Company for the purchase of our line than it had previously been, I, with the approval of the Earl of Macclesfield and Mr. J. H. Westcar Peel, entered into negotiations with the G.W.R. Co., to "make the best terms I could" for the sale of our line. After much negotiation the directors of the G.W.R. Co., offered the sum of £1500 and Bonds for £21,500 for the Watlington and Princes Risborough line, at the same time stating that this was the outside sum they could give for it. I considered that I had full power to accept this offer on the company's behalf, subject to its ratification by the shareholders. In accepting the offer of the G.W.R. Co., I bore in mind the following facts:-

1.— That our company — under the most economical management — is only just paying its working expenses, the balance of £9 15s 9d declared at the Meeting, being nothing to set off against casualties.

2.— That no dividends have been, nor probably ever can be paid to shareholders.

3.— That as long as we retain the line in our own hands there is a little probability of the G.W.R. or any other company forming a junction with it for the West of England, or of securing a more frequent service of trains.

4.— That we shall be saved the heavy and uncertain liabilities which are incident to all Railways from injuries to the permanent way through weather or plant accidents.

5.— That according to our Act we are liable to the G.W.R. Co. for the payment of £600 per annum for running over ¾ of a mile of their line and the use of Risborough Station, and though by an agreement made six years since the G.W.R. Co. have accepted an annual payment of £250 for five years, the term of their agreement having expired they refuse to renew it.

I may mention that the cost of the line has been £50,433 and the whole of this — with the exception of about £8000 raised in shares — has been paid by me, and upon this sum I have received no interest. Also, that the whole of the bonds do NOT go — as stated by Mr. Peel at the Meeting — "absolutely and unconditionally to the Chairman", but, in the words of the agreement, "shall be divided amongst the debenture and other creditors and the holders of stock or shares in the proportion and according to the priorities in which they are respectively entitled to dividends under the existing Act."

With this explanation I do not hesitate to ask your support at the meeting on the 29th inst. to enable me to carry out the proposed agreement with the G.W.R. Co., and thus prevent the possible closing of the line.

I remain, Yours obediently,
THOMAS TAYLOR
Chairman of the W. & P.R.R. Co.

What transpired between Taylor and the shareholders can only be imagined, but that summer his opponents attempted to block the Bill's passage through the Lords. Peel wrote the following letter to the Great Western Board on 26th June 1883:

Dear Sir
The proceedings taken to block (so to say) the Bill before the House of Lords are due as you may know to Mr. Taylor's extreme regard for his own interest to the exclusion of all other, when giving instructions for the framing of the Agreement between the G.W.R. and W.P.R. Railway Companies; & subsequently his breach of faith (coupled with illegality of procedure) so that he has only himself to blame if the Bill is withdrawn. I have appraised him of what you say and am

Yours faithfully,
J.H. Westcar Peel

Nevertheless, the sale went ahead and a letter dated 4th July 1883 from the GWR General Manager's office to their solicitors said:

I have to inform you that the shareholders of the Watlington and Princes Risborough Railway have approved the terms of the Agreement for the sale of the undertaking to the GW Co. I intend reporting this to the Board at their meeting tomorrow. I send you herewith the counterfoil agreement sealed by the Watlington Co.

Later that year, on 29th December, notice was given of an Extraordinary Meeting of Shareholders at the Hare & Hounds Hotel on Tuesday, 15th January 1884 at 11.45 a.m. to pass a special resolution for the winding up of the company 'in pursuance of Section 65 of GWR Act 1883' and to appoint a liquidator.

According to the *Thame Gazette* for 22nd January, a resolution was passed to the effect that the company be wound up voluntarily and that Messrs. J. H. Peel and R. W. Lemmon be the liquidators.

Despite the shareholders' resolution, Thomas Taylor became liquidator of the W&PRR Co. and R.W. Lemmon for the Watlington Rolling Stock Co. The winding up of both companies was protracted and tiresome and, although the two were intimately connected, they were quite separate throughout the liquidation. Indeed, there was apparently little co-operation between them, Lemmon not succeeding in prising an outstanding debt of £177 from the W&PRR Co. until August 1885.

It seems that the agreement incorporated by Act of Parliament for transferring the line to the GWR was executed swiftly enough to preclude alteration to the duration of the five year bonds written into the conditions. Taylor was anxious to have this changed and in a letter to GWR solicitor Nelson on 16th October 1883 wrote:

I supposed that the Bonds would have 20 years to run from the date of payment of the first interest and should prefer them to be so dated if your directors are agreeable. I shall be much obliged if you will push this business forward as rapidly as possible as I am much pressed by those interested to have this business settled as soon as possible.

The matter dragged on with successive misunderstandings of how a settlement was to be achieved, but a letter from Daniel Gooch on 17th January 1884 makes it clear:

My dear Sir,
If you will be good enough to refer to my letter of the 8th November last you will see precisely what was the nature of the arrangement which the Directors of this Company were willing to carry out.

The Bonds having been issued in accordance with the requirements of the Act the proper way to give effect to the contemplated arrangement will be by an endorsement upon the Bond to the effect that it has been agreed between the holder of the Bond and the GWRB that the repayment of the principal sum shall be made on the 1st July 1903 instead of on the date fixed by the Bond and to justify us in making this endorsement we should require that the Bond should be sent to us with the request of the holder of the Bond that this alteration should be made.

Any such application which may be made to us within the time referred to in my previous letter shall at once have the attention of the Officers of this Company and I do not anticipate that there will be any difficulty or delay in effect being given to the arrangement.

But you will see on reference to that letter that it was a condition precedent to this bargain that the arrangement on the terms fixed by the Act of Parliament should have been carried out. I am told however by the officers that the plans &c have not yet been handed over as provided by the Act and that a good deal of inconvenience is caused by the want of them.

I hope you will be good enough to take whatever steps may be necessary to ensure compliance with this part of the agreement and

you will find no reluctance on our part to carry out the extension of time with the holder of any Bond who may desire it.
Yours truly
Dan Gooch

The Bonds continued to form the subject of much correspondence, too tedious to reproduce here, but the following letter from Nelson to Saunders on 24th March 1884 is interesting:

Mr. Taylor's letter to Sir Daniel is as unfortunately most of his communications are very inaccurate.

What was contemplated on the occasion of the completion of the purchase was simply what had been said before, namely that this Company would not object to give to the Transferees of such of the Bonds as might wish them to do so on undertaking to extend the time of repayment to 20 years from June 1883.

Early in July in the present year Mr. Taylor wrote to me informing me that he had sold the Bonds asking that the undertaking referred to might be forwarded to him. In reply I pointed out to Mr. Taylor that he had no right whatever to deal with the Bonds but was merely a Trustee for the Liquidator when he should be appointed.

I also wrote at the same time to Mr. Radcliffe informing him of what it appeared Mr. Taylor was doing and I know that he expressed himself very strongly to Mr. Taylor as to the impropriety of what he was proposing to do.

Mr. Taylor has, I believe, recently been appointed Liquidator of the Company, but I apprehend you will think it right to adhere to what was said before — that upon any transference of the Bonds desiring their period of repayment to be extended you would not object to endorsing on the Bonds a memo to that effect.

On 26th March 1884, Thomas Taylor wrote to Saunders:

I have your letter of 24th inst. and regret very much that there has been any misunderstanding about the Bonds. I am quite aware that the original arrangement was that the extension of the time of payment should be endorsed on the back of the Bonds. But when the Bonds were handed to me in Mr. Nelson's office, I was informed by Mr. Radcliffe that it had been arranged between himself and Mr. Nelson that letters would be given to the holders of the Bonds instead.

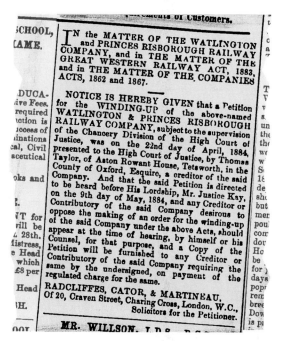

Thame Gazette 29th April 1884

Couching Street, Watlington.

This view of Watlington, taken from a postcard, shows Couching Street, probably in Edwardian days, but one of its charms is that the town changed little over the years.

As you wish them to be endorsed, I will thank you to say when I may forward them to you, and I shall be obliged by your stating how soon I can hear back, as I am pressed very much for the delivery of some that were sold some months since; and as my appointment as Liquidator has been confirmed, I am anxious to get all these matters settled without further delay. All the plans and documents relating to the titles of land purchases by the Watlington Co. were left in the hands of their solicitors, Messrs. Toogood and Jones, and I have Mr. Toogood's undertaking that they should all be delivered to you through Mr. Radcliffe, which I am informed has been done. I beg leave to state that the arrangements for the extension of the time of the Bonds was made unconditionally.

Taylor seems to have been remarkably reluctant to hand over the documentation of the W&PRR Co. as required in the agreement, and whilst this might not be so apparent in the letter he sent to the GWR solicitor, Nelson, on 22nd December 1883 (which follows), it becomes increasingly obvious through subsequent correspondence, as we shall see.

I have your letter of yesterday and now hand you the Directions as to the issue of Bonds.

With regard to plans of the line and agreements for the same I have to state that Mr. Wm. Toogood of London and W. Jones of Watlington were solicitors for the Watlington Company and they had the entire management of the purchasing and conveyancing of the land and paying for the same. Mr. Toogood suggested that we should only take receipts for the purchase money with undertaking to give conveyances if required and to this we agreed.

Mr. Jones was the first Secretary of the Company and continued to fill that office until the line was open when our Manager was appointed Secretary.

Mr. Jones informs me that he does not hold any documents belonging to the Watlington Company but that all were in the possession of Mr. Toogood.

Messrs. Wilkinson and Smith were the Engineers of the line but we have had nothing to do with them since the opening of the line.

Evidently frustrated in their attempts to persuade Taylor to hand over paperwork of various kinds, it is tempting to assume that the Great Western were holding out over the balance due to the W&PRR Co. in order to encourage Taylor to cooperate. A letter dated 2nd June 1884 from Taylor to the GWR explains the situation:

I enclose a statement of interest on the £1,500 which according to the agreement ought to have been paid in December last and also an account of the unused stores, etc. taken by your Company on 29th December 1883 amounting altogether to £63 7s 9d. I shall be obliged by your sending me a cheque for the amount at your earliest convenience as the creditors of the W.P.R.R. Co. we are pressing for a settlement of the Company's affairs . . .

P.S. I shall be much obliged by your sending to Messrs. Radcliffe & Co., 20 Craven Street, Charing Cross, two bonds, viz:

One bond out of the £12,000
" " " " £9,500
which were left with you for endorsement.

In 1886 the Great Western were still pressing Taylor to hand over the minute books and he was still stalling, as shown in a letter to the GWR on 17th September:

In reply to your letter of yesterday's date, I beg leave to state that as soon as the £10 5s 5d due by the GWR to the Liquidator of the Watlington Co. is paid I will endeavour to procure for you the Minute Book you require. The above amount is the balance of an account rendered to you for stores and of the Watlington Co. amounting to £67 8s 4d, an account of which you have only paid £57 2s 11d leaving the above named balance.

His reluctance to hand over the W&PRR minutes persisted until the bitter end. On 7th November 1891 the GWR were still writing to ask for the books and on 29th November received the following reply from Mrs. Helen B. Taylor writing from Bolton:

Mr. Taylor has been severely ill and I should have replied for him sooner to your letter of 7th inst. With regard to the Books and Acts of the Princes Risborough Railway had you applied for them sooner they would all have been handed over to the GWR Co., though Mr. Taylor has no recollection of any 'agreement' on his part to give them up. As it is, when we left Aston Rowant on the 12th June these books were put aside as useless and with an accumulation of other waste paper were sent by the servant to the paper mills. The covers of the books and some sheets of blank paper are all that remain of them.

From the outset until its somewhat sad and acrimonious takeover, the Watlington line had unquestionably been Taylor's railway. With, as pointed out before, only £8,000 raised locally in shares, it seems extremely unlikely that the W&PRR would ever have got built in the first place, let alone have been subsidised to survive and become part of the Great Western Railway and the twentieth century at all. Once Taylor's mind was made up, there was precious little that the other board members could do about it in spite of their efforts to prevent the takeover. He was clearly not a popular man, and his reluctance to hand over the minute books suggests that the company's last years and his marginalisation on the Board were an embarrassment to him.

On 15th March 1892, almost nine years after the death of the Watlington & Princes Risborough Railway Company, Taylor himself passed away. If any shareholder or director of the old W&PRR Co. attended the funeral, they are not recorded among the mourners listed by the press.

The company seal, now held at Swindon Museum.

Engine 1

Built 1857 for Barrow & Furness Coy purchased 2nd hand in 1875 by W&PR. Is in very defective condition, good for nothing but scrap. Copper box appears to be thin and tube plate much eaten away. Both outside frames broken & patched. Brake placed so as to fatigue frame on R. side. Motion old fashioned. No bars but prolonged piston rod, and much worn. D. wheels broken across the rim in several places. Note the openings at the trailing end and position of T. boxes. L & T tyres very thin. Note position of injectors. Three bearing springs broken, wet sand.

Engine 2

Built in 1876 for the W&PR Coy, is badly in want of a thorough overhaul. Loose liners between A. boxes and check plates, all motions want letting together. Tyres want turning (will only turn up once more). R. leading & driving springs broken and cramped together. Left D. wheel boss cracked and a number of spokes in this and the opposite wheel working loose in the boss. Tubes leaking & boiler appears in very dirty condition. Note the short eccentric rods.

Carriage stock

Built by Lancaster Wagon Co. Underframes pitch pine, solebars 10in deep with ¼in iron plate, oak headstocks & cross bearers, diagonals & longitudinals are of deal.

Body framing of teak, cant-rails of pitch pine, panelled in varnished teak, cased inside in deal. These vehicles have suffered very much from exposure to the weather but are otherwise in fair condition for their age. The panels and mouldings require to be stripped off and repinned and the whole of the

vehicles thoroughly repaired and either varnished or painted. They do not appear to have been built with thoroughly dry timbers, many panels are split.

Three old carriages standing at Chinnor consist of Compo, Third & Van. They are perfectly valueless except for the old metal. It will cost as much to break them up as the old timber &c is worth.

Two wagons (Nos. 1 & 2) only are standing at Watlington and two at Chinnor. The other two are from home. They are all light six ton trucks (open goods) with dead buffers and the draw bar pulling on the middle bearers, in some cases with only a half inch iron washer intervening. In each of the wagons at Watlington there is one pair of Kirtley & one pair of Smith & Wylie wheels & in each wagon one sharp flange. The tyres are getting thin. The two wagons (Nos. 4 & 6) at Chinnor are stopped with bulged tyres. Frames pitch pine except headstocks & middle bearers of oak.

The formation of the road is chalk without ballast and in wet weather the engines must suffer severely from dirt thrown up in passing as the road is in very defective condition. The rail 54lbs irons Vignoles fastened with dogs & fished.

The water at Watlington is pumped from the chalk & is very hard. Wood tank 12ft × 7ft 0in × 4ft 4in.

The whole of the engines, carriages & wagons bear the plates of the Watlington Rolling Stock Coy. The greater part of the road is unfenced.

WATLINGTON & PRINCES RISBOROUGH RAILWAY STOCK

Passenger Stock

The 3 vehicles running on the above line, particulars of which are given on the attached Form, were built in 1878 by the Lancaster Wagon Co. and are in fair condition for their age but owing to exposure to the weather the majority of the door panels are split, they should at once be sent into the shops for a general overhaul and to be revarnished or painted, the wheels have wrought centres 9in in diameter, 7in through, the spokes are 3in x ¾in, Tyres (steel) are very hollow and secured by Mansell's fastening, the axles are marked 'Lancaster Wagon Cos faggotted scrap', the side springs consist of 10 7/16in plates 3½in wide, the drawbars and buffers have the ordinary laminated spring consisting of 12 ½in plates, the buffers stand out 1ft 9½in from the headstocks with cast iron buffer guides which allow a stroke of 10in, the buffer rods are 2½in in diameter, the drawbars are 1½in in diameter. Screw connections 1¼in screw 7/8in links. The Compo & 3rd class have continuous footboards but one on the Compo was broken some time back and was never repaired, but this side it is as the doore are never used, full width out to out of continuous footboards 9ft, [. . . ?] step 8ft 4in. The axleboxes are for grease and have solid bottoms.

The first class compartments are trimmed with blue cloth, one cushion the full length, the door trimming American cloth, blue blinds, rail net & hat cords, floor cloth and rug on floor, 6ft 7in between the compartments. The 2nd class are trimmed blue rep, no blinds, but have hat cords and metal rack, 6ft between the compartments, no rug or floor cloth, the trimming is not bad and with a little touching up would look very well. One compartment of each class set apart for smoking. [. . . . ?] the side lights. The 3rd class has also one compartment set apart for smoking at one end, the other 4 compartments have one complete division and two low ones 3ft 4in high, the Composite has a roof lamp in each compartment but the 3rd class is lit by 2 lamps placed in the roof at the two divisions in the same place as the old 1st carriages to light each side. The width of the 3rd class compartments are 5ft, no cushions or blinds but have metal hat racks. The van has a guards compartment 6ft wide. The screw of the break is 1½in diameter square thread, 12in long, the break is out of order and should be repaired at once, the break screw works out of the socket, there is a roof lamp in guards compartment of van but not in the luggage body.

Wagon Stock

The six wagon were rebuilt by the Watlington Co. in 1879, the old wheels and some of the old iron work being used. The wheels were for the most part made in 1858 and the class under the different wagons as follows:

No. 1	1 pr Smith & Willey	1¼ tyres badly worn
	1 pr Kirtly	1½ tyres very hollow
No. 2	1 pr Kirtly	1½ tyres very hollow
	1 pr Smith & Willey	1¼ tyres very hollow
No. 3	2 pr Smith & Willey	1¾ tyres very hollow
No. 4	1 pr Smith & Willey	1¼ bad tyres. Stopped at
	1 pr Kirtly	1¼ Chinnor
No. 5	1 pr Kirtly	1½ Very hollow & square
	1 pr Smith & Willey	1¼ flange
No. 6	2 pr Kirtly	1¼ bad tyres. Stopped at Chinnor.

The journals of these wheels are much worn and the wheels altogether are not worth much. The elevation is 3in deal, the drawbars are light and pull from the middle bearers which are all pine, the India rubbers that were put originally as springs are worn out and only ½in iron washers left.

The solebars and headstock are 12 x 4½in, Nos. 4, 5 & 6 oak, the others pitch pine, the middle bearers and other underframe are pine, the side springs are, with the exception of those on No. 2 wagon, old and consist of 9 3/8in & 1 ½in plates, 3in wide, the springs under No. 2 have an additional ½in plate and have been set up.

Wagon Sheets

There are 6 of these but they are all in a damaged state.

Carriage Shed

There is a shed at Watlington to stand the carriages in, it is 89ft long, 13ft wide and 15ft 4in from rail to centre of roof, it is covered with corrugated iron and also the sides to 6ft 4in from the rails.

? A. Ludgate

CHAPTER THREE

UNDER NEW MANAGEMENT
1883–1921

THE Watlington shareholders may have believed that the Great Western had a bargain in obtaining the line at a fraction of its original cost, but, serving a rural community with farming the only industry, the Watlington branch was hardly likely to yield any dramatic increase in traffic. Furthermore, if the railway had brought any degree of industry and prosperity to Watlington, then it was not reflected in the population figures which fell from 1,943 in 1871 to 1,386 in 1921. The population of Chinnor also fell from 1,379 in 1871 to 973 in 1921. Indeed, judging from the traffic figures, had it not been for the unforeseeable establishment of the limeworks at Chinnor some 27 years later, the line might even have become one of the post-1914 or 1930s candidates for closure.

It would be interesting to know what Messrs. Holden and Ludgate thought when inspecting the line and valuing the W&PRR Co's rolling stock. Coming from the mighty and well-organised Great Western Railway, the sight of the Watlington branch must have intrigued them. The shareholders were told on several occasions of expenditure on rails and sleepers, but, in view of the company's financial position, such purchases were surely only ever essential repair work to patch the line and keep it in operation. The report from Owen, the Chief Engineer of the GWR, only seems to confirm the impression that the impoverished line was very run-down and suffered poor track. Just imagine the impression given by the carriages, bought in 1874, and left abandoned to rot at Chinnor along with two of the company's six wagons which had been stopped with bulging tyres.

As for the locos, the 2–2–2WT was 'good for nothing but scrap' and the newer 2–4–0T was desperately in need of a thorough overhaul. Even the brake van of the coaches ordered new from the Lancaster Wagon Co. in 1878 had an inoperative brake. As this must have doubled for use as a goods brake van, running mixed trains along the line must have been interesting!

The rolling stock was valued at £1,714 and it seems unlikely that anyone could realistically have argued for more. The whole railway must have been a shambles and the sooner the Great Western started to sort it out the better. Indeed the appearance of the railway was probably more akin to some of the ramshackle scenes familiar to students of the Colonel Stephens light railways of the interwar years.

In August 1883, £3,750 was authorised to put the line in order, but it subsequently transpired that the estimate on which this was based was woefully inadequate.

On 14th November 1883 the GWR Board considered a report from Mr. Owen dated 9th November 'on the condition of the Watlington and Princes Risborough line, recently acquired by this company. It is represented that, in consequence of the decay in sleepers and the condition of the rails it will be necessary to expend £7,010 if the line is to be kept up in its present character for light engines, or £9,827 if it is to be made good for the ordinary rolling stock of this company. Mr. Owen was instructed to put the line into a thorough state of repair at the least possible cost.'

Little is known about the work undertaken by the GWR during the first months after the takeover to put the line into proper condition, but it seems likely that all the old lightweight flat-bottomed track was replaced with chaired bullhead laid on proper ballast. In practice, with all the fencing and refencing also required, it seems likely that the GWR's investment had bought little more than the formation. Even the existing earthworks were far from ideal for if the Great Western had built the line, they would surely have eased the gradients by evening out some of the switchbacks, which, of course, remained throughout its life.

The station platforms appear to have had new brick facings and the 11 year old buildings were also probably put into a proper state of repair and perhaps repainted. The offices would

Station	Name	Grade	Date of Birth	Entered Service	Last advance £		Present Salary or wages
Watlington	Lemmon R.W.	Secretary & Manager	May 47	Sep 75	May 77	10	£165
"	Lett R.	Bkg porter	May 34	Oct 72	Oct 87	5	70
"	Charlton H.	Lad porter	July 66	Oct 81	Oct 82	1/-	7/-
"	Cronford A.	Guard	Nov 56	Apr 72	–	–	20/-
"	Almond J.	E. driver	Sep 32	Sep 82	–	–	39/-
"	Robinson F	Fireman & cleaner	Jan 60	May 83	–	–	20/-
"	Green J.	Platelayer	Oct 56	Dec 80	–	–	16/-
Aston Rowant	Day M	Bkg porter	Nov 43	Jan 77	–	–	17/-
" "	Kent T	Foreman platelayer	Oct 39	Aug 79	–	–	20/-
" "	White A	Platelayer	Apr 39	Jan 73	–	–	16/-
" "	Lamborn J	Platelayer	Oct 57	Jan 79	–	–	16/-
Chinnor	Reynolds J	Bkg porter	Feb 48	Aug 71	Jan 82	1/-	15/-
"	Holland W	Foreman platelayer	Apr 38	Sep 72	–	–	20/-
"	Hopkins J	Platelayer	Apr 38	Oct 74	–	–	16/-
"	Swain S.H.	Platelayer	Jan 51	Oct 79	–	–	16/-

List of W&PR Co. staff transferred to Great Western service.

Although taken around 1905, this postcard shows Chinnor station very much as it would have appeared straight after the GWR improvements. It also shows the switchback nature of the line.

doubtless have been restocked with standard GWR stationery, although, curiously, at least some of the old W&PRR tickets were retained and issued by the GWR for many years afterwards.

The staff of the W&PRR were transferred to GWR service (see list) including the secretary and manager R. W. Lemmon who was 'placed on the company's register of clerks'. From 1st January 1884 he was appointed Superintendent at Watlington and in April 1884 he transferred to Norwich as GWR canvasser for goods traffic. He resigned from the railway on 11th September 1887.

It seems likely that the Lancaster Wagon Co's coaches were despatched for sale, whilst the Sharp Stewart 2–4–0T W&PRR No. 2 was sent to Swindon for rebuilding. It emerged as GWR No. 1384 and, with Swindon boiler fittings, had a quite different appearance, but its subsequent service elsewhere in the country has no part in our story for there is no record of it ever returning to Watlington in its new guise.

Although we don't know what engines were provided for the branch at this time, it seems likely they would have been '517' class 0–4–2Ts or 'Metro' class 2–4–0Ts together with two or three 4-wheel coaches, which, although cascaded from more prestigious services, would nevertheless have been more ruggedly built than the W&PRR's stock and quite adequate for this rural outpost.

By the time the Great Western had finished all the relaying, fencing and smartening the stations, issued the staff with the company's uniforms and provided their own properly maintained locos and rolling stock, the line would have presented an entirely different impression and been far more worthy of its place in the greater system.

Despite the improvements, the passenger service saw little change, the basic pattern of three return trips, all of which still ran mixed, enduring until the end of the century. In May 1884, for example, trains left Watlington at 9.0 a.m., 2.10 and 5.40 p.m., returning at 10.30, 3.40 and 6.30 p.m. This was not entirely satisfactory, the *Thame Gazette* for 19th February 1884 reporting:

A numerously signed petition has been presented by the townsfolk, to the management of the GWR, praying for an earlier train than the

CHEAP EXCURSION ON WHIT-TUESDAY, JUNE 3rd, 1884.
International and Industrial Exhibition, Crystal Palace, International Health Exhibition at South Kensington, Horse Show at the Agricultural Hall.

THE Committee of the "Loyal Bud of Hope" Lodge, M.U., I.O.O. Fellows, have pleasure in announcing that they have made arrangements with the Great Western Railway Company to run
AN EXCURSION TRAIN
TO WINDSOR AND LONDON
(Paddington Station), as under:—

	Time of Starting	3rd Class Fares there and back	
		Windsor	London
	a.m.	s d	s d
WATLINGTON	7 20	3 0	4 0
Aston Rowant	7 33		
Chinnor	7 45		
AYLESBURY	8 5	2 3	3 6
Little Kimble	8 12		
Princes Risborough	8 22	2 0	
West Wycombe	8 34	1 9	
HIGH WYCOMBE	8 43		3 0
Loudwater	8 50	1 6	
Wooburn Green	8 55		
Great Marlow	8 33	1 6	3 3
Bourne End	9 5	1 3	
Cookham	9 12	—	3 0
Maidenhead	9 35	—	

First Class Tickets issued at double these fares.

The Return Train will leave Paddington at 8.25 p.m., Westbourne Park at 8.30 and Windsor at 8.50 p.m. the same day.

Crystal Palace — Through Excursion Tickets to the Crystal Palace, including admission, and available for return from Paddington at 8.25 p.m., will also be issued by above Train, as under:—
2s 3d First Class, and 1s 6d Third Class in addition to the London Fares.

For further particulars see Bills.

This staff group at Watlington in 1892 features Robert Lett (third from the left), effectively station master. The other men remain unidentified. Although the GWR had taken over nine years earlier, the station building is shown in its original condition with the open porch which was later enclosed to increase accommodation. This picture also shows goods stock in the platform from mixed train working and a glimpse of what appears to be either a '517' or 'Metro' tank with smokebox wingplates.

present 9 a.m., in business interests, as well as for the later return from town than 4.50 p.m., and for facility for longer stay in Oxford than at present is afforded.

If the petition had any effect on the GWR management, it certainly did not manifest itself for a number of years, but the GWR were disposed to run special trains occasionally, as witnessed by the following examples mentioned in the *Thame Gazette* for 22nd January and 25th May 1884:

GREAT WESTERN RAILWAY — On Wednesday evening this Company ran another train to Princes Risborough, to enable patrons of the histrionic art to assist at a performance given in the National Schoolroom at Risborough. A completely-filled train showed how gladly our townspeople avail themselves of improved travelling arrangements under the aegis of the new proprietary.

EXCURSION TO LONDON AND WINDSOR — Arrangements have been made by the Wycombe "Loyal Bud of Hope" Lodge, M.U., I.O.O. Fellows, with the Great Western Railway Company to run an excursion train to London and Windsor, leaving Watlington at 7.20, Aston Rowant 7.33, Chinnor 7.45. Further particulars will be found in another column.

Perhaps less predictably, a few years later, a petition for a reduction in carriage charges was successful, as reported in the *Thame Gazette* for 30th August 1887:

WATLINGTON — It will be remembered by many readers that a memorial to the Directors of the GWR asking for a reduced scale of rates for carriage of corn and other commodities was initiated some months since by E. Hamersley Esq. of Pyrton Manor, and was very numerously signed. This effort, combined with very great assistance in the matter rendered by our worthy member and near neighbour the Hon. F. Parker, has at length succeeded, and our railway rates from Watlington have been very substantially reduced.

Whether the unspecified reduction in rates was entirely due to the petition or really part of a broader scheme is not clear. By this time the home market for wheat had been devastated by imports from America where the railways had opened up the prairies. Land there was literally given to settlers who were

WATLINGTON BRANCH.
SINGLE LINE.
Worked by Train Staff. Form, Round; Colour, Black.

		DOWN TRAINS.		WEEK DAYS only.	
Dist.	Stations.	Pas. & Gds	Pas. & Gds	Pas.	
		A.M.	P.M.	P.M.	
—	Princes Risboro dep.	10 30	3 40	6 30	
3¾	Chinnor ,,	10 43	3 53	6 40	
6¼	Aston Rowant ,,	10 54	4 4	6 47	
9	Watlington arr.	11 5	4 15	6 55	

		UP TRAINS.		WEEK DAYS only.	
Dist.	Stations.	Pas.	Pas. & Gds	Pas. & Gds	Loads of mixed trains not to exceed 8 trucks for Down Trains and 10 trucks for Up Trains & the passenger vehicles on this branch.
		A.M.	P.M.	P.M.	
—	Watlington dep.	9 15	2 15	5 45	
2¾	Aston Rowant ,,	9 23	2 26	5 56	
5¼	Chinnor ,,	9 30	2 37	6 7	
9	Princes Risboro arr.	9 40	2 50	6 20	

Taken from GWR Service Timetable January to June 1888.

therefore able to grow vast quantities of wheat with minimal overheads. Even after shipping to Britain and Europe in the new larger steam ships, the American wheat was only a quarter of the price of homegrown crops. Furthermore, the American grain, which did not have the same moisture content as home-grown varieties, produced a lighter white bread evidently preferred by consumers.

France and Germany protected themselves from the American grain by imposing harsh tariff barriers, whilst in Scandinavia it was restricted for use as animal feed. Under Britain's free trade policy, it completely undermined the agricultural economy. In Buckinghamshire, for instance, the acreage devoted to growing wheat as good as halved between 1872 (when the Watlington branch opened) and 1890.

Comparison with the picture on page 8/9 shows how Princes Risborough station had been expanded and improved over the years. This picture was probably taken c.1899, before work started on the large modern replacement which was built further south. The bay on the left was for Aylesbury whilst Watlington branch trains used the far side of the island platform on the right. The canopies of the 1894 waiting room are just visible past the footbridge. The unidentified 'Metro' tank and wagons facing against the direction of normal traffic on the up main line, was probably in the course of shunting.

Courtesy Leicestershire Record Office

Furthermore, because the imported wheat was sent to large roller mills for grinding into flour, many local wind and water mills became redundant. In the circumstances, many farmers turned to dairy farming in order to supply demand from the expanding population of London which, of course, the railway enabled them to do.

Incidentally, the population of horses in London also provided a steady market in hay and straw which had become a staple part of farm production, and the vast quantities of manure from London stables were sent out to the country by rail at little more cost to the farmers than carriage charges.

Somewhere around this time, the engine shed at Watlington was 'blown completely over into an adjoining field, while Mr. Lett's two sons, who were inside, had a very narrow escape for their lives'. This recollection from station master Robert Lett was recorded in the *Thame Gazette* as 'a few years later' than 1881, but we can find no other record of the event to help establish the precise date. Mr. Lett also mentioned that 'only the top part of the engines were damaged'.

The shed was replaced by the one featured in the pictures on pages 51/2 but whether it was the new or old building from which firewood was stolen on 12th February 1885 is not known. This was not the first time engine driver Henry Wilshire had missed wood used by him for lighting the engine, so he lay in wait and when he saw the three men concerned in the engine shed at 9.30 p.m., he summoned PC Yates who watched Station Road and caught them red-handed. Labourers B. Almond and Wm Dover, who were caught carrying the wood, pleaded guilty and were sentenced to 14 days hard labour, whilst the third, John Appleby, pleaded not guilty and was fined 5 shillings.

We know frustratingly little about this period of time on the branch, but one snippet which has survived is a statement showing the actual time engineman H. Wilshire of Watlington was employed running his engine between Watlington and Princes Risborough during the week ending 9th May 1891. On Monday the 4th he worked to the times listed below, the figures on the other days being too similar to be worth quoting.

Dep	Arr	Dep	Arr	Time occupied
9 10	9 35	10 36	11 11	1 0
2 15	2 50	3 43	4 18	1 10
5 45	6 20	6 35	7 0	1 0
		Total		3 10
		Hours on duty		9 50
		Time not actually running		6 40

Under the Regulation of Railways Act of 1889, the GWR were obliged to provide block telegraph on single lines controlled by the train staff and ticket system. In the case of the Watlington branch, this would have cost £355, but since in practice the system had not been found necessary, the company realised the expenditure could be avoided by abandoning the system. The GWR therefore wrote to the Board of Trade on 23rd April asking to be released from the obligation:

The Watlington and Princes Risborough Railway Company on 6th August 1872 gave an undertaking to the BoT to work the line from Watlington to Princes Risborough on the train and ticket system, but for several years past there has been but one engine employed upon the branch, and as the traffic can be conveniently worked by one engine, I am to ask that the Board of Trade will allow the undertaking given in 1872 to be cancelled, and accept in lieu thereof an undertaking to work the line by means of one engine in steam or two or more coupled together.

The idea of linking the towns of Wallingford and Watlington was revived in October 1891 when a meeting was held at the Lamb Hotel, Wallingford, to discuss a proposed extension of the Wallingford branch of the GWR to Watlington. It was chaired by the Mayor of Wallingford, Mr. H. Hawkins, who felt it would be 'a great boon to the town and neighbourhood'. Engineered by Mr. Wilkinson of the International Construction Co., the 7½ mile line, which involved bridging the Thames to the west of Benson, was estimated at £50,000. A small committee was appointed to approach the GWR Co. 'to induce them to aid the undertaking'.

In a letter of 12th October, Wilkinson asked the GWR if they were prepared to work such a line if and when constructed on the basis of guaranteeing 3% on the capital cost plus a small allowance for office expenses. The GWR were 'unable to entertain the proposal' and without their support the scheme was abandoned. However, the idea was revived yet again on the back of another scheme to build a light railway from the Oxford and Birmingham line of the GWR at Didcot, 12 miles 6 furlongs to Watlington, to connect with the existing Watlington branch. The Light Railway Order was confirmed by the Board of Trade in 1898, the Didcot and Watlington Light Railway Extensions Order of 1899 subsequently catering for a 1 mile 6 furlong extension from Benson to Wallingford.

It would appear that difficulty was experienced in raising the necessary capital because the scheme was never started and after applying for a revival of powers in 1903, the Didcot and Watlington Light Railways Development Co. received the following letter from the secretary of the Light Railways Commission:

Sir, with reference to the Inquiry held on February 23rd at Didcot, I am directed by the Light Railways Commissioners to inform you that the above named application by the Light Railways Development Co Ltd for a revival of the powers for the compulsory purchase of lands by the Company to be incorporated under the Didcot and Watlington Light Railway Order 1898, should not be granted, and to state that the Commissioners were not satisfied by the evidence that if the application were granted the promoters would be in a position to carry the orders into effect.

Signed. Alan D. Erskine

The junction station at Princes Risborough had been gradually improved over the years, the *Thame Gazette* for 15th April 1884 reporting 'the platform is in course of being covered by an iron roof and other additions are being made'. GWR Board minutes for 2nd January 1884 record the authorisation of £770 for widening and covering the up platform at Princes Risborough. This was followed by more news on 25th November 1890: 'It is stated that some important alterations are about to be effected at the station very shortly. Several new sidings are to be added, a new signal box is to be erected, and a considerable addition made to the levers working signals. These and other alterations when carried out, will tend to greatly facilitate the working of the heavy traffic which has to be dealt with at this station.' The improvements are revealed in Major Marindin's report for the Board of Trade on 25th January 1893:

. . . . There have been considerable alterations in the arrangement of the lines, the points and signals have been interlocked and are now worked from a new signal cabin containing 61 working and 10 spare levers, and from a subsidiary 5 lever ground frame,

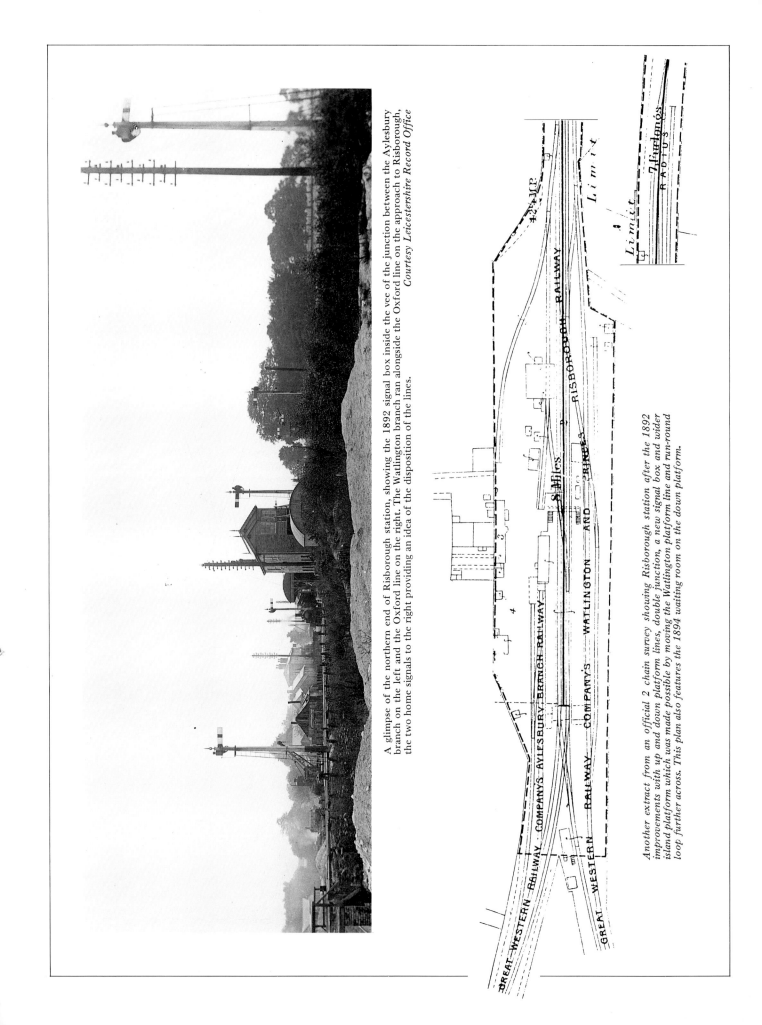

A glimpse of the northern end of Risborough station, showing the 1892 signal box inside the vee of the junction between the Aylesbury branch on the left and the Oxford line on the right. The Watlington branch ran alongside the Oxford line on the approach to Risborough, the two home signals to the right providing an idea of the disposition of the lines.

Courtesy Leicestershire Record Office

Another extract from an official 2 chain survey showing Risborough station after the 1892 improvements with up and down platform lines, double junction, a new signal box and wider island platform which was made possible by moving the Watlington platform line and run-round loop further across. This plan also features the 1894 waiting room on the down platform.

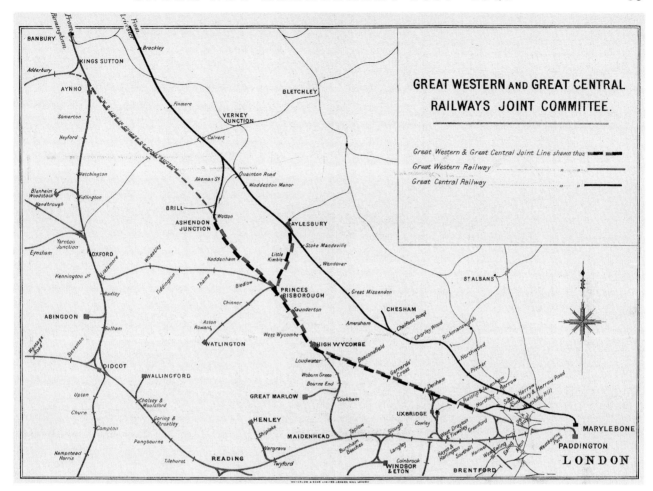

lengthened and widened and a footbridge connecting the two platforms has been erected.

In the signal cabin the 9 lever and No. 36 lever should be interlocked, and No. 65 should lock No. 36 either way. Some shelter is also required upon the down platform.

Subject to the satisfaction of these requirements within two months I can recommend that the use of the new works at Princes Risborough may be sanctioned but the attention of the company should be called to the waiting room accommodation on the up platform which ought to be improved.

Ironically, it was the down platform which received attention next, with the provision of a waiting room and urinal being authorised in November 1893 for £170 17s 6d. In 1894 the *Bucks Herald* for 30th June reported 'the bleak down platform at the railway station here has not hitherto been found an inviting spot by travellers waiting for their trains, but the evil is now being remedied, the company having commenced building a waiting room which will add considerably to the comfort of the passengers.' It was not until March 1895 that £365 was authorised for 'alterations and additions' to the up side. Further to all this, another £387 10s 8d was authorised in February 1896 for 'enlargement of the booking office and general waiting room, a new ladies waiting room with convenience, new parcels office, new urinal and WC for gentlemen, extension of covering over platform up to the footbridge and paving platforms under new covering'.

The photograph on page 32 gives some idea of the result of the piecemeal improvements which made for a very respectable country junction for a secondary line, but after all that expenditure the whole station was soon to be swept away for a much grander scheme. The huge changes which took place at Princes Risborough came about as a result of cooperation between the Great Western and Great Central Railways under which a new main line was built from Old Oak Common to High Wycombe. The two companies agreed a joint arrangement to cover the 16 mile section between a junction at Northolt and High Wycombe, upgrade the eight miles from High Wycombe to Princes Risborough, and continue north from there to the GCR main line at Grendon Underwood.

This had come about because the Great Central was not on the best of terms with the Metropolitan company with whom it shared the heavily congested tracks between Harrow and Quainton Road Junction, a distance of some 35 miles. It was therefore quite logical that the GCR should seek an alternative route into and out of its London terminus at Marylebone.

The newly formed Great Western & Great Central Joint Company took over the single line from Wycombe to Risborough on 1st August 1899 but it was 24th July 1902 before the contract for the doubling work between Wycombe and Princes Risborough and the complete rebuilding of Princes Risborough station was awarded to Mackay and Davies of Cardiff. The contract also included a new goods yard at High

135

WATLINGTON BRANCH.

SINGLE LINE.—Worked by Train Staff and only One Engine in Steam at a time, or two coupled together. Form of Staff, Round; Colour, Black.

DOWN TRAINS.

WEEK DAYS only.

Dist.	STATIONS.	Pass. &Gds.	Goods.	Pass.	Pass.
M. C.		A.M.	P.M.	P.M.	P.M.
	Princes Risboro'......dep.	10 30	12 30	3 40	6 35
3 51	Chinnor............... ,,	10 43	12 45	3 50	6 45
6 11	Aston Rowant...... ,,	10 54	1 0	3 57	6 52
8 69	Watlington.........arr.	11 6	1 10	4 5	7 0

UP TRAINS.

WEEK DAYS only.

Dist.	STATIONS.	Pass.	Goods.	Pass.	Pass. &Gds.
M. C.		A.M.	A.M.	P.M.	P.M.
	Watlington.........dep.	9 5	11 30	2 25	5 45
2 58	Aston Rowant...... ,,	9 13	11 45	2 33	5 56
5 18	Chinnor............... ,,	9 20	12 0	2 40	6 7
8 69	Princes Risboro'....arr.	9 30	12 10	2 50	6 20

Loads of Mixed Trains on this branch not to exceed 6 trucks, 3 passenger vehicles, and Goods Brake Van.

The Mixed Trains must not exchange wagons at Chinnor or Aston Rowant.

Taken from GWR service timetable for June 1895.

Wycombe, the rebuilding of West Wycombe and a new station at Saunderton and 3¾ miles of the new line beyond Risborough. Immediately beforehand the *Thame Gazette* for 22nd July 1902 reported 'There are indications that work on the new line from High Wycombe to Grendon Underwood, via Princes Risborough, is shortly to be commenced here, by the fact that several trucks of material have been unloaded at the station. An office has recently been erected in close proximity to the station.'

However, the new joint line and the new station took 3–4 years to complete, so before we leap too far ahead, let's return to 1900 when 'a very severe and violent snowstorm' blocked the Watlington branch on the evening of Tuesday, 13th February. It seems that it was the guard who had the unenviable job of walking along the line to Princes Risborough in order to deliver the single-line train staff which authorised the snow plough to go down the branch. The first train to arrive at Watlington the following day was at 4.15 p.m.

The line had previously been blocked in 'a fearful snowstorm' in 1881, when, before becoming part of the mighty GWR, the engine and carriages were snowed up for several days at Fairy Furlong★ without the benefit of any snow plough to come to the rescue.

Towards the end of July 1900 the morning train from Watlington was late for a simpler reason, according to the *Thame Gazette* for 31st July: 'the stoker of the Watlington train had absconded and when the engine driver came down to the station expecting to find steam up, he found that the fire had only just been lit'. Passengers for London missed their connection.

Presiding over these problems and doubtless far worse during the independent years of the Watlington & Princes Risborough Railway, was 66-year-old Robert Lett who entered service with the W&PRR in October 1872. From January 1884, under the GWR, he was graded 'booking porter' and from June 1900 'station inspector'. On the GWR, men at such rural outposts were often graded 'booking porter', but effectively did the work of a station master. Lett had served at Watlington for 28 years before retiring in August 1900. He had started his working life on the Shirburn Estate and might even have been recommended for his position by the Earl of Macclesfield. One of Lett's sons, Arthur, worked for Watlington solicitor Augustus Jones, eventually taking over the business, whilst in 1895 his daughter Emma Elizabeth married Mr. Alfred Launchbury, who the press referred to as 'principal engineer of the Watlington train'. According to official records, he was a '3rd class branch engine-man' who served at Watlington from June 1891 to May 1896.

Robert Lett, who lived near the old hospital in Hill Road, must have been a keen gardener because, according to the *Thame Gazette*, he won many prizes from the GWR. He was eveidently very popular because on his retirement, as a token of their thanks, local people subsequently subscribed £45 cash (a substantial sum in those days) and an antique armchair presented to him by the Honorable H. Parker on the afternoon of Saturday, 24th November.

Robert Lett was succeeded by Mr. Fay or Fry† of West Ealing who did not stay for long, and was followed by 29-year-old Walter Colbourne who had started at Bromyard as a passenger

---

★This might refer to Fairny Belt where the line cuts through a 1 chain wide wood near Shirburn.

†Fay is referred to in the *Thame Gazette* at the time of Robert Lett's retirement. Another newspaper report in the Lett family records gives the name 'Fry'. He may have been a relief man as Walter Colbourne had already been appointed to the post.

clerk in 1886 and was appointed station master in May 1900, the two men apparently overlapping. He lived in Letts Alley off the Shirburn Road, Watlington. In October 1903 Ernest Sexton was appointed station master at Watlington. He was born in 1876, and having joined the Great Western in 1892 as a clerk at Windsor, had worked his way up to become chief goods clerk at Marlow for just over six years. He seems to have fitted in very well indeed at Watlington where he was subsequently referred to as 'the popular station master'.

From May 1900 the service was increased to four return trips leaving Watlington at 9.5, 11.30, 3.10 and 6.20, returning at 9.52, 11.10, 3.50 and 7.30, the 1.10 p.m. from Risborough connecting with the 11.15 Paddington to Aylesbury. The early train petitioned for in 1884 was still not part of the regular timetable, perhaps from lack of support for the 7.45 a.m. introduced for the summer timetable of 1893 only. Although it was not repeated in subsequent timetables, from May 1899 it was revived on Mondays only, presumably for those spending a weekend away in Watlington, but was discontinued again in October 1902.

The April 1894 timetable included a return goods train leaving Watlington at 11.30 a.m. However, this was still in addition to mixed working on the 10.30 a.m. from Risborough and 5.45 p.m. from Watlington. Although mention of mixed working disappeared from the winter of 1895/6, they reappeared the following winter.

The January 1897 timetable shows the goods leaving Watlington at 11 a.m., calling at Aston Rowant and Chinnor and returning at 12.20 p.m., but on Tuesdays it left earlier and was shown as 'goods and coaches', perhaps in connection with the Thame market. Goods traffic from Aston and Chinnor was taken into Watlington by the 12.20 p.m. on those days and worked back up the branch on the 6.35 p.m. mixed train.

Mixed working was evidently unpopular with passengers and understandably so when, depending on traffic, the coaches were shunted in and out of the sidings at Aston Rowant and Chinnor, no doubt with the occasional unintentional rough buffering-up, as intimated in the *Thame Gazette* for 16th August 1904.

> It is rumoured that the GWR will eventually have a motor service on our branch line. This will be a great advantage and obviate "the shunting" which takes places at Aston and Chinnor much to the discomfort of the passengers. The goods traffic will be worked from the junction.

The reporter was quite right about the 'motor service' and from that winter, mixed trains were no longer shown in the timetable, although wagons were still occasionally conveyed on passenger trains for many years to come.

The *Thame Gazette* followed this up on 4th October:

> We hear that the GWR intends running goods trains early in the day, instead of having mixed. This will account for the alterations in the time of arrival and departure of passenger trains. The first arrival is now due at 10.10 a.m. instead of 10.35 (in the course of time we may expect our daily papers at the breakfast hour). The afternoon train is to arrive at 4.10 and the last at 7.50. The departure alterations are — The second leaves at 11.45 a.m. instead of 11.30, and the last at 6.50 instead of 6.35 p.m.

Princes Risborough High Street, looking towards Market Square c.1890.

National Monuments Record

Looking south towards London, showing the baulk road of the old Wycombe Railway line from Maidenhead to Oxford on the right and, on the left, the new up line which diverged for about 2½ miles for an easier climb of 1 in 167 over the Chilterns towards Saunderton. The old route had gradients of 1 in 87 and 1 in 100.

The same bridge viewed in the opposite direction, with the new Risborough station under construction in the distance.

This enlargement of the temporary ground frame or signal box provided during construction works, bears an uncanny resemblance to the signal box at Watlington. Could this or a similar structure used elsewhere on the contract have formed the basis for the Watlington building? If so, this raises the question of the pre-c.1902 signal box at Watlington. Risborough's new south box features in the background.

In 1904 an early morning goods train left Watlington at 6.30 a.m. (6.0 a.m. on Mondays because of getting back for the 7.43 a.m. passenger MO) calling at Aston Rowant and Chinnor if required, whilst at the end of the day, another goods was worked out from Watlington at 8.5 p.m., returning from Risborough at 9.40 p.m. and calling at Chinnor and Aston Rowant on the return journey if required.

The impressive new station at Princes Risborough, built 100 yards south of the original, was finally completed in March 1906. Even though it had progressed gradually in front of the regular passengers since 1902, it must have seemed a staggering transformation, especially when Great Central expresses began tearing along the main tracks between the platforms on their way between Marylebone and Manchester.

On 20th March 1905, the *Thame Gazette* had reported:

On Monday the down platform was brought into use for the first time, the old one having been kept in use till then. All three platforms are therefore now completed. The new premises are being given a smart appearance by the finishing touches of paint. The large

This view of the construction of the new station also provides another glimpse of the old establishment. Watlington branch trains used the far side of the island platform on the left.

The old station had completely disappeared by the time this picture was taken of the impressive new north signal box and junction pointwork.

A later photograph, looking north along the new line towards Ashendon Junction with the Oxford line curving off to the left and the Aylesbury branch to the right.

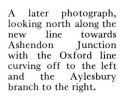

Photos all courtesy Leicestershire Record Office

Great Central Robinson '8B' class 4–4–2 No. 1087 waiting alongside the down platform at Risborough, with a local train, probably in the years before the Great War. GC passenger services to the north of High Wycombe were rather sparse when compared to those of the Great Western. The train pictured here may have been the 11.20 a.m. Marylebone to Woodford which waited at Risborough for the 12.15 p.m. Marylebone to Manchester express to call, then followed it to Woodford, calling at all stations. Built in 1905, this engine was a familiar sight on the London Extension until the class was superseded by LNER designs on expresses in the late 1930s when No. 1087 (by then No. 6087) was transferred away from Leicester to Lincoln. Nevertheless, examples of the class could still be seen on local trains into the war years. The Watlington branch train also features in the West Bay behind the GC engine.

The new station at Princes Risborough shortly after completion. The lines serving the platforms were separated from the up and down main lines so that stopping trains could be held out of the way while higher priority trains sped through the middle.   *Cty. M. Adamson*

footbridge which spans the whole line of metals from the up and down platform will shortly be completed.

Before work on the new line was completed, the Great Western and Great Central agreed to make Ashendon, 10 miles north of Risborough, the northern extremity of the joint line, the 5¾ miles beyond to Grendon Underwood being transferred to the Great Central. This came about because the Great Western, who initially had little interest in the new section to the north of Risborough, had since decided to construct a new cut-off line, laid out for fast running, from Ashendon through Bicester to a new junction at Aynho, five miles to the south of Banbury on the existing Northern main line. This saved 19 miles over the existing route to Banbury via Reading.

The original Great Western plan had been to upgrade the Oxford line through Thame to main line standards, so that in travelling via the new joint line to Risborough, expresses from Paddington to Oxford, Worcester, Birmingham and the north would save eight miles over the route via Reading, although the gradients would not have been so easy. The new Ashendon to Aynho cut-off superseded the idea and the Oxford line thereafter remained a secondary line, only providing an alternative route for West Midland, Northern and other expresses in the event of a major obstruction between West Ealing and Kennington Junction.

The official opening of the Joint Line for goods traffic took place on 20th November 1905, and for Great Western and Great Central passenger trains via Denham, and GCR northwards from Princes Risborough on 2nd April 1906. Inspecting the works of the larger companies was so often a matter of routine that the Board of Trade officer, Colonel Yorke, did not inspect

the line until the following day, when he only found reason to comment on a few minor details.

Not long afterwards, on 28th July, the passengers of the 3.48 p.m. to Watlington had an unpleasant experience when the train was about to leave Risborough. It seems likely that the driver had left the engine in back gear after he had put it onto the train, and, not realising this, propelled the train backwards into the stop block at the end of the bay platform when starting away. According to the *Thame Gazette*:

> The shock was felt by passengers throughout the train, especially those in the last carriage, some of whom were thrown violently from their seats and a good deal shaken. Mr. J. Napier from the office of Wheelers Wycombe Breweries, suffered some injury to his neck and shoulder, and, considerable pain and swelling having developed, he has since been under medical care. A lady was also hurt, but not seriously.

As this was before the introduction of the 'Rail Auto Car Service', it seems likely that the vehicles involved were conventional 4-wheel coaches.

The 'motor service' referred to by the *Thame Gazette* in 1904 doubtless came from news of the intention to open a series of additional halts on the branch as part of a wider scheme being implemented by the GWR in an effort to bring the railway closer to small communities and help combat competition from the roads. This was generally accompanied by the use of specially designed steam railmotors or loco-hauled auto-trailers, both of which were equipped with retractable steps to serve cheaply-constructed rail-level halts. The loco-hauled trailers were normally operated on the well-known push/pull principle, under which the driver controlled the train from the leading end

GWR AND GC TRAINS
PASSING THROUGH AND CALLING AT PRINCES RISBOROUGH

The new GW & GC Joint main line was made good use of by the Great Central who diverted three Marylebone and Manchester and one Marylebone and Bradford expresses in each direction over it, the four or five-coach formations mostly being hauled by Robinson '11B' 4–4–0s, '8B' Jersey Lilies and '8D' 4–4–2s. Of these the 12.15 p.m. Marylebone to Manchester called at Princes Risborough at 1.6 p.m. to pick up passengers for the Midlands and North, whilst the southbound 12.30 p.m. Manchester to Marylebone called at 4.55 p.m.

There were four down and five up GCR local trains calling at Princes Risborough; the 6.10 a.m. and 5.40 p.m. Marylebone to Calvert, and the balancing up workings, and Marylebone & Woodford trains. The shorter workings were run with about four coaches, usually hauled by '9K' and later '9L' 4–4–2Ts.

GC goods services at this time were mostly worked by '9H' and '9J' class 0–6–0s from Annesley or Woodford.

The Great Western ran five trains in each direction between Paddington and Aylesbury and five between Paddington and Oxford, with all except one down Aylesbury and one up Oxford service travelling over the new line via Denham. There were four daily goods trains each way between London and Oxford, two of them routed via Maidenhead in each direction and one return service between London and Aylesbury. The Taplow and Oxford, and Taplow and Aylesbury goods naturally travelled via Maidenhead each way. The only Great Western train over the new line north of Risborough at this time was the London and Aylesbury Goods which ran out to Haddenham and back.

Following the opening of the new Ashendon–Aynho cut-off to goods on 4th April 1910 and to passenger services on 1st July, the character and balance of the GW traffic passing Risborough changed dramatically, more closely shadowing that of the Great Central with express and heavy through goods trains much in evidence.

In the autumn of 1910, Great Western expresses to Birkenhead, via the Joint Line, left Paddington at 9.10, 11.5 a.m. 2.35 p.m., 4.0 p.m. and 6.5 p.m., the 9.10 detaching a slip coach for Risborough at 9.52 a.m. Passing through in the up direction were the 8.30 a.m. Wolverhampton to Paddington and the 6.15 a.m., 8.15 a.m., 9.10 a.m., 11.47 a.m., 12.55 p.m., 2.35 p.m. and 4.35 p.m. Birkenhead to Paddington expresses.

The 11.5 a.m. and 6.5 p.m. Paddington and 2.35 p.m. and 4.35 p.m. Birkenhead trains were regularly hauled by 29XX 'Saint' class 4–6–0s, but the majority of other services were still hauled by 'City', 'Flower', and 'County' class 4–4–0s and later 40XX class 4–6–0 'Stars'. Train lengths varied between four and ten coaches, six or seven of them each way including dining or refreshment cars.

In addition a new service was provided between the Midlands and Victoria (for the south coast and the continent) leaving Wolverhampton at 6.50 a.m., and in the opposite direction leaving Victoria at 8.15 p.m. The following summer, a 12.35 from Victoria to Wolverhampton and 4.15 p.m. Wolverhampton to Paddington (with the coaches for the 8.15 Victoria) were also laid on, whilst the 9.10 a.m. Paddington conveyed an SE&CR brake compo daily from Folkestone to Shrewsbury, the coach being worked by a local service from Victoria to Paddington. The 8.15 Victoria also conveyed an SE&CR brake compo from Queenborough and a GW brake compo from Ramsgate to Wolverhampton.

The Folkestone coach returned on the 2.35 p.m. Birkenhead and the Queenborough and Ramsgate coaches on the 6.30 a.m. Wolverhampton. However, by the summer of 1912 these through Victoria expresses had disappeared.

The five through Oxford line trains in each direction usually comprised four or five 8-wheeled coaches made up with two brake thirds, a third and either a compo or a first, or, in two trains each way, both. These were mostly hauled by tender locos, including 2301, 'Barnum' and even West Midland 2–4–0 classes. Steam railmotors were used on early afternoon and early evening trips from Oxford, strengthened by ordinary stock when required, and on the return journey conveying milk trucks from Aylesbury to Oxford. The railmotors were also used on late evening trips from Oxford on Thursdays and Saturdays only.

On Tuesdays the 9.15 a.m. Paddington to Aylesbury conveyed a brake compo, third and brake van to Princes Risborough for an 11.6 a.m. trip for Thame Market. The coaches returned from Thame at 4.30 p.m.

The six through Aylesbury services in each direction were similarly formed with four or five vehicles, though with a first on each and an additional compo on some. They were hauled by 2221, 36XX and 3150 tank engines, though 'Metro' class 2–4–0Ts were still utilised. These through sets were probably used for the three additional branch trips during their layover at Aylesbury. The Great Central also ran trains over the Aylesbury branch, with a morning passenger to High Wycombe and back and a late evening motor to and from Princes Risborough.

An early morning train, worked from Paddington to Princes Risborough and back by tank locomotives, also comprised five coaches, again including first class accommodation.

Local stations over the new line were served by five auto services to and from Banbury. These were worked by an auto-fitted '517' class 0–4–2T and trailer from Aylesbury, leaving Risborough at 7.17 a.m. and 2.40 p.m., interspersed with a Banbury-based auto train which did three return journeys, making its way back from Risborough at 9.57 a.m., together with the slip from the 9.10 Paddington, 4.5 p.m. and 7.40 p.m.

The 10.25 a.m. and 4.42 p.m. through trains from Paddington to Banbury also called at Risborough and served the main stations for the rest of their journey to Banbury, but, curiously, there were no equivalent up services, the stock working back via Reading.

Great Western goods trains over the new line consisted of the 4.5 p.m. Birkenhead to Paddington meat train, hauled by a 4–4–0, and the 4.30 p.m. Bordesley which, usually hauled by a 28XX 2–8–0, called at Risborough to set down about ten wagons for the Aylesbury and Watlington branches, continuing on to London with sixty wagons. The 11.18 p.m. Banbury Junction, hauled by a 26XX, also called to set down another ten or so vehicles for the Watlington and Aylesbury branches before continuing with a load of fifty onwards to Old Oak. In the opposite direction, the 4 a.m. Old Oak to Bordesley called to pick up empties, running on to Banbury with a maximum load of seventy whilst another 4–4–0 passed through with the 11.15 a.m. Paddington to Wolverhampton vacuum goods.

A local goods, hauled by a tank engine, set out on a return trip from Banbury at 8.20 a.m., arriving at Risborough at 12.20 p.m. This sorted the yard and went back to Banbury with traffic dropped off by the 4.0 a.m. Old Oak, leaving Risborough at 2.50 p.m. and calling at whichever stations wagons had to be delivered to.

By 1911, goods services over the Oxford and Aylesbury branches comprised one train each way between Paddington and Aylesbury, Paddington and Oxford, and Old Oak and Oxford, and two in each direction between Taplow and Oxford.

Princes Risborough North Signal Box.

of the coach while it was being propelled. The Great Western referred to these as 'auto trains'.

We have not discovered any evidence that steam railmotors were ever used on the line, which is hardly surprising when an engine would still have been needed to handle the goods, thus obviating any economy. It is also doubtful whether a steam railmotor could have handled any worthwhile tail load on Chinnor bank. Nor is there any evidence that auto-working was

employed. Auto-trailers were simply provided to serve new rail-level halts at Lewknor, Kingston level crossing and Bledlow Bridge.

Auto working was useful on lines like the nearby Wallingford branch, for example, where the train scuttled to and fro frequently throughout the day, and the advantage of not having to run the engine round to the other end of the train at each end of its short journeys was self-evident. In contrast, the

Another postcard view of Chinnor station c.1905, showing the approach road and a glimpse of the branch train, an unidentified 'Metro' 2–4–0T and four-wheeled coaches.

Chinnor station entrance on the right, and the inclined approach to the bridge carrying the road to Hill Road over the line. The gateway on the left led into 'Aleca' Hill's orchard.

This beautiful postcard view of Chinnor station c.1906 appears to show an unidentified 'Metro' 2—4—0T with a four- or six-wheeled brake third and one of the new auto-trailers provided to serve the new rail-level halts. The building on the right had been Spencer Jackson's iron foundry which remained derelict for many years before eventually being demolished. The old coach body is believed to have been a GWR/B&ER broad gauge first-class carriage of the 1840s. It was brought in from elsewhere around the turn of the century and should not be confused with the W&PRR rolling stock.

The photographer was probably at pains to avoid including Chinnor goods shed (just off the left-hand edge of the picture) when he took this romantic view of Chinnor Hill across stooked corn in Horace Saw's field, Oakley, c.1905. It does, however, show wagons on the two goods sidings and the Chinnor permanent way hut.

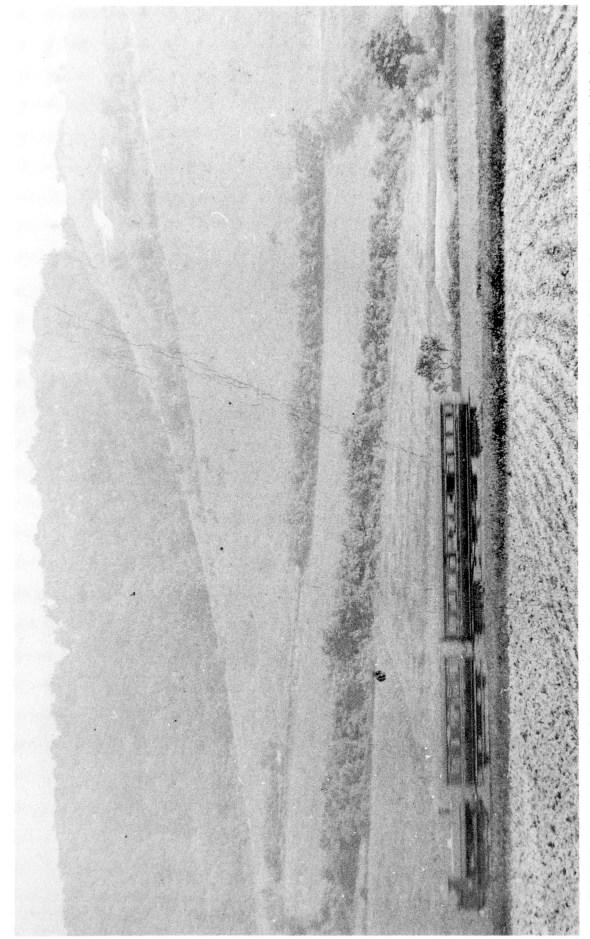

With Bledlow Cross scoured in the chalk hillside above, this poor quality photograph shows an unidentified '2101' class 0—6—0ST heading away from Wainhill Crossing, which was just off the right-hand edge of the print, on its way towards Risborough. The four-wheel brake third and auto-trailer are shown in the all-over chocolate brown livery introduced in 1908. Later coach working notices specified a six-wheel brake third, but whichever, driver Harry Humphreys recalled the engine using more water with the extra vehicle in tow. With the limited tank capacity, he said "You'd have a job to do the 9 miles there and back with it . . . Of course, the engine wasn't always up to scratch."

Watlington branch was only served with five (from 1906) return journeys, at either end of which the engine was often called upon for yard shunting, forming goods trains, placing wagons for traders, pumping water, taking coal, and adding and detaching a strengthening coach. In these circumstances it must have been apparent that auto-working would not have been practicable nor advantageous.

The new halts provided at a total cost of £88 were completed by 20th July 1906 and inspected by the Board of Trade on 11th September, the officer noting the platforms as 6in above rail level, 70ft long and provided with nameboards and lamps, but at this time no shelters. 'Owing to the small height of platforms they are suitable only for rail motor cars with end doors and folding steps.'

GW minute books for March 1906 record: 'Consequent on opening of the new Joint Line to Wycombe on 2nd June, second class bookings were withdrawn over the Watlington and Aylesbury branches'. In any case when the new 'rail auto car service' commenced on 1st September, the auto trailers were one class only. The *Thame Gazette* noted that all trains left Watlington 5 minutes earlier:

> The company have built "halts" at Bledlow Ridge [sic], Kingston Crossing, and Lewknor Bridge, at which places the train will stop for passenger traffic only. The fare from Watlington to Lewknor will be 2d, Kingston 3½d, Bledlow Ridge 7½d. Passengers travelling through the branch will not appreciate the five stopping places, but the "halts" at this end should be beneficial to the trade at Watlington.

In anticipation of the opening of the halts, from the timetable for the summer of 1906, the service was increased to five return trips leaving Watlington at 7 a.m. Mondays only, 9.0, 11.45, 3.15, 4.35 and 7.0 p.m., returning from Risborough at 9.50, 12.58, 3.45, 5.19 and 7.30. Travelling to London over the new GW/GC Joint main line, passengers from the 9.0 a.m. ex-Watlington now reached Paddington at 10.32 a.m.

A six-wheeled brake third was provided to supplement the accommodation of the auto-trailer but was only used for passengers joining or leaving the train at the normal height platforms of the original stations.

Incidentally, 60ft auto-trailers were specified for the Watlington branch, a note being added to coach working books to the effect that 70ft cars were not to be run over the line at speeds exceeding 20 mph. The official maximum line speed was 30 mph. However, at least by 1928 a 70ft trailer and a 6-wheel brake third were specified with no mention of any special restriction.

During the early hours of Sunday, 2nd September, after the first day of the auto-car service, a fire broke out at Watlington engine shed. Normally, with no Sunday service, the engine would have been stabled in the shed after disposal and probably left with a small fire to ensure that the boiler did not cool down too quickly. However, if the engine was required for engineering work on Sunday, this might at least explain the presence of fireman G. Coslett when the building caught fire sometime around 2.0 a.m. Of course, he might have just been sleeping

Although not taken until 1919, this picture, looking south from Lewknor Bridge, admirably shows one of the new rail-level halts with their low platforms and simple wooden shelters.
L & GRP

1569. Watlington Station.

A c.1905 postcard view of Watlington station, showing the recently enclosed porch of the station building, a glimpse of the goods shed and the cattle pen, which at that time was tucked behind the platform fence. The signal box, at the end of the platform, makes an interesting comparison with the building shown on page 38, whilst two of the signals it controlled, the up starting signal behind it and the revolving ground lamp in the foreground, are also featured. Needless to say, there are not many views of Watlington engine shed and this was probably the second (or even third?) building. However, we are fortunate to be able to show a closer glimpse of the roof overleaf, whereas the coaling stage and carriage shed on the right survived throughout the line's existence. The well-pointed brick-work on the chimney of the station building was probably evidence of repair work carried out following storm damage in 1883. The *Thame Gazette* reported that during a thunderstorm 'of unusual severity' on Saturday, 14th July, 'a chimney at Watlington station was struck and some of the bricks &c hurled a considerable distance but fortunately no-one was hurt.'

Photographs like this were usually taken to record a special occasion and, judging from the number of coaches, this was probably a special or an excursion. It shows an unidentified '517' class 0—4—2T at Watlington with a train of close-coupled Holden four-wheeled coaches c.1900 and provides a frustrating glimpse of the roof of the second (or third?) engine shed and a closer view of the old wooden water tank, both of which are at least recorded in official sketches/plans (see pages 54 & 66). The underside of the water tank was 15ft 6in above rail level whilst the tank itself is recorded as 12ft 6in x 7ft 6in x 4ft 4in (or 4ft 6in) and had a capacity at 4ft of 2,340 gallons. It is just possible to make out the 6in delivery hose on this print.

Cty. R. E. Gilbert

This sad picture was taken the morning after the engine shed was destroyed by fire, and shows a 'Metro' class 2—4—0T and a '2021' class 0—6—0ST, the numbers of which are not recorded. The dwarf brick base walls were all that remained to show the position of the building. The station master standing alongside the 'Metro' was Ernest Sexton. This view also shows how conspicuous the station must have seemed amidst the fields at this time. The specially planted trees in the background grew to provide a most effective screen in later years.

there, we will never know, but whatever the reason, official internal correspondence records that but for his 'prompt action . . . the wooden water tank adjoining would also have been destroyed.'

The *Thame Gazette* gives more details:

FIRE AT THE RAILWAY STATION — On Sunday morning last the engine shed at the GWR station was burnt down. The alarm of fire was given about 2 a.m., in response to which the Watlington and Shirburn fire brigades quickly turned out. On arriving at the station it was found that nothing could be done to save the shed, and the efforts of the brigades were directed to confining the fire to the shed, in which they were successful. Fortunately the set of metals nearest the shed was clear of goods traffic, otherwise the fire might have been more serious. The many onlooking willingly helped to move the trucks, &c., to the next set of metals, derailing a truck of coal in doing so, owing to the points not being moved, which prevented the trucks from going any further, but they were able to clear the line sufficiently. Two engines, including the new one for the rail auto-car service, which only started the previous day, were in the shed at the time, and though not completely ruined, were badly damaged. The brigades were much hampered by lack of water; the pumping shed being on fire the engines had to be fed by buckets of water. Mr. Warren placed at their disposal a horse and water barrel which was of great service. Notwithstanding the shortage of water, they rendered very great help in checking the progress of the fire and in extinguishing the smouldering remains. The total damage is estimated at £1,000. The cause of the fire is unknown. A curious incident occurred in connection with the fire which does not reflect very great credit upon the persons responsible. The Watlington fire engine is undergoing renovation, and in case of fire, an engine had been borrowed from a neighbouring town. It is said that on the alarm

being given some members of the brigade did not know where the engine was stationed.

The Great Western Locomotive Carriage and Stores Committee authorised a gratuity of £1 to fireman Coslett as an appreciation for his prompt action. The report mentions two engines and this is confirmed by a photograph of the scene the morning after. It is tempting to suggest the front engine, an unidentified '2021' class 0—6—0ST (probably No. 2081 or 2086), had been used on the auto-car service the previous day, but it could just as easily have been the 'Metro' class 2—4—0T behind, the engines simply having been swapped round.

The presence of the two engines being kept at Watlington at this period, confirmed by the allocation records, is something of a puzzle when the line was worked on the 'one engine in steam' principle, and only one was needed for the day's timetable. The most likely explanation is that they could be alternated to allow more frequent boiler washouts. Elsewhere at this time, at Shipston-on-Stour for instance, the boiler of the branch engine was washed out every fortnight, on Sundays, when the engine was out of use. However, the chalk in the hard water at Watlington would not allow such a long interval between washouts and gave much trouble with priming. Watlington driver Harry Humphreys later recalled "after two or three days you could see the chalk in the engine". It is therefore possible that the boilers were washed out every few days and, if this was the case, a second engine to maintain the service would have saved light engine mileage to and from the parent shed at Slough even though this would have exceeded the more general Loco Department provision of a spare engine for every two in use.

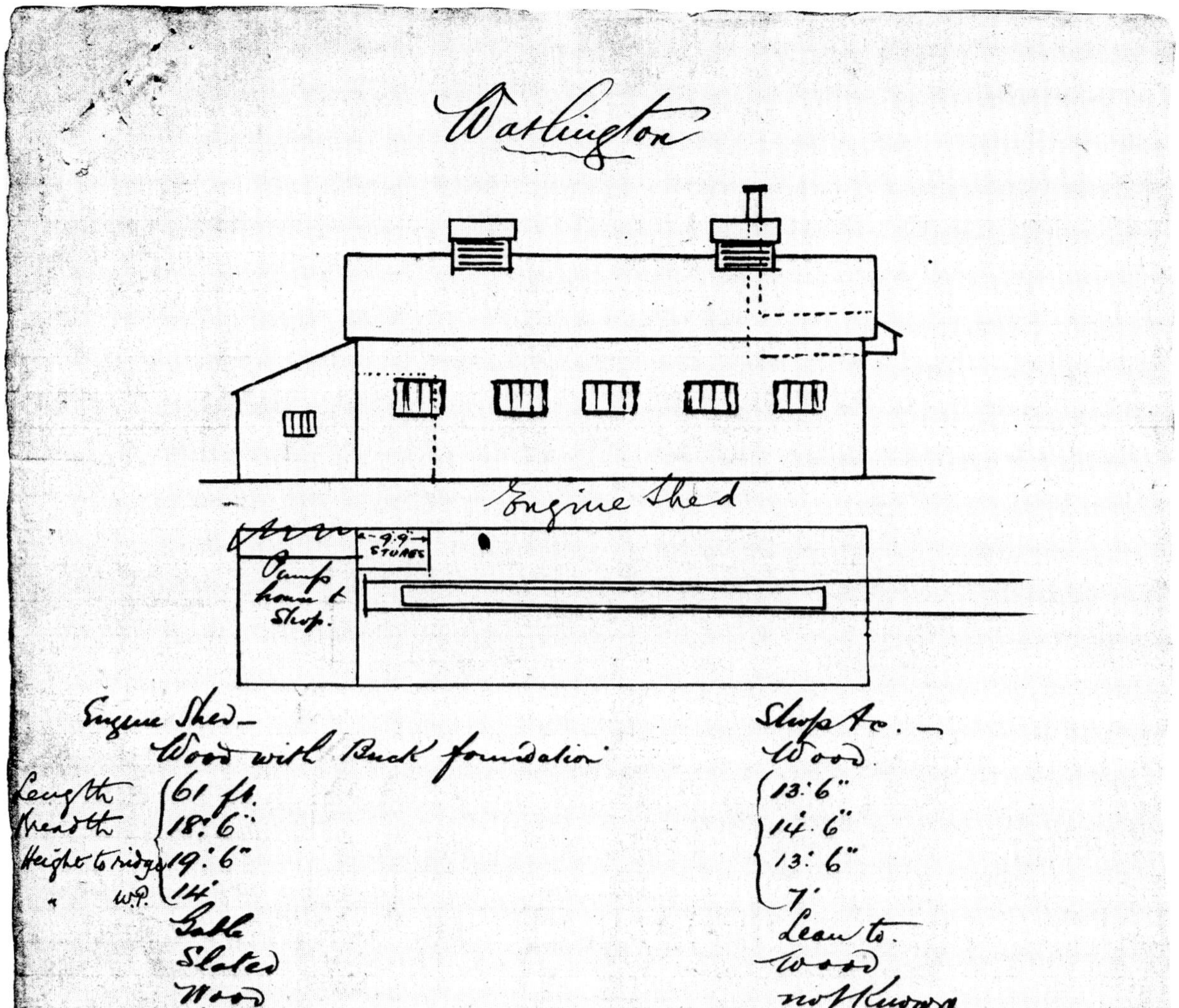

Watlington

Engine Shed

Pump house + Shop.

Engine Shed —
Wood with Brick foundation

Length   61 ft.
Breadth   18: 6"
Height to ridge 19: 6"
   "   w.p. 14'
             Gable
             Slated
             Wood
             For. 13' ft
             Not Known
             20 ft - inside

             42'

Shops &c. —
Wood.
13: 6"
14: 6"
13: 6"
7'
Lean to.
Wood
not Known

Outside Shed
Line avail. for standing engines
60 ft
no pits, no turntable

Wood store

Coal Stage —
Wood.
date not Known.
no tips —

Sand furnace —
Nil.

This 1892 sketch of Watlington engine shed was drawn up for the official records held at Swindon.

Locomotives used on the line since 1902 included '517' class 0–4–2T No. 1465 and '2021' class 0–6–0ST No. 2081, but in 1904 'Metro' class 2–4–0Ts Nos. 5 and 467 and '2021' class 0–6–0ST No. 2083 also feature in Watlington's official allocation. In 1905 only 'Metro' class 2–4–0Ts Nos. 4 and 467 are listed whilst in 1906 '2021' class 0–6–0STs appear again, Nos. 2081, 2083, 2132 and 2150, along with 'Metros' Nos. 4 and 981. Hauling the down branch goods up Chinnor bank was no light duty, so it is hardly surprising the 0–6–0 wheel arrangement of

the dogged '2021s' were preferred for branch work and increasingly allocated to Watlington.

However, to return to the question of the engine shed, it seems that the Great Western were unwilling to simply erect another on the existing site, undoubtedly because they were considering the establishment of a larger depot at Princes Risborough. If that had materialised, the Watlington branch would have been worked from that end of the line, thus obviating the need for any shed at the terminus. The earliest

This postcard view, taken one evening after the demise of the engine shed, provides more evidence of two engines at Watlington. They appear to have been '2021' class 0–6–0STs. It also shows some of the old post and rail fencing, subsequently replaced by standard GWR post and wire.

Another postcard view taken around the same time, showing another '2021' class 0–6–0ST and auto-trailer, and the original location of the pair of lamps huts at this end of the station garden.

Lower Station Road, Chinnor, looking east towards the railway during the Edwardian years. The prominent two-storey building on the left was Tom Witney's bicycle shop. This was taken over by Fred Gomm who, in the 1920s, also had a 14-seater Overland coach which was kept in a garage at the back and used for private hire work. Gomm later became landlord of The Crown public house where he adapted the outbuildings (featured in the middle distance) for his motor coach business. The striped blinds adjacent to the bicycle shop shaded the window of Balls, chemist and general store, whilst in the 1920s the dwelling immediately beyond the arch was used as a surgery by a doctor from Thame who visited Chinnor twice a week. The Black Boy public house was rebuilt in 1932 following a serious fire.

evidence of this is in a letter from J. W. Armstrong to G. J. Churchward, CME, in January 1904: "I am not particular as to the shape of the shed, so long as it is a turntable shed, but I propose a round shed as I am of the opinion that it will cost less to build than one of the rectangular shape." A subsequent letter (6th January) reveals "This could be half built, which would be quite enough for present needs, and of course would allow for future extension . . . I propose to put at present about 5 or 6 engines at Risborough, but of course when all the alterations are complete it will no doubt be necessary to stable a much larger number of engines there."

The provision of a new shed at Watlington was therefore held in abeyance.

Other improvements to the branch through this period included the provision of telephonic communication between Watlington and Princes Risborough, authorised 19th October 1904 at an estimated cost of £236, and in March 1906 the introduction of the 'economic system of maintenance' was authorised for the permanent way. The most far-reaching of all, however, came in 1910 when on 14th April the GWR agreed to provide a connection at Chinnor to serve W. E. Benton's lime kilns, the estimated cost of £298 being met by him and refunded by a rebate on his traffic payments. The work was completed by 11th August 1911 and inspected on 18th October 1911.

Few people in Chinnor could have imagined how the new lime works would expand and contribute to the growth and prosperity of the village, but it must have been eagerly welcomed in the light of this extract from the *Thame Gazette* a few years earlier on 30th April 1901:

DECLINE OF THE VILLAGE OF CHINNOR
(Specially contributed)

When a village like Chinnor, which beyond a doubt is "beautiful for situation", is weighed in the census balances and found wanting to the extent of about 250 in population, the startling fact demands a pause for reflection. Such a pause is lengthened in the light of the statistical barometer of the last 60 years.

In 1851 the population was 1257
" 1861 " " " 1296
" 1871 " " " 1371
" 1881 " " " 1237
" 1891 " " " 1247
" 1901 " " " 1000 (unofficial)

When a drop of nearly 400 occurs in a village of great scenic attractions, it surely is high time that any remaining spark of enterprise should be fanned. The village has had a name for being progressive (in some quarters a bad name), whilst in truth it is almost delusively stationary if not actually reactionary.

This view, taken further east along Station Road, shows the inclined approach to the railway bridge, with the station entrance just hidden by the hedge on the right. The house on the left with the porch was called 'Ivy Bank' and was occupied by the Jarretts. More of the Jarrett family lived opposite in a house which, in the 1950s, was used as offices for Siareys (see Vol. 2). Chinnor porters Joe and Ivy Bateman lived in a property hidden in this view between 'Ivy Bank' and 'Old Cott'. Their garden and privvy were on the opposite side of the road. Porter George Howlett remembers children playing by 'the gulley' on the right and watching matches float downstream.

Cty. George Howlett

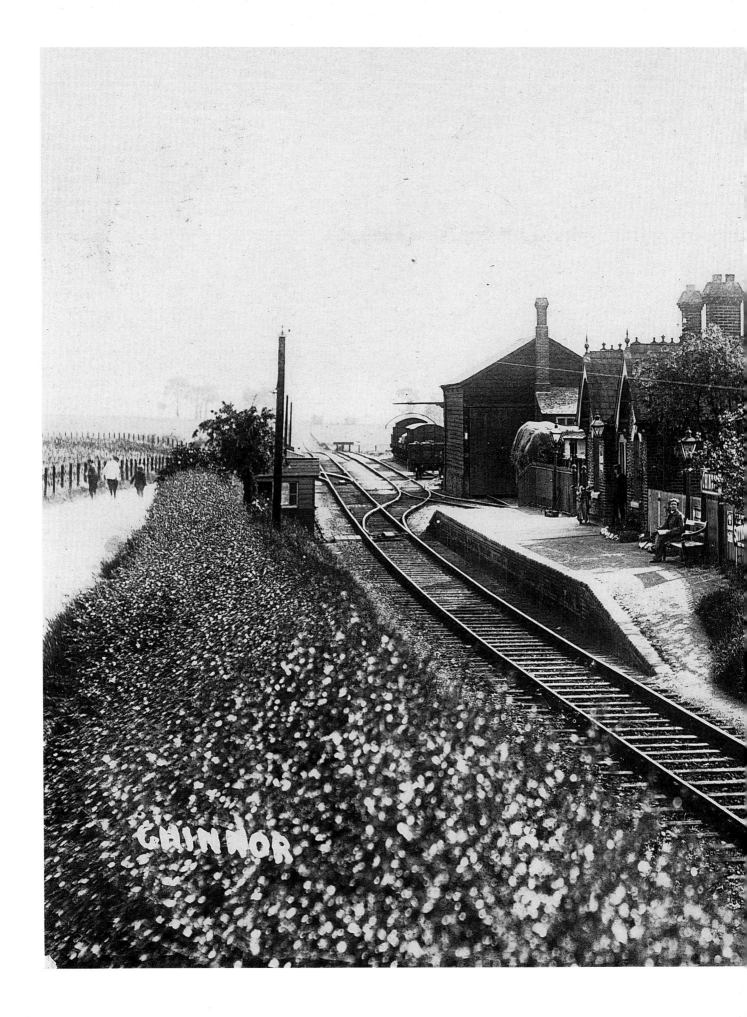

This postcard view of Chinnor station shows the new private siding connection for Benton's lime works, the access road to which features outside the railway boundary hedge on the left. The tall yard lamps by the private siding connection and the station forecourt were recent additions, but the goods shed was demolished in 1912 to make way for improvements to the goods yard.

Aston Station.

An unidentified 'Metro' class 2—4—0T calling at Aston Rowant station one morning on its way back from Princes Risborough with a train of four-wheel coaches. This picture was probably taken c.1905 before the introduction of auto-trailers on the line.

A c.1906 staff group at Watlington station, showing Jimmy Nelms (seated on the left), who joined the railway as a porter at Watlington in 1904, and next to him Ernest William Harry Sexton, who had previously served as clerk at Windsor, Aylesbury and Marlow, and transferred away to Staines in 1911.
Cty. Mrs. P. Shorter

Battalions of youths, the strength of its loins, have been reared and as constantly passed on to further inflate the million-massed bubbles in the wilderness of walls. This outflow of the best and strongest has met with no check, but rather has been encouraged. No attempt has been made to disillusion young minds with the apparent terrors of town life. The voice of Empire locally demands that health should stand before wealth, and here we have a village that is so healthy that a doctor cannot be found to reside in it. It is all "right-about-face march"; no one has been found sufficient to say "right-about-heart stay". We have a station; sometimes a train; sometimes that slow impulse lands a visitor (it would be hundreds if we had accommodation). The first vision that visitor has of any masonry is an engineer's dilapidated foundry. Surely there are capitalists in Wycombe, for instance, who could utilize such a spot for a chair factory in a village where the beech-wood is and can be plentifully worked up in parts . . . We have still amongst us men of ideas, but they are mostly of the winged species; these ideas want toning down to "earthfulness". For instance, one hears of golf-links on the Hills, of a palatial boarding-house, of GWR excursion trains, of a fortnightly market, of a Rifle Range, of a horticultural show, or an allotment competition. It has been said, notably at our district centre, that we are a most hardly-pleased, dissatisfied community; now if this can be more politely phrased and charitably interpreted, it means that we are tired of the "down grade", have still some ambition and believe in a prospect of advancement. The fact is we are at the low ebb-tide. The question is, can there be a flowing tide? Upon the sea-shore the ebbing tide reveals the mud-banks, the flowing tide reveals the many mighty waters bearing commerce.

W. E. Benton was a welcome saviour and the story of the lime kilns and their expansion into the mighty Chinnor Cement Works is told in an appendix to Volume Two.

Even during the first year of Benton's siding, the traffic to and from the lime kilns had evidently developed sufficiently to tax the capacity and layout of the old goods sidings at Chinnor. Accordingly, on 10th October, £530 was authorised to lengthen the sidings and connect one of them with the running line (forming a loop siding) "to enable the practice of tow-roping to be dispensed with", demolish the old goods shed (providing a

goods lock-up on the platform instead) and metal additional roadway surfaces. The work was completed exactly 12 months later on 10th October 1913 and eventually inspected by the Board of Trade on 4th March 1914.

Similarly, one of the sidings at Aston Rowant was lengthened and provided with an additional connection to the running line to form a loop siding. The work, authorised on 3rd June 1912 for £230 (not including land), was completed on 17th December 1912 and inspected on 25th March 1913. Incidentally, the roadway along the back siding at Aston Rowant had been extended in 1902 to provide extra accommodation for loading, the work, involving the purchase of 24 poles of land, totalling £70.

In May 1911 Ernest Sexton transferred from Watlington to Staines to take a higher grade station master's position. He had held office at Watlington for 7½ years during the 'whole time' of which, according to the *Thame Gazette*, he had been 'most courteous and attentive and in addition has taken an interest in every movement in the town'. The *Thame Gazette* for 2nd February 1909 mentions him playing a piano solo at a Conservative dinner one Wednesday evening at the Hare and Hounds Hotel.

In a manner reminiscent of Mr. Lett's departure, 'as an acknowledgement and appreciation of his courteous manner and ability in business transactions, it was decided to invite donation to a testimonial fund, and with little difficulty sufficient money was raised to present Mr. Sexton with a gold watch and a purse of gold.'

Mr. Sexton was succeeded by William Thomas Yeates who coincidentally later also transferred to Staines when Sexton moved on from there. Yeates, almost six years junior to Sexton, had joined the GWR as a clerk at Shrivenham in 1899. He had been promoted to Watlington from the position of goods clerk at Didcot which he had held since 1908.

Few towns and villages can have escaped the effect of the First World War, but at this distance in time we have not managed to find many first-hand memories. However, the following extract from the *Thame Gazette* for 8th September 1914 conveys something of the mood:

ENLISTING FOR THE ARMY — Since its commencement recruiting has been going on in a quiet manner, and we wish to take this opportunity of denying the report of scaremongers that the parish has done nothing in this direction. Sergeant H. Kirby, of the Working Men's Club, when war broke out, at once placed his services without pay at the disposal of Cowley Barracks, and the Committee of the Working Men's Club were only too glad to relieve him of his duties so that he might do the work. The difficulty, up to this week, has been conveying recruits to the barracks. It occupies all day to go to Cowley and back by rail. Now the owners of four motor-cars have undertaken to help, so not only money but hours of valuable time will be saved. It is no uncommon thing to hear, when too late, of men actually walking to Reading or Oxford to offer themselves for the Army. On Monday one young fellow from an outlying village left his home, and poor as he was took a ticket for Paddington to enlist. All this may be avoided by applying to Sergeant H. Kirby, who will either supply a free third-class railway ticket to Oxford, or secure the loan of a motor-car, to enable men to join Lord Kitchener's Army.

Jim Clarke, who spent his life in Chinnor, said most men from the village went off to the Great War. He recalled evacuees from the East End of London arriving by train. They apparently stayed in some of the run-down empty houses in the village. He also

remembered fusiliers from a camp 'down the main road' using the village shops.

In common with most railways throughout the country, the service on the Watlington branch was reduced, the *Thame Gazette* for 4th January 1916 reporting:

The train service has been seriously curtailed, one of the most useful trains, the 11.40 a.m., disappears. Also the 4.35 daily, and that leaving Paddington at 9 a.m. on Wednesdays and Saturdays, arriving here at 10.50 a.m.

The late-night service connecting with the 9.0 a.m. from Paddington had been introduced on Saturdays only in October 1909 and additionally on Wednesdays from February 1910. Leaving Risborough at 10.25, this train was run with the engine from the 8.20 p.m. Watlington goods which, on the other weekdays, returned with goods traffic.

From January 1916, the service consisted of three return trips leaving Watlington at 8.45 a.m., 12.55 and 6.55 p.m., returning from Risborough at 10.0 a.m., 4.5 p.m. and 7.43 p.m., although from May 1916 the 11.40 a.m. was reinstated, but only on Fridays.

From May 1917 the early and late goods trains were replaced by an 11.0 a.m. from Watlington (except Fridays) calling at Aston Rowant and Chinnor and returning from Risborough at 12.30 p.m. with '29 minutes allowed to work at Benton's Siding' on the

Shunting was going on in the revised goods yard when this picture was taken at Chinnor on 16th August 1919. The base of the 125ft chimney for Benton's new chamber kilns can just be made out in the left background.   *L & GRP*

This companion view of Aston Rowant station was taken looking towards Watlington on 16th August 1919, and just shows the road entrance gates alongside the bridge. *L & GRP*

**WATLINGTON BRANCH
PASSENGER COUNT
week ending 20th September 1913**

From Watlington	Count at P. Risborough Average
(MO) 7.35 a.m.	13
8.40 a.m.	21
11.40 a.m.	28
? .55	18
4.35 p.m.	9
6.55 p.m.	27

From P. Risborough	
(MO) 8.6 a.m.	4
9.57 a.m.	16
12.59 p.m.	15
3.0 p.m.	26
5.24 p.m.	12
7.43 p.m.	37
(SO) 10.25 p.m.	16

**WATLINGTON BRANCH
PASSENGER COUNT
Week ending 27th January 1917**

From Watlington	Average Watlington	Bledlow
8.55 a.m.	8	20
(FO) 11.40 a.m.	5	16
2.55 p.m.	5	14
6.50 p.m.	9	9

From P. Risborough	P. Risboro'	Lewknor
9.48 a.m.	8	2
4.5 p.m.	45	13
7.43 p.m.	24	8

down journey. On Fridays the goods left Watlington at 4.45 p.m. and returned at 6.0 p.m.

By 1920 the goods workings reverted to being run at the beginning and end of the day's timetable, leaving Watlington at 5.50 a.m. and 5.0 p.m. and returning from Risborough at 7.0 a.m. (calling at Chinnor only) and 6.15 p.m. (engine and van) respectively. Aston Rowant was served by a 12.15 p.m. return trip from Risborough (returning from Aston Rowant at 1.10 p.m.) which was later adapted to become the midday Chinnor goods.

From 1913 to 1916, '1076' class 0–6–0ST No. 1172 was used on the line and from 1913–15 '1854' class 0–6–0ST No. 1770. Under the 1919 engine classification scheme, the Watlington branch was designated as a yellow route, with an axle weight limit of 16 tons. Officially, the '1854s' were 'blue' engines, which meant No. 1770 exceeded the official axleweight for the bridges on the line. Conversely, however, the '1854s' had an axle weight of just 15 tons?

By 1918 the old wooden water tank, which narrowly escaped the fire at Watlington engine shed, was getting into bad condition and in need of replacement. If, as we believe, this was the original W&PRR structure, it was now 46 years old.

The replacement of the tank provides an insight into GWR interdepartmental affairs and shows how such a barely significant branch line fitted into the huge Great Western empire.

In a letter from the Locomotive and Carriage Department that March, C. Crump of Old Oak Common said:

> You may probably think it desirable to take this opportunity to provide a steel tank. A 3000 gallon pillar tank would do excellently at this place, and if you have no use for the one which will shortly be taken down at Bishops Road, I suggest that it should be re-erected at Watlington.

As nothing had come of the proposal to establish a new engine shed at Risborough, plans had been prepared in 1912–13 for a replacement shed at Watlington. Even then the matter was held in abeyance. However, in order to ensure the new pillar tank was erected in a position to suit the anticipated new arrangements, the plans for the replacement shed were

This less formal picture of a Risborough-bound train approaching the station platform at Chinnor one summer evening, is thought to have been taken shortly after the First World War.

Cty. George Howlett

consulted. These provided for a long overdue extension of the run-round loop. Although improved, Watlington station was little different to when it was first built in 1872 and the short run-round loop inherited from that time frequently restricted operation. Even after the shed building had gone, the site of the inspection pit with adjacent well, hydrants, drainage, etc, effectively blocked any extension of the loop, so the proposed new shed was to be outside the existing boundary fence, involving the purchase of a small piece of extra land along the station's eastern boundary. The 1 rood 26½ poles concerned was on property rented by farmer Alfred Cooper from the Earl of Macclesfield.

Just to complicate things, Loco & Carriage Department correspondence reveals 'During our enquiries it was learned that the Military Authorities had also been making enquiries respecting the land and there appears to be a possibility of its being taken for Army purposes'.

A subsequent letter from one of Churchward's officers dated 27th January 1919 said 'in the circumstances, I suggest that the pillar tank be erected in the position shown on the accompanying plan No. 57197 [presumably for the position adopted] as should the branch ever be worked from the Princes Risborough end, the necessity for an engine shed at Watlington would disappear.'

In the meantime, the Bishops Road tank was evidently not available for Watlington, and, according to a letter of 10th August 1918 from the Loco Department at Swindon, 'The only 2000 gallon pillar tank we have in stock has been marked off for Pembridge. There is, as you are aware, a 3000 gallon barrel standing on timbers at Marlow which you might like to have removed to Watlington, or would either the pillar tanks recently removed from Hereford suit the purpose with a steel column?' Coarse blue pencil markings on the original of this letter show 'Hereford' underlined and a large 'no' scribbled in the margin.

By June 1919 it transpired that a pillar tank at Taunton was about to be replaced by a water crane. One of Churchward's officers wrote 'I shall be glad if you will arrange to take this work in hand to plan No. 57197 as soon as possible utilizing the pillar

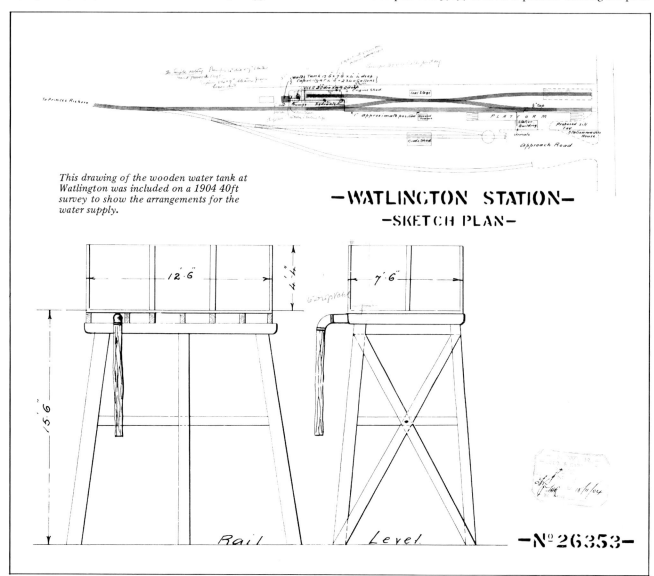

This drawing of the wooden water tank at Watlington was included on a 1904 40ft survey to show the arrangements for the water supply.

—WATLINGTON STATION—
—SKETCH PLAN—

—N⁰ 26353—

tank I have instructed you to remove from Taunton. This is an urgent matter, as the existing tank is now in a defective condition and leaking badly.'

In another letter on 31st July 1919 one of Churchward's men said 'we are hoping to bring the new pillar water tank at Watlington into use in the course of a week or so. I understand the underneath portion of the existing tank is used as a stores, and perhaps you will kindly let me know if you wish this accommodation retained. If so, it will be necessary to ask the engineer to roof over the structure when the tank is removed.'

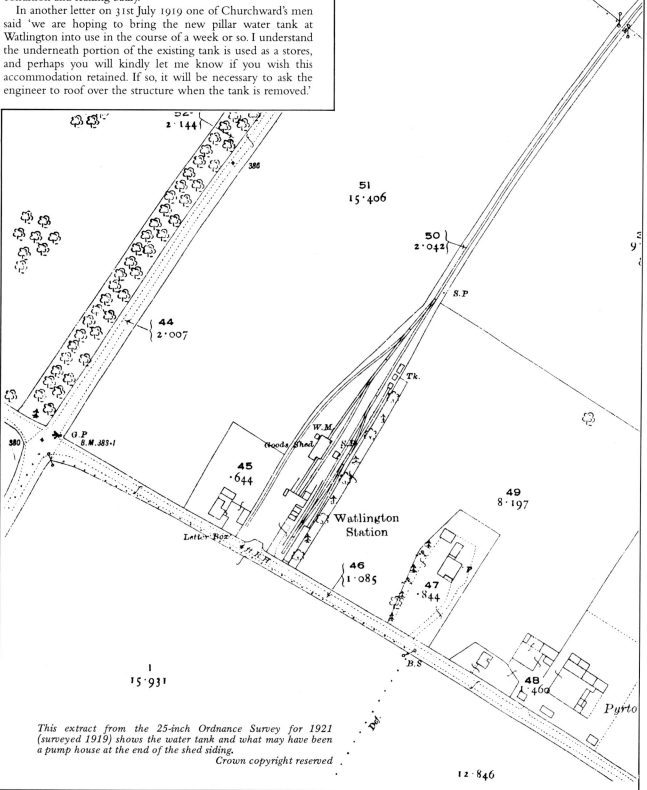

This extract from the 25-inch Ordnance Survey for 1921 (surveyed 1919) shows the water tank and what may have been a pump house at the end of the shed siding.
Crown copyright reserved

It transpired that the cabin under the old tank had a roof on it and so the old tank supports were cut off level with the top of it. However, it is not clear how long it survived.

The provision of the pillar tank 'in lieu of existing wooden structure' was first authorised on 1st August 1918 at an estimated cost of £621. In May 1919 the amount had changed to £592, whilst in practice the use of the tank from Taunton had resulted in a final cost of £426, a saving of £154.

In January 1919, in the wake of the Great War, the Watlington Parish Council had petitioned the GWR to reinstate the prewar train services, at the same time complaining about 'the long and unnecessary delay' in leaving Risborough after the up and down trains had departed. The GWR replied that it was not possible to make any modifications or improvements in the existing train services 'until the staff and locomotives had been returned'.

The Parish Council then urged for an 8.40 a.m. train as soon as possible to enable businessmen to reach London at 9.55 a.m., and from at least July 1920 the 8.40 a.m. connected with the 6.50 a.m. Wolverhampton express which ran non-stop from Risborough and arrived at Paddington at 10.0 a.m. As Watlington branch driver Harry Humphreys later said, "Good going that was".

However, this excellent service was interrupted (at least the return journey) by the 1919 railway strike which lasted from 26th September until 5th October, when an emergency service of two trains a day were run from Watlington to High Wycombe at 8.55 a.m. and 12.45 p.m., returning from Wycombe at 10.30 a.m. and 2.20 p.m.

Although Watlington had been provided with the public telephone at the Post Office since March 1914, news of the strike reached Watlington by a telegram sent to the newsagent on Friday evening. Farmers sent their milk to the station on Saturday morning as usual, only to find that although the local railwaymen were loyal, no train could enter Princes Risborough. According to the *Thame Gazette*:

A third view taken at Watlington on the 16th August 1919, showing the branch auto-trailer, supplemented by the brake third and one or more siphon vans.

L & GRP

A local postcard view, looking east over Kingston Crossing with the halt on the left and the crossing cottage partly obscured by foliage on the right. The flint and brick walls of the cottage were subsequently rendered.

The milk was taken back and disposed of to the best advantage. The ordinary foodstuffs are plentiful and all emergency arrangements for supplies have been made. Lord Macclesfield has offered meat and rabbits to the town should they be required. On Sunday, and since, the milk churns have been collected and taken to London by motor transport. On two occasions pickets have been sent to urge the men to strike, and on Tuesday a dozen men at least came but found their efforts were in vain.

It must have seemed all too familiar when the train service was curtailed again in October 1920, this time by a national coal strike which lasted from 18th October to 8th November. The *Thame Gazette* reported:

> The train service has been altered as far as the fast trains are concerned and the midday train. The 8.40 a.m. leaves at 8.50 and arrives at Paddington at 10.52. The 11.40 is not running. Passengers are advised not to rely upon the 3.25 p.m. ex Paddington (slip) but to catch the old 2.25 p.m.

Trains left Watlington at 8.50 a.m., 3.0 p.m. and 6.50 p.m., returning from Risborough at 9.55, 4.20 and 7.47.

The 3.25 p.m. Paddington to Birkenhead which slipped a coach to enable passengers to connect with the 4.20 to Watlington, had been restored by 11th November, but the pre-strike branch service was not restored until the 15th. However, coal remained in short supply for some time, and according to the *Thame Gazette* of 17th May 1921:

> The lack of coal has created another industry, one from which hard and laborious work is needed. There are thousands of tons of 'dead' branches of timber in the woods, and it is all free to those who will respect the existing trees and not create any disturbance and all it needs is carting. From the villages crowds are to be seen obtaining the wood, and these 'wise virgins' recognise that they will have to depend upon this for heating purposes right up to the autumn. The exercise today is not 'physical jerks' but saving and chopping up wood.

Crossing keeper Mrs. Lambourn at Kingston crossing c.1920 with her granddaughter Joan Pearson. Her husband Jim was the branch ganger and they lived at the crossing from about 1918 until about 1926/7 when they were succeeded by the Bills family. The Lambourns' daughter Dorothy, known as Dolly, married branch fireman Arthur Pearson who moved away for promotion in 1919 and returned to Watlington as a driver in 1929. *Cty. Joan Jones*

Aston Rowant station around 1928, looking much as it did when Reg Pocock took the position of station master in 1922.

C. L. Mowat

CHAPTER FOUR
POCOCK'S PRIDE
1922–1939

AS we have already seen, the way to promotion for many GWR employees was to move around the system in order to take up more senior posts as they became available. This not only provided the opportunity for betterment but also gave staff a broader experience which, as they rose in the ranks, was of benefit to the company.

Nothing is permanent in this life, but when Reg Pocock took up the post of station master at Aston Rowant in 1922, he

Reg Pocock in 1922.

evidently found contentment and, in remaining on the branch for 24 years, brought a sense of stability both to the staff and local people.

Born in Moulsford in 1886, Reg joined the GWR as a telegraph messenger at Reading in September 1900. In March 1901 he became a telegraphist at Reading station, in September 1904 a porter and in January 1907 a porter signalman at Wheatley. The following September he returned to Reading and appears to have spent the next fifteen years as a relief signalman, covering boxes from Sonning to Didcot. In 1910 he married his first cousin, Beatrice Winifred, the daughter of his uncle, Edward John Pocock, who had looked after him throughout his childhood in Moulsford. The couple set up home at 15 Curzon Street, Reading, and later at 35 South View, Caversham.

By the time he was appointed station master at Aston Rowant, he had four children, Cecil, Leslie, Maurice and Gwen, and they all moved into a cottage in Weston Road, Lewknor. Previous station masters had apparently lived at Woodway Cottages, Woodway Farm, Aston Rowant, the properties concerned at the time being rented from farmer Morris.

Reg's daughter Gwen remembers that her father inherited a number of chickens which the previous station master had left

at the station. On Sunday evenings Reg used to take her on circular walks to Aston Rowant to see them. 'They seemed to nest everywhere', but she particularly remembers them congregating in the goods shed and opposite the station platform, near the ground frame hut.

Whether Reg Pocock had complained about his family's accommodation at Lewknor or whether there was some other problem is not known, but in 1923–4 GWR Traffic Committee minutes record the sanctioning of a new house for the station master at Aston Rowant for £700 (including £75 for land). However, this never came about, as when W. T. Yeates left Watlington, the posts of station master at Aston Rowant and Watlington were merged as an economy measure, and Reg was moved to Watlington where he became very much part of the local community.

Just three days prior to taking up his new appointment on 4th March 1924, the family moved to Watlington, taking over a property in Gorwell previously occupied by station masters Sexton and Yeates. It is said to have once been a public house (the Peacock?) but, although rented at first, the Pococks later purchased it from the Rev. Hilgrove Coxe and christened the house 'St. John'.

Reg had taken a keen interest in First Aid and the ambulance movement since at least 1908 when he attended classes at Reading and gained his St. John Ambulance certificate and subsequently a gold medal for ambulance efficiency. He appears to have joined the brigade in 1922 shortly after his arrival at Aston Rowant and the following year he was giving a series of First Aid lectures at the Memorial Church Hall in the High Street, Watlington, with the assistance of Dr. T. King Edwards. Said to have been attended by the local police and 90 per cent of the Watlington branch railwaymen, the lectures received the official recognition of the St. John Ambulance Service with the subsequent formation of a local brigade on 27th March 1928. Reginald was most proud to be the founder and superintendent of the Watlington Division, by which time 70 per cent of the Watlington branch railwaymen were still regular class attenders.

In addition to the hall in Shirburn Street, use was also made of the Rev. Coxe's 'tin hut' adjacent to the Pococks' house at Gorwell. Reg's daughter Gwen remembers how in the early 1930s she used to light the fire to warm the building in readiness for meetings and First Aid practice.

The brigade flourished under Reg's leadership. The Earl of Macclesfield became President, and Sid Pratley, clerk at Watlington station from 1928 to 1933, was appointed Secretary. Again, thanks to the generosity of Rev. Coxe, from 1st September 1935 the Salvation Hall in Shirburn Street became the headquarters of the St. John Brigade and subsequently became known as the Ambulance Hall.

The Watlington Brigade even had its own ambulance — a Model T Ford which was later replaced by a 25hp Vauxhall, funded principally from public donations, including the Rev. Coxe and the Earl of Macclesfield. A one-shilling share entitled people to a free ride if the need arose. The new ambulance was dedicated at the old town hall in March 1937 during a snowstorm!

Reg Pocock and his staff at Watlington, probably in August or September 1924. From left to right this picture shows: *Back Row*: Albert Brown, permanent way; 'Darkie' Sowden, permanent way; Harry Humphreys, driver; George Baker, porter; Edward ('Rumper') Jones, driver; Cecil Evetts, fireman; Peter Robinson, fireman; unidentified; Tommy Johnson, permanent way; *Front Row*: Charlie Hopkins, porter; Jimmy Nelms, guard; Miss Winifred Siarey, clerk; Reg Pocock, station master; W. G. 'Nobby' Clarke, guard; Harry Blackwell, porter at Aston Rowant; and Bill Gomme, porter at Aston Rowant. George Baker transferred to Watlington in August 1924 and remained there until June 1929 when he left to take up a porter/guard position at Oxford. W. G. Clarke, who had served at Watlington from at least 1921, went to Abingdon in October 1925, whilst Cecil Evetts, who had been at Watlington since August 1924, transferred away to Slough in June 1929.

Gwen Clarke & Rita Watts

This picture from the Pocock family collection was also probably taken around 1924 and shows Watlington station at its most cared for. The window boxes and flower tubs do not appear in later views.   *Gwen Clarke & Rita Watts*

On 10th May 1938 Reg became a serving brother of the Order of St. John of Jerusalem. His investiture took place in London on 22nd July 1938 and the occasion was marked by the railway staff who arranged a line of detonators on the rails in readiness for his return. As the branch train ran into the station, the explosions were accompanied by loud cheers from a number of friends and colleagues waiting to congratulate him.

In addition to the St. John Ambulance, Reg had joined the Royal Ancient Order of Buffalos in 1923 and besides serving as a sidesman and church warden, also became a lay preacher, sometimes standing in for the Vicar at St. Leonard's Church. He was secretary of the Parochial Church Council, member of the Ruridecanal and Diocesan Council, an active member of the British Legion, a school board manager, a member of the hospital management committee, and, for a short time, librarian.

After moving to Watlington, Reg and his wife had two more children, Bernard and Rita. His daughters remember him as strict but kind, and their house 'had an ever-open door', with a constant flow of visitors in connection with the railway or his numerous voluntary activities. Even Mrs. Pocock found time to belong to the WI and Mothers' Union and collected for the blind. The whole family were involved, the children polishing the buttons on his St. John uniform and cleaning out the ambulance. Reg always looked smart and wore wing collars which were starched at the laundry.

His children frequently visited the station, even as early as 6.0 a.m. to pick mushrooms in the fields. They would play in the goods shed, have very unofficial rides on the engine during shunting movements, and were generally fussed over by the staff. Gwen loved to sit in the office with her dad; in fact both girls were very proud of him and his position in the community. They loved visiting the station in the afternoons of the school holidays and might sometimes get a lift home 'on Mr. Tappin's coal lorry'. However, we have leapt ahead in our story.

When Reg first took over at Watlington in 1924, the staff comprised:

Clerk	Miss W. M. Siarey
Porters	George W. Baker
	Charlie Hopkins
Guards	Jimmy Nelms
	W. G. Clarke
Drivers	Harry Humphreys
	Edward Jones
Firemen	Cecil Evetts
	Herbert Henry Hearn
	Peter Robinson

Miss Siarey's time at Watlington is not entirely clear. The *Thame Gazette* for 1st February 1921 records a presentation to mark her departure from the booking office at Watlington where she had served throughout the war, whereas not only does she appear in the 1924 group photo, but there is also a gap in the records between the departure of J. F. Richardson, who left the post in

The centre of Watlington in the 1920s, very much the scene which the Pocock family enjoyed.

Watlington High Street in the 1920s with Trindall's garage in the right foreground, followed by Cooks newsagent, 'Peady' Green's house (with the prominent pattern of headers in the brickwork) and Wilsons jewellers. The large light-coloured building housed a club.

July 1923 when he transferred to Oxford, and the arrival of Percy Peyman from Marlow in 1925.

Charles Harry Hebourn Hopkins, known to everyone as Charlie, was born of Welsh parents at Chinnor in 1892. His father worked for farmer Hickman at Chinnor. Interestingly, Charlie went to Wales to start his working life at Gwinear Ystrad Colliery, but after about two years he returned to Chinnor to live with his brother Tom and joined the railway as a porter at Watlington shortly before the Great War. Both of their parents had died by this time. He was a 'crack shot' and is remembered for scoring ten shots through the same bull's-eye with a Lee Henford 303 on Watlington rifle range. It was hardly surprising therefore that he should have served with the Royal Warwickshire Regiment during the Great War on Lewis guns. After his left arm had been partly riddled by machine-gun fire, he was discharged from the army in August 1918 and returned to the railway as a porter at Watlington, lodging with his wife at the Royal Oak until 1933 when he bought a house in the High Street where they remained for the rest of their lives.

He was a conscientious and loyal man whom Reg Pocock could depend on, and, as he served the rest of his career at Watlington and Aston Rowant stations, Reg never knew the line without him.

James Cornelius Nelms was born in Watlington in 1880; his father ran the Red Lion public house in Couching Street. Jimmy started out as a stable lad on the Shirburn Estate and joined the railway as a porter at Watlington station in January 1904, later marrying the daughter of Henry Cheney, one of the Watlington branch guards, in 1906. He became a guard on the branch in December 1912.

He was an extremely shy and reserved man and would never eat in company, even at home. He ate in the guard's van between trips and if anybody approached him he would immediately close his box and stop. He was a happy and jovial man, good-hearted and very thoughtful.

The Nelms family lived in a succession of different houses in Watlington, Shirburn Street, Hill Cottages, Hill Road, the bottom house in the High Street, and finally Watcombe Road. Percy Peyman and George Baker were among the lodgers they

WORKING OF GUARDS
Notice dated 14th July 1924

Turn		Guard	
194	5.35 a.m. – 2.30 p.m. (MX)	Nelms	
	6.30 a.m. – 2.30 p.m. (MO)		Change weekly
195	2.40 p.m. – 10.40 p.m.	Clark	
194	5.50 a.m. – 2.14 p.m.		
195	3.0 p.m. – 10.20 p.m.		
	11.15 p.m. (SO)		
Sundays			
365	7.0 a.m. – 12.0 noon	Nelms	Alternate
		Clark	Sundays

This view of Church Street somehow encapsulates the feel of Watlington with its humble brick-and-flint dwellings. A number of the railway staff lodged with the Dover family who lived at No. 2, at the opposite end of the street on the right-hand side.

took in, Percy finding the Nelms household a vast improvement over his previous accommodation "and there was always toast for tea!".

Jimmy was a great reader and was always having books out of the library, "he particularly liked a good novel". In private he smoked a pipe (but never on duty) and he was a keen vegetable gardener. However, his colleagues might have been surprised to learn that he could play several musical instruments well. He is also said to have been very proud of some land he owned in Watlington.

Little is known of driver Edward Jones who started as a cleaner at Gobowen in 1892 and transferred to Watlington as driver on 21st February 1916. According to official records, he was engineman 3rd class and suffered from 'defective form vision'. He should not be confused with 'Jim' Jones, who according to the *Thame Gazette* had been a driver on the independent Watlington & Princes Risborough Railway and died in 1925.★ As a child in the 1920s, George Howlett (who later became a porter and guard on the line) remembers Edward, or 'Bumper Jones' as he was known, as short, with a white moustache, a larger-than-life character with 'a bit of a short fuse'. He is also believed to have

run into the buffer stops at the end of the line at Watlington, which might account for his nickname, but at this distance in time, it is difficult to tell. He lived in Watcombe Road.

Henry George Humphreys, known to everyone as 'Harry', was "a quiet sort of man", a Londoner, who, born in 1887, had started out as a cleaner at Old Oak shed in 1905. He became a fireman in 1907 and driver in 1919, transferring to Watlington on 7th May 1923 and remaining on the line until he retired. During his first 12 months at Watlington he lodged with the Dover family at No. 2 Church Street.

By all accounts, Harry was a good engineman, meticulous, extremely conscientious, "always busy with the engine", and "an expert at frying bacon on the shovel". He did everything properly, insisting on doing the oiling himself and never leaving the fireman to do the shunting on his own. He was a "very dapper little man" who wore corduroy trousers which squeaked as he walked to and from the station in short methodical steps with his head down and carrying his tuck box.

The combination of his reserve and shyness with the responsible attitude he showed towards the job, was not always understood, one of the women interviewed regarding him as "a miserable old devil", "you could never get a smile out of him". Similarly, some of the local youngsters referred to him as 'Humpo', but his concern for safety and propriety tended to veil

★ We have been unable to trace Jim Jones in GWR staff records and, of course, it is possible that he never became a GWR employee.

his kind and courteous nature, and such misunderstandings are easily outnumbered by instances of his willingness to stop the train and reverse back into Watlington station for latecomers, through to his arranging lodgings for a new fireman and even unofficially taking porter Harold Blackwell's daughter from Watlington to Risborough and back on the footplate while working a special cattle train.

Reading and Oxford. Conversely, other traffic figures rose for a while, with an increase in the numbers of parcels handled — 38,000 in 1913 to nearly 54,000 in 1929. General merchandise forwarded rose from 6,000 to 17,000 tons and coal received from nearly 9,000 tons to over 20,000, not least in connection with the increased consumption of coal at the new Chinnor Cement Works (see Volume Two), but we are leaping ahead again.

This poorly produced coloured postcard provides a glimpse of Reg Pocock's new sleeper-built milk platform, probably not long after it was built c.1924.

Peter Robinson was serving as a fireman at Watlington at this time. He was born in 1902 on the Shirburn Estate, where his father farmed for the Earl of Macclesfield, and is shown in GWR staff records as starting in the loco department as a cleaner at Slough in January 1919. He became a fireman there in March 1920 and transferred to Watlington in April 1921.

Peter lived at 1–2 Mafekin Road, Shirburn, which was virtually alongside the line. His daughter Doreen, who was a bit of a tomboy, recalls walking from there with him to the station at about 4.30 a.m. to help light up, then travelling out to Risborough and back on the engine with the first train before going to school, but not when Harry Humphreys was on duty!

Cecil Evetts was born in Watlington in 1903, the son of a baker in the High Street. He joined the GWR as a cleaner at Slough in 1918 and, having transferred to Cardiff Docks to gain promotion to fireman, managed to get to Watlington in August 1924. He married a local girl, Dorothy Rose Hobbs, in 1926 and for a while lived at the bakery before renting a council house at 4 Britwell Road. He remained as a fireman at Watlington until June 1929 when he transferred to Slough.

Sadly, almost nothing has been discovered of George Baker (who moved to Oxford in 1929), W. G. ('Nobby') Clarke (who moved to Abingdon in October 1925), or Herbert Henry Hearn, who transferred from Salisbury in July 1924 and remained at Watlington until March 1934, but many of their successors are recalled as this account progresses.

When Reg Pocock arrived, passenger figures were already set in decline, tickets issued falling from nearly 25,000 in 1913 to just over 16,000 in 1923 in the face of the increasing use of the motor bus. The popularity of the bus services did not come from offering any direct competition between Watlington and Risborough, but simply because of the wider choice of more desirable destinations on offer to the inhabitants of the neighbourhood, who now had easy access to High Wycombe,

In 1920, following the severe cut-backs of the Great War, the timetable provided four return passenger trains leaving Watlington at 8.40 a.m., 11.40, 3.0 p.m. and 6.50, returning at 9.55, 1.50, 4.20 and 7.47 respectively. Times varied slightly in subsequent years, but, following the introduction of an additional train from Watlington at 4.33 p.m., returning at 5.45, the pattern established remained virtually unchanged until the Second World War.

Not long after taking charge at Watlington, Reg Pocock managed to arrange to have a wooden extension built onto the south end of the short passenger platform to ease the congestion in the mornings when the milk arrived for the 8.40 a.m. which had two milk vans, or siphons, attached to the rear of the train, one for Paddington and one for Kensington.

Reg's idea was simple enough and inexpensive, requiring only a modest quantity of second-hand sleepers and labour, which might even have been provided by the permanent way gang as the details have not been traced in official GWR records. The only complications were the removal of a pair of corrugated iron lamp sheds to the opposite end of the platform, the re-arrangement of a wooden paling fence, and the excavation of an access bay to enable carts to back up to the side of the new platform. The transformation must have proved an enormous relief to all concerned.

Every morning some six to eight farmers brought their milk to the station in either 2- or 4-wheeled horse-drawn carts. At this time they included farmers Harry Tew from Brightwell Baldwin, and Jimmy Smith who kept a small dairy herd 'next door to the station' at Pyrton Field Farm. Jimmy's brother Sydney of Stoke Field Farm and Robert of Manor Farm, Clare, also brought in supplies, as well as 'Old Frank' Nixey of Clare Hill Farm and his two sons, Bert of Easington Manor and Frank of Manor Farm, Cuxham. Others were Jimmy Brown of Cornwall Goss Farm and Frank Joslyn of Stoke Grange Farm.

This picture, taken at Risborough one morning in August 1930, is believed to show vans being put onto the Watlington branch train by 'Star' class 4–6–0 No. 4057 *Princess Elizabeth*. Carrying 'B' headlamps, the engine was probably on a Paddington to Oxford service on which Old Oak (and Oxford) often utilised 'Star' class engines. Around this period, the 8.10 a.m. Paddington to Oxford was scheduled to call at Princes Risborough from 9.41 to 9.49 a.m., carrying a number of empty 'milk trucks' in addition to three coaches; those trucks destined for Watlington, Banbury and Aylesbury were detached at the station for onwards conveyance by other services. The bay signal over the engine can be seen set for a return to the down platform line, where the remaining vehicles of her train would be standing.

Dr. Ian C. Allen

'Bimbo' Spicer, who worked for young Frank Nixey, helped with the milking each morning before loading the cart and setting out for Watlington about 7.30 a.m. He recalls how the timing was critical as 'the milk train' had to make the connection for London at Princes Risborough. The farmers would often arrive around the same time and queue to back up to the milk platform to unload their churns.

Bimbo recalls Reg Pocock standing on the platform booking the churns, while Charlie Hopkins skilfully rolled them, almost upright, to the doors of the relevant siphon. Each of the heavy churns had a label bearing the name of the consignor wired to one of the handles.

Everyone helped each other to speed the loading, and the horses, which brought the milk, were trained to move the carts as commanded, but the star turn was Jim Smith's pony which would take the milk to the station and back it up against the milk dock without a word of command, and often without Jim Smith even being present!

Empty churns were kept at the end of the timber platform and put into each cart for return to the farm as soon as the milk had been unloaded.

A Sunday milk train was provided for in the timetables from February 1923 until the end of the 1933 summer issue, but regretfully this never arose in our conversations with those who would have experienced the arrangements, so whether it was always run is not known. In most timetables the return working is shown as a goods train calling at Chinnor and Aston Rowant.

When there were no trains on Sundays, there was extra milk on Monday mornings; Nixeys of Eastfield farm, for example, usually took about eight churns of milk on normal weekdays whereas on Mondays they might send ten or twelve.

While all this was going on, parcels were also loaded onto the train and passengers started to arrive, some buying tickets from Miss Siarey in the office, whilst others had season tickets. There

WATLINGTON BRANCH PASSENGER COUNT week ending 24th January 1924		
From Watlington		Count at P. Risborough Average
(MO)	7.35 a.m.	14
	8.40 a.m.	12
	11.40 a.m.	14
	2.15 p.m.	12
	4.35 p.m.	6
	7.55 p.m.	10
From P. Risborough		
(MO)	8.6 a.m.	8
	9.57 a.m.	11
	12.59 p.m.	12
	2.0 p.m.	1
	5.21 p.m.	7
	7.43 p.m.	20
(WSO)	8.25 p.m.	13

were "usually no more than about twenty passengers on the first train", and the regulars looked out for one another, peering down the road for any sign of an absentee. A number of them caught the Hare and Hounds motor bus from the town hall, which for years was driven by Dick Smith. Some arrived on bicycles which they left in the waiting room.

Reg Pocock used to stand on the end of his new milk platform peering over the fields to see if he could spot any stragglers. Sometimes if a farmer was late, the others would look out and jeer him on. The anxious man would tear through the gates and everyone would unload the heavy churns and help manoeuvre them onto the train which "often left a couple of minutes late but always made up time", even though there were similar situations in despatching the train from Aston Rowant and Chinnor. As Harry Humphreys said, "it was a scramble sometimes if we were late". Inevitably, there were times when things were fraught and 'Bimbo' Spicer still remembers a row he had with Mr. Pocock one morning in the early 1930s when he arrived late due to bad weather.

In 1925 Miss Siarey left and was replaced by Percy Peyman who remained there until 1928 before continuing on the promotion ladder, which for him eventually culminated in his becoming station master at Paddington. Jimmy Nelms, whom he had lodged with, made such an impression on Percy that he was kind enough to say that his ultimate success was due to Jimmy's influence.

On 1st August 1925 the GWR opened an additional halt at Wainhill, "better known as Winnall". There was only a handful of houses there, the *Thame Gazette* remarking 'It will serve the hills chiefly'.

By this time, road competition was becoming firmly established and biting hard, forcing the GWR, among other things, to review the future of some of its less remunerative branch lines. It commissioned a report on 53 lines to investigate practicable economies, but in the case of the Watlington branch, the recommendations published in 1926 were confined to the recovery of signals and signalling equipment at Watlington station, to give an annual saving of just £8. Harry Humphreys said this was Reg Pocock's suggestion — "he got a gratuity for that — it saved so many pints of oil a week anyway". The report as such is hardly significant to this account, but the statistics for the branch in 1925 are interesting and reproduced in Appendix 6.

The 1926 report certainly did not recommend closure but J. V. A. Kelly of the Advertising, Publicity and Excursion Department at Paddington, recorded that he had 'heard of the intention to close it down for passenger traffic when I could see there was every chance for development on popular lines.'

This rather optimistic view of the effect a handful of excursions would make to the line's future seems rather naive, but, on the other hand, any extra receipts were worth having. In this connection, he travelled to Watlington in March 1926 "to inspect the publicity arrangements". He met Reg Pocock and

After visiting the quaint old town and its interesting surroundings, realising there was no Sunday service of trains I enquired if he thought a Sunday excursion from London would be a success. He

This picture of a northbound LNER express on the down platform line c.1930 was taken from the foot of the West Bay platform ramp and shows the crossover used to transfer milk and cress vans from the back of the Watlington branch auto-car to main-line trains. It was also used by the branch engine to gain access to the water column between the down platform and down main lines. *Roye England*

immediately agreed it was a good proposition. I returned to Paddington and handed in my report and proposed to run the Bluebell Express on Sunday, April 25th, 1926.

I had also discussed with the Princes Risborough Station Master Mr. A. Gozney, my proposal to run the last four coaches of an Oxford Excursion via Thame, to be detached at Princes Risborough and run through to Chinnor, Aston Rowant and Watlington, including all halts with a motor trailer at the rear for this purpose.

On hearing my proposal at Paddington, I was laughed to scorn, but I assured Mr. Stanley Downing that if he failed to agree he would have the surprise of his life. The first Sunday train was duly advertised, and with a special postcard announcement (my own idea) to invite friends in London to make the inaugural trip I circulated 5,000 in the towns and villages adjacent to the railway and on Sunday, April, 25th, 1926 carried over 400 passengers at a fare of 4/6 return.

Reg Pocock attributed the success of the trip "largely to the advertising ability of my friend, Kelly and also to a large placard displayed at Paddington Station which said: 'Come to Watlington and see the bluebells'." Since we have been unable to confirm the existence of any official printed handbills, it would be interesting to know whether these trains received proper official blessing, or whether they were confined to some kind of local arrangement, dependent on Kelly's postcards and perhaps a chalk-written billboard on the lawn at Paddington?

Reg recorded that the trip was the fourth Sunday excursion to reach Watlington in 67 years and it was followed by one or two others during the season. "Watlington was, perhaps for the first time, 'put on the map', at Paddington, and the Bluebell Excursion was an event for several years."

Recollections vary: Jimmy Nelms' daughter, Mrs. Shorter, recalls one arrival of a Bluebell Special with people streaming off the train at Watlington and going to Christmas Common to pick the bluebells, whereas Mary Read, who has lived at Shirburn for most of her life, recalls the travellers to Watlington were visiting friends and relatives rather than picking flowers. It seems that most of the people in search of bluebells alighted at other stations on the branch. The woods at Watlington were some way from the line so it would not have been feasible to spend long

Looking south-east up Chinnor Hill with Hillside Cottage on the right.

The beechwoods above Chinnor, looking down from Goose Neck.

An unidentified '2021' class 0–6–0PT shunting a train of excursion stock at Watlington c.1936/7. Whilst the occasion is not recorded, it is reminiscent of the scene when the Bluebell Specials were run.
Cty. Gwen Clarke & Rita Watts

there anyway. From exploration today, this certainly appears to be the case, and whilst blue glades can be found in the beech woods on the hills above the line, the walk up the steeply graded roads is not inconsiderable and could be quite taxing for some.

Percy Peyman said there was an enormous protest in the *Bucks Free Press* over the invasion.

Tom Saunders, a cleaner at Aylesbury shed throughout the 1920s, stood in as fireman on the branch at various times and later served as a Watlington branch fireman between 1935 and 1937, so his memories spanned most of the years of the Bluebell Excursions. He said they ran for some three or four Sundays each spring, the branch locomotive being kept in steam from Saturday night for an early turn crew to take the engine and empty trailer to Risborough on Sunday morning to meet the trippers. He seemed to think that the trains employed two or three coaches from the Aylesbury branch, supplemented by the branch trailer for rail level halts, and that passengers from London transferred to the branch train rather than stock from the main line train being worked through. This differs from Kelly's account of the coaches working through, and Hugh Harman, clerk at Princes Risborough for many years, said "I'm certain the London train had a separate portion for Watlington which was attached to the branch car to serve the halts." He remembers trains of eight or nine coaches routed via Ealing Broadway and Greenford, four of which were collected for Watlington whilst the others were stabled. Whilst Tom could have confused some of these trains with other excursions run

during Mr. Pocock's reign, it seems more likely that the arrangements simply varied over the years.

He said passengers from London travelled to see the bluebells at various locations along the branch, but the ramblers certainly had ample opportunity to explore the Roman Ridgeway, the gentle countryside or the bluebell woods as the train left Risborough mid-morning and the return working did not leave Watlington until about 7.0 p.m.

Both early and late turn crews were needed to work either end of the day, the early turn men leaving the loco 'on shed' for the late turn, that is after the laborious task of running round the unusually long train in sections. Not all of the train would fit within the run-round loop (let alone the platform!) so after the passengers had got off, the train was divided outside the station, run round in portions and reassembled in the spare road. Then it was stabled in the platform, that is providing that it did not foul the points providing access to the shed road. Tom remembers how there was often only just enough clearance to ease past the end of the last coach when putting the loco 'on shed'.

As we have seen, for many years a spare coach, an old 4-wheeler, was kept at Watlington to supplement the 70ft auto-trailer. By Reg Pocock's time, it was rarely needed, the trailer providing more than enough accommodation for the regular passengers. The standby coach was kept opposite the platform beneath the old corrugated-iron carriage shed, which resembled a Dutch barn, especially as the sides only extended about halfway down from the arched roof. In truth, the appearance of the

Watlington station around 1928 after the removal of the signals. The redundant post in front of the signal box had carried the arm of the starting signal. This view shows that oil lighting for the station had included a lamp on the coaling stage, and it also serves to show how the presence of the engine inspection pit on the left and its associated hydrants and drainage which remained from the former engine shed, effectively blocked any extension of the painfully short run-round loop. Empty siphons for the milk and watercress traffic can be seen in the spare road behind the signal box. When discussing these with driver Harry Humphreys, he remarked "We used to call them milk trucks".

C. L. Mowat

whole station at Watlington was rather quaint and rustic and, whilst it was more than adequate for the purpose — even appropriate — this delightfully rural outpost hardly conveyed the image pursued by the mighty Great Western Railway!

During the spring of 1926 or 1927, the spare coach had been left undisturbed in the back of the carriage shed at least long enough for a thrush to select as a cosy nesting place. The corrugated-iron sheeting provided shelter from the wind and rain which drifted so freely across the open landscape, and when the sun shone, it steadily absorbed the heat. Following this discovery, the national press had a field day, Reg Pocock later writing:

'I was astounded one morning when a friend rang up and said "Congratulations old man, I didn't know you were an ornithologist." I replied "Neither did I". He protested "But it is in this morning's papers". This is what I read:

NEST IN RAIL COACH
MOTHER THRUSH'S DISTRESS WHEN
TRAIN MOVED

When a GW train was about to start from Watlington, Oxfordshire, for Princes Risborough on Thursday a Thrush, apparently greatly distressed, was seen circling round the coaches. The station master, who is an ornithologist, investigated and in the roof of the last coach, which had stood in a shed, found a nest containing two eggs.

When the train returned from its journey to Princes Risborough the coach was shunted back to the shed to allow mother thrush to hatch out her eggs during the holidays.

The thrush's nest built on one of the end steps of the spare coach, evidently not called upon much by this time to supplement the accommodation of the auto-trailer.

THAT HORRID EXCURSION.

STATION STAFF ON TENTERHOOKS.

THE BIRDS.

To-day an excursion train—a big blustering train from London with a large, noisy engine and hundreds of passengers—will enter Watlington Station, Oxfordshire, a beautiful spot tucked away at the foot of the Chilterns.

And Mr. R. H. Pocock, the station-master and his small staff are very worried about it.

They do not mind the train itself, but the noisy, snorting intruder will disturb the birds which have made their homes in the pretty little station.

A BIRD LOVER.

Mr. Pocock is a bird lover, and his station is something more than a terminus. It is a bird sanctuary. Every year the same birds come back to build their nests and hatch their young somewhere in the station.

At the present time a tom-tit is busy building a home inside one of the lamp-posts, a starling is preparing to lay its eggs in the roof of the waiting-room, and Mr. Pocock is anxiously awaiting the return of the thrush which selects a brake handle on a coal truck on which to erect her home.

There is very little indeed at Watlington to distract the birds. The station is planted in a beautiful stretch of country-side, and not even the village of Watlington is visible to spoil the view. The only train is a single coach with a small engine which comes into Watlington five times a day. The birds have got used to this.

There have been only three trains in six years at Watlington on Sundays. So that it is on Sundays when the birds come in flocks and sit on the little station house, the signals, the rails, and on the deserted platform, pouring their hearts out in song.

BRITISH HISTORY

HARE & HOUNDS
HOTEL BUS

The Hare & Hounds Hotel
in the centre of Watlington.

The Hare & Hounds Hotel was used by businessmen and commercial travellers, but it was also very much a social centre of the town. The hotel had handled parcel deliveries since at least 1887 when, under proprietor T. Brunton, the local trade directory says 'omnibus meets all trains'. The establishment changed hands over the years, owners listed including James Whiting 1891, Richard Billing 1899, William Walters 1903 and Edward Jackson 1907. These are dates of directories rather than occupancy.

In 1922, when R. H. Sales took over as proprietor, he inherited Dick Smith as driver of the horse bus, which, plying between the station and town hall, had become such an integral part of the local community. It met all down trains, a signboard at the station giving details. The fare to the town was 6d. In the mid 1920s this was replaced with a Ford T bus which was kept in a small garage behind the hotel. The bus also ran to other places like Cuxham.

In the late 1920s the Ford was replaced by a Morris Oxford bus, and Dick Smith, who had become a conductor for House Brothers buses, was replaced by Sales' son Harold.

When R. H. Sales retired c.1930, the Hare & Hounds was taken over by a Mr. Bush who had been in the army, but the bus service ceased in the mid-1930s, it is said because the hotel lost the GWR parcels agency.

Dick Smith with the Hare & Hounds horse bus. Born in Watlington in 1887, Dick started at the hotel as a stable lad in 1902. He is believed to have taken over driving the horse bus when the previous driver, Arthur Dover, went to serve in the Great War. Dick drove the hotel's motor bus until its withdrawal, after which he became a conductor for House Brothers coaches and eventually became a porter at Watlington station.

The Hare & Hounds motor bus. *Cty. Mrs. C. Collins*

'Be that as it may, we came in for a good deal of good-natured leg pulling, but my amusement was apparently not shared by headquarters as the coach was withdrawn and the birds advised to build elsewhere.'

In his memoirs, Reg says that he suspected that his friend Kelly, who inaugurated the bluebell specials, may have had something to do with the story. If this was the case, then in seeking publicity he ended up subjecting the line to ridicule and hardly enhancing the progressive image of the GWR in the manner which might have been expected from someone in the publicity department. It is difficult to believe this impressed his superiors at Paddington.

However, while considering the more farcical aspects of the Watlington branch, this seems an appropriate place to present another of Reg Pocock's recollections:

'When I took office at Watlington in 1924 there were still some old Watlington and Princes Risborough Railway first class paper tickets in use, and I remember the late Sir Claude Severn used to have these tickets whenever he travelled to London, and on one occasion when I was writing out his ticket Sir Claude said: "What, again that joke?"

When asking Sir Claude what he meant, he said: "Do you know that the last time I went to London with one of these tickets your travelling ticket collector on the express doubted the validity of the ticket, and I had great difficulty in convincing him that everything was in order." You see, apart from being headed Watlington and Princes Risborough Railway (a railway long since absorbed by the Great Western Railway Coy.) these tickets had the paper portions perforated ready for separation, one each for forward and return journeys, and it so happened that the Watlington and Princes Risborough Railway forward and return portions were printed in reverse order to the GWR standard paper ticket, so that the travelling ticket collector was nonplussed in having to hand Sir Claude back the portion for his return journey which he normally would of course have collected as the forward half. I subsequently had these tickets withdrawn from stock and standard GWR printed tickets supplied. I believe the old Watlington and Princes Risborough Railway tickets found their last resting place in the Great Western Railway museum at Paddington.'

It might have only been a railway backwater suffering a slow decline but Reg Pocock was a staunch company man who took great pride in his work. He was in his element supervising the

Sydney Pratley (clerk), his brother Arthur Pratley (guard), Reg Pocock and Charlie Hopkins alongside the branch auto-trailer at Watlington station c.1930. Sydney Pratley was clerk at Watlington station from 1928 to July 1934, then station master at Chinnor until 1942, when he moved to Wooburn Green. Arthur Pratley transferred from Southall to replace A. W. Sollars, who is believed to have served at Watlington from March 1926 until August 1927 when he moved on to Reading. Arthur Pratley remained at Watlington until July 1934, when he returned to Southall.
Gwen Clarke & Rita Watts

An unidentified '2021' class 0–6–0PT pulling away from Aston Rowant with a Watlington-bound train c.1929. Traffic statistics reveal that the presence of the cattle wagon behind the engine could not have been a particularly common sight by this time. *J. E. Kite*

duties of the enginemen, guards and station staff. He kept up morale and, as already mentioned, encouraged them all to attend First Aid classes. Once a week he visited Aston Rowant to see the men there and check the books.

Apart from taking part in the social and public life of the district, he also prided himself in the way he dealt with passengers. In those days when businessmen and commercial travellers used the railway as a means of visiting their clients, the duration of their calls was governed by the railway timetable. Again in his memoirs, Reg recalled how he pacified a commercial traveller whose visit one morning was somewhat shortened when the 10.0 a.m. to Watlington arrived some twenty minutes late. He had apparently recalled a series of four pictures in the *GWR Magazine* portraying a station master who remained cool and calm when approached by a passenger in a towering rage. The gist of the example was that by not inflaming the situation the passenger calmed down, the caption to the pictures reading 'The soft answer turneth away wrath'.

Reg had chance to put this into practice when the traveller returned a few minutes before the departure of the 11.30 a.m.

'He was still very irritable and cross as each time I had occasion to pass him I was greeted with a pugnacious glance. Suddenly my friend, standing nearby, bawled out: "I know you don't damn well care." Said I, "I am sorry, Sir, are you addressing me, my friend?" "Yes, you know very well I am, even when our train is on time it barely gives me time to call on my clients and catch the 11.30 back. How the blazes can you expect me to do my business satisfactorily when your down train is so confoundedly late?" I replied: "My dear Sir, I quite appreciate your annoyance and sense of frustration, but it is no use losing your temper with me. I am not responsible for the late arrival of the down train and I would suggest that you report the facts to the Divisional Superintendent, Paddington, who will have inquiries made into the cause of the delay and send you an explanation, and take such steps as will prevent a recurrence if possible. The 11.30 will leave here to time.

'There was an immediate change in his attitude and getting into the train, he apologised, shook hands, smiled and thanked me for my forbearance and sound advice.

'Nett result: one railway servant exercising tolerance and trying to give helpful advice and one client appeased and satisfied.

'I have often been glad I saw those pictures.'

Reporting on the 1926 General Strike, which began on 3rd May, the *Thame Gazette* for 11th May said: 'Peaceful picketing is being observed at the GWR station . . . no trains are running . . . as many as 14 lorries daily are engaged conveying milk to London.' On 13th May the same paper reported 'The

Charlie Hopkins, Sydney Pratley and Reg Pocock in the yard at Watlington at the end of May or beginning of June 1929, with a giant walnut butt. The other two men have not been identified. The *Bucks Free Press* reported: "This tree, reputed to be the largest in South Bucks, was about 600 years old. The butt weighed nearly seven tons and the girth was 25 feet." A crane was sent from Reading to handle the load. This is one of very few pictures taken in the yard and the only one to show the corrugated iron pump house (in the right background) which stood at the end of the loco siding until 1935.
Cty. Charlie Hopkins

This picture of the Watlington station staff c.1929 shows from left to right: *Back row:* porter Harold Blackwell, who served at Aston Rowant; guards Jimmy Nelms and Arthur Pratley; and porter George Baker. *Front row:* driver Harry Humphreys; porter Charlie Hopkins; station master Reg Pocock; porter Alf Taylor, who served at Chinnor; and driver Arthur ('Geoff') Pearson.

first passenger train from Watlington since the strike left for Princes Risborough and Aylesbury, Mr. Benton of Chinnor Lime Works being the amateur driver' (believed to have run on 11th May). Harry Humphreys said he didn't work but two porters stood in as firemen with the other driver (presumably Edward Jones?).

Evidently there were no organised connections to get milk to London so it was taken by road. Ernie Forte, a young hand from Nixey's Farm in Chinnor, recalled taking milk to Watlington station where it was picked up by army lorries. This is confirmed by the *Thame Gazette* for 18th May: 'The usual routine continued during the past week. Milk was conveyed to the GWR and there transferred to lorries for Hyde Park'.

Despite the recommendation in the 1926 branch line report, it was not until 1928/9 that the signals and signalling equipment were recovered to effect a saving of just £8 per year.

Tickets issued had fallen from the 16,000 in 1923 (already referred to) to 12,000 in 1929, then, although they remained at a similar level until 1932, they dwindled again down to 9,000 in 1938.

An interesting survey conducted in 1928 (right) shows the handful of people carried on most trains.

From the winter of 1927, late evening travellers, on Saturdays only, were provided with a train from Risborough at 10.52 p.m. in conjunction with the 10.32 from High Wycombe to Oxford. This late train utilised the engine of the 8.50 p.m. Watlington goods which had formerly returned engine and van. The winter timetable for 1929 also provided an additional train on Monday mornings for the benefit of returning weekend visitors, typically spending Saturday and Sunday with their families. Leaving Watlington at 7.30 a.m., this connected at Princes Risborough with the 7.45 a.m. Aylesbury to Paddington and returned down the branch without calling at the halts, no doubt to ensure the prompt departure of the 8.40 a.m. milk. Incidentally, the 7.30 a.m. was run in place of the early morning goods which had

WATLINGTON BRANCH PASSENGER COUNT
Week ending Saturday 17th March 1928

	From	Mon 12th		Tu 13th		Wed 14th	
		1st	3rd	1st	3rd	1st	3rd
8.40	Watlington	—	33	—	10	—	56
10.6	P. Risborough	—	20	—	5	—	11
11.30	Watlington	—	7	—	3	—	12
1/49	P. Risborough	—	5	—	3	—	5
2/58	Watlington	—	16	—	10	—	13
3/58	P. Risborough	—	5	—	4	—	6
4/33	Watlington	—	8	—	3	—	1
5/45	P. Risborough	—	20	—	13	—	26
6/50	Watlington	—	6	—	2	—	5
7/57	P. Risborough	—	9	—	7	—	35
		Th 15th		Fr 16th		Sat 17th	
		1st	3rd	1st	3rd	1st	3rd
8.40	Watlington	—	12	—	14	—	18
10.6	P. Risborough	—	11	—	4	—	12
11.30	Watlington	—	8	—	10	—	13
1/49	P. Risborough	—	6	—	4	—	15
2/58	Watlington	—	3	—	11	—	25
3/58	P. Risborough	—	7	—	5	—	28
4/33	Watlington	—	7	—	8	—	19
5/45	P. Risborough	—	12	—	18	—	18
6/50	Watlington	—	12	—	2	—	21
7/57	P. Risborough	—	6	—	13	—	24
Empty	Watlington (SO)						
10/32	P. Risborough (SO)					—	17

Counts were made leaving Princes Risborough in the down direction and leaving Bledlow in the up direction.

HOUSE BROTHERS BUSES

WATLINGTON & HIGH WYCOMBE SERVICE. 14

	SUNDAY SERVICE.			DAILY SERVICE.				Friday only	Sats. only	
					Not Wed.					
	a.m.	p.m.	p.m.	p.m.	a.m.	p.m.	p.m.	p.m.	a.m.	p.m.	p.m.
WATLINGTON (dep.) ..	1015	215	640		945	1 0		615	830	5 0	8 0
Shirburn Village ..	1020	220	645		950	1 5		620	835	5 5	8 5
Lewknor Village ..	1025	225	650		955	110		625	840	510	810
Lambert Arms	1030	230	655		10 0	115		630	845	515	815
Stokenchurch (P.O.) ..	1045	240	710		1015	130	255	645	9 0	530	830
Beacon's Bottom ..	1050	245	715	825	1020	135	3 0	650	9 5	535	835
Piddington (P.O.) ..	11 0	255	725	830	1025	145	3 5	655	915	545	845
W. Wycombe ..	11 5	3 0	730	835	1030	150	310	7 0	920	550	855
H. WYCOMBE (arr.) ..	1115	315	740	845	1040	2 0	320	710	930	6 0	9 0

WATLINGTON & THAME SERVICE. 15

Via Christmas Common, Stokenchurch & Sydenham. TUESDAYS ONLY.

	a.m.			p.m.
WATLINGTON (dep) ..	10 30	THAME (dep)	3.45
Howe Hill (X Rd) ..	10.40	Sydenham	3 55
Christmas Common ..	10.50	Stokenchurch	4.25
Stokenchurch ..	11 0	Christmas Common ..	4.40
Sydenham . ..	11 20	Howe Hill (X Rd)	4.45
THAME (arr)	11 30	WATLINGTON (arr) ..	5.15

WATLINGTON & WALLINGFORD SERVICE.

FRIDAYS ONLY.

	p.m.			p.m.
WATLINGTON (dep)	1 30	WALLINGFORD (dep) .. .	4 0
Cuxham	1.35	Benson (the Crown)	4.10
Brightwell Baldwin ..	1 40	Ewelme (Shepherds Hut) ..	4.15
Ewelme (Shepherds Hut) ..	1.50	Brightwell Baldwin	4.25
Benson (the Crown)	1.55	Cuxham	4.30
WALLINGFORD (arr) ..	2.5	WATLINGTON (arr)	4.40

One of House Brothers buses at the Coach & Horses public house, Stokenchurch.

Arthur House's father with a 1922 Dennis. The company had another two of these which were built in 1923. The 26-seat bodies were built by Vincents of Reading onto new 2½ ton chassis delivered straight from Dennis, fitted with early pneumatic tyres.
Cty. Arthur House

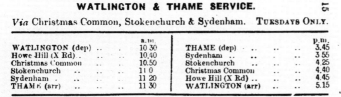

Henry House and Dick Smith with House's 16-seater Chevrolet which was first put into service in 1930. Dick Smith had previously driven the Hare & Hounds bus and later, during the war, was employed as a porter at Watlington station. *Cty. Arthur House*

been brought in on Sunday as the return working of the milk train.

While the figures held steady, the service continued, but when they fell in 1933, the early train was withdrawn, as was the Sunday milk train and the 10.52 p.m. from Risborough, none of which appear after the end of the summer timetable.

Unfortunately, in his memoirs Reg Pocock did not provide many clues to enable us to date various incidents. However, it is tempting to suggest that the following story may have occurred during this period, or at least while milk traffic was still being carried.

'The "one engine in steam" system suffices for the normal train services but during emergencies such as derailments, snowstorms, etc., it presents considerable difficulties. On several occasions we have had to rapidly implement bus services in place of the train and to advise and instruct each station and halt along the line what is being done and I cannot remember any occasion on which the main line connections have not been maintained. Snowstorms were, however, a tougher proposition and the branch line is peculiarly liable to snowdrifts.

'The "one engine in steam" system of working railways means that the engine driver carries a wooden staff which is his only authority for being on the single line, there is only one staff supplied for the branch line, and on no account must he hand it over to anyone unless his engine is derailed or "dead" for some other reason. The wooden staff has then to be handed to the station master or someone authorised by him to take possession of it, and it is then carried by the most expeditious and available means to Princes Risborough and handed to the engine driver of the relief engine or breakdown train as the case may be.

'I remember some years ago the branch line being covered by deep snow, and every road in the district completely blocked by snowdrifts for some days. The branch train managed to reach Princes Risborough, but snow was still falling and drifting, and on its return journey to Watlington at about 10.0 a.m. it spent hours battling against deep snowdrifts, one of the worst places being Kingston Crossing Halt, where the snow buried the level-crossing gates. Some time was spent on this spot alone fighting against the monotonous and ceaseless snowdrifts, which filled up the clearances as fast as they were made. At last the train got under way and managed to get as far as Lewknor, where another impassable drift was encountered and eventually the engine became derailed just this side of Lewknor Bridge Halt. Slough, being our depot for the breakdown train and crew, was immediately advised, and one of my porters was sent to Princes Risborough with the wooden staff to allow the breakdown to come through. The man was told to get to Princes Risborough by the best route he could find but after many hours passing before I received news of his safe arrival, I began to doubt the wisdom of sending him, especially as very deep drifts were subsequently reported at various points on his line of route.

'Eventually he reached Princes Risborough and the breakdown train left for the scene of the derailment and after a journey more difficult than the branch train experienced some hours earlier it eventually reached the derailed train. The storm was still raging and after many efforts the derailed train was got on to the line only to slip off again after going only a few yards. By this time it was the early hours of the next morning and bitterly cold, when I received an "S.O.S." to send some refreshment to the breakdown train men and our own gang of permanent way men, who had been on duty since the previous morning and were still hard at work on the site of the derailment.

'There happened to be some full churns of milk on the platform, waiting despatch by the next available service, so I purloined one of these and sent it along to the men, who were kept sustained by drinks of hot milk. The consigner of the milk was rather concerned at its disappearance, but when I explained the circumstances to him

Tom Saunders pictured on a '22XX' tank when he was a cleaner at Aylesbury.

and told him he would be fully compensated for the loss, he was quite happy.

'The combined Watlington branch train and the breakdown train stormed into Watlington Station about 6 a.m., some twenty hours after leaving Princes Risborough, and normal service was resumed.

'This is the only occasion that I can remember on which the Post Office mail was sent from Watlington by train, this being the only means of transport as all the roads in the district were completely snowbound.'

This was not the only occasion on which the line was blocked along the same stretch as Harry Humphreys recalled "a terrible snowstorm" when he was driving the 10.06 a.m. ex Risborough away from Aston Rowant one day. The bridge under the A40 was full of snow but "we thought we'd be able to get through it — we didn't. We got stuck in it and the coach got derailed." Unfortunately, Harry could not remember what year this was.

Tom Saunders' appointment as fireman at Watlington from March 1935 provides us with the earliest detailed account of daily operation on the branch, although it is undoubtedly coloured by his earlier experiences in the 1920s when, as mentioned before, he was serving as a cleaner at Aylesbury and stood in as a temporary fireman at Watlington.

Without wanting to move around the system to gain promotion, he had to wait from 1920 until 1935 to become a fireman locally, and even then he had to move to Watlington where he lodged "with Mrs. Dover in a house behind the Royal Oak". His predecessor, F. Gould, who came from St. Blazey for two months before moving on to Reading, had stayed there, and porter Frank Gough shared the same lodgings too. Tom's future wife worked in a nearby shop and it was there that they first met.

The other firemen serving with him were Peter Robinson and J. B. Cummings, who transferred from Oxford in July 1935 and remained at Watlington for a slightly longer time than Tom, eventually following him to Aylesbury in May 1938.

The two drivers were Harry Humphreys and the younger Arthur Alfred Pearson, known as Geoff to at least the later Watlington staff, and Arthur at home. Born in 1894, Pearson was no stranger to the branch. He had started as a cleaner at Southall in 1911, where he became a fireman the following year. He first went to Watlington in 1913, remaining there until 1919 before transferring back to Southall, then Aylesbury. After being made a driver in 1923, he transferred to Glyn Neath, then back to Aylesbury, before finally taking up the driver's vacancy at Watlington on 6th May 1929 following the death of Edward Jones on 1st March at the age of 51.

Tom Saunders, who must have known the amiable Arthur Pearson from their days at Aylesbury, described him as 'quite a lad', 'rough and ready' and an entirely different character to the particularly sober and steady-going Harry Humphreys, a view which has been consistently expressed by others.

Jimmy Nelms, who was always early on duty, apparently often helped the fireman to get the engine ready in the mornings when driver Pearson, "who he was usually rostered with", was late. This is said to have been quite often as he was "somewhat notorious for leaving things to the last moment"!

Porter Aubrey Jarmaine's daughter Audrey says Pearson was "a real jokey sort of man who used to have a lot of fun", and Risborough clerk Hugh Harman says that he "spoke like a cockney".

Not long after Tom's transfer to Watlington, Pearson demolished the pump house at the end of the shed siding on 11th August 1935. According to official records: 'After failing to be alert and satisfy himself the points were set for the proper road before moving his engine, he ran into the stops at the end of the pit road and struck the pump house wrecking the pumps.'

The three firemen provided 24-hour coverage in three shifts: 12.30 a.m. – 8.30 a.m., 8.30 a.m. – 4.30 p.m. and 4.30 p.m. – 12.30 a.m. in weekly rotation.

The fireman on night duty booked on at 12.30 a.m. and took over from the late-turn man who might just give him a hand filling the bunker from the coal stage before stabling the loco on the pit and signing off. The night man cleaned the fire and built up a smaller one with fresh coal placed under the firehole door. This was tended to keep the boiler hot through the night and maintain enough pressure to pump water from the well to fill the pillar tank. George Nicholson recalled how the 2021s "gave tremendous trouble with leaking tubes at night when the fire was pulled back under the door". On Saturday nights, water was usually pumped to fill the tank before the last trip because as the engine was not normally in use on Sundays, there was no overnight fireman and in the small hours of Monday mornings it had to be lit up from cold.

Before the accident, the pump was driven by a small steam engine housed inside a standard GWR corrugated iron shed and powered by steam from the loco via a flexible pipe (probably an articulated pipe with swivel joints at this time) coupled in place of one of the whistles. A minimum of 100lb of steam had to be maintained for this operation which could take two hours or so if the tank was low. Keeping the tank full, so that water was always available at Watlington, was a vital requirement which fell to the night man. He kept the little pumping engine lubricated and once a week greased the moving rods, which extended right down into the dark depths of the well. There was a small servicing landing at the foot of an almost vertical iron ladder and the pump itself was submerged beneath the water. The pick-up pipe had a filter which occasionally became clogged, and clearing it was another of the night man's less attractive duties. Needless to say, with all the effort involved in maintaining the 3,000 gallon tank of water at Watlington, the branch engines,

with their small capacity, were topped up at Risborough on every trip.

While the little pumping engine was running sweetly inside the iron shed, the night man would clean the frames and motion ready for the driver to inspect and oil. If there was time, he would also clean the paintwork of the tanks, cab, etc.

Working out in the open on dark nights could be a grim and lonely duty with only the wind sweeping across the fields and rustling the leaves on the trees to break the silence. However, Tom Saunders did not mind the quiet and said "there was always plenty of work to get through". Apart from varying degrees of moonlight, the only light to work by was from the smoky flame of a paraffin flare lamp. Although electric lighting was provided in 1936, the yard was illuminated with only a few strategically placed lamps equipped with shades and 60-watt bulbs, so the flare lamp remained a vital companion.

Other tasks included cleaning the tubes with a steam lance on, say, a Thursday night, or sometimes earlier during the engine's week at Watlington. This was carried out soon after the loco came on shed while the steam was still 'dry'. If the tubes needed cleaning on Sunday night when the engine was not in steam, they were rodded before lighting up, either way the operation being carried out standing on a board or plank laid across the buffers to provide a platform. Then there was the task of unloading the coal wagon, again before 1936 with only the light from a flare lamp. Usually two ten-ton wagons were sent to Watlington each week. They were apparently sent down the branch one at a time and unloaded onto the coal stage single-handed by the night man. If the coal arrived in one of the twenty-ton wagons instead, they were only half emptied in a single shift. These wagons were moved into position by the fireman using a pinchbar.

On other branch lines it was common practice to load the bunkers of engines directly from coal wagons, but Tom said that at Watlington the wagons were only emptied onto the coal stage, which apparently held about 20 tons, and the empties were returned straight away.

When Tom was on night duty, he used to 'take a breather' around 4.0 a.m. when he had a meal break. Before the pump house was demolished, loco crews did not have their own mess, so they shared the nearby platelayers hut, where they also signed on and filled out all the necessary paperwork associated with the loco department, using the desk provided there. At Watlington the locomen got on well with the members of the permanent way department, so this proved a congenial arrangement. It was a cosy place and Sergeant Middleton, or one of the two constables from the local police force, would often call at the station and shelter in the hut, enjoying a brew with whichever night man was on duty.

The fire was spread across the gate and built up in time to raise steam for the driver's arrival at 5.0 a.m. Harry Humphreys was always punctual and, after signing on, went underneath to carry out his inspection and oil up. He was very conscientious and there was never any problem with the loco being ready well in time for the first train. On the other hand, Tom remembered Arthur Pearson as "not too good in the mornings!"

When Arthur was on duty (Tom is the only railwayman we have met who referred to him as Arthur), Tom would build up the fire and soon after 5.0 a.m. leave the engine and "cycle over to the council houses" to 'knock up' his driver. When Arthur was on, Tom would oil up and have the engine absolutely ready to come off shed as soon as he turned up. The anxiety about leaving punctually with the 5.50 a.m. morning goods was due to the need to perform this duty and get back in time for the 'milk train' which, as already explained, had to make main line connections. The return working was booked to leave Risborough at 7.0 a.m. and a note in the service timetable underlined the situation: 'Important this Goods trip works to time to enable 8.40 a.m. passenger train from Watlington to start punctually.'

Goods traffic varied and at this time the up goods traffic was more often than not worked out to Risborough in the evenings as the 8.50 p.m. which 'ran as required'. If this was the case, the early morning goods was run engine and brake van to collect the down traffic.

The guard, Jimmy Nelms or Tom Bowler (who transferred from Wycombe on 7th May 1934) arrived at about 5.45 and unlocked the signal box, operating the lever frame to release the engine from the loop and admit it into the yard to pick up the brake van from the back siding or 'coal road'. On cold mornings the guard then lit the stove in his van, which later on made it quite a cosy place to travel. When it had been pulled out clear of the yard access points, the guard waiting in the box reset the road and retrieved the wooden train staff from the lever frame. This staff, carried on the engine as their authority to be on the single line between Watlington and Risborough, also incorporated a key to unlock the various ground frames on the branch, including the one at Watlington.

The engine and van were taken straight to Risborough and put into the bay platform where the engine was uncoupled, released via the engine release crossover, and run off behind the station to the down sidings at the London end to sort wagons for the branch from those left earlier by the Aylesbury goods. When this was done, the wagons were brought up to the station, past the brake van left in the bay, and backed onto it. If, instead of being worked the night before,

the up goods was conveyed by the first train, all the up traffic was left in the bay with the brake van, and after collecting the down traffic, the whole lot was then drawn out of the platform and propelled back behind the station to the down sidings where all the vehicles from the 5.50 were left for transfer to the main line.

The branch goods, which was really only for Aston Rowant and Watlington, usually comprised anything between four and twelve wagons. It hastened away down the branch, calling at Chinnor "for station truck purposes only" and Aston Rowant, where traffic was put off, any empties being collected and taken on into Watlington (ready for the following morning).

A station truck for Aston Rowant and Watlington was also conveyed, so when the branch goods reached Aston, the early-turn porter (Tom remembered Albert Rowe), was there to meet them and unload the smalls traffic onto the platform, including provisions for the local shops. This was all done with haste, and if the porter did not get there in time, the train crew unloaded the goods themselves and left them stacked beside the station door while they continued on their way.

By the time the train returned to Watlington, the early-turn porter, Aubrey Jarmaine or Frank Gough, would usually be waiting to help unload the town's provisions. The early-turn fireman would also be waiting on the platform to take over from the night man and at some point Arthur Pearson's daughter Betty would call at the station on her way to school to deliver a bacon sandwich! Generally, the station truck was unloaded while the engine ran round its train, but if the porter was not actually there waiting to do it, there was no time to dally and the whole train was shunted out of the way into the back road before collecting the auto-trailer and milk siphons from the spare road behind the signal box and propelling them into the platform. Sometimes, if the crew had time, the

Taken from GWR Service Timetable 1st October 1934 to 7th July 1935.

stranded station truck was then collected and pushed up to the end of the spare road or dock siding for unloading alongside the cattle pen. The engine then rejoined the train in the platform for the bustling 8.40 departure described earlier, except that by this time, the milk was being lost to road competition, notably Wests of Thame.

Unloading the station truck through the cattle pens was not ideal, but this was the only place it could be left accessible from the platform and, in any case, the inconvenience was the price paid by the early-turn porter for either arriving late or for not ensuring he was available when the goods arrived back from Risborough. Incidentally, the dock side of the cattle pens was rarely used in Tom's day, the few cattle still handled being loaded or unloaded via the passenger platform.

Tom said the first train carried about twenty or so passengers, including schoolchildren for Chinnor and Risborough, workmen, particularly for the chair factory at Risborough, and businessmen for the London train.

At Risborough, the branch engine ran round its train in the bay, collected the siphons from the rear, and waited on the down main, clear of the crossovers, at the north end of the station, for the arrival of the 8.18 a.m. Oxford–Paddington, which was booked to allow 10 minutes at Risborough. The Watlington engine then propelled the

siphons over to the up platform for attachment to the rear of the train. By this time, if there were not enough churns to justify transferring the siphons to the London train, the churns were unloaded and barrowed across to the up platform. Jack Rutland, who began as a staff runner at Risborough North Box in 1937, recalls just 4 or 5 cans being barrowed across.

Having got the 8.40 a.m. safely to Risborough in time for the booked connection, the engine was taken to the down sidings at the London end of the station to carry out any shunting required. Harry Humphreys remarked "We were on the go all the time, practically speaking." If there was time after the engine had been put back into the bay and coupled onto its trailer, this was a good chance for the crew to 'open their boxes' and enjoy their bottles of cold tea before heading back to Watlington with the 10.06 a.m., which carried passengers for various stations along the branch.

When they were back at Watlington, the yard was sorted and the trailer was taken into the back siding to collect the brake van, which was taken on the rear of the 11.30 a.m. Sorting the yard involved placing the wagons for unloading in the goods shed, putting traders' wagons, usually coal, wherever they were needed and, if required, leaving empty wagons accessible for loading with agricultural produce, etc. The up goods train was also formed and left on the back road ready for the late-turn men.

This picture, taken soon after the installation of electric lighting at Watlington station in 1936, appears to record the scene after the 10.6 a.m. from Risborough had been unloaded onto the platform. The engine had probably just backed the trailer clear of the engine release points prior to running round. This is the only view discovered which features the elusive Weedon Brothers coal office in the left background, albeit only the roof.
Cty. Gwen Clarke & Rita Watts

'2021' class 0−6−0PT No. 2098 alongside the platform at Watlington with the 11.30 a.m. for Risborough with goods brake in tow on 6th June 1934. The guard looking back along the platform was Tom Bowler who had only just transferred from High Wycombe to replace Arthur Pratley when he moved on to Southall. The fire-iron propped up between the cabside handrail and injector waste pipe was left there to cool before being stowed inside the cab across the front of the bunker. Fortunately, there was rarely any need to clean the fire, clinker generally only being removed at night. Fireman Tony Benham said "It was bad coal if the chisel bar became necessary". Incidentally, once the engine was oiled up in the morning, it was left all day, unless Harry Humphreys was on the late shift, in which case he would walk round with the oil can at lunchtime.
F. M. Butterfield

Harry Humphreys recalled that before working the 11.30, there was an opportunity to pump water, but this was probably in the 1920s and before the provision of electric pumps. Tom did not remember that as part of the routine in the two years he was there, particularly as water was always taken at Risborough. In fact, the only times he could remember taking water at Watlington was last thing at night and coming off shed in the morning, unless, of course, it was really needed, as full tanks at Risborough would comfortably last the round trip.

After arrival at Risborough with the 11.30 a.m., the engine was uncoupled from the trailer and again taken, via the release crossover, to the down sidings at the south end of the station to sort wagons for the next train, the Chinnor goods. Before 1924 the midday goods left Risborough at 12.15 and ran through to Aston Rowant, but the growth of Chinnor Cement Works traffic denied them the time to serve Aston Rowant as well, so it simply became the Chinnor goods, largely comprising wagons of coal, gypsum (which Tom referred to as 'gippy'), and any general goods. The maximum number of wagons allowed up Chinnor bank at the time was twelve, so anything in excess of that was left until the next day.

The train of wagons was set back into the bay to collect the brake van, which had been left on the back of the trailer, before leaving for Chinnor at 12.20 p.m., but Tom could not remember whether the trailer was put on the line behind the station to leave the bay clear for the return of the Chinnor goods or for any intervening arrival from Oxford.

Tom Bowler in his guard's uniform.
Cty. Bryan Bowler

An everyday scene at Risborough in the 1930s. This picture shows goods trains held in both up and down platform lines, no doubt for numbertaking purposes (as detailed in Volume 2) and for the engines to take water, leaving the main lines clear for the passing of higher priority trains like this 'King'-hauled London-bound express. The Watlington bay was behind the canopy on the left.

Cty. Jack Rutland

Looking south through the station, with Princes Risborough North Signal Box on the right and a glimpse of the Aylesbury bay (left) and West Bay (right). All of the Watlington passenger services used the West Bay, which was also used by a number of Oxford trains. The three GWR wooden-posted triple bracket signals were all replaced with LNER upper quadrants by 1937.
Cty. Wally Mitchell

Another 1930s view of a London-bound express speeding through Risborough while up and down goods trains were held on the platform lines.
Cty. Jack Rutland

Pictures of goods trains are rarely easy to come by, so this view looking north-east across the south sidings at Risborough is particularly welcome because it shows Watlington branch traffic. The wagons in the foreground were mostly empties from the branch, but those on the adjacent line were mainly for Chinnor with four GW 20T shed mineral wagons (dedicated to Charrington, Gardner, Locket & Co. Ltd.) loaded with fine coal for the rotary kiln at Chinnor Cement Works, a GW van (possibly an empty destined to be loaded with bags of cement?), a Southern Railway open loaded with coal, perhaps for one of the traders, and three assorted opens with what appears to have been crushed gypsum rock which was described to us as "walnut-sized lumps, pinky-white in colour". Gypsum arrived, two or three wagons at a time, from Easthill, near Nottingham, or Kegworth in Staffordshire. The vehicle on the extreme right was one of Weedon Brothers 8-ton coal wagons which have always proved frustratingly elusive in pictures.

S. H. Freese

At Chinnor, gypsum and coal for the cement works were put into the private sidings, and traffic collected from the works. The cement produced there was packed in sacks and generally despatched in covered goods vans to the cement company's depots at Small Heath and Greenford. The small yard at Chinnor was also sorted, and the return working left for Risborough at 1.18 p.m.

Back at Risborough, the train was put into the south sidings and the Watlington brake van was put on the back of the branch trailer, together with any odd coal wagons that traders at Watlington might be waiting for. In fact, when the 1.55 arrived at the terminus, the coalmen were sometimes hanging around waiting for them.

The 3.0 p.m. passenger was the last return trip for the early-turn men, the late shift booking on at 4.30 p.m. for the return passenger. The men were usually there earlier.

The only other passenger trip for the late-turn men was the 6.50 p.m. which during the watercress season conveyed one or two

Geoff Pearson with 2112 in the south sidings at Risborough preparing for departure at 12.20 p.m. with the Chinnor goods one summer day in 1939. The Mendip Mountain Quarries wagons on the far siding probably contained roadstone for delivery to one of the branch stations. No. 6362 in the middle of the picture was being held on the up main with the 9.40 Banbury–Old Oak coal which was scheduled to arrive at 11.44 a.m. and drop off traffic (only) at the yard, connecting for the 12.1 a.m. Oxford to Taplow train (due at 1.33 a.m. the following morning) as required. It was also nominated "to shunt for (or follow) another train, and also to perform work" before departing at 12.36 p.m. No. 5961 on the right was almost certainly on the 11.20 a.m. Oxford to Paddington passenger (via Greenford) which called at Risborough from 12.19 to 12.25. *S. H. Freese*

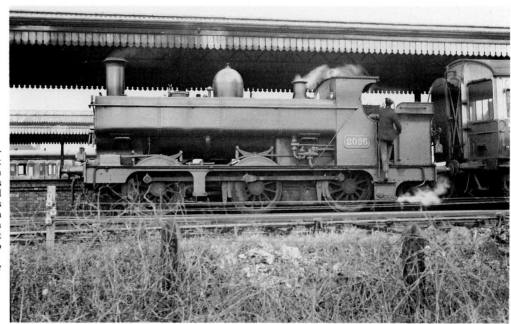

No. 2026 with the Watlington auto-car in the bay at Risborough on 10th February 1938. This engine, officially allocated to Watlington in 1939, was one of Slough's allocation of shunting engines from 1929–32 and 1935-38. It was transferred to Hereford in 1940.
S. H. Freese

A post 1936 scene at Watlington station taken shortly after the arrival of what was probably the 5.45 p.m. from Risborough.

Lens of Sutton

Ken Cox, in the platform gateway at Watlington station, during his time as clerk from 1936 to 1937.   *Cty. Joe Nicholson*

siphons on the rear. At Risborough these were collected from the rear of the train by the engine of the 6.25 p.m. Paddington–Oxford stopper. This traffic is detailed in Volume 2. After arrival back at Watlington at 8.22 p.m, the trailer was put on the spare road behind the signal box and presumably coupled to, or at least left buffered up to, the milk siphons ready for the morning. Unfortunately, after a number of independent interviews with Tom, we both forgot to ask which train the empty siphons were brought in with, but the picture on page 78 indicates they were taken on the 10.06, although arrangements probably varied and Percy Peyman recalled that in 1925 at least they usually arrived with the goods.

The up goods was then collected from the back road where it had been left earlier, the brake van was put on the back of the formation, and the crew made a fairly smart departure at 8.32 p.m. Tom recalled that the train was usually made up of five or six empties, some of which had been brought down from Aston Rowant in the morning, together with any loaded opens of locally grown produce according to the time of year. The 8.50 p.m. was booked to call at Aston Rowant and Chinnor as required, but in practice this seems to have been largely unnecessary in the years

Tom was there. The engine and van returned any time after 10.0 p.m. and sometimes very late if there was work to do at Risborough.

According to official records, Tom transferred back to Aylesbury in June 1937, yet his replacement, George Nicholson, went to Watlington on 26th April. Presumably, therefore, either Cummings or Robinson were off sick or away for some other reason at the time, otherwise this unexplained overlap would have resulted in four firemen there for the weeks concerned.

George Nicholson's transfer to Watlington was the beginning of a long and very happy association with the branch. Born in 1917, he had begun as a cleaner at Old Oak Common in 1935 and Watlington was his first appointment as fireman.

This cheerful cockney character made quite an impression on some of the local girls; porter Aubrey Jarmaine's daughter Audrey,

Above: Porter Aubrey Jarmaine, station master Pocock and clerk Ken Cox.
Above right: Clerk Ken Cox, porter Aubrey Jarmaine, guard Jimmy Nelms and porter Frank Gough.
Cty. Audrey Griffiths

Right: Ken Cox again, with Jimmy Nelms and Reg Pocock.
Cty. Audrey Griffiths

Left: The original St. John Ambulance at Gorwell with Cecil, Maurice and Leslie Pocock. *Right:* The body of this vehicle ended its days in use as a garden shed in Watlington.

Left: Frank Willoughby, Reg Pocock, Arthur Pearson and Ernest Young with the Daimler ambulance at the brigade headquarters in Gorwell. The Pococks' house 'St. John' features in the background on the right. *Right:* Arthur Pearson in his garden wearing his St. John Ambulance uniform.

This St. John Ambulance group photo is believed to have been taken c.1937 and shows (from left to right) *Back row:* Unidentified, Henry House, Bill Rymell, Bill Brian, Unidentified. *Front row, standing:* Frank Willoughby, Harry Humphreys, Reg Pocock, Arthur Pearson, unidentified. *Front row, seated:* Bill Collins, Len King, Cecil Pocock.

When Frank Saunders and George Nicholson went down to the White Hart after they had finished work, they often found Reg Pocock in there. He went to most of the pubs on a variety of business, but the White Hart was his regular because it was the lodge for the Buffs. Although they would all be in their railway clothes, Reg wore a trilby hat whenever he was off the railway. When Frank and George walked in he would say "Everything alright then?" and sometimes buy them a drink. "He was a gentleman." They would not disturb him if he had anyone with him, and he would never let them buy a drink for him — he would just say "No thank you, I'm alright." Frank remembers there were three pubs in Shirburn Street alone — "We'd patronise them all".

for instance, was one of the smitten, as mentioned later, whilst Jean Saunders says "George was a smashing bloke — always smiling." Such was his personality that everyone we have spoken to has smiled and conveyed a warmth in their recollections of him.

George's brother Joe had also joined the GWR, but as a porter at Gerrards Cross. When he went to Watlington to see his brother, he says he "liked the Watlington set-up". At the time the porters were 'Taffy' Heathfield and Tommy Tuck.

Charlie Hopkins had moved to Aston Rowant in May 1935 and appears to have been replaced by Frank Gough, who is believed to have gone to Calne later. However, it has been difficult to establish quite when Charlie's opposite number, Aubrey Jarmaine, left the post. It might have been towards the end of 1936 or early 1937 because after he left the railway he worked at the cement works for about 18 months and in 1938 he died from an illness.

Of course, working at Watlington did not suit everyone, and there are many instances of firemen in particular staying only a few weeks. Evidently it was not porter Tommy Tuck's ideal, so when Joe Nicholson discovered Tom was anxious to leave, he told him about his position at Gerrards Cross and the two porters eagerly exchanged places. Joe moved in with his brother George who was lodging at the Dovers, at No. 2 Church Street. Later on they lodged with platelayer Charlie Adby.

Joe regarded George as a "bit of a card" but he was quite a joker himself and among other pranks remembers blocking the chimney of the permanent way cabin while the gang were "sat in there

having their breakfast round a roaring great fire — they used to get smoked out!"

It is difficult to believe that such high jinks were always appreciated by everyone, but Joe found it a friendly place and the brothers were willing workers and popular.

Quite how much of this came to Reg Pocock's attention is not clear, but Ken Cox, clerk at the time, remembers some of the things that used to go on in Reg's absence. For instance, Geoff Pearson used to slip off down to the White Hart and leave his fireman to do the shunting, and on one of these occasions on a Saturday afternoon, Ken suddenly realised that the engine had disappeared too! It later transpired that Peter Robinson had left his wellington boots at home, and as he needed them to watch a football match later on, he had driven the engine out to Shirburn to collect them. Ken remembered this happening on another occasion when the engine crew ran out of sugar, and collected some from Peter's home. He also remembered that the line between Watlington and Shirburn was strewn with coal where the crews had taken pot-shots at the pheasants from the engine.

When porter Taffy Heathfield left in July 1937, his place was taken by Frank Saunders, whose clear memories and agile mind have enabled us to present a detailed picture of a working day at Watlington, which is presented separately in Volume 2.

Frank lived in Didcot and, as there was not much work around at the time, went to the railway where he was interviewed by the station master George Kerno and offered the choice of a job in the

No. 2055 shortly after arrival at Watlington with the 10.6 a.m. from Risborough on 17th March 1939. The cress baskets were piled up here or by the gate, never inside. If they arrived back in the station truck, they were unloaded in the goods shed and carried over here, otherwise they were unloaded from 'the car' in the platform. 'The car' was always used for the more fragile pheasant baskets.

H. C. Casserley

No. 2026 approaching the tiny platform at Bledlow Bridge with a train from Princes Risborough on Sunday, 21st May 1938. We have not established its purpose, but it was presumably in connection with an excursion. *S. H. Freese*

Loco Department, where he would have started as a cleaner, or a porter's job at Watlington.

His father took him to Watlington to arrange lodgings before he actually started there. At first he stayed with 'Trader' Horne, who had a small general store in Couching Street, opposite the Three Tuns, but after a while he moved to cheaper lodgings with the Dovers in Church Street where the Nicholson brothers were staying. He earned £1 19s 6d on days or £2 0s 10d on nights and Mr. and Mrs. Dover looked after him for £1 per week.

The Dovers had a fish shop, Messum & Dover, in the High Street, Bert collecting the wet fish from the station most days in a *c.*1934–5 Ford 8 van, which he also used for deliveries to villages around the area like Weston, Turville and Christmas Common.

Frank worked under Reg Pocock whom he remembers as very regimented towards his work. He liked to see that everything was done properly and kept up-to-date. "He spoke his mind to you and never went behind your back." "He was a good station master." Needless to say, it was not long before Frank was recruited for the St. John Ambulance!

Joe Nicholson, working on the opposite shift, extended his hours to show Frank what to do, and Mr. Pocock helped a lot, too. Frank says "Joe was a real cheerful cockney, a bit of a joker and good to work with", and recalls that "Mr. Pocock was happy with him".

Frank took his bicycle to Watlington so that he could "get about". It was particularly useful in the evenings for getting to Britwell, or even as far as Princes Risborough, with Joe and George for a drink.

When Frank started at Watlington, Ken Cox was clerk. He had been there since about March 1936 and was lodging in Gorwell with Mr. and Mrs. Simmonds for 18 shillings a week full board. Mr. Simmonds was manager of Weedon Brothers' Watlington coal depot.

Not long after Frank arrived, Ken transferred away and was replaced by Eric Nash, who moved from Falmouth to Watlington on 15th November 1937. His father was senior lineman at Risborough. Eric was "happy-go-lucky" and enjoyed playing football in the yard with Frank and Joe, while Mr. Pocock was away visiting Aston Rowant, which he usually did a couple of times a week.

The two guards were Tom Bowler and Jimmy Nelms. Tom was "a country man with a real old Oxfordshire country accent". He was also "happy-go-lucky" and whilst he could be a bit quick-tempered,

Fireman Maldwyn Jones from Aberystwyth, porter Frank Saunders and fireman George Nicholson at Watlington with No. 2055 in 1938/9. *Joe Nicholson*

"it passed over quickly". They all worked as a team and "nobody ever fell out".

Jimmy Nelms was a nice old gentleman to get on with, "a railwayman through and through". He did not have much conversation, "he'd say only what he needed to".

Frank complies with the consistent impression of the two drivers in saying that Harry Humphreys was "always busy on the engine and his cloth was always in the same place in the cab", "but he was good for a joke", whilst although Geoff Pearson "would do no more than he had to", he would "always help if asked". Frank always "found Geoff OK", "he took everything in his stride".

Besides the three regular firemen, Frank also recalled Reg Stoneham, a Slough fireman who came over on his motorbike to stand in when required. "He was a damn nice chap."

Frank Saunders enjoyed his time at Watlington. It was an ideal place to learn all about railway work because the porter there covered virtually all duties. All the staff got on well and there was tremendous teamwork. He made lots of other friends, and when he was on the late shift he earned himself extra money in the mornings by working as a driver's mate to haulier Aubrey Tappin. There was lots of road work during the 1930s and Frank helped Aubrey loading gravel from a pit at South Weston and delivering it to whichever roadbuilding site it was needed for at the time. He enjoyed the work, and with all the shovelling involved, the return trip usually included a stop at a convenient pub.

Taking on extra work was not uncommon; even Geoff Pearson supplemented his wages when he was on the early shift, by working for Tappins when he came off the engine. He apparently helped loading parcels, etc. for the agency round.

Harry Humphreys with 2112 on the Horsenden curve, between Risborough and Bledlow Bridge, in June 1939. Both the engine and the driver saw many years service on the line, so this beautiful study is probably as representative as any of the Watlington branch train. Porter Frank Saunders said Harry "always wore a soft cap on the engine . . . unless anyone in particular was coming down, then he wore the official driver's cap" whereas "George Nicholson always wore the proper fireman's cap". A lamp on each end to show the train was complete was all that mattered on this and many other less formal branches. Officially the engine headlamp should have been put on the bracket in front of the chimney to denote a stopping passenger train, but Frank says he could not remember the lamp ever being put there, and this is borne out in most pictures, whilst the train featured on page 87 was not carrying a headlamp at all!

S. H. Freese

The two Watlington porters regularly earned extra money on Sunday mornings when they went in to clean the auto trailer, whilst the permanent way gang were often called out for relaying on the main line which sometimes required the Watlington branch engine.

Sunday excursions and special trains from Watlington provided another opportunity for overtime, some of those run in the 1920s and 30s including trips to places like Southend, Weymouth, Ramsgate and Margate, the return train often getting passengers back in the early hours of Monday morning. Harry Humphreys

recalled that on these occasions two or three extra coaches were sent down from Old Oak to take passengers up the branch, the auto trailer ("the car") being used to serve the halts. "We'd pick up about fifty people from Chinnor." "We had over four hundred people one Sunday in four coaches and the car but it was about as much as the engine wanted because of the heavy bank at Chinnor."

Michael Webb of Shirburn went on a combined schools train to the GWR's Swindon Works. Leaving about 9.0 a.m., the train was not only seen off by a party of local dignitaries, including station

This photo of passengers for the Bertram Mills Circus special in December 1937 appeared in the *GWR Magazine*. Reg Pocock features in the back row.

Station Master's Office,
Watlington.

24th January, 1939.

Dear Sir,

      Government Store - Watlington.

      Further to my report of the 30th ultimo hereon, work has commenced on this building this week. I find the chief contractors are Messrs. Wilson Lovatt & Co. of London and Wolverhampton. I have made contact with their foreman, Mr. Green, and actively canvassed for traffic to rail.

      Yesterday, I had a visit from a representative from the War Office regarding a supply of water from our Locomotive Department water tank and I referred him to Mr.C.B.Collett of Swindon. I also took the opportunity of asking him to use his influence in favour of the railway and he very agreeably promised to do so.

      To give you some idea of the position of the site, I beg to attach a rough sketch plan.

              Yours truly,
              (signed) R.H.Pocock.

master Pocock, but the departure was even marked by the sound of exploding detonators.

The teachers in charge of the parties, some with their husbands or wives, included Mrs. Scott, who taught at Lewknor School. Incidentally, she was the sister of Winifred Siarey, former Watlington station clerk. ·

As mentioned before, the Bluebell specials have not so far been traced in official records, but they are believed to have continued until about 1937, by which time they were apparently not so well supported. Sunday trains were not always a success, station clerk Ken Cox recalling that, in his day, "excursions to the seaside never seemed to be well patronized". However, one outing of particular note was a special with through coaches to Bertram Mills Circus in December 1937. It was organised by the Buffaloes and merited a photo in the *GWR Magazine* (see opposite).

Life is not always easy and when things were not right between Joe Nicholson and his girlfriend, he forsook the camaraderie at Watlington and applied for a post at Addison Road, Kensington, George Howlett replacing him from 1st May 1939.

George was no stranger to the branch, having been born at Chinnor and spending many hours with the staff there when he was a lad. Like Frank Saunders, much of his experience as a porter at Watlington is related in Volume 2. We have been fortunate indeed to be able to speak to both the men from opposite shifts.

In these final months before the outbreak of war, an Ordnance Depot or 'Mobilization Shed' was established about 300 yards from the station, at the end of Pyrton Lane. Known locally as 'The Dump', it is believed to have been a sub-depot of the huge establishment at Didcot and had been started in January 1939. It was built by Wilson Lovatt & Sons Ltd of Victoria Street, SW1, 'Public works and building contractors'.

Frank and George recall wagons of loco ash arriving for the foundations and steelwork for the building, whilst Ernie Tappin recalled components for the huge doors being unloaded through the goods shed that "only just cleared the door". According to him, it was "one of the rare occasions the goods shed was used at this time."

Some of the stores which came in by rail included such diverse items as uniforms, and emergency generators mounted on lorry trailers arriving on 'lowmac' style wagons and being collected by government personnel using Thornycroft lorries, which hauled them off the wagons at the end loading dock. They think this was around the time Hitler was invading Czechoslovakia. Ernie Tappin remembers 20–30 brand new lorries were stored at 'the dump' for quite some time.

The railway was a reserved occupation, so while the storm clouds of war were gathering, Reg Pocock gave Frank the opportunity to apply for a shunter's job at Risborough to avoid the call-up, but Frank declined and left the railway in September to join the services. George Howlett was also called up and left three months later in December. George Nicholson transferred to Old Oak shed in November 1939.

No. 2055 in the Watlington bay at Risborough on 21st June 1939. This engine, often used on the line between 1939 and 1946, was readily recalled by George Nicholson as alternating with 2112.   *Collection P. Winding*

Mrs. Scott (formerly Siarey), headmistress of Lewknor School, cycling along the B4009 through Lewknor in 1941.

Cty. Lewknor School

CHAPTER FIVE

THE WAR YEARS

THE prospect of another war and the apprehension of what it would all come to, may well have been at the back of everyone's mind, but the likelihood of it happening was certainly brought home to householders in Watlington when, according to the *Oxford Times*, they were canvassed as early as February 1939 'by a volunteer band of ladies under the Chairman of the Parish Council. The instructions of the District Council have been carried out to the letter, every courtesy and consideration being shown to the holders.'

On a nationwide scale the sheer magnitude of the evacuation must have been a nightmare to plan, so it is hardly surprising that there were a few unknown factors. The *Oxford Times* for 12th September conveyed some of the anxiety at Watlington:

> After waiting for several hours on Friday week the committee were informed that no children from London would arrive although complete arrangements had been made for 300 children. The following day, another period of waiting, and then nearly 100 women and infants came unexpectedly. The committee eventually obtained billets and by Sunday order prevailed. It was noticeable how hard the ladies of the committee worked and in addition provided hot meals for the evacuees, at their own expense. Too much has been heard in praise of the headquarters staff, but the real thanks and appreciation, in addition to the ladies, should a thousand fold go to the homes who, without reserve, welcomed those evacuated from London. Many stories have been told of the amazing habits of the Londoners and their mode of living. The country folk score every time.

One of the mothers included in the party directed to Watlington that Saturday must have been Mrs Doris Beech of North Kensington. On the day before war was declared, she and her three daughters, Joan, Sylvia and Josephine, met up with other mothers and children and travelled to Paddington by special bus. They arrived there around 9.0 a.m. and, in the charge of a woman official, a group of them was taken by train to Princes Risborough. The official saw them onto the Watlington branch train which they virtually filled, and at the other end of the journey they were met by more officials who took them to Watlington town hall.

Since no children had been received at Watlington on Friday, it caused some surprise when this group arrived accompanied by their mothers. Watlington branch porter Frank Hyde's daughter Barbara recalls the local people's amazement when instead of just children, mothers were seen waiting with their families at the town hall. Some locals were not keen to take them, so temporary arrangements were made to put them in the Memorial Club in the High Street. She says some were moved out to Russells Water but many went back to London. Joan Beech (now Joan Hunt) says that many Londoners were struck by the quietness and the narrow pavements. "Many evacuees returned on Monday — their cases were not even unpacked . . . they just couldn't stick the quietness."

Mrs. Beech made every effort to keep her family together and, following some difficulty, they were eventually billeted with the Hughes, 'an army family' at Barn House in Hill Road. However, because there was not enough room, her eldest daughter Joan had to stay with Mabel Lett. Some of the other evacuees were not so lucky and had to sleep in the church hall for at least one night until accommodation could be sorted out. Mrs. Whittaker of Britwell House, Britwell Salome, organised

some of the billets and it is believed she was connected with the Soldiers and Sailors Association.

Mrs. Beech was upset about her family being divided and recalls crying when her daughter was pointed out to her at the Letts' bedroom window. However, the following year, after the period referred to as the 'phoney war', another evacuee staying at the Hughes' house returned to London and Joan was able to move in with the rest of her family. Indeed, many families returned to London. Mrs. Beech stressed how friendly the people of Watlington were towards her. She socialized with many of them and regularly met other evacuees at the recreation ground in Shirburn Street.

Her husband Leslie, who was a reservist in the Royal Signals and a despatch rider for Field Marshal Montgomery, visited her

Joan, Josie and Sylvia Beech on their father's motorbike c.1940.

whenever possible, usually on his motorbike, and sometimes without warning while he was on his rounds. Mrs. Beech says he was taking messages to and from a large house in Chiselhampton where Churchill, Montgomery and even Eisenhower had meetings. It was certainly a happy coincidence that her husband's duties took him to the area. She would sometimes learn that he was about when friends told her they had seen her daughter on the back of a solider's motorbike.

Her fourth daughter Virginia was born at Watlington in 1944 and the family settled there and after the war lived in Church Street.

After the evacuation from London, the *Oxford Times* for 24th October 1939 conveyed the following message:

> The London County Council on behalf of the people of London has conveyed to the Billeting Authorities in Oxfordshire an expression of gratitude to those in the reception areas who have cheerfully taken on the responsibility for the reception of a large number of evacuees, and on whose shoulders has fallen the task, which commenced when the London parties were detrained, of caring for them, extemporising social benefits, and of educating the children.

Joan Beech says the first evacuees arrived before the outbreak of war. These included two families of Austrian Jews who took large houses in Hill Road, Madam Lowe and their two daughters, and the Branns, who had two sons, Dieter and Florien. The Branns, who lived at Hill House, were puppeteers and gave some shows before the war. Frank Hyde's daughter

A wartime scene at Paddington station in 1942.

Barbara recalls that Czech evacuees had stayed at the hostel in the old brewery for a few months in 1938 at the time of the Munich crisis. "I remember feeling sorry for them as they couldn't speak any English."

A number of families refuged at Watlington during the war through family connections. Violet Turner from Ealing was one of the first to arrive. Her husband, who knew fireman Peter Robinson's mother when she worked in the telephone exchange at Shepherds Bush, was about to join the RAF so the Robinsons invited him to bring his wife and one-year-old son to stay with them in their home at 1–2 Mafeking Road, Shirburn. It seems likely this was a tied cottage as Peter's other three brothers all worked on the Shirburn Estate.

Violet later worked at the Miles aircraft factory at Risborough, travelling in on the train with work colleagues Eileen Woodley from Pyrton and Eileen Foley from Chinnor. Going home at night, Arthur Pearson and George Nicholson would unofficially stop to drop her off at Shirburn at the top of Blenheim Road, to save her the walk back from Watlington. However, she didn't like to ask the conscientious Harry Humphreys who she felt had an "officious attitude", so she walked or cycled back to Shirburn when he was driving. When her husband was on leave, he caught the train to High Wycombe and made the rest of his way home by bus to Shirburn.

Violet remembers how the children used to get on the gate at the bottom of Peter Robinson's garden and wave to the drivers whenever the train went by. "Mr. Pearson would drop a lump of coal off to help the Robinsons as that was the only way they could cook."

Another family billeted at Shirburn were moved away because the children were a nuisance.

Local Civil Defence arrangements were often viewed with a mixture of resentment and amusement, doubtless dependent on the suitability or otherwise of those individuals, mostly volunteers, endeavouring to enforce the regulations. Air raid wardens were not popular with the public, but they were only part of the local government bureaucracy. The following extracts from the *Oxford Times* during 1939 record happenings in Watlington and convey something of the mood of the town during the preparations for the inevitable war.

11th April: 'Watlington ARP — During last week members of the St. John Ambulance Brigade, British Red Cross and other organisations took part in the general rehearsal held over a wide area.'

15th August: 'Blackouts that are not black — The efforts made in the town and district were well responded to and no complaint can be made in that direction, but the condition and position of certain lights would not for one moment be tolerated in actual warfare. It would then be a state of 'gross darkness' in reality. It was noticeable the very small numbers of cars on the road, testifying to the good sense of the owners.' [Refers to ARP blackout exercise for South East England including Oxfordshire on 9th/10th August.]

29th August: 'ARP — One or two over-zealous members of the ARP rather exceeded their instructions in ordering darkened blinds on Thursday. The matter, surely, is one, when the time arrives, for the Police alone.'

12th September: 'The air raid — Quite a scene was that of Wednesday morning [6th September] when the warning came. It was a good rehearsal, but perhaps a little overdone. Here is an illustration: People going to Oxford were solemnly told that they would not be allowed to enter the city unless carrying gas masks. Another town, it is said Wallingford, penalties were to be enforced for such a crime! In one important centre a warden turned up wearing the gas mask! But with the morning cool reflection came.'

14th November: 'Air Raid — The muddle on Friday [10th November] over the private warning must be placed at the door of the local ARP. Much resentment and annoyance had been caused by the fact that the council school children were turned out into the street when no air raid warning had been officially given by the police. The managers of the schools should insist upon a better and more sensible arrangement being brought into readiness should an actual air raid occur.'

5th December: 'Petty Sessions — Insufficient Blackout — An innkeeper on the hills was fined £2 for not blacking out to perfection. The case was one brought by a special constable from Ewelme. The penalty should be a caution to others.'

The same paper also records that the cinema at Watlington was reopened in September 1939, which must have been a comfort to many and something to look forward to, whereas, for reasons not explained, the local shopkeepers were unanimous in their decision to close for an hour at midday and earlier in the evenings.

After the so-called 'phoney war', some women and children had returned to London, but, when the Blitz started in September 1940, there were further evacuations. These included 11-year-old Roy Millen and his sisters Lillian, 12, and Maureen, 5, who left Bermondsey to live with their aunt and mother in rooms above Hoddinuts Electrical Store in Couching Street. This had all been arranged through a distant relative who owned Edwards garage in Lewknor High Street.

Although they left London by train, they used one of House Brothers' buses from Reading to Watlington. At first, Roy was disappointed with living in a town house in Watlington, which did not compare with his first billet at Kellaton, near Kingsbridge in Devon, where he had been sent a year before. However, he grew to love the area and has remained there ever since.

He recalls there were few civilian motor vehicles in the locality during the war, but the rumble of military vehicles was regularly heard through the town, particularly later on in the war with the establishment of Chalgrove Airfield. McAlpine and Trenthams were two contractors involved in the construction of the aerodrome. Ernie Tappin recalled that coal supplies for heating the contractor's accommodation kept one of their lorries busy ferrying supplies from the station to Chalgrove for six months. Manned initially by American airmen, the airfield also brought paratroops and other army units.

Roy Millen remembers Canadian troops passing through the town in general vehicles and tanks. "We used to wave at them as they went by . . . it's a wonder they didn't hit the town hall." He also recalls that some Americans from Chalgrove brought doughnuts, chocolate and gum on a lorry "for the kids". They also organised parties at Chalgrove for the children and took lorries around the villages to collect them. Les Tappin recalls that doughnuts arrived by train for collection by the Yanks who typically gave some to the staff. They would "turn up at the youth club in the High Street and hand out sweets and doughnuts . . . They got invited into some of the homes."

Whilst the Americans were also undoubtedly welcomed by the younger women because of the shortage of male company of their own age group, they were not always popular with the older drinking population who supported the thirteen pubs in Watlington, because the Americans collectively succeeded in drinking the pubs dry!

The Blitz drove many Londoners to seek refuge away from the City. They were desperate to get away from the bombing. Some of those who went to the booking office at Paddington

The Pineapple Tea Rooms shown in early postwar years. During the war, Messum & Dover fishmongers, not far off the left of the picture, fried fish and chips on selected nights.

National Monuments Record

asking where to go to escape were apparently told "Go to Watlington station!"

Some of them stayed at the Pineapple Tea Rooms which had been bought by Mr. and Mrs. Davies just before Easter in 1939. It had formerly been run by two ladies who were retiring.

The fine weather of Easter 1939 brought a large number of visitors to the area, many of them cyclists or ramblers, looking for accommodation, which led to the Pineapple becoming a guest house. There were five bedrooms but after the outbreak of war, the numbers of evacuees billeted there, even for one night at a time, increased, so guests frequently ended up sleeping on the dining room floor and were pleased to do so. Members of the Metropolitan Police, who had been on almost continual duty for several days, came with their families, sometimes just for a few hours rest from the chaos, many of these people arriving by train in the early evening.

During the Blitz Mr. and Mrs. Davies were given an open ration voucher because of the large number of evacuees they catered for. Their three daughters, Connie, Judy and Phyllis, made friends with many of the younger guests and there was always a friendly atmosphere, long-standing guests in particular becoming very much part of the family. There were doubtless other such hostels similarly used in the area, but another one brought to our attention during research was the Wheatsheaf at Oakley, Chinnor, where Mrs. Webb, the landlord's daughter, remembers evacuees sleeping on the landing.

Some railway staff also lodged at the Pineapple, one of the first of whom was George Thomas, who was clerk at the station in 1939/40 before being called up for the forces. He was a Londoner who Connie Davies remembers tap-dancing in a charity concert in the vicarage hall.

His place was taken by 16-year-old Joan Saw. She really wanted to be a nurse, but in 1940 applied for the clerk's job at Watlington station because it looked more interesting than the clerical job she had taken in Princes Risborough when she first left school. She remembers Mr. Pocock interviewing her in his office and giving her some columns of figures to add up "just to see if I could do it!" After another interview at Paddington, and a medical at Oxford, she was taken on as a temporary clerk at eleven shillings a week, "and no uniform".

At first she worked from 7.0 a.m. till 3.0 p.m. but later this was changed to 10.0 a.m. until 9.0 p.m., with a two-hour break during which she wandered around the town while Mr. Pocock held the fort. "Mr. Pocock was always very much in charge" but kind and helpful. She sat next to him in the office with her back to the ticket window. When he was not there and she needed help with anything, like complex ticket routeings, she could ring the Risborough station clerks. "Hughie Harman was particularly helpful."

Joan cycled in from Chinnor but caught the train back to avoid the dark, stowing her bicycle in the guard's van. During two winters she lodged at the Pineapple where she was very happy and got on well with Connie Davies. She remembers how the cafe was used by Air Force personnel.

During her time at Watlington, the two porters were Dick Smith, who had formerly driven the bus from the Hare and Hounds, and Tom Tunnicliffe who had been a chauffeur for Lady Sueter of How Hill. He joined the GWR in the early war years and, after a spell in the forces, went back to being a porter at Watlington again around 1944.

Dick Smith was always helpful and "a kind of father figure". She had little contact with the train crews but remembers the

guards were Jimmy Nelms, who retired while she was there, Tom Bowler and Frank Hyde.

During the war, there were no fewer than three factories at Risborough contributing to the national effort, "the munitions", Belling & Lee, and Miles. The latter two made aircraft components, Belling & Lee apparently moving out of London for the war. Mabel Howlett worked for Sadgroves, who she believes had been London dressmakers, who had taken over part of the furniture factory and made fabric engine covers for

Dick Smith.

bombers. She says Belling & Lee occupied premises in the town centre, whilst Audrey Griffiths remembers they made "fuses and small components". The Miles Aircraft Co apparently took over the machine shop of Goodearl's furniture factory where they made parts for trainer planes.

These establishments drew extra workers from Watlington and elsewhere along the branch to the extent that from December 1940 an early train was reintroduced at 7.25 a.m. At first it returned from Risborough empty stock, but from October 1941 it also conveyed passengers when required.

When the 7.30 train of 1929–33 had been run on Mondays only, the early goods was cancelled, but now that it was a daily feature of the timetable, it was necessary for the goods to leave earlier at 4.20 a.m., returning at 5.30 a.m. and calling only at Aston Rowant. Harry Humphreys remarked "The branch was turned upside-down".

The number of passengers booked from Watlington rose steadily from 9,296 in 1939 to a staggering 37,228 in 1944, so it is not surprising that an extra coach was sent to Watlington to strengthen the first train. In Joan Saw's experience, the need for the extra vehicle was not necessarily evident when the train left Watlington where she thinks about ten workers used the 7.25 (she says there were about eight on the 8.45). However, passengers boarding the train as it progressed along the line resulted in people standing from Chinnor where the largest number joined. Mabel Howlett says "Thirty people joined the first train at Chinnor".

The number of passengers booked from Chinnor rose from 4,513 to 25,015 in 1943 and even the sleepy station at Aston Rowant experienced an increase from a meagre 434 tickets sold in 1939 to 2,903 in 1944.

Even with the increased importance of the first train, Phyllis Davies from the Pineapple sometimes ran a little late. She cycled in from the town each day to catch the train for Risborough

Unusually, during 1941, 5ft 2in-wheeled 0—6—0PT No. 5417 was sent for use on the branch. Designed for working auto-trains, the larger wheels of this engine would not have been welcomed by the crews when hauling the goods up Chinnor bank, neither would its screw reverser have made shunting any easier. It is therefore hardly surprising that the class does not recur in the allocation list on page 216. No. 5417 is featured here at Aston Rowant and again on the opposite page.   *Cty. Lewknor School*

and, when she was behind, her mother telephoned the station to tell them she was on her way, and the train was held for her!

One morning when she was sick, Mrs Davies failed to let them know and instead received a telephone call from the station to find out where Phyllis was as the train was waiting for her!

Sylvia King (now Sylvia Bird) of Lewknor was another regular who travelled in to work at Princes Risborough on the first train during the 1940s. She remembers how they climbed into the trailer at Lewknor bridge halt, but whenever possible she and her travelling companions would quickly transfer to the compartment coach at Aston Rowant. When the return of the 7.25 arrived back at Watlington, the engine ran round to the other end of its train and shunted the spare coach into the siding behind the signal box. In the evening it was retrieved and taken out to Risborough again for use on the rear of the 5.50 p.m.

January 1941 brought deep snow to the area and, during the whole of the afternoon of the 18th, the Engineering Department men were out clearing the line. However, the weather was so severe that the snow drifted as fast as the men cleared it away. That night Mr. Pocock stood out in the dark station yard anxiously waiting for the arrival of the 5.48 p.m. from Risborough. In the distance he could hear the train climbing the bank out of Shirburn, but then it became obvious that it had come to a stand.

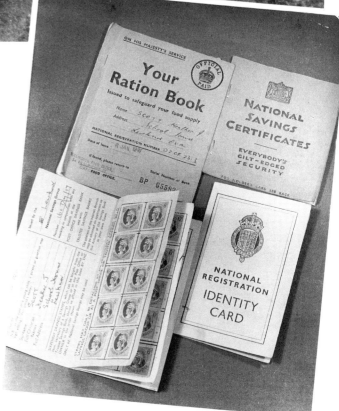

This publicity shot for National Savings stamps, featuring Mrs. Scott at Aston Rowant, is the best portrait we have discovered of Geoff Pearson. He smoked Woodbines and, suffering severe cracks in his tough hands, was always rubbing or massaging the fist of one in the cupped palm of the other. He used cream to soothe them but without curing the problem. He was quite a character; Frank Saunders says that if the engine was off the ramp at Watlington, Geoff would 'move the train along the platform to save climbing down'. Porter Frank Hyde, seen in the background, became a guard when Jimmy Nelms retired later in 1941. Note the regulation blackout sheet tied above the cab entrance.

Cty. Lewknor School

He went to investigate and found the train stuck in a deep snowdrift about 500 yards from the station. There were thirteen passengers on the train and they decided to alight and walk along the top of the bank to the nearby Middle Way level crossing, from where they were able to reach the main road into the town. Mr. Pocock stayed to help clear the line and the train eventually reached the terminus at 9.05 p.m.

The combination of the deep snow and working the branch train in blackout conditions was proving too much for 61-year-old guard Jimmy Nelms, who felt he was getting too old for climbing steps to attend to the lights at the halts along the line.

A few years earlier, in 1935, he had transferred to Marlow where not only were duties lighter, but he and his wife wanted to move close to her father, former Watlington guard Henry Cheney who had transferred there and retired. However, it is not difficult to imagine their disappointment when, after only seven months, guards were abolished on the Marlow branch auto-trains and Jimmy had to transfer back to Watlington to resume the more demanding guard's duties there. Apparently without the stamina he had previously enjoyed and now working in the blackout, he had recently experienced one or two narrow escapes from serious accidents and this worried him. He had had

Mrs. Scott again at Aston Rowant selling savings stamps for the war effort to Cecil Tutty (from Aston Stud), watched by Charlie Hopkins in 1940.

Cty. Lewknor School

Although posed for the promotion of National Savings certificates, this evocative classroom scene at Lewknor School in 1941 was real enough and amply conveys the day-to-day atmosphere.

Cty. Lewknor School

This beautiful composition, another of the National Savings publicity pictures, was taken during haymaking at Church Farm, Lewknor, in 1941. It shows Alice Amor selling savings stamps to farmer Robert Graham with farm workers Arthur Geifkin on the trailer and Neddy Amor and Audrey Graham on the haystack.

Cty. Lewknor School

Aston Rowant station, looking towards Watlington in 1941. *J. H. Venn*

enough. Rather than wait until he reached 65, which, as things turned out, would have been the duration of the war, he retired early in 1941.

Incidentally, the line was blocked again by snow the following year, this time near Wainhill Halt, on the night of Tuesday, 3rd February 1942. A bus service was substituted, normal service resuming with the 1.35 p.m. train from Risborough to Watlington. George Nicholson thought it was in 1942 when, on an icy day, a goods train arriving at Watlington crashed through the buffer stops and ended up through the hedge at the roadside. He says the wheels 'picked up' on the ice and, with the weight of the train, the engine just slid along the rails. The rear of the engine remained 'on the buffer stops' and they immediately "ballasted the fire and sent for the steam cranes". George thought the load might have been "armament for the nearby army dump" and recalled that the engine suffered a broken front buffer spring on the driver's side.

Throughout the 1940s there was a high turnover of firemen at Watlington, most of whom seemed keen to move on, not least because of the overnight duty without shelter, and the feeling of being so cut off. One young man taking up a vacancy was Donald Brown, an 18-year-old engine cleaner from Exeter, who went to Watlington to take up his first appointment as fireman on 25th April 1941.

Taking lodgings with Mrs. Willoughby in Brook Street, he was paired with Geoff Pearson, and took up his first duty the next day, working the 8.30 a.m. to 4.30 p.m. shift on 0-6-0PT No. 2055.

No. 2112 near Lewknor Bridge Halt in 1941. *J. H. Venn*

This picture gives some idea of the conditions around Chinnor in February 1942.

Sadly, on the Friday morning of his first week, owing to a misunderstanding between him and the driver, Brown met with a distressing accident which could easily have been fatal. It was a fine sunny day and shortly after arriving with the 10.18 a.m. from Princes Risborough, the train was set back into the loop, the engine was uncoupled and run forward clear of the release crossover alongside the platform. When the points changed, it ran bunker first onto the loop and was brought to a stand. A milk truck which had been brought in on the front of the train was then uncoupled "and pushed by hand onto the stop block". Pearson then took the engine back to the platform to couple onto the vehicle with the intention of taking it over to the yard via the run-round loop. He noticed that an ash wagon standing on the loco siding looked as if it was not sufficiently clear of the loop and told his new fireman to watch the clearance on his side.

Brown shouted for him to stop when they were about a foot from the wagon, when he could see it was definitely just foul. Brown then got down with the intention of pushing the wagon clear, and, after taking the brake off, started to move it with a wooden pinchbar that was lying around. He had heard Pearson shout, but thought he was talking to the traffic staff. However, Pearson, who had no idea what Brown had in mind, had shouted to him to keep out of the way because he would push the wagon clear with the engine. He then reversed 2055 and drove it back to the coal stage so the porter could change the points to the loco siding and allow the engine towards the wagon. He thought his mate, who was on the blind side of the engine, had gone to the other side of the wagon to take the brakes off, but, when he was about 8ft from the wagon, he saw it move and, straightening up to apply the brake, he heard Brown shout.

Brown had the pinchbar under the tread of the rear outside wheel of the wagon and was standing with his back to the

engine. By the time he heard it behind him, there was no time for him to get out before being pinched between the buffers. The engine stopped about 2ft from the wagon and Pearson rushed across the cab to see his mate come out from the bunker holding his chest. Brown said "You've caught me" and fell to the ground, evidently fainting.

Pearson, who held a St. John Ambulance medal, quickly loosened Brown's clothing, then took him into the loco cabin and sent for Mr. Pocock, who took him to the booking office and treated him for shock after examining him. He was conveyed to the local hospital at about 11.40 a.m. and from there he was taken to the Radcliffe Infirmary, Oxford, by the Watlington Division St. John Ambulance. He suffered a wound on the underside of his left arm and severe bruising to his left shoulder and chest. It had been suspected that he had fractured ribs, but happily this was not so, and he was taken back to Watlington Hospital on 6th May and discharged on 13th May.

Firemen wishing to remain in the GWR's service were obliged to study and take the examination to become drivers. They had three separate chances to pass, after which unsuccessful candidates were usually dismissed or given work as shed labourers. According to official paperwork, Fireman Peter Robinson was 'removed from the footplate' and reduced to shed labourer on 3rd November 1941 'owing to his failure to pass the technical examination for promotion to a driver'. He remained on night duty at Watlington until 29th May 1944 'when, owing to an alteration in the working, there was no suitable employment which he could be offered at that depot, and his transfer to Aylesbury as a General Shedman was effected.' We have failed to establish what the alteration in the working was.

In addition to the high turnover of firemen, Slough shed was often called upon to send crews to cover for any absentees. One of those despatched to Watlington without notice was Slough fireman Ron Grantham:

"My first encounter with the Watlington branch was on Boxing Day 1941. I was on 'spare' and called from my home to cover for a fireman who was sick. On arrival at Princes Risborough during the early afternoon there was not a soul about, so I decided to go into the porters room on the up side to keep warm by the fire. Some time elapsed and I became aware of an engine on the down side which collected a staff at the North Box. There was another long period before a double-headed train appeared and ran into the Watlington bay. After the locos were released, the second was shunted aside; I can't remember where, but it might have been the Research Laboratory siding. The other engine then attached to the other end of the trailer. By this time, the porter had arrived and it transpired that on the previous run into Watlington, the fusible plugs had gone and the engine had to be withdrawn from service. A fresh engine had therefore to be requisitioned from Slough which ironically had left after me!

"I only did a couple of trips with the late-turn driver Harry Humphreys, who we nicknamed 'Vinegar Joe' because he ate vinegar sandwiches — he used to say he couldn't afford anything else . . . he was always moaning. There was no lodge available for me so I slept in the old horse-box body they had there and returned home 'on the cushions', arriving back at about 10.30 a.m."

Evacuee families continued to arrive at Watlington, and we are fortunate in meeting Martha (known as Millie) Lawrence (now Millie Batten), a teenager at the time and one of the later arrivals. Despite all the activity at the nearby fighter airfield, she was not moved out of her home at Gravesend in Kent until 1941, after the Battle of Britain. Her mother understood that she and her children were to be sent to 'a hotel in Oxford' and was asked if her seven children had slippers! It transpired that instead of Oxford, they were sent to Watlington to stay in a hostel rather than a hotel. When they arrived at Watlington station, Millie's mother spoke to the staff who pointed out that it was quite a walk to the town, and took pity on them struggling with heavy luggage. Millie recalls how one of the staff said reassuringly "That'll be alright my dears", and kindly arranged for it to be delivered to them.

Their billet, arranged by Mr. McFarlane of Watcombe Road, was the old brewery at the bottom of Couching Street, opposite the police station. By this time, it was in use as a youth hostel for cyclists and ramblers. Millie remembers the rather grand appearance and decor of the whole place, which was under the care of Mr. and Mrs. Parker, who lived next door. "There was a wall around the building with spikes on top and a conservatory on the Couching Street side which we were not officially allowed in because the weak glass roof was in need of repair." The accommodation, all on the first floor, consisted of four bedrooms equipped with bunk beds, a sitting room at the front, a dining room and kitchen behind, and a lavatory off a landing on the stairs. "There was a beautiful marble floor in the hall and at the back a lovely oak staircase. It was a beautiful place". However, although it was clean, when they first arrived, her mother was taken aback by the sparsely furnished rooms, the bare mattresses, grey blankets and soiled pillows. Millie remembers her mother pinned freshly aired nappies to the pillows so that the babies had something clean to put their heads on. Desperate for linen, she rang Northfleet bus garage, where her husband Bill was based as a Greenline conductor, to ask him to send a trunk of items by train. Subsequent to their immediate needs, he later arrived with a van load of furniture and visited them as often as possible.

A few months later, they were joined by the Cook family from London, who took one of the upstairs rooms, then the Smiths, who occupied part of the divided dining room, and later two of the upper rooms were occupied by other families, including the Dietts who had previously stayed with relatives at Ewelme.

Millie's family subsequently shared the large sitting room with the Fords from Ashford, Kent, four pairs of bunk beds being arranged on either side of the room for the two families.

Although there was a bathroom off the landing, only the WC was in use, the only water supply being drawn from the tap over

An Oxford City 1937 Weymann-bodied AEC Regal 1 on what was probably either the No. 76 or 88 Thame–Watlington service during what seems likely to have been the 1942 floods.
Cty. Cyril Hopkins

the sink in the kitchen at the back of the house. The water for the tank supplying the sink and the WC was pumped by hand each morning from the scullery at the back of the Parkers' house. "We all took it in turn to do this."

"There was a kitchen range for us all to use, but this was in the Smiths' room and we didn't like to disturb them." Instead they improvised with two primus stoves stood on a table under the front window. One was used for preparing meals, which were cooked in a biscuit tin, whilst the other heated a bucket of water for washing, including boiling the babies' nappies. There was a bowl for washing themselves and "we had a tin bath and all us kids shared the water".

Millie said "I fell in love with Watlington . . . you used to be able to get everything there — even a pram". She recalled Mrs. Snow, the wife of the vicar of St. Leonard's, "riding around the town on a 'sit-up-and-beg' bike, blowing a whistle to warn of air raids . . . and Major Munroe who worked for Cable and Wireless and walked to the station each morning for the 8.40 a.m. to London."

The family used the railway a lot, the pushchair or pram being left at the station while they were away. They could not afford any holidays so they went to Princes Risborough for the day 'to walk around', Chinnor for the woods, and Bledlow. Millie also recalls travelling to Gravesend to visit her father who, subsequently, from early in 1943, was employed at the Morris factory in Cowley. Relatives from Crayford, Thornton Heath

Swyncombe Downs being cleared during the early part of the war for corn growing. This had been shrubland which farmer Richard
Roadnight rented from Christie Miller.   *Cty. Mrs. D. Roadnight*

and Norfolk occasionally travelled by train to Watlington for the
weekend and were collected from the station by Cecil Tappin.
She also remembers her mother buying watercress grown by Mr.
Coles and taking it to the station for despatch to her relatives. If
they missed the train, they handed it to the conductor of the
High Wycombe bus.

By 1946 the Lawrences were the only family left in the hostel,
and had moved into the back of the building, occupying a
bedroom upstairs and dining room downstairs. Clement Ives★
took over the building and, much to Mrs. Lawrence's disgust,
used the sitting room as a furniture factory and three of the
upper floor rooms as stores. The Lawrences now rented from Ives
and entered the building from the back, via the kitchen, instead
of using the front door. However, Millie got married in August
1946 and moved into a Nissen hut on Chalgrove Airfield whilst
the rest of her family moved to Headington in 1948, leaving the
remainder of the building free for Ives' business. But we are
jumping ahead again in our story.

The more casual way of life on the Watlington branch will by
now be quite evident, but it is interesting to have this confirmed
through the first impressions of a 19-year-old member of the
Women's Land Army. Audrey Davis, an East End girl ("a
cockney from Ilford") had joined up at the outbreak of war
when she was sixteen, attending Writtle agricultural college at
Chelmsford and learning practical farming in the area. On Lady
Day in 1942 she was posted to Manor Farm, South Weston, the
nearest station to which was Lewknor Bridge Halt.

Being more used to main line trains in the London area, she
was fascinated when on arrival at Princes Risborough, she was

told she had to catch the 'Watlington Donkey' and even more
surprised when the porter pointed to what struck her as a toy-
town train with a little engine and single coach.

She must have presented quite a spectacle to the regular
passengers as she entered the auto-trailer in her fawn-coloured
uniform, which consisted of breeches, a three-quarter length
woollen greatcoat, a felt hat similar in style to an Australian
soldier's, and thick-soled black boots, which needed considerable
breaking in!

Everyone was friendly and helpful, particularly the guard,
Frank Hyde. As if to underline her relaxed impression, the train
had hardly started out on its journey when it came to a stand,
then reversed back to Princes Risborough. It transpired that the
crew had forgotten to take water! Everyone seemed to take this
state of affairs for granted, one of the other passengers
commenting that, the day before, they had stopped along the
line to pick mushrooms, something to which Judy and Connie
Davies independently testified.

With an eye for a pretty woman, the engine crew also made
themselves known to her during the short journey. The fireman
was George Nicholson.

To complete her first impression, the train seemed to have
stopped in the middle of nowhere when it reached Lewknor
Bridge Halt, where Frank Hyde lowered the steps and helped
her down with her kit bag and several cases. She made a big
impression on the train crew who gave her a cheery wave as they
pulled away and thereafter always looked out for her.

Audrey was met at Lewknor by a Mr. Austin, the manager of
Manor Farm. She was the only woman there, she and four men
covering all sorts of work. Audrey got up at 5.30 a.m. and, after
a quick cup of tea, set off to the fields to gather in the cows,

---

★Ives' business is detailed in Volume 2.

which were milked twice a day at 6.0 a.m. and 2.0 p.m. Manor Farm had a prize herd, Bill Slater, the head cowman, taking them to shows.

During the long hours of daylight in the summer, she was often in the fields until 10.0 p.m. and she also remembers exercising the bulls, by leading them along the roads around South Weston with ropes through the rings in their noses.

Audrey was paid fourteen shillings per week (with lodgings and food), had Monday afternoons off, and every three months went back to Essex for the weekend to see her parents.

As one of the longest-serving members of the Land Army, she was presented to the Queen at the Mansion House, London, in December 1945, travelling from Lewknor on the first train and returning in the early evening.

She was not the only land girl in the area, some from a camp at How Hill, for instance, worked for farmer Schwier whilst others were employed at Roadnights Farm.

Another recollection of the time was recorded in the diary of railway enthusiast Charles Bayes, who travelled out to Watlington on 19th August 1943:

'GW trailer saloon No. 87 in bay platform at Princes Risborough 10 minutes after our departure time. A goods train behind 2078 came in from Watlington; 2078 shunted its train into a siding, removed the brake van which it attached to the saloon, and then set off for Watlington some 20 minutes late. About 20 passengers were carried, but only 6 as far as the terminus. The PW was surprisingly well kept, with no weeds visible (as on the Aylesbury branch). All the halts are at ground level, but the three stations Chinnor, Aston Rowant and Watlington neat and charming. [At Watlington] The locomotive shunted; there were loaded guns and tanks in the yard. Soldiers loaded a lorry, and an upside-down notice warned owners of heavy vehicles not to pass over a certain unspecified bridge. 2078 added an ex 1st class compt coach to the saloon and so I sat on brown velvet for the return journey. The guard warned me against embarking the first compartment in case it was off the platform at Princes Risborough! On arrival I had a brief chat with the driver who told me of the rigours of branch line life; in a few minutes he was due off on a run to Thame, returning after 19 minutes, and then to Watlington again. Two engines were kept at Slough for the working, and changed once a week, breakdowns were frequent, and replacement engines came from Southall shed.[?]'

In subsequent correspondence, Charles Bayes recalled that the coach added to his train was a non-corridor 'unremarkable elliptical roofed bogie coach' which was put on the Risborough end of the train, next to the engine. He thought it was steel panelled. On an earlier occasion in the summer of 1942 James Venn recalls seeing a downgraded first class clerestory accompanying the branch trailer, whilst Chinnor porter Bryan Bowler referred to the spare coach variously as 'a compo' and 'a suburban coach with compartment doors', and fireman Tony Benham says that it had eight compartments and was kept in the carriage shed.

Details are hazy, but the official coach working book for 1943 shows the Watlington branch as being provided with a 70ft auto-trailer and a brake third when required. It seems that a supplementary bogie coach continued to be used for workers to Risborough until at least 1945 and was still included in the coach working book for that October.

Special trains were apparently run on Sundays during the war to enable relatives to visit evacuees. Aubrey Jarmaine's daughter Audrey thinks these were run about once a month. They were arranged in a similar way to the Bluebell specials, arriving with two or three extra coaches in the middle of the morning and returning in the early evening.

The first train on Monday mornings also continued to be well used by weekend visitors making their way home.

The nearby Ordnance Depot, the new airfield at Chalgrove and the aircraft and munitions factories at Risborough were largely responsible for a dramatic increase in traffic, which kept everyone busy, and at Watlington resulted in a higher level of clerical work for Joan Saw who recalls that it was the goods paperwork that kept her occupied. Goods forwarded rose from 516 tons in 1939 to 5,098 in 1944, and goods received from 5,564 to 17,497, coal received rising from 2,873 to 5,098. Even Aston Rowant's forwarding rose from an extremely poor 108 tons in 1939 to 2,755 in 1943. Chinnor's fell from 17,643 tons in 1939 to 3,626 in 1941 (climbing to 10,919 in 1944) and goods received in the same years from 31,998 to 14,687 (climbing to 26,736 in 1942). As traffic at Chinnor was dominated by the cement works, it appears that its output was curtailed by the war.

Just before traffic peaked, Joan's hours were reduced when, in the autumn of 1943, Esme Jarmaine, Aubrey Jarmaine's daughter, started as a clerk at Watlington station, enabling the work to be covered in two overlapping shifts.

Joan Saw, photographed at Watlington at the side of the cart bay which gave access to Reg Pocock's milk platform.

Cty. Joe Christie

Porter Tom Tunnicliffe at Watlington station c.1940/1. The GWR handbill on the wall read 'Join the GWR Spitfire Club and help to buy a fighter'. The idea for the fund was explained in a letter dated 19th August 1940 from the GWR Divisional Superintendcnt's Office: 'Gift of Aircraft to Royal Air Forcc. It is felt that the staff of the Company would like to have an opportunity of raising a fund for presenting one or more aircraft to the Royal Air Force in recognition of the magnificent achievements of that Force, and the Directors who wish to be associated with the movement have promised to subscribe £500 towards the cost of the first machine. The method of collection will be by means of Collecting Boxes at Stations and Depots.' The *GWR Magazine* for September 1940 subsequently publicised the appeal.

Cty. Joe Christie

Above: Joan Saw and Tom Tunnicliffe at Watlington station c.1940-1.
Joe Christie

Left: Esme Jarmaine at Watlington station c.1943-4 when she worked there as a clerk. During this time, Esme met her husband Joe Christie while he was collecting coal for the searchlight battery at Watlington Hill.
Cty. Audrey Griffiths

Joan was still keen to fulfil her ambition to become a nurse, and in the spring of 1943 she managed go get a place in the West London Hospital Preliminary Training School prior to starting a three-year course. Her place is believed to have been taken by Sally Matheson from Wainhill.

Chinnor porter Bryan Bowler recalled Sally Matheson travelling into Watlington on the return of the first train and his father Tom forgetting to retract the steps after picking her up at Wainhill. Bryan had to pick up the pieces after the steps struck the platform at Chinnor!

According to Bryan, traffic for the Ordnance Depot was such that the midday goods to Chinnor was sometimes sent through to Watlington. He also recalled seeing about three special trains each week carrying guns and other equipment destined for the ports. Largely comprising machine wagons, together with a fitted brake van, these trains were run after the last passenger train and often in the moonlight. Loads included tanks and "guns with rubber tyres". Reg Pocock also recalled "It was frequently necessary to arrange two or three special trains over the branch during the day".

In order to ease the handling of all the military equipment, the old rope-worked 1-ton fixed hand crane in the goods shed was replaced with a more convenient 1-ton overhead 'runway' with hand-operated pulley block. This must have made it a lot easier to transfer the diverse items to waiting military lorries. The installation was reported as complete in March 1942, but the new works order reveals that this was first authorised by the Locomotive Committee minutes on 21st January 1937 and 27th October 1938.

Tom Saunders said he thought the cattle pens were removed for the military traffic, but, whilst we can find no evidence of this, he might have been confusing them with Weedon's coal pens which, situated at the south end of the goods shed sidings, would probably have been regarded as an obstacle. However, although they had disappeared by the end of the war, a photograph in Volume 2 shows them still in use in 1943/4.

The volume of traffic for the air force and army at Watlington station varied during the war years, but there must have been times when it looked more like a military base, and not without incident. On 5th June 1944, while ammunition was being unloaded by soldiers, an army lorry 'fouled and knocked down some of the brickwork at the side of the steps leading to the Goods Shed office', and on another occasion, on 19th February 1944, when the American Air Force★, based at Chalgrove airfield, sent their own mobile crane to unload heavy cases beyond the capacity of the crane in the goods shed, the jib fouled the telephone wire which was secured by stays around the station chimney stack. This brought the whole chimney crashing down on the office roof, smothering Mr. Pocock and his clerk in soot and dust. Mr. Pocock recalled, "We thought we were being bombed and were glad that it was not worse." The US officer in charge said "Waal boss, I guess we shall have to make this good", and they did.

★The official accident report states 'American Army'.

During the war, many of the engines undergoing overhaul at Swindon Works were turned out in plain black with the letters 'GWR' along tanksides or tenders. No. 2112 is seen here at Watlington in wartime black livery which it received at Swindon in 1942 (as did 2055). The traditional GWR green was restored in June 1946.

Cty. Gwen Clarke & Rita Watts

Mr. Pocock also recalled the arrival of a pedigree duck in a very elaborate case addressed to a member of the USAF at Chalgrove. As was customary with livestock, he rang the aerodrome to advise of the arrival, but no-one knew the addressee. Mr. Pocock kept the bird for another day and rang the station master in Norfolk where it had come from. He could not help, so, in accordance with GWR regulations, Mr. Pocock sold the bird to a poultry dealer.

The following morning, he recalled, "two Yanks" came for the bird, which it transpired was the company mascot and called Donald Duck. When Mr. Pocock told them it was probably already "in the pot", one of them "danced round the office, waving his arms and shouting". Luckily, he contacted the dealer in time and got it back for them!

Throughout Reg Pocock's reign, the line was run using '2021' class 0–6–0 tanks, most of which had been converted to pannier tanks. Classified as power group A, these rugged little engines had been quite adequate for work on the branch, especially in the skilled hands of Harry Humphreys and Geoff Pearson. However, they were built between 1897 and 1905 and by this time were dwindling in numbers as they were displaced by the larger and more powerful (group C) 57XX 0–6–0PTs introduced in 1929.

Officially these were not allowed on the line because they exceeded the axle weight on the underbridges. As mentioned in Chapter Three, the Watlington branch was designated a 'yellow route' whilst the 57XX were only permitted on 'blue routes'.

As there is no evidence of the bridges being strengthened at this time, it would appear that the Locomotive Department obtained special permission from the Engineers Department to use the larger engines on the line, but whether this was prompted by the heavy wartime traffic, which peaked around this time, or simply because one of the regular engines, No. 2078, was condemned, is not known. The RCTS history *The Locomotives of the Great Western Railway* records that in 1950 it was decided to allow the class over yellow routes due to their negligible hammer blow. The Watlington branch might simply have been an earlier instance.

No. 2078 had been used on the line from 1939 to 1944, alternating with 2112 whilst a third member of the class, No. 2055, largely remained at Slough.

With the restriction evidently lifted, Slough were able to send any of their more numerous allocation of 57XXs to Watlington, or one of the three older but equivalent 27XXs stationed there.

The earliest recorded evidence of a 57XX stationed at Watlington was 5783 which was sent there in 1944, followed by

Nos. 5715 and 5737 the same year. No. 2757 was recorded in use on the line in 1945 and 2787 and 2790 in 1946, (see Appendix 9 for more examples).

These larger classes made hauling the goods up Chinnor bank much easier as Harry Humphreys reflected: "When I was thinking about retiring, they gave us a bigger engine — of course they were more powerful, it was child's play then; you see you could take double the load to Chinnor." But 2112 was still

Although this portrait of Reg Pocock appeared in the *GWR Magazine* in 1946, comparison with other photos indicates that it was probably taken before the war. *Cty. Rita Watts*

used for a number of years and by Harry at least, held with some affection — "Good engine, that was".

By the spring of 1945, Montgomery was crushing the last resistance in the lower Rhineland and German defences in the Eifel collapsed, the war was nearing an end and there was reason for optimism. However, a serious accident, which occurred on 15th March, gave Harry Humphreys a nasty shock and more than dampened the spirit of the rest of the branch staff when they heard of the injuries sustained by Tom Bowler, the guard.

Harry Humphreys and Tom Bowler had worked the line together for years, and the 4.20 a.m. goods from Watlington, the first train of the day, was just part of their familiar daily routine, a procedure they had carried out hundreds of times before. That morning there were two wagons to pick up from Aston Rowant, so, when they arrived there, the train was brought to a stand alongside the platform. The engine, 4617, was uncoupled and run into the middle road, then Tom reset the crossover controlled by the ground frame so the engine could run into the dock to pick up the first vehicle. He then walked across to the goods shed and altered the hand points leading into the mileage

siding or 'coal road', and told Harry Humphreys to proceed there while he went back to the ground frame to alter the crossover for the main line.

When the engine entered the coal road, it trailed through the points which were controlled with a weighted or 'Turk's head' lever, which maintained the previous setting for the goods shed. It was very dark and Tom did not notice the points were set for the shed instead of for running back out of the coal road, which they normally were. After coupling No. 4617 to the wagon being collected, he rode on the step of the engine as it left the sidings. Before Tom realized they were heading towards the goods shed, he was struck by the rail post of the loading gauge and the goods shed wall as the engine smashed through the wooden doors of the building. He suffered a fractured pelvis and ribs, and injury to his lungs, wrist, arm and head. It was a dreadful experience for all concerned and not easily forgotten.

According to Tom's son Colin, Harry Humphreys was so shocked that he just froze in the cab whilst fireman George Nicholson rushed off to the station building and smashed the window to reach the phone and summon an ambulance. He then returned to comfort Tom who was taken to the Radcliffe Infirmary, Oxford, by Watlington St. John Ambulance.

The incident ended Tom's railway life, which must have been a bitter blow to suffer on top of the physical injuries. He was never able to use his left arm properly again and had to be content with it in a fixed position away from his body. He received compensation and spent the rest of his life "busying himself on his garden" and doing what jobs he could around his home, 'Glentromie' in Hill Road. As well as being a keen gardener, he also kept pigs, rabbits and chickens.

The whole episode must have had a tremendous effect on the conscientious and steady-going Harry Humphreys who had got on so well with Tom in the ten years or so they had worked together, apparently on the same shift. He felt so bad about what happened that he never went to see Tom afterwards. He probably did not know what to say. George Nicholson often visited Tom at home, but his closest friend from the railway, Charlie Adby from the PW gang, kept in touch with him most, particularly through the difficult years that followed, no doubt keeping him up to date with the goings-on at the station, until Tom died in 1951.

Harry Humphreys was particularly unfortunate in experiencing a more dramatic incident just a few months later in the summer. On 3rd August he was driving 2757 on the 10.22 a.m. from Princes Risborough, again with fireman George Nicholson. He had just climbed Shirburn bank at about 20 mph and was about to pass over Middle Way accommodation level crossing (8m 57ch) just outside the terminus, when a 5cwt Morris milk van appeared from behind a 20ft hedge on the right and ran onto the level crossing directly in front of them, without warning. There was no chance of stopping and the engine struck the vehicle, which was completely wrecked.

The driver, Miss Lilian Rule, suffering from shock and extensive abrasions, was put in the train and taken on into Watlington station, then to the hospital by car, accompanied by Harry Humphreys. She had had a lucky escape. The van (registration No. BGF 496) was owned by F. Simmons of the Swan Dairy, Brook Street. Both the engine and auto trailer 187 sustained damage and were replaced, the trailer suffering smashed steps and damaged vacuum cylinder.

The postwar scene at Watlington, the station now looking more functional than cared for. This picture, taken on 13th June 1947, shows the corrugated asbestos-clad bicycle shed provided for the extra wartime workers and the rebuilt chimney after damage by the American Air Force. During research, we noted an entry in a small register at the Divisional Engineer's Office at Reading dated 17th July 1947 'Watlington repaint of station buildings and signal box'.

J. H. Russell

CHAPTER SIX

ALL CHANGE

THE postwar years are remembered by many, both for the harsh winters and the hardships of rationing. Having kept going throughout the war, even the weekly Saturday market at Watlington could not survive. The upsurge in traffic on the branch, brought about by the war, was soon to fall away to reveal the declining trend that was previously apparent, particularly in the face of increasing road competition and, of course, the spread of the private motor car.

The daily ritual of a regular band of twenty or so travellers walking down Shirburn Street soon after 6.15 p.m. each night on their way home from the station may have been mildly reassuring, but, as far as the vast majority of inhabitants of Watlington were concerned, the buses were more convenient. Princes Risborough's modest High Street paled in comparison

131

The two portraits on these pages were both taken at Slough shed on 13th July 1946 and show Slough shunting engines used on the Watlington branch. No. 2112 was based at Slough from 1928 and is shown here about a month or so after being outshopped from Swindon in GWR green.

F. M. Gates

The larger and more powerful 2757, stationed at Slough from 1938-1947, was recorded on the branch in 1945 and 1946.   *F. M. Gates*

with Oxford and Reading, which had become so conveniently accessible through House Brothers coaches, whilst some Thames Valley buses to High Wycombe took London-bound passengers into the forecourt of Wycombe station and connected with main-line services. It is therefore hardly surprising that branch trains were not crowded.

For a while, workers still travelled to and from the factories in Risborough on the 7.25 a.m. and 5.48 p.m. trains which continued to be strengthened with the spare coach, but the only other notable patronage came from the people of Chinnor, who, on Saturdays, travelled in to Risborough for shopping or the matinee at the cinema. The 12.25 Saturdays Only from Chinnor was easily the busiest of the week and was so crowded that many people had to stand or sit on their companions' laps. An extra coach was eventually found for this one train, as detailed in Volume 2.

Traffic statistics are given in the appendices, but, as an illustration of the postwar decline, the 37,228 passengers booked at Watlington in 1944 fell to 28,740 in 1945, 18,103 in 1946, and 14,924 in 1947, whilst goods tonnage at Watlington fell from 22,595 in 1944 to 12,609 in 1945, 8,313 in 1946, and 7,850 in 1947. Conversely, goods traffic for the cement works increased through this period, presumably reflecting the needs of the country to repair war damage and build new houses.

By its nature, goods traffic varied, but it is interesting to note from an account of a minor derailment on 12th March 1946 that the 5.30 a.m. from Risborough consisted of just five wagons and a van.

It was a time of change, but before we move too far ahead in our story, we ought to mention that the branch train was involved in another sad incident, this time with Arthur Pearson in charge of No. 2757 on the 4.20 a.m. freight from Watlington on Monday, 7th January 1946. Arthur and his fireman, William Galliozzie (from Merthyr), were quite unaware of hitting anyone, but later discovered that while passing through Chinnor in the 'pitch dark' at 4.50 a.m., they had struck 73 year old Mrs. E. J. Willoughby, whose body was discovered 'lying in the 6ft way between the running line and the Watlington end of the goods yard sidings'. She had been missing from her home at Chinnor since the evening of Saturday, the 5th, when police were informed and a search was made, which included the railway line. Lengthman William North found the body when coming on duty at about 7.15 a.m., whilst the first the crew knew of it was when they were stopped and informed by platelayers on approaching Chinnor with the 7.25 a.m. ex Watlington.

Life is essentially a process of continual renewal, and despite the disruption of the war and the turnover of staff in the unsettled aftermath, the Watlington branch kept going. However, Reg Pocock's retirement in 1946 not only marked the end of an era, but was symbolic of the change and sad decline which followed. He had held office at Watlington for 22 years and made the post very much his own, at the same time becoming an established and respected member of the local community.

One of the young evacuees, more familiar with the mainline stations of London than such a rustic outpost, found it rather amusing to witness Reg constantly checking his watch for the arrival of the branch train, especially since it could be heard and seen coming from such a distance. However inclined we might feel to smile, it was Reg's conscientiousness, dedication and pride in office which contributed so much to the whole establishment and its stability. Everyone agrees he was a good man and everyone we've spoken to has had something good to say about him or something to thank him for. Furthermore, as we shall see, things were never the same after his departure.

Harry Humphreys and Geoff Pearson retired soon afterwards and even 2112, the line's most familiar engine, did not have that long to go, but in the meantime Joe Nicholson and George Howlett returned from the army to resume their positions on the railway. At this time the two porters at Watlington were Tom Tunnicliffe and Dick Smith.

After transferring to Kensington Addison Road before the war, Joe had married his Watlington girlfriend at Paddington in April 1940. Sadly he can no longer remember the details of his return, but he was trained as a guard on the branch which somehow displaced Frank Hyde, causing some ill feeling. Frank, who had served as a guard on the line following Jimmy Nelms' retirement in 1941, transferred to Wallingford in September 1946 as leading parcel guard, Joe taking his place.

Aylesbury guard George Newman is said to have stood in for Tom Bowler in 1945 immediately after his tragic accident, followed by relief guard Percy Smith, who lived at Wainhill crossing and presumably remained on the duty until Reg Watkins transferred from Newbury in December 1946.

Whatever the detail, Joe remembers feeling very unsettled after the army – "the rest of the world was out of step", so he did not stay long and left the railway about 1947.

It has not been easy to establish the exact sequence of staff in various posts at this time, particularly firemen, but the combination of recollections and some official records has helped patch together a reasonable picture. For instance, a brief record of a Miss Crocker spraining her ankle when slipping off the bottom step when alighting from auto-trailer 185 at Bledlow Bridge Halt on the 8.0 p.m. ex Risborough on 22nd May 1947 confirms relief guard Percy Smith on the branch again, presumably after Joe Nicholson's departure. Percy subsequently transferred away to take a position as station foreman at Thame. Certainly by December 1947 his place seems to have been taken by Reuben Davis of Bledlow, then Frank Hyde, who transferred back from Wallingford on 17th January 1949 and remained as a guard on the line until closure. Incidentally, at this time the guards were working in shifts of 7.0 a.m.–3.0 p.m. and 3.0 p.m.–11.0 p.m.

When George Howlett came back from the war in 1946, he applied for 'the porter's job' at Aston Rowant, but, as explained in Volume 2, this went to Laurie Johnson. He therefore decided to try for a relief porter's position based at Thame, covering the main line from Northholt Junction to Ardley, and the Watlington, Thame and Aylesbury branches. He continued to live in Chinnor, using the train whenever he could, or cycling to whichever station he was posted to. If the work involved staying overnight he was paid a lodging allowance. There were two relief porters, the other one being Len Howse.

It seems that guards' absences had often been covered by relief signalmen, but by 1948 Mr Rumble, the district inspector at High Wycombe, must have experienced trouble in covering the Watlington branch and asked George and Len to learn the guards' duties. He arranged for them to be passed out for work as relief guards on the Watlington branch only. Apart from learning the rules and procedures concerned, they also had to spend time when they were not needed elsewhere riding with the Watlington guards in order to familiarise themselves with the route and, of course, all of the gradients for braking loose-coupled goods trains. Who they were with depended on the shift concerned, but George Howlett remembers learning a lot from Reg Watkins who, by all accounts, was a good guard.

After Reg Pocock's retirement, the post of station master was only maintained for another three years. There are said to have been a number of short-term stand-ins before a successor, Sid Jarvis, was found, and, starting in November 1946, even he kept his home in Ardley and only for a while lodged in Watlington during the week with the Bowler family in Hill Road.

Sid Jarvis had been a guard at Aylesbury and, according to Bryan Bowler, covered station master's duties at Haddenham, then Ardley, and worked at the booking office at Risborough during the war. He is said to have been a decent enough chap, but evidently no match for Reg Pocock. Chinnor station master Eric Humphrey, who transferred there in October 1947, recalls that Sid did not excel with accounts so Mrs. Jarvis used to help with the books. Mr. Humphrey was also consulted frequently for help and advice for anything from book-keeping to, on one occasion, how to manhandle a 30cwt case which had been unloaded onto the platform without a trolley underneath it.

When Eric Humphrey stood in for him during one holiday, Jarvis asked for help with pages of outstanding amounts on the books, and when he returned Eric had 'squared the lot' for him.

When keen 18 year old Tony Benham arrived to take up a fireman's vacancy at Watlington in March 1947, he brought a fresh youthful enthusiasm and romance to the branch. He was no stranger to the line for it had been his ambition to become a fireman since he had first arrived at Chinnor as an evacuee to live with his aunt and uncle at 41 Station Road.

In 1942 when he first left school, he was employed at Basils grocery shop, then Adnetts, a small timber company handling pine at the side of Siareys yard (see Volume 2). In 1943, when he was 15, he took a job with Chinnor Cement Works, driving a narrow gauge diesel between the quarry face and the works. At lunchtimes he used to meet the Watlington branch crews in the canteen where they usually enjoyed a cup of tea and a sandwich. He was very keen to join the GWR and, being all too aware that there was a need for local men, they encouraged him, particularly Geoff Pearson, who didn't like all the swapping about resulting from the high turnover of firemen, few of whom wanted to remain at Watlington for longer than they had to. He arranged an interview with Mr. Portsmouth, the foreman at Slough, who travelled down with the Chinnor goods to see him. The interview was carried out during the crew's routine visit to the cement works canteen and resulted in Tony being sent to Cardiff for a medical.

As soon as he was 16, he joined the GWR, starting as an engine cleaner at Aylesbury in October 1944, cycling there from Chinnor each day for a 5.30 a.m. start. While he was at Aylesbury he worked with Peter Robinson who he recalls as "about 5ft 8 inches with a stocky figure, a round face and big hooded eyes". Tony found him a "solemn character . . . a good beer drinker" and "a good mate of Geoff Pearson". In December 1945 Tony took a fireman's vacancy at High Wycombe, serving on relief turns which occasionally included Watlington.

After a spell at Aylesbury, from September 1946, the fireman's vacancy he had been waiting for arose at Watlington when, in March 1947, Trevor William Wells (known as 'Taffy') transferred back to Aylesbury after only a month at Watlington.

Tony was fortunate in getting to Watlington while both Harry Humphreys and Geoff Pearson were still there and he even remembers something of Mr. Pocock from his earlier relief

Fireman George Nicholson looking on while 9789 was providing steam to the injector pipes to raise water from the well at Watlington on 13th June 1947. The steam supply was taken from two connections; the 40lb supply from the carriage warming pipe raised water to ground level whilst the steam supply pipe, coupled in place of one of the whistles, carried steam at boiler pressure to drive it up to the pillar tank. *J. H. Russell*

turns. As a young fireman, Tony was full of confidence and even a bit cheeky, and remembers the old drivers being referred to as 'Mutt and Geoff', comic cartoon characters of the day. Nevertheless, he respected them, particularly Harry, and gained more than a flavour of the old GWR establishment and tradition of the interwar years.

Tony worked with Harry for some of the time during the last six weeks of his service (and previously on relief duties), and remembers him as "popular . . . a most respected man with a clean record . . . a very upright character who never swore . . . punctual and extremely conscientious". He never let the fireman drive and would not put up with anything irregular.

The job meant a great deal to Harry, and Tony's memory of his retirement is most poignant. "He patted the engine and said goodbye to it with tears in his eyes."

Harry's successor, Frank Tredwell, transferred from Oxford to start on 21st April 1947.

At this time there were still three firemen working in shifts, 7.0 a.m.–3.0 p.m., 3.0 p.m.–11.0 p.m., and 11.0 p.m.–7.0 a.m. These rotated on a weekly basis with a sequence of 11.0–7.0, 3.0–11.0 and 7.0–3.0, which meant the firemen worked with both drivers and each of them had a long weekend every third week. George Nicholson worked opposite Tony who does not have much recollection of the men who filled the third fireman's duties. According to official records, these were: Colin Bowler, 21st October 1946 to 30th June 1947 (when he left for military service); Lionel Andress, 14th July to 17th November 1947; David Charles, 8th December 1947 to 5th April 1948; William

Beddoe, 5th April 1948 to 19th February 1949 (resigned); Phillip Phillips, 22nd August to 19th September 1949; Colin Bowler, 19th September 1949 (on return from military service) to 23rd January 1950; John ('Sam') Neighbour, 6th February 1950 to 5th April 1951.

George Nicholson became 'temporary driver' in April 1948 and subsequently transferred to Tyseley, his place being taken by John Cummings from 19th September 1948 to 9th January 1950. Some of the gaps evident in this list might have been filled by men not yet traced, but then the official dates cannot always be relied upon; for instance, Frank Tredwell's diary records John Neighbour's departure from Watlington on 21st March instead of 5th April. However, the turnover of men is apparent, and when a third fireman was not available, Tony and George covered the work in two 12-hour shifts, 7.0 a.m.–7.0 p.m. and 7.0 p.m.–7.0 a. m., and they were very glad of the overtime. Furthermore, the early morning goods was no longer being run around this time, so the night duty was easy. He remembers working the 12-hour system for about six months and the gap in the records of any third fireman between 19th February and 22nd August 1949 would tie in with his recollections of the season when he secretly used the engine to get back to Chinnor each night!

When Tony Benham went to live with his aunt and uncle in Chinnor, he could not have imagined how much this was to change his life. He did not just manage to get a job which he wanted, but he just happened to find himself living next door to a particularly attractive young lady – Janet Croxford.

When Slough fireman Doug Quartermaine covered relief turns at Watlington, he stayed at a pub in the High Street. There was no night duty, the early man booking on at 4.30 a.m. Nevertheless, he found it "an eerie place", on dark winter mornings and remembers owls hooting in the trees alongside the station. This beautiful portrait shows 2112 on shed out of steam and abandoned one Sunday in May 1949. It must have been wonderful for the photographer and his wife not only to have stumbled across Watlington station while out for a drive, but to have the whole place and 2112 to themselves to explore without any interference. The engine was not always left there on Sundays; sometimes it was needed for PW trains which were run as far as High Wycombe to pick up men and equipment for work on the main line, or the branch, the Wycombe and Risborough gangs often working together. Firemen George Nicholson and Tony Benham split the overtime between them, one working 12.0 midnight to 6.0 a.m. to prepare the engine, the other 6.0 a.m. to 6.0 p.m. with the train. The engine and brake van left early to get the men to their site of work at 7.0 a.m. Permanent way work varied; it might occur every Sunday for months, then ash loading and coal stocks at Watlington would fall behind and need even more Sunday work. They were always glad of the overtime. The *Railway Observer* reported 2055 and 2112 were stored at Slough during the summer of 1949 but brought into service again in November when 2055 was in use as a stationary boiler and 2112 used for shunting.

J. H. Ahern

Eventually, the two of them fell in love, and just could not be kept apart to the extent that during the summer of 1949, Tony on many occasions secretly sneaked back to Chinnor with the engine during the small hours to spend more time with Janet!

That really did take nerve. As a young fireman, he was not officially authorised to move the engine, let alone drive it along the line single-handed as his personal transport. His action could never be explained away and whatever would Harry Humphreys or Reg Pocock have made of that?

At Chinnor he left the engine under the bridge and banked-up the fire carefully so that it would not blow off while he was absent. This apparently went on for weeks until he was eventually heard by the station master who, living nearby, had a quiet word with him.

Driver Frank Tredwell thinks the early morning goods was first abandoned around the end of 1947, and this is confirmed by an incident which shows the 10.15 p.m. ex Risborough running as a freight rather than just engine and van. Details were as follows:

On 9th March 1948 Pearson and David Gwyn Charles were bringing in the branch goods, which comprised ten wagons and the brake van. The run-round loop could only accommodate eight wagons and the brake, but instead of dividing the train outside the station and running round twice, they ran into the platform as usual and took the engine over the engine release crossover and into the loop. Because the train was too long, the rear vehicles were fouling the loop exit, so the guard, 45-year-old Reuben Davis, released the brakes he had pinned down on the first two wagons, and waited for the train to gravitate down the slight gradient towards the buffer stops. However, although they moved, they only rolled far enough to block the engine release crossover and did not clear the loop exit, so the engine remained trapped.

The guard searched around for the pinch bar or 'truck lever', "but it was very dark and there were no yard lights", so he could not find it. He tried using a brake stick in the wheel but this was unsuccessful, so Pearson suggested they used an iron bar placed between the back of the engine buffer and one of the wagons to give them a push.

Unfortunately, the bar slipped and struck the guard's right hand against the engine framing, then dropped on his right big toe. Pearson got down and helped him across to the ground frame steps where he left him while he phoned for the doctor and transport to Watlington Cottage Hospital. In the meantime, the fireman obtained the ambulance cabinet and helped to dress his hand.

The guard was taken to Watlington Hospital and from there to the Radcliffe Infirmary, Oxford, where he was retained and the top of his fingers amputated. His big toe was also fractured.

According to official records, David Gwyn Charles transferred to Didcot from 5th April, yet once again the date is in question because on 7th April 1948 he was recorded with Frank Tredwell on the footplate of 8750 on the 10.20 ex Risborough.

Incidentally, despite the frequent use of these larger pannier tanks since 1944, it was not until some three years later that GW minutes record £850 being authorised in December 1947 for 're-flooring' a bridge on the Watlington branch at Princes Risborough 'to admit the use of heavier engines'.

Later, on 26th August 1948, the PW cabin at Watlington was destroyed by fire. According to ganger William Kendall, "Driver Tredwell had previously cleared out some rubbish from the loco cabin and store shed and had set fire to it on the piece of ground between the loco and PW cabins just before he left on the 11.30 a.m. ex Watlington to Princes Risborough train. A south-westerly wind, the velocity of approximately 15–20 mph, was blowing at the time".

The fire was first noticed by Mrs. Perry who lived in the large house adjacent to the station. She rang station master Jarvis at 12.20 p.m., who in turn rang the Watlington Fire Brigade, which arrived at 12.30 and remained there until 2.30 p.m.

Frank Tredwell had watched the rubbish "burn almost out" but there must have been some smouldering waste which the wind had caught. Tools, mackintoshes, leggings, coats and other personal effects belonging to the gang were all lost, but the item that caused the most paperwork was a new lady's bicycle which patrolman T. Johnson had only recently purchased for his daughter and which he was using to travel to and from work at the time. He was eventually awarded £10 towards the cost of £11 11s 0d.

With the turnover of firemen and differing arrangements, it has been difficult to be precise about changes, but from the listing on the previous page, it would appear that January 1950 was the last time when there were three firemen based at Watlington.

We have already pieced together a typical day for the loco crew in the 1930s, but at the risk of some repetition, it is interesting to hear what it was like for Tony after the shifts were changed to 4.0 a.m.–11.0 a.m. and 11.0 a.m.–9.0 p.m.

At this time, Tony still lived with his aunt at Chinnor. She would get up and cook him a good breakfast of bacon and eggs at 3.00 a.m. before packing his black tin box with sandwiches and a bottle of cold tea. The box also contained detonators, gauge glasses, soap and towel, and a tea billy. On the engine the cold tea was often warmed on the tray over the firedoor, and, when this had been drunk, he often brewed more, boiling water in the billy can which he covered in thick oil to stop it burning while it was held in the firebox with a pricker.

Tony set out at 3.30 each morning on his bicycle, arriving at Watlington at around 4.0 a.m. One morning he remembers being chased by the local policeman after calling out a very cheeky response to the question "Where's your rear light?" He pedalled furiously and lost the policeman somewhere around Kingston, but was later fined £3 – just a week before his wedding.

On arrival at the station, he would invariably find the engine with about 10–20lb of steam on the clock and the remains of the banked-up fire, which he pushed halfway across the grate and built up with fresh coal. Later, when Tony was married, he got this down to a fine art and didn't get there until about 5.30 a.m. when, instead of leaving the fire to come round on its own, he would speed things up with the blower. If he needed to get the fire going even quicker, he would burn some old sleepers.

While steam was being raised, he would go into the pit beneath the engine to clean the motion and oil up. This is where once again we come across the contrast in the two drivers. He still remembers that Harry Humphreys had always oiled up and inspected the engine himself whereas Geoff Pearson did not turn up for duty until the last minute. He relied upon the fireman checking and oiling everything. From Tony's point of view, the compensation for the extra work and responsibility was a more easy-going time with Geoff and plenty of driving whenever he wanted it. Geoff would slip off home around 11.0

a.m., or 6.0 p.m., and leave young Tony to do all the shunting on his own. He would even visit the pub for a quick drink. On the other hand, Tony could occasionally do the same and leave Geoff to do the shunting.

The pair of them kept snares alongside the line between Middle Way Crossing and the cottages at Shirburn and one of them would go to collect the rabbits they caught (often one or two per day) and reset the traps. This was a long-standing tradition but particularly welcome during the longs years of rationing, and, if the rabbits were not needed at home, they were swapped with friends and colleagues for other food.

When he had first started at Watlington, the electric pump had been removed from the well for attention and a temporary steam injector system was in use to lift water from the well to the storage tank. The engine was connected to the pump by means of two steam pipes, one to the carriage-warming pipe and the other in place of one of the whistles, as described in Volume 2. This was "a lousy job" as the pump was difficult to start and it was not easy to tell if it was working properly. In the daylight it was at least possible to see steam pouring out of the pillar tank, but, to establish whether it was actually raising water, it was necessary to climb up the ladder and open the door in the conical tank cover to look inside. When it was dark, this was done with a flare lamp. It was a tremendous relief when the electric pump was back from overhaul later that year.

When Tony had been on the night shift, 11 p.m.–7 a.m., this job was done in the middle of the night, when the engine was also coaled either from the wagon or the coal stage. He would also get the cleaning and oiling out of the way early on, so that he could lock himself in the mess (the old grounded horsebox body) and enjoy a good sleep.

The early-turn porter usually arrived round 7.0 a.m. At this time it was Dick Smith or Tom Tunnicliffe, who would unlock the station and operate the ground frame to let the engine onto the train. In the winter, the porter also lit the fires in the station and goods shed offices so that they were warming while they put the engine onto the train.

In Geoff's absence, Tony used to move the engine off shed and over to the pillar tank to take water before putting it onto the auto-trailer which was left ready in the platform. In winter months the steam heating was turned on to warm the coach ready for the passengers.

With everything ready, Tony and either Tom or Dick would sit down in the station master's office for a cup of tea and wait for the passengers to arrive for the 7.25 a.m. The guard, either Frank Hyde or Reg Watkins, depending on shifts, arrived about 7.15, but driver Pearson cut it fine – sometimes even to the whistle! Tony recalls one occasion when Geoff overslept, and so he drove the first train to Risborough and back with Tom Tunnicliffe as his fireman! Needless to say, this was all very unofficial and Geoff, who was waiting when they got back, was grateful.

Guard Reg Watkins did everything as quickly as possible so that he could enjoy tea in the van or a game of cards. He was tall and smart, with swarthy skin, a moustache and had something of a Spanish or Italian appearance. Tony thinks he would have been in his early thirties and was "a bit of a ladies man", with "black, swept-back hair always glistening with Brylcreem". "He never wore a cap". He lodged at the Pineapple, was good at his job and quite popular. Audrey Jarmaine from Kingston Crossing recalls "I was mad after a guard with a pencil slim moustache. He was

posh, and I spent hours going up and down on the train when he was on".

If Reg saw any passengers running for the train, he would wait or go back for them. He was sociable and easy to get on with, he smoked Players and enjoyed gambling, especially on horses, and he would do anything for anybody.

The 7.25 was a workmen's train, typically conveying about 10 from Watlington, 2 from Lewknor, 1 from Aston, 1 from Kingston, 10–15 from Chinnor, 2 from Wainhill and 2–3 from Bledlow.

This train always got to Risborough on time, and on arrival in the bay the engine ran round straight away and returned to Watlington with the trailer, which was usually empty except for station master Jarvis who, at one time, came from Ardley each day.

When it got back to Watlington, the engine simply ran round and left again with the 8.42, which conveyed office workers, "the bowler hat brigade". Up to ten travelled from Watlington each day, none from Lewknor, but, at Aston Rowant, Sir Edward Cadogan joined the train. As he was a director of the GWR, as far as the staff were concerned everything had to be "just so". One passenger usually joined the train at Kingston, ten at Chinnor and another two at Wainhill, which was regarded as well-to-do because of the large houses. There was not usually anyone from Bledlow for this train. At Risborough they nearly all crossed the footbridge to catch the 9.18 to Paddington, which was apparently one of the best trains of the day, giving the shortest journey time from Watlington to London.

The timetable provided for a coal train to Chinnor at 9.20 a.m., but Tony thinks this was only required about once every couple of months or so. Frank Tredwell remembers that if they were required to run it, they were informed on their arrival at Risborough with the first train, so they could bring the brake van out from Watlington on the following trip. The 9.20 usually conveyed coal and sometimes gypsum for the cement works, but, because time was tight, the engine went straight back to Risborough with just the brake van, which was left in the down sidings while the 10.22 was run.

Normally the engine ran round the trailer and sat in the bay until 10.22 unless they were required for a shunt at the research laboratories. This layover time was an eagerly awaited opportunity for a break with enough time to make fresh tea and cook breakfast (Tony's second!) on the shovel. If Reg Watkins was guard, they would join him in the van after that meal and enjoy a game of patience, otherwise Tony and Geoff generally stayed in the cab. This break was also a good opportunity to slip off for a haircut. Tony was always clean and smart on the engine and was always washing himself. He had three pairs of overalls which were in constant rotation.

Again, the next train back from Risborough had few, if any, passengers. It generally only conveyed parcels and, on Tuesdays and Thursdays, fish for Tom Snow, who was the step-son of Messum, the Watlington fishmonger. Frank Tredwell remembers that one regular passenger was a solicitor from Aylesbury who had chambers at Watlington (once used by Letts, the Watlington solicitor).

Back at Watlington, there was time to collect the brake van from the yard (this was needed for the Chinnor goods) and go on shed to top up with coal. After the electric pump had been repaired, coal was shovelled straight from the wagon, which was then kept on the end of the shed siding, beyond the pit.

Tony Benham filling the tanks of 2112 at Watlington on 10th September 1949 prior to working the 11.30 a.m. to Risborough. It was during this layover at Watlington that after his retirement Harry Humphreys would call at the station to see them all. Tony recalls seeing "his little smiling face" when he strolled over to the pit. Harry was fit and healthy and was one of those men who could have worked for years past the arbitrary age limit.

E. S. Russell

COUNTRY BRANCH LINE

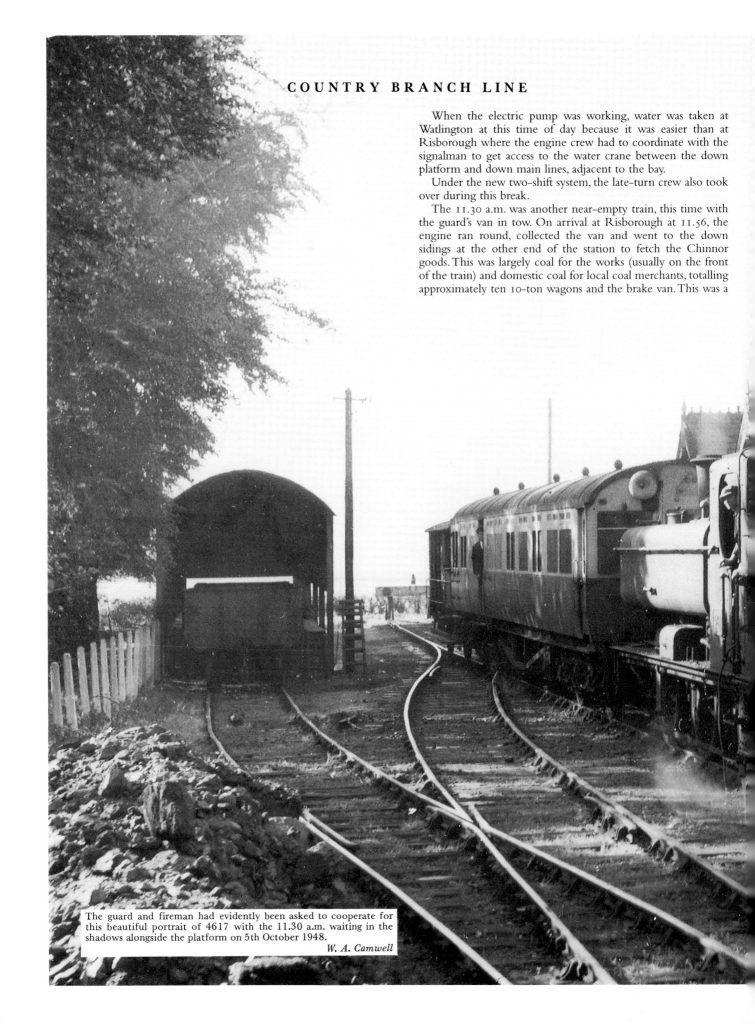

When the electric pump was working, water was taken at Watlington at this time of day because it was easier than at Risborough where the engine crew had to coordinate with the signalman to get access to the water crane between the down platform and down main lines, adjacent to the bay.

Under the new two-shift system, the late-turn crew also took over during this break.

The 11.30 a.m. was another near-empty train, this time with the guard's van in tow. On arrival at Risborough at 11.56, the engine ran round, collected the van and went to the down sidings at the other end of the station to fetch the Chinnor goods. This was largely coal for the works (usually on the front of the train) and domestic coal for local coal merchants, totalling approximately ten 10-ton wagons and the brake van. This was a

The guard and fireman had evidently been asked to cooperate for this beautiful portrait of 4617 with the 11.30 a.m. waiting in the shadows alongside the platform on 5th October 1948.

W. A. Camwell

struggle for one of the smaller 2021 class 0–6–0PTs, which was down to a crawl by the top of the bank, whereas the larger 27XX and 57XX engines handled the load much more easily. Tony recalls that leaving Risborough with the Chinnor goods called for a large wedge of fire under the door, both dampers open and the little-and-often technique of firing the engine on the climb. At the top of Wainhill bank one of the dampers was closed to help calm the fire and the injector was turned on to fill the boiler and keep the engine quiet while shunting.

On arrival at Chinnor, the engine ran round its train and shunted the works and yard, to place the new traffic and collect empties. The return train might have 10–15 wagons, including two or three vans loaded with bags of cement for Greenford. When the work had been done, there was usually time for tea and a sandwich in the canteen which, for Tony, was where it all started.

If there was a lot of traffic, loaded vans were collected from Chinnor and taken into Risborough after the last train, but this did not happen often because anything extra could usually be taken with the late goods.

On returning to Risborough, the branch trailer was already occupying the bay, so the wagons were left alongside or behind the station while the engine ran round to the other end via the down main platform. After putting the wagons in the down sidings, the van was retrieved and put into the bay via the engine

release crossover. The engine was then put onto the Watlington end of the trailer, which was subsequently backed onto the van ready for the 1.55 p.m. This was another quiet train, generally carrying the ganger back to Chinnor or Watlington. On the 12-hour duties, this had also been the last trip for the early-turn men. Either way, on arrival back at the terminus, the van was taken over to the yard where they sorted the wagons ready for the evening goods. Any coal wagons that needed placing or removing were dealt with at this time of day.

In season, sugar beet was loaded by Schweirs at the end of the back siding, which was the most convenient place for them, although the whole of the back siding had to be cleared to reach it. It is not entirely clear at this distance in time, but Schweirs

Passengers waiting to board the trailer which is shown being propelled back into the platform ready for the 3.10 p.m. departure. The engine on this occasion was one of the smaller '850' class. When they were sent from Slough, perhaps two or three times a year, the crews were stuck with them for the whole week. Complaints to Slough shed were usually met with "You've only got one coach to pull around — what do you want, a Castle?" This picture also shows the patchy result of washing the trailer clean with a broom and plain water. The ends used to get covered with dirty smoke from the chimney, so, as porter Frank Saunders says, they would wash the ends in the middle of the week "if they got bad", the opposite end being cleaner because the porter could stand on the front of the engine to do it. *Lens of Sutton*

might well have been the last farmer to have been sending beet away by rail.

The 3.10 to Risborough may have had the occasional passenger and one or two from Chinnor, but it was otherwise quiet. It arrived at 3.36 and at 4.12 the Watlington engine and trailer worked out to Thame to collect children from King Alfred Grammar School. The branch train arrived at Thame at 4.27 and left again at 4.45.

The 5.48 was mainly used by the workers who had travelled out on the first train, whereas the 7.15 from Watlington was another quiet run, but then, as Frank Tredwell said, "Who would want to go to Princes Risborough at that time of night?" After arrival at 7.41 and running round, the train was often left in the bay while Geoff and his fireman had a quick pint with Bill Allaway, the landlord of the Railway Tavern opposite the station.

The 8.0 p.m., the last passenger train, conveyed the businessmen back home, some being dropped off at the various halts on the way. After getting back to Watlington at 8.26 p.m., time was their own for the train crew. They could run the goods train to suit themselves, which was usually as quickly as possible so they could finish and get off home. Everything was off to a fine art. They put the trailer out of the way in the carriage shed to free the run-round ready for their return, then they ran into the yard to collect the train which they had left ready to draw out of the back siding.

The trip to Risborough was 'smart', calling only at Chinnor if required to collect any empties or vans of cement not dealt with earlier by the lunchtime goods. On arrival at Risborough, the train ran into the bay where it was run round and then put in the down sidings, any wagons for the London direction sometimes being run over to the up sidings ready for collection.

Traffic for the branch was collected from the down sidings and the crew set out back to Watlington as soon as they could, regardless of any timetabling. The only call on the way back was at Aston Rowant where there was only the occasional wagon or two of coal to drop off. Any empties waiting there were taken into Watlington where, after running into the platform, the engine ran round and the train was put away unsorted into the back siding. The trailer was then collected from the carriage shed and put into the platform ready for the morning and the engine was taken onto the pit for disposal.

Cleaning the firebox and throwing out the clinker was easy because the fire had been run down on the return journey. Tony always remembered how Harry Humphreys had nursed the engine along on the last trip whereas Geoff Pearson was "a bit heavy on the regulator" and Tony had to allow for that while running the fire down on the way back.

Before leaving the engine, the late-turn fireman filled the bunker from the wagon left at the end of the pit.

On Saturday nights the engine was left without a fire as there were no trains on Sundays. The porters went in on a Sunday morning to clean the auto-trailer in the platform, and Tony and the other fireman also went in sometimes to earn extra money, loading the accumulation of ash and clinker into an empty coal wagon, and/or unloading a 20-ton loco coal wagon onto the stage. They were each allowed four hours overtime for this work.

Each night, the contents of the smokebox, ashpan and clinker from the fire were thrown onto the blue brick paving on the east side of the pit, against the boundary fence, where it was allowed to accumulate until it justified a wagon load. Fireman Colin Bowler said the ash and clinker were piled up alongside the engine "like a volcano". He said it was often hot underneath and

PRINCES RISBOROUGH and WATLINGTON.

(ENGINE AND BRANCH CAR, ONE CLASS ONLY.)

SINGLE LINE. Worked by Train Staff and only one engine in steam at a time, or two coupled together. Form of Staff, Round. Colour, Black.
Passenger Trains to carry "B" Head Code   Freight Trains to carry one Headlamp in centre of buffer plank.

Week Days only.

Down Trains.

Distance.		STATIONS.	Ruling Gradient 1 in	Time Allowances for H, J & K Head Code Freight Trains. (See page 346.)			Freight	Empty Auto.	Freight	Pass-enger.	Freight	Pass-enger.	Pass-enger.	Freight	Pass-enger.	Pass-enger.	Freight
				Point to point times.	Allow for Stop.	Allow for Start.	K	¶	N RR	SX		SO		SO			
M.	C.			Mins.	Mins.	Mins.	a.m.	a.m.	a.m.	a.m.	p.m.	p.m.	p.m.	p.m.	p.m.	p.m.	p.m.
—	—	Princes Risborough ... dep.	—	—	—	1	5 30	7 57	9 20	10 22	12 40	12 50	1 54	3 55	5 48	8 20	10 15
1	52	Bledlow Bridge Halt ... ,,	107 F.	—	—	—				10 27	12 45		1 59	—	5 53	8 25	—
2	75	Wainhill Halt ... ... ,,	68R.	—	—	—				10 30	12 48		2 2	—	5 56	8 28	—
3	57	Chinnor ... ... ,,	68R.	12	1	1	CR		CR	9 30	10 33	12 34	12 51	2 5	4 9	5 59	8 31	—
5	17	Kingston Crossing Halt ... ,,	61 R.	—	—	—	Q			10 37	12 55		2 9	—	6 3	8 35	—
6	16	Aston Rowant ... ... ,,	116 R.	8	1	1	6 35		CR	10 40	12 58		2 12	—	6 6	8 38	CR
7	4	Lewknor Bridge Halt ... ,,	117 F.	—	—	—				10 43	1 1		2 15	—	6 9	8 41	—
8	75	Watlington ... ... arr.	78 F.	8	1	1	6 45	8 20		10 48	1 6		2 20	—	6 14	8 46	10 45

¶—May convey passengers from Princes Risborough when required.   K—Suspended.   N—Will run as "light engine" if required.   Q Aston Rowant arrive 5.52 a.m.

Up Trains.

STATIONS.	Ruling Gradient 1 in	Time Allowances for H, J & K Head Code Freight Trains. (See page 346.)			Freight	Pass-enger.	Pass-enger.	Engine and Van.	Pass-enger.	Freight	Pass-enger.	Pass-enger.	Freight	Pass-enger.	Freight
		Point to point times.	Allow for Stop.	Allow for Start.	K			V RR		SX		SO		SO	
		Mins.	Mins.	Mins.	a.m.	a.m.	a.m.	a.m.	a.m.	p.m.	p.m.	p.m.	p.m.	p.m.	p.m.
Watlington ... ... dep.	—	—	—	1	4 20	7 25	8 42		11 30		1 15	3 10		7 15	9 0
Lewknor Bridge Halt ... ,,	78 R.	—	—	—		7 30	8 47		11 35		1 20	3 15		7 20	Z
Aston Rowant ... ... ,,	117 R.	8	1	1		7 33	8 52		11 38		1 23	3 18		7 23	9 25
Kingston Crossing Halt ... ,,	116 F.	—	—	—		7 36	8 55		11 41		1 26	3 21		7 26	—
Chinnor ... ... ,,	61 F.	8	1	1	CR	7 40	9 0	10† 0	11 45	1 18	1 30	3 25	4 55	7 30	CR
Wainhill Halt ... ... ,,	68 F.	—	—	—		7 43	9 3		11 48		1 33	3 28		7 33	—
Bledlow Bridge Halt ... ,,	68 F.	—	—	—		7 46	9 6		11 51		1 36	3 31		7 36	—
Princes Risborough ... arr.	107 R.	10	1	—	4 48	7 51	9 11	10†15	11 56	1 30	1 41	3 36	5 5	7 41	9 45

K—Suspended.   V—Will run as "light engine" if required.   Z—Aston Rowant arrive 9.10 p.m.

Taken from Service Timetable 25th September 1950.

The photos on these two pages show Slough shed, which was responsible for providing an engine to be outstationed at Watlington each week. This view, taken c.1947, shows the south end of the shed with some of Slough's allocation of pannier tanks used for shunting the yards. The one in the foreground, No. 5715, was often used on the Watlington branch. Locos arriving on shed for disposal were taken to the coal stage at the opposite end of the shed where the fires were dropped and coal and water were taken. However, during the war, 'the Smokebox' Road, on the outside of the shed, was provided with the shelter apparent above the cab roof of 5715, so that fires could be dropped there without attracting attention during air raids. Slough fireman Ron Grantham recalls 'the Smokebox' had a pit "shallower than those in the shed . . . but we only used the covered area for a short time while the heavy air raids were on". The shed was used to its fullest capacity when locos and men were temporarily transferred from Old Oak during inner London air raids. "Like so many sheds, Slough was always a dingy place, especially when it was gaslit. In the war they blackened the skylights and windows with black paint, but they really needn't have bothered because they were already sooted up!", After disposal, locos were stabled in order of going off shed for their various duties. The earliest was positioned at the north end of 'the smokebox' which, in this photograph, was occupied by 61XX class 2—6—2Ts. The other engines were put in sequence behind it and when that line was full, they were similarly put in order along the adjacent No. 1 Road through the shed, then No. 2 Road, occupied by the row of pannier tanks, was reserved for repairs whilst No. 4 Road, off the right of the picture, was left clear to provide access to the others.

R. K. Blencowe

he thought that had led to the horse-box body catching fire (see Volume 2).

Because the engine was cold, the early-turn fireman went in early on Mondays as extra time was needed to raise steam. Also the engines were changed on Mondays at Princes Risborough, where, after arriving with the first train, the Watlington crew uncoupled and as usual left the bay platform via the engine release crossover. The Slough men, who had brought the fresh engine, then drove it out of the down sidings, where they had been waiting, and put it onto the branch trailer. The fresh engine had been given a boiler washout at Slough and arrived with a

week's supply of stores which included oil in a 5-gallon drum with handles and a coned neck.

The engines were looked after by the fitting staff at Slough shed, and every Tuesday Mr. Portsmouth, the shed foreman, travelled out to Watlington to keep in touch with the men and see all was well. His 'afternoon out' was timed to catch the 1.55 p.m. from Risborough and, wearing the traditional dark 'mac' or suit and black bowler hat associated with his office (or an inspector), he usually rode with the crew on the engine, but sometimes on the cushions. The cab was generally clean for the crew's own pride and comfort, but, on Tuesday afternoons, the

The south end of the shed on 18th June 1952, showing (from left to right) 'the Smokebox' Road, No. 1 Road, No. 2 Road (known as the Dock Road, which terminated inside), and Nos. 3 and 4 Roads. The small brick building on the right housed the lavatories, the shed master, shed foreman and clerks sharing the privilege of a cleaner one which was kept locked at this end of the building. When women cleaners were employed during the war, they were provided with their own lavatory and mess room against the shed and cut into the bank alongside No. 4 Road.
National Railway Museum

Watlington branch engines were returned to Slough each week for a boiler washout and any attention necessary from the fitters. The pannier tank receiving attention on No. 2 Road from Ted Wisdom, one of many shunting engines, might well have been despatched for service on the branch but it has not been identified. During the day, No. 1 Road was used for boiler washouts. The shed doors were normally left open, except the ones at the south end of No. 1 Road which the boiler washers closed for their own comfort.
National Railway Museum

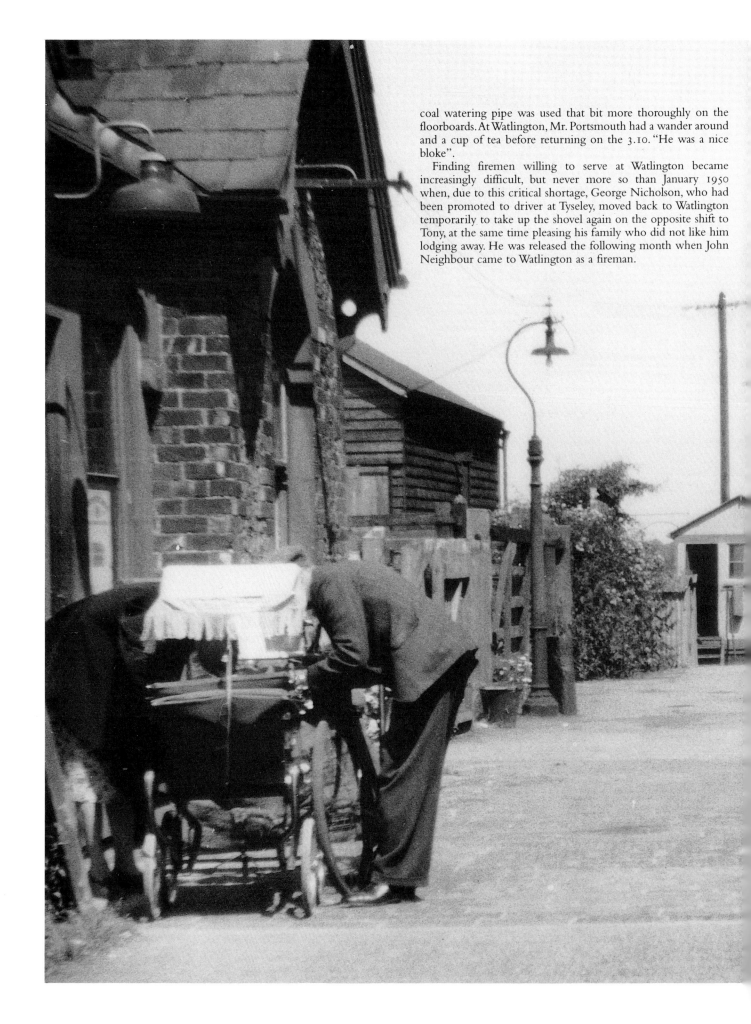

coal watering pipe was used that bit more thoroughly on the floorboards. At Watlington, Mr. Portsmouth had a wander around and a cup of tea before returning on the 3.10. "He was a nice bloke".

Finding firemen willing to serve at Watlington became increasingly difficult, but never more so than January 1950 when, due to this critical shortage, George Nicholson, who had been promoted to driver at Tyseley, moved back to Watlington temporarily to take up the shovel again on the opposite shift to Tony, at the same time pleasing his family who did not like him lodging away. He was released the following month when John Neighbour came to Watlington as a fireman.

Sadly, by this time, Geoff Pearson's eyesight was deteriorating and, according to his daughter Betty, his career as a driver was brought to an end when he was reported for wearing glasses on the footplate. When he was transferred to Oxford, presumably for shed duties, in April 1950, George Nicholson transferred back from Tyseley again, this time as a driver.

Shortly before this, two brand new pannier tanks, built in January and February 1950, were sent to Slough, the *Railway Observer* for April 1950 noting that 74XX pannier tanks Nos. 7441 and 7442 had 'taken over from 2112' on the Watlington branch. The 74XX class, introduced in 1936, had not been used

No. 7442, one of the 74XX panniers sent new to Slough, perhaps specifically with the Watlington branch in mind. This picture shows the engine as it had just finished backing out of the platform in order to run round 'the car'. Porter Tom Tunnicliffe can also be seen beyond the platform on his way to uncouple. *Lens of Sutton*

This picture shows 7442 in the bay at Risborough in 1951. Although the engine had already run round the trailer and backed it up to the buffer stops, the crew had yet to transfer the headlamp from the back of the engine.   *Lens of Sutton*

on the line before and, for that matter, did not remain for long. Fireman John Neighbour was not impressed with these new engines which were "not as good as 2112", but, in contrast, Tony Benham had little affection for 2112, not least because "you couldn't move on there". He liked the larger cab of the new engines which were "good steamers". "Everything was better".

Around this time, the branch was put under the control of the Chinnor station master, Eric Humphrey, the station master's position at Watlington being dispensed with and a clerk, Bob Williamson, put in charge.

Eric Humphrey went to Watlington every afternoon to sort out any problems and take over from the clerk, who went home on the 3.10. Eric travelled out on the 2.5 p.m., from Chinnor and stayed to book the last train, the 7.15 p.m. on which he returned. He particularly recalls one fine Thursday afternoon when he was taking the wages to Aston Rowant and Watlington on the 2.5 p.m., hauled by the familiar 2112 which, freshly painted and overhauled, and driven by Frank Tredwell, suffered a broken con rod running down Shirburn bank. According to the fireman, John Neighbour, the engine nearly derailed. The train was stranded and Eric remembers escorting the passengers along the track, with the fireman, who apparently carried a suitcase belonging to an attractive girl (it was heavier than he expected!). Eric's main concern was hiding the wages he was carrying. The details are not recalled, but a bus was substituted for the 3.10 ex Watlington, and by the end of the day a fresh engine from Slough had taken over. Although we have no date for this incident, the record card for 2112 shows the engine returned to service after a heavy intermediate overhaul at Derby on 24th February 1950 when it had been in BR black livery. As the engine was stopped on 19th May, it seems likely the incident took place on 18th May.

Tony Benham's girlfriend Janet worked in Risborough and had occasionally travelled with Tony and Geoff Pearson on the engine, so the staff, and no doubt many of the locals, were well aware of their romance. Few would have been surprised when they announced their marriage, but after Tony had booked 12 days leave, the railway could not find anyone to stand in for him.

No. 7442 with the 5.48 p.m. from Risborough near Middle Way Crossing between Shirburn and Watlington on Thursday, 21st June 1951. Earlier that afternoon, travelling in his 1932 Austin Seven, the photographer had already taken pictures on the Woodstock branch, then one of this train at Bledlow Bridge Halt, and went on to Wallingford afterwards.   *R. H. G. Simpson*

The shortage of firemen was, of course, aggravated by the call-up of young men for national service. When the threat of the train service being suspended came to light, Eric Humphrey says he was besieged by the national press for three days. "I did nothing but answer the telephone."

The papers had a wonderful time with the story, apparently beginning in, of all places, the *Manchester Guardian* on 9th March 1951.

Fireman's Honeymoon

Train services between Princes Risborough, Buckinghamshire, and Watlington, Oxfordshire, have been suspended until March 17, because railway fireman A. V. Benham, of Chinnor, has been granted twelve days' leave to get married. The wedding takes place at Chinnor

It was not often that there were two trailers at Watlington but these views taken on Saturday, 23rd June 1951, show 7442 with what is believed to have been the stock for the unusually well patronised 12.25 ex-Chinnor. The purpose of the move into the spare road is not known but it was probably to deliver (or collect) what appears to have been a horse-box.

Collection R. S. Carpenter

on Saturday, and there is no one to carry on his job as fireman, his relief having been called up.

Four trains run daily, with five on Saturdays, from Princes Risborough to Watlington, and five daily, with six on Saturdays, in the reverse direction, and they all stopped running on Monday. Passengers are being carried from the stations at the normal train times by buses.

and in the *Evening News:*

The Line of Romance is Open Again

Shy sunbeams danced on the bright metalled track of the Watlington to Princes Risborough branch line today. Birds sang in the neighbouring Chiltern Hills. The railway of romance was open again.

Love, which it is well known makes the world go round, stopped the trains for three days this week. One of the two firemen working the 'Watlington Flier' had been granted leave to get married – and there was no relief available.

Neither 23-year-old Tony Benham of Chinnor, Oxon, the affianced fireman, nor Janet Croxford, aged 19, his pretty next-door neighbour, wanted their wedding to stop the trains.

Young Man's Fancy

And, of course, it did not for long. Romance, or the memory of it stepped in again: George Nicholson, once a fireman on the line, came home unexpectedly and volunteered for his old job.

Clattering through the sunlit fields today George thought of the day, eight years ago, when his young man's fancy turned to thoughts of love.

From his cab window he saw a girl crossing the fields on her way to a bus stop. They exchanged waves – and married.

Only Cupid can tell whether George was as shy a swain as Tony: He made his first date four years ago through the agency of a porter.

Wolf-whistles

One of the happiest men on the line today was driver Frank Tredwell of 'The Flier', a strong believer in railway romance. He met his wife to a background of wolf-whistles from trains when she was a passenger guard at Reading.

At each of the seven wayside halts on the nine-mile stretch connecting the two counties there was a welcome for the flier and a wave for Frank and George, who know what it feels like when you get the go-ahead signal in the spring.

Foot (plate) note: Eighty years ago, Janet's great grandfather helped to lay the line of love which her romance threatened to stop for a fortnight.

and the *Daily Mirror* on 8th March.

Driver George Restarts Train Stopped by a Honeymoon

The Railway Executive has found George. As soon as horrified high officials found romance had entered the life of the little train that runs from Watlington, Oxon, to Princes Risborough, and that it wouldn't run for a fortnight because the fireman was taking time off for his honeymoon, they decided that only one man could solve the situation.

He was George Nicholson, who for seven years stoked the Watlington Flyer on its rustic route.

They knew George had been promoted to drive a shunting engine at Tyseley, Birmingham, and they started to phone. All the weekend they phoned. But it was George's off-duty time.

He'd Been There

Despite the conferences and the searching, Monday came and the Watlington Flyer stood silent in its shed. And for the first time anyone could remember, the folk of Watlington had to go by bus to Princes Risborough.

Then on Monday night George arrived back at Tyseley, ready to spend a noisy night shunting. "George", they cried, "where have you been?" Innocently George replied: "I've been home at Watlington."

Then they told him how Cupid had jammed the throttle.

"George", they said, "we know you're a driver, but would you please be a fireman on the Watlington train, just for a fortnight?"

'I'm Fond of It'

Last night George told me happily: "I jumped at the chance. For seven years I fired this train. It's just one coach and a little engine, but I'm fond of it."

George, born in the sooty shadows of Paddington Station, hated the day when the railway sent him into the country and put him on the Watlington train. But he married a local girl.

"Now I think it's the best service of the lot", he said.

This morning, the 7.25 for Princes Risborough will pull out of Watlington Station again.

Tony and Janet Benham.

Tony and Janet Benham enjoyed a very happy life together and Tony still looks back on it all with a sparkle in his eyes. When first married, they lived in a flat in Risborough, then a cottage in Duck Square, Chinnor, a property owned by Janet's grandfather, Walter Hopkins. Tony, borrowing a sty at first, kept about four breeding sows at the cottage, feeding them before he went to work each day. He later built a sty using railway sleepers which staff were allowed to buy (ten a year) at 6d each. During the rationing, pigs fetched somewhere between £20 and £30 each, so it was a worthwhile sideline.

Before leaving this chapter, we should perhaps mention some of the special trains still being organised for Sundays during the postwar years. These were mostly run from Watlington to the coast but the incoming Bluebell and Rambler specials featured in the list were not on the same scale as their predecessors. The branch trailer was apparently quite adequate to collect passengers from Risborough while others in the main-line train went on to other destinations.

And happy thirty-three-year-old Cockney accented George will give that tug on the whistle which will let the folk of little Watlington know the five-trains-a-day service is running again.

George will be happy firing the Flyer – for his name is on the waiting list to be its regular driver – and there will be peace in the Railway Executive office.

It is very clear from interviews with George and accounts of him that he really did love the line, so it is not surprising that when he was asked to return to Watlington again and stand in as fireman to cover Tony's absence, he agreed – it was that sort of line.

According to official records, he started there on 7th March and saved the situation, but it was a close thing because John Neighbour, the other fireman, was called up for National Service that April. Tony and Janet got married at Chinnor on Saturday 10th March 1951 in the middle of Tony's two weeks leave and the crew of the Chinnor goods that day, Geoff Pearson, George Nicholson and Reg Watkins, abandoned the train during a layover at Chinnor to call in at the reception.

5/6/49	Brighton	25/6/50	Southend
3/7/49	Southend	16/7/50	Eastbourne
10/7/49	Bluebells	30/7/50	Ramblers
28/5/50	Southend	17/9/50	Worthing

The usual procedure for the excursions to the seaside was for the branch train to leave at some time around 7.30–8.0 a.m. to connect with the main line special at Princes Risborough. Afterwards the engine and trailer returned to Watlington, where they remained, running out to Risborough again in the evening to meet the return train.

Frank Tredwell's wife and mother-in-law sometimes went on these excursions, especially to the south coast, and occasionally, after working the empty trailer back to Watlington, Frank would get on his motorbike and ride to the coast to meet them, returning again in time to work the return train in the evening!

These excursions were not that well supported from Watlington. Sometimes there were only half a dozen passengers, so it is hardly surprising that there is no trace of any more specials after 1950.

No. 9789 and auto-trailer 190 near Bledlow on 15th March 1952. *J. F. Russell Smith*

CHAPTER SEVEN

THE 7.25 A.M. FROM WATLINGTON

ALTHOUGH individual stations along the branch are examined in Volume 2, it would be as well to look at the route as a whole by joining Geoff Pearson and Tony Benham on the footplate of 2112 on the first train of the day in the summer of 1948, the 7.25 workmen's. By this time, without the aircraft factories, the number of workers travelling to Risborough had fallen to pre-war levels, so there was no longer any need for an additional coach to supplement the accommodation of the single auto-trailer.

About a quarter of an hour before departure, much of the platform at Watlington was still in shade, largely deprived of the soft rays of early sun by the foliage of the narrow spinney planted along the eastern boundary, and the carriage shed, the auto-trailer alongside the platform further blocking many of the stray shafts of light. In contrast, the fields to the south, the approach road, forecourt and back siding positively basked in the kind light and mild warmth that often precedes a really hot day.

Tony had been on duty since soon after 4.0 a.m. and had now finished cleaning and preparing the engine, filled the tanks, put it onto the train and carried out a vacuum brake test with the guard, Reg Watkins. Now everything was quiet, with only the gentlest sound of the blower, just cracked open to draw the fire, breathing life into the thin grey smoke drifting from the chimney.

M. E. J. Deane

Looking south towards the terminus from Middle Way accommodation crossing in 1941 and showing the Watlington fixed distant signal.
Ganger Charlie Adby referred to this crossing as Beechwood Crossing.   *J. H. Venn*

Having worked hard on his own to get the engine ready, Tony now had chance to stop and lean against the platform fence. In this idle moment he gradually became more aware of his surroundings, and found himself enjoying the birdsong which had passed almost unnoticed throughout his solitary duty. He watched the few workers for Risborough randomly appear as they made their way from the bike shed to the waiting room for a ticket, then cross the platform and step into the freshly swept-out carriage.

In the distance, the occasional call of a pheasant on the Earl of Macclesfield's estate echoed across the landscape, and all the while Tony breathed the fresh morning air, now and then seasoned by the faintest trace of that characteristic but fleeting scent which results from the combination of burning coal, steam and hot oil.

When Geoff finally arrived, Tony would precede him into the cab as there was not much room to pass one another inside,

especially when Geoff moved the reversing lever into back gear. In fact, the area was so confined that there was even a cut-out in the bunker to accommodate the handle of the lever in that position.

At just past 7.25, with the tip from the guard, Geoff gave a tug on the whistle chain and opened the regulator for a reasonably brisk start, the engine barking away from the platform on the 1 in 333 gradient out of the station, and into the sun — "It was a fair old climb out of Watlington". About 400 yards past the neck of the yard, the line began to fall, so when he had built up sufficient speed, Geoff shut the regulator and the train drifted past the fixed distant signal and over Middle Way accommodation crossing (8 miles 57 chains).

Tony and Geoff kept snares along the low grass banks either side of the line along this stretch, but there was no time to think about that now. The engine was beginning to get a move on, and, with a grey haze drifting out of the chimney and the

Looking in the opposite direction from Middle Way Crossing, towards Shirburn, again in 1941. The very low cutting side on the left gave way to an equally shallow embankment beyond the rarely used occupation crossing which is just discernible in the middle distance and featured overleaf. Tony Benham said the farm crossings were quiet — "It was rare to see anyone". The line from here to Lewknor passed through some of the simplest yet most beautiful countryside, and this stretch is easily one of the most romantic in the summer evening sun.

J. H. Venn

freshly-filled vacuum pump spitting loudly as the crossheads slid backwards and forwards deep inside the frames, they rattled down the 1 in 102 bank and over another occupation crossing by the cluster of brick-built estate cottages at Shirburn.

Mary Read, daughter of the Earl of Macclesfield's head gamekeeper, lived at Shirburn for most of her life. She says they always knew when a train was approaching "because the crockery used to rattle on the mantelpiece". As a youngster, she used to play on the line here with her friends. They used to see how far they could walk, balancing on the shiny rail tops and felt quite safe because they knew the timetable and "the trains always ran to time"! She also used to collect lumps of coal which the train crews had used as missiles in their attempts to poach pheasants.

Although there was no halt, trains nevertheless occasionally stopped here to oblige the locals. The 1937 working timetable even included the footnote '8.40 a.m. Watlington stops at Shirburn Farm Occupation Crossing (near 8 m.p.) when required to pick up passengers, and the 3.55 p.m. Princes Risborough when required to set down'. However, this did not last for long and in subsequent years crews who stopped trains here did so unofficially and at the risk of getting into trouble for it. Even so, Michael Webb of Shirburn recalled that during the war he had no trouble in getting drivers to drop him off at the end of Blenheim Road whenever he had a 48-hour leave, and, as mentioned elsewhere, former branch fireman Peter Robinson was regularly picked up and dropped off here.

The line climbed away from Shirburn at 1 in 78 so Geoff opened the regulator again to maintain speed across the grazing

No. 9653 climbing Shirburn bank on 30th September 1948 with the 1.55 from Risborough which conveyed the goods brake back to the terminus. This is another of the few photographs to show the head-lamp carried in the correct position to denote a stopping passenger train. Down trains climbing Shirburn bank could be heard on the approach to Watlington, which was rapid if Geoff Pearson was driving. Tony Benham said Geoff was always eager to get off on his tradesman's bike, leaving Tony to run round, take water, etc. This view also shows the backs of the houses along Mafeking Road. Peter Robinson lived in the one nearest to the line and his children waved from the garden. It is just possible to discern Shirburn Farm occupation crossing in the bottom of the dipped track.   *M. F. Yarwood*

pastures of Field Farm, the shadows of exhaust steam reaching out across the fields to the west and drifting far beyond the shorter, more crisp image of the engine and trailer flickering along the lineside in view of both passengers and crew. In the distance, the occasional car or van could be seen speeding along the B4009 which, skirting the hidden grounds of Shirburn Castle, was paralleled by the branch nearly all the way to Risborough. The road was about a quarter of a mile away from the branch along here.

As explained in the history, the line was virtually laid directly across the fields, along the foot of the Chilterns in this quiet corner of Oxfordshire. There is nothing spectacular to seek out, no dramatic or obvious topographical features of the kind that lure travellers to the Lake District or Scotland. Here there is just simple, but no less precious, gentle farmland stretching for miles, patterned with hedges and trees and narrow lanes, each beckoning those who feel the call of this ancient landscape from which many a heart can find no release.

Geoff shut off steam as they neared Lewknor, where, after curving to the right through a shallow cutting, the barely

It has not been easy to find photographs of the line between Lewknor and Watlington so we were particularly pleased to discover this pair of a Risborough-bound train passing Field Farm Crossing in 1953. At this time, Farmer Graham was the tenant of Field Farm, his son-in-law George Suckling taking the pictures while the family were out walking. "The crews always waved." Notice the absence of any lamp on the engine again. The row of trees in the background of the left-hand view is believed to have been known as 'Fairny Belt'.

significant Lewknor Bridge Halt (6m 75c) came into view, and the engine was brought to rest on the road bridge immediately beyond the tiny rail–level platform.

To save time recreating vacuum when pulling away, Tony wound the handbrake on gently to prevent the train from moving, while the guard used the lever to swing the steps out for the two workers waiting to board. Geoff looked down towards the village from his side of the engine — "you could see anybody coming up that road". Tony shovelled a little more coal on the fire, taking care not to catch his knuckles on the corners of the tall sandboxes so inconveniently mounted against the front of the bunker either side of the coal hole, then looked out of the

Another picture showing the switchback nature of the line, this time looking north from Lewknor Bridge Halt towards Aston Rowant. The line disappeared into a cutting on the other side of the brow.

M. J. Esau

A postcard view of Lewknor.

Edwards garage/post office alongside the B4009 at Lewknor. Edwards also kept hire cars.

The only known view of the cutting south of the bridge carrying the A40 over the line at Aston Rowant.   *G. D. Parkes*

cab for the guard's 'right away', which he relayed to Geoff, releasing the handbrake as they started away.

The regulator was only kept open for a short distance, the train running freely the rest of the way over the undulating trackbed to Aston Rowant, with more grey smoke drifting back over the trailer. The little village of Lewknor could be seen below the line, on the driver's side, the sun already warming the red tiled roofs. The brick and flint dwellings of the little community were entirely typical of this Chilterns countryside. For hundreds of years, the nodules of flint, which occur naturally in the surrounding chalkland, had almost exclusively provided the building material in the area. The flint, of ideal size and shape, and valued above all for its easy availability, was used in combination with red-brick quoins and reveals. This style, seen in classic form at the station buildings on the branch, was, every bit as characteristic of the area as millstone grit in the West Riding or timber framing in East Anglia.

The view from Tony's side of the cab was quite different. Looking into the light, he could see the beechwoods in shadow on the slopes of Beacon Hill.

As the village receded, both views were soon interrupted by the sides of the cutting taking the line down the 1 in 335 gradient to pass beneath the plate girder bridge carrying the busy A40 over the branch.

The line emerged through a shallow cutting into the quiet little station serving Aston Rowant (6m 7c), the familiar figure of Charlie Hopkins already out on the platform with the one

The view from the other side of the bridge, with Aston Rowant station nestling in tranquil surroundings.   *J. N. Faulkner*

regular passenger for this train. The drivers had their own stop marks, so that when they pulled up, the central door of the trailer would be somewhere near the station building. At Aston Rowant the engine was brought to a stand alongside the station nameboard.

The station here was one of the prettiest to be found anywhere, and well groomed because the two staff had little else to do besides look after the gardens. The most noticeable adornment was the climbing roses which around the station

building produced a mass of white and yellow blooms, and pink flowers around the nameboard. Tony particularly recalls the flower beds from which he used to cut white 'pinks' for Janet.

From behind the station, the village could only just be seen in the distance, some half a mile away across the sun-drenched fields, on the far side of the B4009, whilst in the opposite direction the platform overlooked a once well-kept grass bank, a short distance above which a row of mature horse-chestnuts and sycamores screened the railway from the ancient Icknield Way.

With the platform on his side, Geoff would take the 'right away' from the guard, pulling away quite vigorously up the 1 in

This view from the platform looking back towards Watlington, on 16th August 1955, clearly shows how the line dipped through the cutting to provide sufficient headroom for the road bridge which was built in place of the originally intended level crossing.

J. N. Faulkner

No. 2112 pulling away from Aston Rowant on its way to Risborough on 23rd July 1951. The trees and hedges on the horizon lined the side of the A40 which can be seen starting to climb at the foot of the formidable Aston Hill. The trees in the left foreground separated the line from the Icknield Way which, from here to the other side of Kingston Crossing, the line closely paralleled.

Collection R. S. Carpenter

282 gradient out of the station, easing off shortly afterwards and letting the train run on the gentle down grade towards Kingston Crossing. While trees flanked the line's eastern boundary, the sunlight flickered on Tony's side of the cab, but they were soon out in the open and running right alongside and more or less level with the Icknield Way, which was popular with ramblers and horse riders, but not at this time of the day.

Kingston Crossing was under a mile away, and intending passengers could usually hear the train leaving Aston Rowant. As they coasted along this stretch, Tony put some more coal on, and more thin grey smoke trailed behind them.

Lineside fires were nothing new and compensation claims from farmers no doubt kept the railway's legal department busy in many parts of the country. However, one documented incident occurred along this stretch of line on Tuesday, 19th August 1947, when workers from Woodway Farm were out in the fields cutting barley. After Geoff Pearson had passed by with 9789 on the 11.30 a.m. ex Watlington, a fire in a field to the south of the line destroyed 4¼ acres of straw and one third of an acre of growing barley which had been combine-harvested.

The distant signal for Kingston Crossing was usually off, but the crew knew Mrs. Jarmaine had been sent a bell signal from Aston Rowant to advise her of their departure, and in Tony's time took it for granted that, whether the signal was on or off, she would have the gates open for them and be outside the lonely cottage to wave to them.

Looking west towards Kingston Blount from the edge of Grove Wood, with Grove Farm in the middle distance. Kingston Crossing is just hidden behind the group of trees to the right of the farm, although it is just possible to make out the back of the halt nameboard. The dark hedgerow running horizontally across the picture divided the single line track from the Icknield Way which the line closely paralleled from Aston Rowant (left) to Crowell (right).

J. H. Venn

Kingston Blount village. In the late 1930s the house on the right was occupied by Mr. Meeks, dairy farmer. The hedge running off the right-hand edge of the picture bounded the road from Kingston Crossing.

Kingston Crossing Halt, looking towards Chinnor.   *M. J. Esau*

The halt (5m 7c) was on the east side of the line, immediately beyond the level crossing, so it was Tony's responsibility to keep an eye on the platform. There was usually only one passenger for this train and he was soon on board, Reg Watkins giving Tony the 'right away' from the doorway of the trailer and retracting the steps while they were pulling away.

Like Aston Rowant, the villages of Kingston Blount and Crowell lay some half a mile away to the east, the sun highlighting some of the rooftops, which could be seen across the fields from the train.

Again the line climbed from here and veered away from the Icknield Way, which, bordered by hedging, gradually became less distinct in the overall view across to Crowell Hill. After leaving the halt, Tony was busy adding more coal to the fire, which, throughout most of the rest of the day, was kept fairly thin in a saucer-like shape, i.e. thicker around the sides and corners. However, this first trip was different, the speedy journey and quick turnround time at Risborough enabling him to build a thicker wedge-shaped fire, but still thin at the front. He also put one of the injectors on to top-up the boiler. He'd left Watlington "with a full glass" but now it was down to two-thirds, and in any case, the cold water from the tanks would stop the engine blowing off in the platform at Chinnor.

Kingston Crossing Cottage, viewed from alongside the down distant signal, looking south towards Watlington on 16th August 1955. The brick-built PW hut on the left dated from the Second World War when the old sleeper-built huts at Lewknor, Kingston and Bledlow were replaced by Mr. Williams of the Risborough repair gang. Bryan Bowler said that a local landowner complained about the one at Kingston, so the PW Department planted thirty bushes to hide it.

J. N. Faulkner

Looking east towards Crowell Hill, this postcard view shows how the line gradually parted company with the hedge-lined Icknield Way.

On the mile or so to Chinnor, the line again followed the contours of the land, as it did for much of the route, but it was particularly noticeable across the open landscape here. Passengers waiting on the platform at Chinnor could hear the train's progress and even see it for much of the stretch until, in switchback fashion, it almost disappeared into the dip, only coming into view again beyond the end of the yard and running down the bank into the station (3m 48c), where the engine was brought to a stand alongside the station nameboard.

In contrast to the overall impression of unspoiled farmland along the rest of the line, the linear sprawl of the kilns, silos and associated structures of the cement works along the eastern boundary on the final approach to Chinnor, gave a convincing impression of an industrial landscape, quite distracting the eye from the beautiful wooded slopes of Chinnor Hill above the quarry. Likewise the functional improvements to the goods yard opposite, and the adjacent wood yard, changed the whole character of the station, which, judging from the old postcard views on pages 44/5 and 58/9, had presented a rural idyll on a par with Aston Rowant. Now just the station building, platform and garden allotments remained as a picturesque cameo of its past.

Geoff and Tony had made good time, so they now had a few minutes at Chinnor to chat with the station staff. Of course, this was the only station on the branch besides Watlington that produced any worthwhile volume of passenger traffic, so they gave intending passengers every chance to reach the station. Some 10-15 joined the 7.25 while parcels and other passenger-rated traffic were being loaded, and, throughout their wait, the blower sounded up the chimney, keeping the fire bright for the climb ahead.

As the platform was on his side, Geoff watched out for the tip from the guard before sounding the whistle which heralded the train's departure. Incidentally, this was only the second time the

The switchback approach to Chinnor, viewed from the station platform.   *M. J. Esau*

whistle was used on the journey; Tony says it was only really sounded leaving Watlington, Chinnor and Risborough. Geoff took the train briskly out of the platform and down towards the road bridge in order to gain speed for the short climb which followed on the other side.

As soon as they were on the move, Tony sprinkled some more coal around the fire, then put his head out into the fresh air and listened to the sharp bark of the exhaust ricocheting loudly off the sides of the cutting which took the line round the curve and out of Chinnor. It was a reassuring sound and Geoff kept the

Chinnor station, looking towards Risborough with the climb up through the cutting on the other side of the bridge quite evident. This picture was taken on 23rd September 1951.   *R. C. Riley*

A closer view of the Chinnor road bridge (3m 44¼c) which, according to official records, had a 14ft span of wrought iron girders and curved plate decking, supported on brick and flint abutments. The jack arches are just discernible in the shadows.   *Brian Morgan*

regulator open until the other side of Donkey Lane Crossing, where "the two Heybourne girls" usually waved at the train from the garden of one of the two cottages which stood on the left of the track beyond the gates. This was the noisiest part of the journey.

From here the blower was opened again, to hold the flames from licking back into the cab, now that the fire had been roused by the vigorous exhaust up the bank. Some more grey smoke issued from the chimney while the train rattled down the long bank towards Wainhill. Inside the cab the reversing lever, dropped into full back gear, rattled noisily with each revolution of the wheels, and the intrusive vertical coil springs over the rear axleboxes vibrated and flexed over the rail joints as the speed increased until finally checked with the vacuum brake, its single application producing the familiar sound of air rushing through the perforated brass face of the control valve and into the train pipe.

At Wainhill (2m 75c) the gates were normally closed across the road and, in any case, could be seen from a good distance, so Geoff approached without concern and brought the train to a stand with the engine across the road, leaving the trailer steps somewhere near the middle of the platform.

Without the need to open the gates, Mrs. Smith, the crossing keeper, did not always appear, and only had the occasional chat with the crews. The crossing was particularly exposed, with little shade from the hot sun later in the day, circumstances in which it was difficult to imagine the harsh winters experienced here, but, even so, Mrs. Smith needed coal for cooking and heating water, so Tony would drop off a few large lumps onto the side of the track by the house, especially when they had a harder coal more suited to her needs.

Only two passengers joined the 7.25 here, Geoff watching them climb the steps of the trailer, and taking the 'right away' as soon as they were safely on board. The start away from here was

Wainhill Crossing Halt, looking south-west, viewed from the back of a departing train.   *Lens of Sutton*

Looking west over the landscape with the tiny little community served by Wainhill Crossing in the centre of the picture. The four trees, at the end of the lane winding through the centre of this view, mark the site of the junction with Lower Icknield Way, the B4009. The small village of Henton is largely hidden by the clusters of trees in the centre of the picture.   *Ronald Goodearl*

View from Halt Bridge Steps, Bledlow

'Bledlow City' bridge (2m 0¼c) which marked the line's passage below the little village of Bledlow. It had a 20ft span (21ft 3in skew) with, according to an 1893 drawing, 1ft 9½in wrought iron main girders and 10¼in cross girders, and timber decking supported on brick and flint abutments, each of which incorporated a single jack arch. Timber parapets are also shown. According to a note written on the 1893 plan, it was 'strengthened in 1927 by the addition of rail bearers &c'.

gentle as the line continued to fall away down Chinnor bank, crossing the Cuttle Brook which marked the boundary between Oxfordshire and Buckinghamshire at this point. Still falling on gradients of 1 in 72, 1 in 69, 1 in 183, 1 in 73, and 1 in 107, the engine ran like a well-oiled sewing machine towards the bottom of the dip where Geoff opened up again to maintain momentum over a short 1 in 151 climb over the second of the line's underbridges, just below the small village of Bledlow, which was just apparent on Tony's side.

The line then levelled out on the approach to Bledlow Bridge Halt (1m 43c) where another tiny rail-level platform lay on the west side, just beyond the bridge carrying the line over the narrow road from Pitch Green to Bledlow Ridge. Anyone waiting on the platform would have heard the train climbing from the other bridge, but although two passengers joined the 7.25, the halt was otherwise "pretty dead".

Regulars would obviously only get there just before the train was due, but anyone who missed the first train, or, for whatever unlikely reason, was waiting in the tiny shelter when the empty-stock return of the 7.25 came back, would have had quite a surprise when it rushed by so closely, at anything up to 60 mph on its way to Watlington non-stop!

Tony says this was a fast stretch of line and anyone who has witnessed any pannier tank running at speed will have little problem imagining the stirring sight of the small-wheeled 2112

Above right: Bledlow Bridge Halt viewed from the branch trailer and providing a glimpse of the steep approach steps. *Right:* The 'Bledlow Road' bridge (1m 44½c), looking east towards the village. The steps to the halt had led up the side of the left-hand abutment. The bridge had wrought iron main and cross girders (1ft 9in and 12in respectively), and timber decking spanning 19ft 9in (21ft skew). According to an 1893 drawing, the brick and flint abutments each incorporated a single jack arch, but only engineers blue brick is evident today. In 1949 a crack in the brick face of the east end of the southern abutment was secured with bolts and 6in square anchor plates. Unfortunately, apart from the view across the top of Lewknor bridge, we have not come across any pictures showing any of the line's underbridges in their earlier condition, but the steel-frame parapets sheeted with corrugated iron probably replaced timber ones, although we haven't yet discovered any details.

After climbing up the formidable flight of steps from the road below, travellers were faced with a sharply contrasting landscape. Suddenly they were in the middle of what seemed a vast expanse of crops or ploughed fields, depending, of course, on the time of year. This evocative view was taken on 16th August 1955.

J. N. Faulkner

No. 2112 passing over the Horsenden curve farm crossing in 1939 on its way back from Risborough, with the goods brake in tow at the rear of the 1.55 p.m., and fireman George Nicholson looking out of his side of the cab.

S. H. Freese

racing across the fields, with the rapid beat of the vacuum pump and the deep metallic click-click, click-click from the wheels of the single auto-trailer pounding over the rail joints as it swayed behind. Viewed from the platform of the halt, the rear of the trailer, complete with tail lamp, receded into the distance, but more gradually than might be expected, in view of the speed. Pulling away from the halt on the slight down grade towards Risborough called for little effort from the engine, Geoff using a modest regulator setting while Tony sprinkled more coal around the fire for the last time before reaching Risborough, the

amount depending on the layover time. They did not want the safety valves blowing all the while the engine was waiting in the bay there, but this was not a problem on this trip with the hasty turnround.

Passing over the last occupation crossing, at Horsenden curve, the line veered to the right and entered a cutting. Somewhere along here Tony put the injector on again to fill the boiler and stop the engine blowing off at Risborough. At the end of the curve, the branch joined the line from Oxford, the two tracks running alongside one another the rest of the way into

The point at which the Watlington branch (left) curved tightly to parallel the Oxford line (right) on the approach to Princes Risborough. *M. Wallen*

A Watlington branch train nearing the western end of the Horsenden curve. *M. Wallen*

The single line of the Watlington branch features on the right of this picture of No. 4985 *Allesley Hall*, leaving Risborough with a stopping train to Oxford c.1947. The signal in the centre of the picture was the Watlington branch up home, the bracketed centre pivot arm on the right signalling moves onto the goods loop round the back of the station. There was no track circuitry to show when the Watlington branch train was approaching the home signal, but Dave Pinfold recalls "We saw the smoke of the branch train, but he usually blew up [whistled] anyway."

H. K. Harman

Risborough where many of the Oxford trains shared the same bay platform.

Skirting past the end of the long gardens of the houses stretching along Summerleys Road, the line maintained its gently curving course towards the spacious junction station, the branch train lessening pace as it slipped anonymously behind the impressive North Signal Box and into the modest bay platform, stopping short of the engine release crossover.

The 7.25 was "always on time" and while the passengers made their way out of the trailer and along the platform, past the engine, Tony climbed down from the footplate on his side and worked quickly to uncouple so the engine could be run round to the other end of the trailer and make a hasty return to Watlington for the 8.42.

The fireman's view of the final approach to the West Bay, which accommodated Watlington branch trains at Princes Risborough.
David Madley

On arrival in the bay, Watlington branch trains would normally stop clear of the release crossover where the engine was uncoupled. This picture captures the scene well.
Collection J. Scott-Morgan

Watlington station on Sunday, 23rd September 1951, with No. 2076 on shed.

R. C. Riley

CHAPTER EIGHT
THE FINAL YEARS

THE Watlington branch was in the newspapers again on 19th June 1951 when the *Oxford Mail* carried news of closure.

The passenger services on the Princes Risborough to Watlington branch line are to be withdrawn, and a bus service by the City of Oxford Motor Services substituted.

This was stated in a letter from the Western Region Railway Executive to Mrs. J. M. Gould, Clerk to Watlington Parish Council, read by Mr. A. R. Harrison, the chairman, at last night's meeting.

The service was suspended for two days last March because the train fireman, Mr. Anthony Vincent Benham, of Chinnor, had 12 days' leave to get married. No substitute for him could be found, and buses were hired from the Thames Valley Bus Company. When the train again ran after the stoppage it was named "The Train of Romance".

The letter stated that the date of the change had yet to be decided.

The road service would start at the Town Hall, Watlington and end at Princes Risborough Market Place, via Watlington Town Hall, Shirburn, Lewknor, "Leather Bottle", "Lambert Arms", Kingston Blount, Crowell, Oakley, "The Wheatsheaf", Chinnor, "The Bird in Hand", Bledlow, "The Corner House", Princes Risborough Railway Station and Market Place.

Five Double Journeys
There would be five journeys in each direction on weekdays, with an additional one on Saturdays, and the fares will be on the basis of 1¼d a mile. The journey would take 40 minutes compared with 26

minutes by rail, but there would be advantages in that the service would start and end in the centre of the town as well as serve Princes Risborough Railway Station to connect with the main line trains.

Arrangements would be made by the Railway for parcels to be taken by lorry. There would be no change in freight traffic.

Mr. B. C. Lewis said that it seemed to be a better service.

Mr. Harrison said it would save people going to Watlington Station.

Mr. B. Ingram said that the nationalised railways were not paying, and so lines were being cut out.

Mr. J. Trindall said he didn't think they could do anything about it. It was all cut and dried. It was agreed that the letter should be acknowledged without comment.

The threat of closure was subsequently mentioned in the *Daily Telegraph* of 14th September.

MORE BRANCH RAIL LINES TO BE CLOSED
More railway branch lines are to be closed soon because they do not pay. In each of the six railway regions a committee has been examining traffic returns and receipts of all uneconomic branch lines.

About 150 local services are to be investigated before the end of the year. In many cases, services are being maintained for other than economic reasons.

Four services threatened with closure are:

Leominster, Herefordshire, to Bromyard, 11 miles. Highbridge, Somerset, to Burnham-on-Sea, two miles. Princes Risborough,

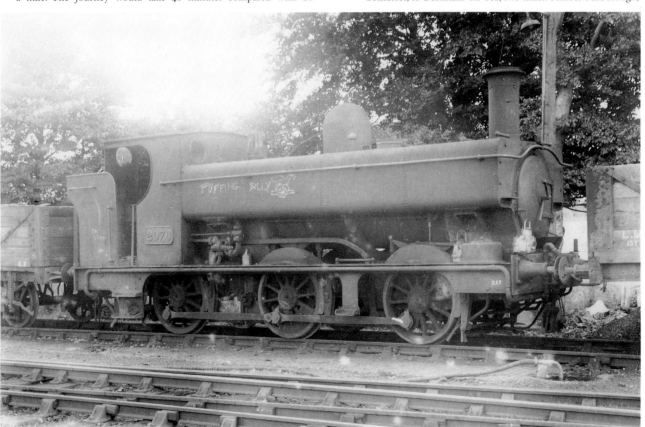

This portrait of No. 2076, also taken on 23rd September 1951, shows this Oxford-based engine minus its safety valve cover and otherwise in a very sorry state shortly before withdrawal the following month. It was presumably a shortage of engines at Slough which brought about this loan. The chalk graffiti says much about the mood of the time. *R. C. Riley*

Bucks, to Watlington, nine miles. Pontypridd, Glam. to Ynysybwl, four miles.

Final decisions concerning these services have not yet been taken. Local opinion is being consulted and alternative means of travel are being reviewed ....

. . . Since the railways were nationalised, 253 miles of railway have been closed completely and a further 314 miles closed to passenger traffic.

With hindsight it is difficult to see how the Watlington branch survived for so long. Perhaps the buoyant traffic generated by Chinnor Cement Works, in being attributed to the branch as a whole, somehow obscured the dwindling traffic at Aston Rowant and Watlington, and perhaps even a blind eye was turned while the line was still useful to 'the Ordnance'? Whatever the reason it would have been difficult to justify the line's retention beyond Chinnor when Aston Rowant station was hardly used, and only a handful of Watlington's 1,500 or so inhabitants actually used the line at all. For that matter, by this time, the majority of local supplies arrived at Watlington by road.

Even the Great Western had effectively removed some of the traffic carried over the line when its Zonal delivery system was introduced in 1947. Smalls traffic which had been sent down the line in the station truck each day, was instead delivered and collected by road, a Reading-based lorry delivering items to Watlington and district from the sub-railhead at Wallingford, whilst Aston Rowant and Chinnor and their outlying areas were covered by a lorry from Thame. Parcels traffic for Chinnor and Watlington was shared with Messrs. Tappins. News of the threatened closure continued to appear in the local press, the *Oxford Times* for 22nd February 1952 reporting:

RAIL CLOSURE OPPOSED
Chinnor Protest Overwhelming

Chinnor residents meeting in the Village Hall on Wednesday instructed their Parish Council, by 61 votes to seven, to oppose a

suggestion that the existing passenger rail services should be replaced by a bus service.

Mr. R. H. Siary, chairman of the Parish Council, who presided, said the reason that British Railways wished to close the branch line between Princes Risborough and Watlington was that there was a big weekly operating loss. The figure, not official, was thought to be £150 a week.

The meeting voted in favour of the following amended resolution, proposed by Miss Evelyn Gibbs and seconded by the Rector of Chinnor (the Rev. S. Day):

Watlington station forecourt in June 1951. The brake van against the end loading dock was provided for use as a mess room after the grounded horse-box body had been destroyed by fire earlier that year.   *Derek Clayton*

'This parish meeting, after close consideration of all the arguments for and against the proposed substitution of a bus service for the existing passenger rail service between Princes Risborough and Watlington, calls upon the Chinnor Parish Council to oppose any such substitution.'

Mr. Siary said that last summer the Council received a letter from British Railways intimating they wished to close the Watlington branch rail service and substitute a bus service.

The three parish councils affected – Chinnor, Watlington and Aston Rowant – were asked for their observations, and these they had made, pointing out possible difficulties which might arise.

Might be Left Stranded

British Railways had told the Council they had invited the City of Oxford Motor Services, Ltd., to provide an alternative service, but, Mr. Siary commented, it was customary to invite tenders for such services, and said some members of the Council felt this might have been done.

There was also the fact that in closing down the present service the railways would then automatically discharge its liability to provide any service. But the question arose that if the bus company found it did not pay to operate an alternative service it would be able to withdraw, leaving the people of Chinnor to walk or get along as best they could.

The chairman then told of a conference arranged between the three parish councils, the railways and the bus authorities. The bus company said it wanted to try the services before committing itself, and the railway was asked if a trial period of substitution could take place, after which, if the bus venture was not successful, the existing rail services could be resumed.

British Railways were unable to give this guarantee on the question of the maintenance of the permanent way. But the ultimate decision on whether or not the line would be closed would come from the Road and Rail Transport Consultative Committee, and the Council would have an opportunity of presenting its case to that committee before any decision was made.

and in the *Oxford Times* again on 20th June 1952:

"WOULD SAVE £4,500"
IF WATLINGTON LINE CLOSED

The proposed withdrawal of passenger train services on the Princes Risborough—Watlington branch line was discussed at Monday's meeting in Derby of the East Midland Area Transport Users' Consultative Committee.

"We feel that the British Transport Commission can arrange a bus service as good as the present passenger train service and the economy would be to the public's advantage", commented Mr. C. A. Galley, Railway Executive spokesman.

The report of the Railway Executive on the withdrawal of the service asked for by the committee, was referred to the subcommittee investigating the matter, which is to report to the next meeting of the full committee.

The 'inability' of a bus service to cope with sudden and unexpected increases in passenger traffic, its comparative lack of reliability in keeping to schedule, and the withdrawal of through tickets to villages on the line were the main objections made to the withdrawal of the service by a meeting of Chinnor Parish Council.

Mr. J. H. Criddle, a member of the sub-committee, in a letter dated May 20, asked the Railway Executive for a further breakdown of figures already supplied, and fuller details on staff saving.

"Figures of train loading should be available from the guards' journals for each and every day and I cannot see why we should be asked to accept figures nearly two years old", he said.

"I am by no means satisfied with the case submitted by Paddington."

A staff of nine would be saved by the closing of the line to passenger traffic, according to figures supplied by the Railways

Executive and the financial saving would be £4,500 a year, "if anything a conservative estimate".

Train loading figures supplied by the Executive showed that the average number of passengers in each train varied between two and 32.

Should the City of Oxford Motor Services, Ltd., operate the proposed road service, 42-seater buses, with standing room for eight, would be available, accommodating 50 persons.

"I must say that these figures are rather staggering" commented the chairman, Prof. R. Peer, on the Executive's report.

A later Western Region report records: 'The Local Authorities were consulted in connection with the original proposal in 1951 and no objections were forthcoming except in the case of the Chinnor Parish Council, who were supported by the Aston Rowant Parish Council'.

In the meantime the branch lingered on, with the usual shortage of firemen willing to be transferred to such a remote outpost. When the problem was announced in a circular, it caught the attention of Brian Pugh, a cleaner at Swansea shed who recalls:

The first time that I became aware of the existence of Watlington was in the summer of 1951 when I was an engine cleaner in Swansea East Dock loco shed. A notice appeared in the office one day which said in effect "There is an acute shortage of firemen at Watlington and applications are invited from firemen and passed cleaners to transfer there for a limited period on an 'on loan' basis."

At first I imagined Watlington to be an important depot with a large allocation of engines, and it was only after further enquiries that I discovered its true location and the fact that two of its three firemen had either transferred away or been called up for national service.

In the autumn of that year I was 'made' as fireman to Slough and soon discovered that Watlington was one of our out-stations along with High Wycombe, Marlow and Aylesbury. For the first few months of my time I was in Slough's pilot link and did not venture far on the main line. However, promotion was fairly fast in those days and I was soon made up to No. 4 Control link. One day we had to go to Princes Risborough 'on the cushions' to relieve an up goods, and it was then that I saw for the first time the Watlington branch train awaiting to connect with the train we had just arrived on. It was in its usual position in the south bay and was headed by 2112, a Slough engine but one that I had not worked on yet due to the fact that it was used almost exclusively at Watlington and was not all that popular due to its advanced age, narrow cab and limited power.

As we waited for our train, 2112 puffed out and I followed its course as it ran parallel to the Oxford line, then turned to the left. I remember asking my driver what sort of line it was, and, after giving me a description, he said "The blokes working there don't know how lucky they are, a nine-mile line all to themselves with no-one to bother them".

I was filled with curiosity and could not wait to 'have a go' on the line myself. In May 1952 I was elevated to No. 3 link which, although it was termed the goods link, contained many spare and relief turns as well as some passenger runs. It was while on a morning spare turn that I finally had my first trip to Watlington. My driver had been given work and I was in the enginemen's cabin alone when the foreman came in and asked if I knew where Watlington was. After assuring him that I did, he told me to catch the next train to Risborough and relieve the fireman who had become ill and had requested relief.

It took me over an hour to reach Risborough, and by the time I did, the fireman had made a recovery from what was probably a hangover and did not want relief! I was quite disappointed, of course, but his driver intervened to the effect that he had better accept it or face a dressing-down for wasting people's time and BR's money. So off we all went with the auto coach to Watlington. I had the benefit

Another portrait of No. 2112 at Slough shed in August 1951 in BR black livery after return from overhaul at Derby.

of being able to 'learn the road', a privilege not often available to mere firemen, and what a road! The place names themselves I found fascinating, Bledlow Bridge, Chinnor, Aston Rowant and the rest. Later on, when I came to work the line for perhaps a week at a time, I found that one of the guards was also Welsh and he told me that Wainhill was usually called Wynhill. 'Wyn' or 'gwyn' is Welsh for white and there at Chinnor was the white hill being turned into cement! This was quite interesting as Cores End at Bourne End had a familiar ring to it, 'cors' being Welsh for bog or fen and it was not difficult to picture that area of Thamesside being marshy in Celtic times.

At Watlington we dropped off the 'sick' fireman, ran around the coach and went into the non-existent 'shed' for water and to top up the bunker from the coal wagon. By the way, the engine was No. 9653. This was done fairly regularly in order that the right duty fireman would not have to fill the entire bunker by himself. The engine buffered up to the wagon and I had to climb in and throw the coal from the wagon bottom and over the bunker top; this was quite heavy work, so 'little and often' was the order of the day. The coal stage was never used in my time as it was considered to be double handling to throw coal out of the wagon, then back into the bunker.

Soon it was time to go back to Risborough, where we left the coach in the bay, collected the brake van and took a train of coal to Chinnor. These were shunted into the cement works and a train of empties was collected for Risborough. There was time for a quick cup of tea in the canteen before we left. No sooner had we put the empties away than it was time to collect the coach and work into Watlington again! By now I was beginning to realise that the line, far from being sleepy, was really quite busy, at least as far as we were concerned. Although the track undulated somewhat, it tended to be harder work going to Watlington than Risborough, especially as the loaded coal trains all went to Chinnor. The fairly heavy shunting work also explained why 14XX and 54XX locos were rarely used on the line; their screw reversing gear made them highly unpopular with drivers.

On arrival at Watlington, we were relieved by the afternoon crew and I returned to Slough as a passenger. The next day I was on a suburban passenger working to Paddington, quite a contrast in the two days!

The link that I was now in had a Sunday turn entitled '4.0 a.m. Watlington'. This involved preparing an engine and working it light to Watlington to bring the branch engine back to Slough, performing

any necessary duties en route. The branch engine would be left with a banked fire and we were required to drop ours and leave it for the night fireman In practice, this very rarely happened; the engine would be brought to Slough on Saturday night and a fresh one taken down early on Monday morning as we did with the Wycombe pilot which was changed by pilot link men from 1.0 a.m. on Monday morning. One Sunday, this 4.0 a.m. turn was converted into a ballast train and we had to collect the token from Risborough North Box and go light to Watlington to collect the brake van, then back to Risborough for the wagons before proceeding to Bledlow Bridge for the work. Eventually we had to go to Chinnor, run around and come back to the site, leave wagons at strategic intervals to be filled with spent ballast, then go all the way to Slough light engine for relief!

For the rest of my time at Slough, until early 1954, visits to Watlington came at fairly frequent intervals, including one occasion when it was decided, because of lack of a driver, that I would have to stay the night alone at Watlington to service the engine. Visions of Fal Vale station in the film 'The Ghost Train' were easy to conjure up, but, having been brought up in the country, I was not afraid of the dark nor of isolation.

The Watlington fireman stayed for a while to show me the ropes, then left me to carry on. After doing my chores on 4650 and making a can of tea, I managed to get my head down, only to be awakened at about 3.0 a.m. by a policeman who had called to see that all was well. By the time I got back to Slough, I had 'gone over the top', i.e. worked for more than 12 hours, which meant that, as we had to have a minimum of 12 hours rest between turns, I missed the turn on the following night.

There was one story concerning these night turns which, although I do not remember the name of the person concerned, is true to the best of my knowledge. One day a phone message was received at Paddington from the country seat of a certain Earl to the effect that a locomotive whistle had sounded continuously for several hours in the vicinity of Watlington station in the early hours of the morning. The foreman at Slough was told to investigate and, together with 'an official' from Paddington, drove to Watlington by road the next night and took up an observation position near the station. Shortly after midnight, the night duty fireman was seen to leave on his bicycle and did not return until well after 4.0 a.m. His reason was that his child was sick and he had gone home to see to it. Questioned about the whistling, it emerged that he had placed a can of cylinder oil on top of the steam fountain. This had later slipped and caused the whistle to blow until all the steam and most of the water had vanished. Frantic efforts had then to be made to restore the situation in time for the first train. In view of the labour shortage, he got off with a 'strong verbal caution' for what would have been a sacking offence in former years.

One unusual load I remember taking to Watlington was a 3.7in anti-aircraft gun. It was rumoured that the aforementioned Earl wanted it for shooting pheasants. There was plenty of game in the area and rabbits would often break cover and run in front of the train. One Slough fireman had a .22 Webley air pistol that he would take with him and try a few potshots at them!

As you can see, I never actually lodged at Watlington, but always worked from Slough, which was comparatively easy due to the frequency of trains. I lodged in the railway hostel at 27 Upton Park, Slough, for fourteen shillings per week for room, bed and change of towels and linen once a week. Food was paid for when eaten at either the hostel canteen or at the Slough staff dining club canteen by the station. This was shared with LT busmen. The hostel canteen was open 24 hours, 7 days a week, a roast dinner and sweet cost 1s 6d whilst a bottle of Mackinson stout at the shed canteen cost 1s 3d. Happy days! Most foodstuffs were still rationed when I went to Slough and we used to live like kings with our extra tea, sugar and cheese rations! There was also a network of 'suppliers' on the line who could get you almost anything, at a price.

When Cyril Saunders joined the staff as a porter at Watlington during the winter of 1951-2, things were very different from Reg Pocock's day. After national service in the army, Cyril took the place of Dick Smith, who retired on 3rd January 1952. Tom Tunnicliffe was on the opposite shift.

Cyril lived in Love Lane and had spent all his life in Watlington. He says that in the mornings he would "get up at 6.15 and be at the station for 6.20 a.m.!" By this time, the main gate was not even closed, let alone locked, and the trailer was left overnight in the platform. "It was never put in the shed."

On arrival, he would unlock the station building, light the stove in the office, then the open fire "in our office in the goods shed". The driver and fireman were already over with the engine. Cyril was usually on the same shift as George Nicholson and guard Reg Watkins, whilst on the opposite shift Tom Tunnicliffe usually worked with driver Frank Tredwell and guard Frank Hyde. Reg Watkins left in 1952 apparently transferring to Bridgend. His place was taken by Ron Williams who moved from Dolgarrog to Maidenhead to try for a bus driver's job, but there were no vacancies so he joined the railway as a shunter at Maidenhead, transferring to Old Oak Common and eventually becoming a passenger guard at Watlington. He lodged at the Pineapple and later married a local girl. The two firemen were Tony Benham and Ron Bowden, who had succeeded John Neighbour. Ron lodged at the Pineapple and also married a local girl. The firemen worked with both drivers but Tony preferred to work with George, a combination which Cyril's wife regarded as "a couple of laddoes together".

In fact Cyril met his wife Jean at the station on Saint Valentine's day in 1952 when he was fooling around playing snowballs with Tony Benham and George Nicholson. A stray snowball hit Jean when she was walking along the lane from Pyrton Field Farm to the station, and they were married that October.

Passengers for the first train, the 7.25 workmen's, included Joe Mathews, Sid Norcutt and his brother, "and a woman for the research place", all travelling to Risborough. There were about six of them altogether, one regularly getting to the station 10-15 minutes beforehand and the rest arriving at the last minute.

The return of the 7.25 still officially ran as empty stock but now picked up Bob Williamson, the clerk in charge of Watlington station. He lived at Kingston Blount and joined the train at Kingston Halt, but Cyril recalls that as he and guard Frank Hyde did not get on well together, there was "some fun" over this arrangement and Bob was left behind on more than one occasion.

Eventually, an official note was put in the working timetable to the effect that the train would pick up a member of staff at Kingston, but the relationship did not improve, especially when Bob's bike had to be loaded in the van on the occasions when he took it with him for collecting money from traders around Watlington. The empty stock train was also used by former branch fireman Peter Robinson on his way home from his shed duties at Aylesbury. He travelled out each night on the 7.10 pm, usually walking along the track to Watlington station to catch the train. If he was running late, the branch train picked him up anywhere along the lineside, but, if he didn't show up at all, they would pull up at the end of his road. If he was ill, his wife would signal that he wasn't coming. Incidentally, certainly by this time, Peter spent some of the day sweeping chimneys, carting his brushes and rods around on a trolley behind his bicycle.

Following an accident in which Peter had been injured by the flap of a coal wagon falling on him, driver George Nicholson regularly stopped at Shirburn to drop him off by his home. George thought nothing of this and the unofficial stop at Shirburn was nothing new, but it was reported to Paddington and he was 'carpeted' for it.

Passengers for the next train at 8.42 included three or four businessmen and quite often shoppers for London who, on the main-line train, had to stand all the way from Risborough.

The 10.22 brought in fish each day, except Mondays, when the fish shop was closed. This was collected by Tim Messum or his stepson Tom Snow. "Sprats arrived in a tub with no lid on them". Sausages arrived from Trowbridge on two days a week and Walls or Lyons ice cream was also received for the Co-op. At this time, Tappins only called once a day, so if the ice cream arrived on a later train and missed their collection, it was sometimes too late. The insulated containers used at the time only kept it for a while, so the manager of the Co-op would tell the railway staff to eat it!

The Zonal lorry would call at Watlington each morning around 11.0 a.m. with parcels and 'smalls' deliveries which regularly included cartons of tobacco for Worleys, tobacconists. According to a later Western Region report in 1958, H. E. Worley, wholesale tobacconist, was receiving about 40 cartons of tobacco each month. Cyril recalls how Tappins would usually arrive within five minutes of the Zonal lorry's departure "as if he'd sat round the corner waiting", calling at the waiting room for anything to be delivered around the town.

Cyril went home for lunch each day from 12.0–1.00, leaving Bob Williamson on his own. When Cyril was on the early turn, Tom Tunnicliffe came on duty about 2.20 p.m., when the train crews also changed over, the two porters overlapping duties for about 20 minutes. It was during this time that the yard was shunted to form up the 3.55 p.m. goods on the spare road. It was so much quicker with two of them, one operating the hand points and uncoupling the wagons being sent down the sidings, whilst the other one "could catch them". When the porters were

Sep 51

298

PRINCES RISBOROUGH and WATLINGTON. (ENGINE AND BRANCH CAR, ONE CLASS ONLY.)

SINGLE LINE. Worked by Train Staff and only one engine in steam at a time, or two coupled together. Form of Staff, Round. Colour, Black.
Passenger Trains to carry " B " Head Code Freight Trains to carry one Headlamp in centre of buffer plank.

Week Days only.

No. 1

Down Trains.

Distance.	STATIONS	Ruling Gradient 1 in	Time Allowances for H, J & K Head Code Freight Trains. (See page 346.)			Freight	Empty Train.	Freight	Passenger.	Freight	Passenger.	Passenger.	Freight	Freight	Passenger.	Passenger.	Freight
			Point to point times.	Allow for Stop.	Allow for Start.	K	¶	N RR			SX	SO			SO	SX				K
M. C.			Mins.	Mins.	Mins.	a.m.	a.m.	a.m.	a.m.	p.m.	p.m.	p.m.	p.m.	p.m.	p.m.	p.m.		p.m.	p.m.
— —	Princes Risborough .... dep.	—	—	—	1	5 30	7 57	9 20	10 22	12 20	12 40	1 54	3 55	3 55	5 48	..	8 20	....	10 15
1 52	Bledlow Bridge Halt .. ,,	107 F.	—	—	—				10 27		12 45	1 59		—	5 53	....	8 25	...	—
2 75	Wainhill Halt ... ,,	68 R.	—	—	—				10 30		12 48	2 2		—	5 56	....	8 28	...	—
3 57	Chinnor .. .. ,,	68 R.	12	1	1	CR	CR	9 30	10 33	12 34	12 51	2 5		4 9	5 59	....	8 31	...	—
5 17	Kingston Crossing Halt.. ,,	61 R.	—	—	—	Q			10 37		12 55	2 9		—	6 3	....	8 35	...	—
6 16	Aston Rowant ... ,,	116 R.	8	1	1	6 35	CR	..	10 40		12 R58	2 V12		4 T32	6 R6	..	8 R38	...	CR
7 4	Lewknor Bridge Halt .... ,,	117 F.	—	—	—			..	10 43		1 1	2 15		—	6 9	....	8 41	...	—
8 75	Watlington .. arr.	78 F.	8	1	—	6 45	8 20	..	10 48		1 6	2 20		4 42	6 14	..	8 46	....	10 45

¶—May convey passengers from Princes Risborough when required.   ‡—Aston Rowant arrive 4.17 p.m.   K—Suspended.   N—Will run as " light engine " if required.
Q Aston Rowant arrive 5.52 a.m.   R—Treated as a Halt.   V—Treated as a Halt on Saturdays only.

Up Trains.

STATIONS	Ruling Gradient 1 in	Time Allowances for H, J & K Head Code Freight Trains. (See page 346.)			Freight	Passenger.	Passenger.	Engine and Van.	Passenger.	Freight	Passenger.	Passenger.	Freight	Freight	Passenger.	Freight
		Point to point times.	Allow for Stop.	Allow for Start.	K			N RR		SX	SO		SX	SO			K
		Mins.	Mins.	Mins.	a.m.	a.m.	a.m.	a m.	a m	p.m.		p.m.	p.m.	p.m.	p.m.		p.m.
Watlington .... dep.	—	—	—	1	4 20	7 25	8 42	11 30		1 15		3 10	4 55	....	7 15	....	9 0
Lewknor Bridge Halt .. ,,	78 R.	—	—	—		7 30	8 47	11 35		1 20		3 15		—	7 20	....	Z
Aston Rowant ...... ,,	117 R.	8	1	1	—	7 R33	8 52	11 38		1 R23		3 V18		—	7 R23	....	9 25
Kingston Crossing Halt.. ,,	116 F.	—	—	—	—	7 36	8 55	11 41		1 26		3 21		—	7 26	....	—
Chinnor ...... ,,	61 R.	8	1	1	CR	7 40	9 0	11 45	10† 0	1 30	1 18	3 25	5 T23	4 55	7 30	....	CR
Wainhill Halt ...... ,,	68 F.	—	—	—	—	7 43	9 3	11 48		1 33		3 28		—	7 33	....	—
Bledlow Bridge Halt ... ,,	68 F.	—	—	—	—	7 46	9 6	11 51		1 36		3 31		—	7 36	....	—
Princes Risborough .. arr.	107 R.	10	1	—	4 48	7 51	9 11	11 56	10†15	1 41	1 30	3 36	5 35	5 5	7 41	....	9 45

K—Suspended.   N—Will run as " light engine " if required.   R—Treated as a Halt.   V—Treated as a Halt on Saturdays only.   Z—Aston Rowant arrive 9.10 p.m.   ‡—Chinnor arrive 5.13 p.m.

Taken from Service Timetable for September 1951.

on their own, the engine had to run down with the wagons into each siding.

As the goods shed was hardly used by this time, the heavy doors across the track at either end were often left closed and, after the doors were smashed in a shunting accident a few years earlier, they did not use the goods shed siding much during shunting in case the wagons could not be brought to a stand safely before they reached the new door!

On Mondays, after the departure of the 3.0 p.m., the late-turn porter walked out to the distant signal to replace the vessel in the lamp with a freshly filled and trimmed one to last the next seven days.

As the 3.55 freight was run from Risborough, the brake van was now kept there instead of at Watlington. Although the train did not call at Chinnor, which was still catered for by a dedicated working, it did call at Aston Rowant to drop off any traffic, usually coal, and collect any empties which were taken into Watlington.

Despite the accident described on page 137, if the train was just too long for the loop, it was still run into the platform where the engine was released and held by the coal stage while the train was gravitated towards the buffer stops to clear the opposite end of the loop. "We had to lever the train down if it was too long . . . they didn't need a lot of moving, but they wanted some stopping."

When the engine had been coupled onto the other end, the train was drawn back up to the neck of the yard, and the empties from Aston Rowant, which were on the front, were sent down the spare road onto the outgoing train. The rest of the 3.55 was then put in the back road and left there.

The engine then collected the outgoing train from the spare road and set it into the back road to collect the brake van before pulling it out onto the running line and back down to the ground frame to pick up the guard and the single line staff.

When the engine returned with the 5.48 from Risborough, which brought back the workmen, it had an hour at the terminus, during which any wagons left in the back road could be placed if required; this often included a delivery of loco coal.

On the late shift, Cyril did not have a meal break and booked off at 9.10 p.m. after the return of the last passenger train, often going down the road into Watlington with George Nicholson.

Cyril recalls that incoming goods traffic at this time was mainly coal for Tappins which he thinks averaged a couple of wagons a day. However, wagons often bunched on the way from the collieries to Watlington, with the result that whereas they might not receive any supplies one day, some four or five wagons might arrive the next. In these circumstances, Cyril says they "didn't bother them with demurrage".

In the sugar beet season, around November, as soon as Tappins had emptied the coal wagons, they were reloaded with sugar beet, "often about eight trucks or more".

Tappins also handled the delivery of miscellaneous supplies to 'the Ordnance' which, even six years or more after the war, ranged from clothing to crated beds and arms.

The familiar scene after the arrival of the Watlington branch train in the bay at Risborough. When this view was taken, the engine had already been uncoupled and moved up to the buffer stops ready to run round. Having retrieved the tail lamp from the rear of auto-trailer W179W, the guard can be seen leaning over to hang it on the other end ready for the return journey.   *Norman Simmons*

"Supplies were always in and out" but Cyril particularly recalls a consignment of Bofors anti-aircraft guns which arrived one week and were sent out the next!

When 100 wheeled guns had to be delivered to 'the Ordnance', they were brought down the branch, 8-10 at a time, on the branch goods. However, when the first consignment arrived, Cyril found the guns were on 'low loaders' (well wagons) instead of 'platform trucks', so they could not be wheeled off at the end loading bank. In the absence of a yard crane, the only way round the problem was to return them all to Greenford for reloading onto wagons more appropriate for their destination.

News of the predicament evidently travelled fast because before anything could be done about it, B. G. Gaster, trading as B. G. Plant, of Pyrton Farm Lane, approached the station staff and offered to unload the guns using a large ex-army crane he owned. He quoted £10 each or £11 delivered to the depot using his Landrover, and the railway accepted. Gaster normally handled items like saw benches, despatched from the station in sheeted opens, fork-lift trucks and other equipment.

The dwindling traffic, working under threat of closure, and the problems in finding firemen willing to put up with being stranded at Watlington without proper facilities, may have all conspired to deprive the staff of some of the sense of pride, achievement and service felt in the pre-war establishment. It is

therefore quite possible that a personality clash between one driver and guard, set against a background of low morale may have led to a dispute which delayed the 3.5 p.m. by half an hour one day.

It seems that the driver had insisted on a green flag for the 'right away' whereas the guard protested that a wave of his arm was perfectly sufficient. There were no passengers on the train, which is just as well in view of the delay, but the driver's argument was that "It could be anybody giving me the signal". Eventually, the guard used the flag and the dispute was settled, but the situation did not improve relations.

It appears that the driver was not consistent, at least on a subsequent occasion at Aston Rowant, when the guard was on the platform giving a passenger directions with his arm! Needless to say, the driver took this as a 'right away' and left the guard behind. The train was then held at Watlington until the guard could get there by taxi and normal service was resumed.

An unfortunate combination like that could also result in a late-running train being 'run by the book', with the strictest observation of the speed limit and stopping at every halt even when there were no passengers in sight and none on the train. Therefore, a train which left ten minutes late would still be ten minutes behind at the opposite end of its journey. Furthermore, late-running passengers could no longer feel sure the train would be held for them. It was all a far cry from the spirit of the past when staff, passengers and traders would do anything to help one another.

During 1953, Cyril Saunders and his wife moved in to the crossing cottage at Kingston (see vol. 2). Cycling in from there to Watlington each morning for 6.30, he sometimes caught up with Tony Benham who was supposed to have been there for about 4.0 a.m. "The antics they used to get up to to raise steam", said Cyril, recalling Tony and George together. "They used to get the engine moving and run down to Shirburn and back to pump up some pressure and get the fire drawing. Then they'd try and leave with the first train and run out of steam by the ground frame!" "They must have had a lovely time together."

Sometime around 1954 Ron Williams transferred from Watlington to become a passenger guard at Reading, and in 1956 he left the railway to become a postman. His place as guard at Watlington was taken by Don Gray, who learned the road with relief guard Percy Smith. Don had joined the railway in 1945, his interest having developed while working at a furniture factory alongside the line in High Wycombe. He made friends with the signalmen in High Wycombe South signal box, where he spent his lunch hours. One day, the District Inspector called into the box and asked him if he would be interested in joining the railway, and Don started as a lad/runner at Risborough North signal box, going on to become a porter/signalman at Blackthorn c.1946. Subsequently he served as a signalman at Brill, then West Wycombe, before becoming a guard on the Watlington branch, working on the opposite shift to Frank Hyde, 7.10 a.m.–3.10 p.m. or 1.05 p.m. to 9.5 p.m.

At this time the branch stations were manned in a single shift, so Frank and Don often finished the early turn by helping Charlie Hopkins at Aston Rowant. When required, the early turn guard travelled out on the 3.0 p.m. and came back on the goods, along with Charlie Hopkins, who travelled home each day with his bicycle in the brake van. There wasn't always much goods traffic and Don recalls one occasion when, as there was nothing to deliver beyond Aston Rowant, they decided to propel

the brake van the rest of the way to Watlington. This confused one farmer at Middle Way Crossing, who, seeing the end of the brake van, assumed he was crossing the line behind the train which came very close to hitting his Landrover.

Sometimes, if there was only one wagon for Aston Rowant, it was attached behind the trailer, using the screw coupling of the coach. At Aston it was uncoupled in the platform and simply gravitated into the yard. Don even remembers one occasion when on an up journey the auto-trailer with only a few locals on board, was set back into Chinnor Cement Works to collect a box van of cement for Greenford.

At some point before Tony Benham left the railway in February 1954, Frank Tredwell must have been absent, because the serious shortage of men led to buses being substituted for the first and last trains so that the rest of the day's timetable fell within the hours of one crew, George and Tony, based at Watlington. Frank Tredwell also left the railway in February 1954. The buses, provided by Surmans of Chinnor, did not venture towards the town, but picked up and dropped off in the station forecourt. Not long afterwards, George Nicholson was left as the only member of the loco department still based at Watlington, so the engine was kept overnight at Slough and travelled light to Watlington and back each day. Brian Maynard, a young Slough fireman at the time, recalls the early-turn Slough crew booked on at 4.0 a.m. to prepare and water the Watlington engine which was due off shed at 4.45. Drawn from its stud of shunting engines, regulars included 5755, 5766 and 9789, but this varied and on the week ending 3rd March 1956, for example, 5755 was used on Tuesday, 4680 Wednesday, 3740 Thursday, 4680 Friday and 5755 again on Saturday.

When they arrived at Risborough, the engine waited behind the North box while the fireman went to collect the single-line train staff and use the signalmen's kettle to fill the tea can. During the summer months some crews would stop in the dip alongside the cress beds between Bledlow and Chinnor to enjoy their breakfast, often taking the opportunity to pick some of the cress. There was usually plenty of time, so long as they arrived at

The Watlington goods brake van seen opposite the platform on the approach to the Timber Research Laboratory's private siding at Risborough in the mid-1950s. How long this vehicle was in service on the line is just not known, but, because of the short run-round at Watlington, it was always one of these shorter 20ft vans. Porter Frank Saunders thinks that before the war the van was changed from time to time and that the verandah was usually at the Risborough end.
A. Attewell

Watlington in time to take water, and couple onto the trailer for the first train, the 7.25 a.m. which still took workers to Risborough.

When they returned to Watlington at 8.20 am, George Nicholson relieved the driver, who travelled all the way back from Watlington to Slough 'on the cushions'. The early-turn fireman was relieved at 11.30 a.m. by a middle-turn man, who booked on at Slough at 9.40 a.m. and caught the 9.50 passenger train to Risborough where he began his duty with George on the Chinnor goods. Another Slough driver and fireman booked on at 2.40 pm and travelled to Risborough on the cushions, the fireman taking over on the 5.48 pm and the driver taking over from George when the train reached Watlington. The Slough men then completed the rest of the day's timetable and took the engine back with them.

This was a wonderful arrangement for George who no longer had any preparation or disposal to do, but quite how much satisfaction he derived from the job during these sad final years is open to question. It was all a far cry from the pre-war years.

As it had all meant so much to him, it is difficult to believe that he did not think back to his days as a young fireman working to the exacting standards of Harry Humphreys who would not even let him drive. Reg Pocock ensured the rest of the staff maintained standards and in doing so kept up pride and morale. Having earned his place in the old order and progressed to the position of driver, George must have felt something of the hollowness which now followed. The bustle and activity was all but over, and sadly all the loyal old company servants, the very embodiment of the line itself, had departed.

Still, all things change, and now George had an easy time driving the familiar pannier tank and single auto-trailer to and fro over the branch he loved so much. Don Gray remembers him as a very popular character – "Nothing was too much trouble for George" – whilst relief guard George Howlett regarded him as "a damn good driver", which was probably in no small way attributable to Harry Humphreys. Some drivers were reluctant to put themselves out, or to do something that was not absolutely by the book, but not George. Typically, on an occasion when there was a train of 22 loaded coal wagons to be taken to Chinnor, George Howlett expressed his concern to George, who, as obliging as ever, just replied "That'll be alright boy!"

Cyril Saunders left the railway in January 1955 to take a job at Pressed Steel in Oxford, although both he and his wife remained living at Kingston Crossing until 1962.

Before he resigned, the Slough crews often used to give him a lift home to Kingston on the light engine on Saturday nights. The cab of a pannier is not the most commodious place, especially with the intrusion of large coil springs for the rear axleboxes and the reversing lever, so it is not difficult to picture the scene with the two Slough men, Cyril and his bicycle inside!

Cyril says the Slough men were in no hurry to get back and lost time in the dip between Kingston Crossing and Chinnor where they stopped to enjoy their sandwiches.

On one of these occasions, a Saturday night in August, the crew invited him to drive the engine back to Kingston while they got on with their sandwiches. Apparently, it seemed no time at all when, after passing under the bridge at Aston Rowant, the engine crashed through both sets of gates!

Cyril said that as the driver had already received one or two warnings, the accident would take some explaining if he was to avoid dismissal. They certainly could not admit Cyril was driving, but, as luck would have it, Cyril had previously reported defective gate catches, so the incident was attributed to the gates swinging out of control while the engine was passing through!

While the replacement gates were being made, Cyril was posted at Kingston with ropes and lamps, cycling into Watlington each day to sign on duty, and returning to the crossing to take up his position. Ironically, he profited from all the overtime involved during the protracted absence of any gates.

The closure of the branch was evidently decided following a report of the Western Region Branch Lines Committee, dated July 1954. The following extract explains the deteriorating situation since 1951:

> When the original report recommending the withdrawal of the passenger train service was submitted in June 1951 (based on 1949 figures) it was pointed out that the Watlington Branch was in the nature of a "border line" case and that the *net* annual economy was not likely to exceed £2,000 per annum.
>
> Since that date, however, there has been a decrease of £1,524 (33%) in passenger revenue, due chiefly to the increased use of private cars and the fact that a number of people who moved to the Watlington area during the war have returned to London.
>
> Similarly, there has been a decrease of £1,509 (48%) in parcels revenue, due chiefly to one of the principal traders at Watlington having gone out of business, in addition to which there has been some diversion of small parcels to parcels post.

George Nicholson and Don Gray in the summer of 1956.

Concurrently with this decrease in revenue, there has been a steady rise in wages and operating costs, with the result that the withdrawal of the passenger train service would now result in an increase in net revenue of approximately £4,300 per annum, even after allowing for the subsidy required by the City of Oxford Motor Services.

It will be recalled that in 1952 the B.T.C. desired consideration to be given to the introduction of a diesel car service with a view to reducing operating costs, but it was demonstrated that, instead of producing an economy, this would result in increased expenditure.

In June 1953 the B.T.C. decided that the branch should continue to be kept open for a further twelve months but asked for special enquiry to be made regarding possible operating economies.

The Chief Officers reported in September last that no operating economies were possible but some extension of the cheap ticket facilities would be introduced with a view to increasing revenue. The net result of these extended facilities was an increase of .£13 only during the 7 months ended April 30th last.

In view of the foregoing, it is recommended that the passenger train service be withdrawn and substituted by a road service, provided by the City of Oxford Motor Services Limited.

On the run up to closure, a survey was conducted of the number of passengers using the 7.25 a.m. and 8.42 a.m. trains for the six days Monday 19th to Saturday 24th March 1956. On the

Looking south-west towards the buffer stops at the end of the line on 4th August 1956. There is a tale about an auto-trailer which was pushed through the buffer stops and ended up in the lane. This is said to have happened during the postwar years when an empty trailer for an excursion was being propelled into the platform without the crew realising that the other one had been left there. We have been unable to confirm this, but the buffer stop illustrated here appears to be different to the one illustrated in the 1947 photograph on page 6 of Volume 2.

Alan A. Jackson

A. Attewell

Despite the appeal of this wonderfully rural scene, photographs of the station entrance are extremely rare. We were thrilled to discover this one which, taken on 4th August 1956, apparently with the driver's co-operation, shows the rustic appearance of this remote outpost of the GWR. Reg Pocock's sleeper-built milk platform had been sited alongside the front of the engine and with careful study it is possible to identify the fence posts which marked its extent. There is no mistaking the air of slumbering neglect here, a contrast to the heartening scenes of the 1920s when the station mattered to the local community and passengers hurried to catch the 8.40 a.m. while farmers arrived with horse-drawn carts loaded with churns of milk for London. *Alan A. Jackson*

Various auto-trailers were provided for the Watlington branch through the years, and some of them feature throughout both volumes of this book. The change of vehicles is mentioned on page 127 of Volume 2. This one, W179W in BR maroon livery, is shown here at Watlington in 1957 (top) and c.1955/6 below. Not surprisingly, interior photos are rare but this one should bring back memories to local people.

N. C. Simmons and A. Attewell

The 1957 staff group features (from left to right) David Madley (Slough fireman), Ted Kennedy (C&W assistant at Risborough), Frank Hyde, Jack Grace (C&W examiner at Risborough), Tom Tunnicliffe, Joe Ireland (an Aylesbury driver learning the road) and George Nicholson in the cab.

Cty. Don Gray

busiest day, in the case of the 7.25 on Monday, there were four passengers on the train when it set out from Watlington, four joining at Lewknor, none at Aston Rowant, three at Kingston, eight at Chinnor, none at Wainhill and six at Bledlow, making a total of twenty-five. Saturday was the busiest for the 8.42, with six passengers from Watlington, one from Lewknor, none from Aston, fifteen from Chinnor, none from Wainhill and nine from Bledlow, a total of thirty. The poorest totals on other days were eight and nine.

The survey bears out the poor support from the people of Watlington and Aston Rowant, so there really was little case for maintaining the passenger service, as explained in a letter dated 16th April 1956 from the General Manager of the Western Region to the National Union of Railwaymen:

Dear Sir,

Proposal to withdraw the passenger train
service from the Princes Risborough/Watlington branch

The circumstances of the Watlington branch have been carefully investigated and, from an examination of the passenger train traffic, it is clear that the use made of the services provided is insufficient to justify their continuance especially as reasonable alternative facilities can be made available. It is, therefore, proposed to withdraw the passenger train service and arrangements are being made for the

The branch engine taking water after running round the trailer in preparation for another trip to Risborough in 1957.
Norman Simmons

A closer view of the pillar tank.   *A. Attewell*

matter to be submitted to the East Midland Area Transport Users' Consultative Committee. The annual savings in traffic and train working staff alone will amount to £4,076 and, with the further savings to be realised from maintenance and renewal of rolling stock, permanent way, etc., and also from train working expenses, a substantial economy will be secured.

Yours faithfully,
K. W. C. Grand

Although Thames Valley Traction Co. and the City of Oxford Motor Services each covered a small part of the route, there was no bus service between Watlington and Princes Risborough. The British Transport Commission therefore arranged an alternative service which the City of Oxford Co. were prepared to provide for a subvention of £3,806 per annum. Assuming receipts from the bus company of £1,200 per annum, the net cost to the BTC was calculated to be approximately £2,600 per annum.

The bus would conform to the existing train service and operate from Watlington town hall to Princes Risborough market place. Parcels traffic would continue to be dealt with at Chinnor, Aston Rowant and Watlington, with the existing Zonal lorries and Tappins. Freight traffic was unaffected by the proposals, although engine power was to be provided by the Eastern Region from Aylesbury shed.

Much of this was explained by the DOSO at a 'consultation meeting' with the branch staff at Princes Risborough on 26th May 1956.

At this time the Watlington branch staff comprised:

Chinnor: station master (class 3) and two female crossing keepers at Wainhill and Kingston
Aston Rowant: one leading porter
Watlington: one clerk (class 4), two porters★, two passenger guards and one driver

After the withdrawal of passenger services, this would be reduced to:

Chinnor: one clerk, one goods porter, one crossing keeper at Wainhill

★Tom Tunnicliffe is the only porter recalled at Watlington during the final years, so it seems likely that the second porter was the one based at Chinnor.

Aston Rowant: one goods porter
Watlington: one goods porter
Risborough: one goods guard

In preparation for the goods only service, an Eastern Region J68 0–6–0T No. 68650 was tried on the branch as detailed in the following report:

7th September, 1956.

Dear Sir,

Engine Test—Watlington Branch
NE 68650. J68 Class

The above engine was used in a load test on the Watlington Branch on 6th September. The load for this engine is 12 Class (1) the load for the WR engine is 19 Class (1).

This engine would be all right if the Watlington Branch was closed for Passenger Service as it could then make two trips to Chinnor, but while passenger service remains the NE engine would not be a success.

With the present working load to Chinnor 19 Class (1) we are unable to keep Princes Risborough clear, as 24 Chinnor coal has been in No. 2 North End Princes Risborough for over a week and the 12.15 has had a full load each day.

One of the objects of this test was to see if this engine would work from Princes Risborough to Watlington and back without taking water at Watlington, so as to do away with the Water Column at Watlington.

I would not recommend this as during the dry weather water is often in short supply at Princes Risborough which would mean going to Thame or Aylesbury for water.

The test was carried out arriving back at Princes Risborough with a ¼ tank of water.

The load to Watlington was 5-21 tons and 2-16 tons coal (7=13) Class 1, and the return was the same coal and 8 empties.

Time was lost at Watlington in running around wagons and shunting, but we did not call at Chinnor on the way back to prevent delay to the 5.48 Princes Risborough Rail Car.

We arrived at Princes Risborough 5.46, 9 minutes late.

Yours truly,
(Sgd.) W.J. Thompson

N. H. Briant, Esq.,
Paddington

In September 1956 Slough enginemen appealed to keep the Watlington branch goods from being transferred to the Eastern Region. They proposed: 'the 57XX class engine used to work

With the steps of the auto-trailer already retracted by the guard, this photograph shows No. 4650 starting away from Lewknor Bridge Halt after dropping off one of the locals.
Les Nicholson

WESTERN  **BRITISH RAILWAYS** REGION

DAY EXCURSION BOOKINGS

TO

LONDON

(PADDINGTON or MARYLEBONE)

ON

WEDNESDAYS, THURSDAYS and SATURDAYS
SEPTEMBER 19th and until further notice

LEAVING	DEPART		Return Fares (Second Class Only)	RETURN SAME DAY		
	a.m.	a.m.	s d		p.m.	p.m.
WATLINGTON ... ... dep.	7A 0	8A 30	9/3	PADDINGTON ... dep.	4 34	—
LEWKNOR BRIDGE HALT „	7A 12	8A 42	8/9	MARYLEBONE ... „	—	6 50
ASTON ROWANT ... „	7A 18	8A 48	8/9			
KINGSTON CROSSING				BLEDLOW BRIDGE		
HALT ... ... „	7A 25	8A 55	8/6	HALT ... ... „	5A 53	8A 25
CHINNOR ... ... „	7A 34	9A 4	8/3	WAINHILL HALT ... „	5A 56	8A 28
WAINHILL HALT ... „	7A 37	9A 7	8/0	CHINNOR ... ... „	5A 59	8A 31
BLEDLOW BRIDGE HALT „	7A 50	9A 10	7/9	KINGSTON CROSSING		
				HALT ... ... „	6A 8	8A 40
PADDINGTON ... ... arr.	9C 34	10 10		ASTON ROWANT ... „	6A 15	8A 47
MARYLEBONE ... ... „	9SX 17	—		LEWKNOR BRIDGE		
				HALT ... ... „	6A 21	8A 53
				WATLINGTON ... „	6A 33	9A 5

A—Change at Princes Risborough.   C.—Arrives at 9.36 a.m. on Saturdays.   S.X.—Saturdays excepted

Children under Three years of age, Free; Three and under Fourteen years of age, Half-fare

Notice as to Conditions.—These tickets are issued subject to the British Transport Commission's published Regulations and Conditions applicable to British Railways exhibited at their Stations or obtainable free of charge at station booking offices. Luggage allowances are as set out in these general notices.

Tickets can be obtained in advance at Booking Stations

Further information will be supplied on application to Stations, Agencies, or to Mr. N. H. BRIANT, District Operating Superintendent, Paddington Station, W.2; or Mr. A. C. B. PICKFORD, Chief Commercial Manager, Paddington Station, W.2. (Telephone: Paddington 7000, Extension, "Enquiries" 8 a.m. to 10 p.m.).

Paddington Station, W.2.
August, 1956.

K. W. C. GRAND,
General Manager.

L.D. 599 D.   Printed by W. A. SMITH (Leeds) LTD., Carlton Printeries, Leeds.

Last day scenes at Watlington.
Les Nicholson and Hugh Davies

the 5.38 a.m. Parcels Reading to Princes Risborough, then work the 'Q' trip, 9.20 a.m. Princes Risborough to Chinnor and back (uncovered under the former proposals) with the existing set of Slough men and a second Slough set (vice ER Aylesbury men) work the remaining goods trips and bring the engine to shed'. The correspondence also mentions that the district inspector 'considers that an ER J68 Class engine would require water at Watlington and if a supply has to be maintained (it would not be necessary if a 57XX class engine worked the trips) the Chief Mechanical & Electrical Engineer will have to renew one pump and repair the other at Watlington'.

It was October 1956 before the public announcement was finally made that the branch was to close to passengers on and from 1st July 1957. Former branch driver Geoff Pearson, who

retired from Oxford shed in 1954, had told Cyril Saunders "They've been talking about closing the line for years, but it'll never close in my lifetime". This was prophetic indeed for he died suddenly in an Oxford hospital during the last week of passenger services.

By 24th June 1957, internal correspondence records that despite overtime from Slough, 'Eastern Region locomen have been across the Watlington branch in strength learning the road'.

In that strange tradition that people turn out in force to celebrate the demise of a line, crowds gathered to give the last train "a wonderful send off". Jean Saunders, keeper of Kingston Crossing, recalls "I just stood there open-mouthed at all the arms out of the windows – it was packed."

The last train at Kingston
Crossing and Chinnor.
Hugh Davies

The local newspapers provided traditional coverage of the occasion:

Farewell to the "Flyer"

On Saturday night at 8.20 p.m. a group of people at Princes Risborough railway station said goodbye to the 'Watlington Flyer'. The train, which has taken people on the eight-mile journey through the Chiltern Hills for over 85 years will never again carry a passenger.

The service has been withdrawn by British Railways, because it was found to be uneconomical. The single-track line will continue to operate, carrying goods and freight instead of passengers. A bus service has been substituted, to run from Princes Risborough to Watlington.

The train, which only had one coach seating 72 people, used to run four times a day. But for its last journey into the country there were two coaches, carrying members of the Chinnor Parish Council. Guided by the steady hand of 53-year-old Mr. Bill Thomas, a relief driver from Slough, it pulled out for the last time and headed towards the Chiltern Hills.

Nineteen-year-old Brian Strickland, of Burnham, was on board as fireman, with Donald Gray, of 55 Lower Road, Chinnor, as guard.

Enthusiasts

Earlier in the day members of the Railway Enthusiasts Club had come to Princes Risborough to take pictures of the old 'tanker'.

A man who rode on his first train 50 years ago on the same line came to see the 'Watlington Flyer' off on its last journey with passengers. He is Mr. C. G. Goodchild of 'Lorette', Chontrey Road, West Wycombe. For him the occasion was a very sad one.

"It's a tragedy to see this little line go", he told us, "I well remember how excited I was 50 years ago in 1907 when my parents took me out on this train. It was my very first train ride. But in those days things were different. There were always plenty of people travelling on the line, but of course in later years it has been different."

One of the last people to buy a 1s 5d ticket was Mrs. Jean Braginton of 19 Wee Cot, Chinnor. Together with her husband she boarded the train and said: "We'll always remember this last journey."

And so will many other people, who knew and loved this railway.

THE SENTIMENTAL JOURNEY OF THE 'WATLINGTON FLYER'
Lively Scenes at Train's Last Trip

The Watlington Flyer made its last journey from Watlington Station on Saturday along the eight and three-quarter miles of track to Princes Risborough. The line has been closed to passenger traffic and a bus service is now in operation.

The reason for the closing of the line has been one of finance. It had not been paying, but it certainly paid on Saturday when the last train from Risborough carried all of the 200 passengers packed into two coaches as the little tank engine whistled and hooted its way along the edge of the Chilterns.

Railway enthusiasts from many towns came to have their last ride on the Flyer, but the final parting was made by local people, the passengers to whom the train has been familiar for many years.

At Princes Risborough there were photographers and crowds to take a last look at the train, questions were asked and answers given before the Flyer left on its last trip on the branch line. Engines on the main line and in the sidings of the station whistled their farewells and from the houses and gardens near the track groups of people waved and cheered.

At Wainhill Crossing a crowd had gathered, among them Mrs. Jessie Smith who had closed the gate across the line for the Flyer's four daily trips with the extra journey on Saturday.

The journey slowly became a triumphal procession as the Flyer entered the area where it has been an institution for so many years. There were cheers at Chinnor as the crowds lined the station approach and Mr. R. H. Siarey, chairman of the Parish Council led a party of over 70 Chinnor residents into a special coach which was added to the train.

The driver, Mr. William Thomas, and the fireman, Brian Strickland, invited Mr. Siarey to join them on the engine as they turned to pull the train out again. The guard, Mr. D. Gray from Chinnor, gathered up his loading lists and his ticket punch and there was a general leave-taking by the members of this very happy railway.

Opened as a private line in 1872, the Watlington Branch was taken over by the Great Western Railway in 1883. Since then it has served the villages from Watlington to Princes Risborough. Its staff have

Preparing for the final departure from Chinnor . . .

. . . and heading away towards Risborough.
Hugh Davies

been few but they have all stayed. Mr. Frank Hyde of Watlington, started as a porter at Watlington in 1920 and although his shift was over he rode as a passenger in the Flyer on its last journey.

One person who missed the closing was Mr. Jeff Pearson, of Spring Lane, Watlington. Mr. Pearson, who was 63, had driven the Flyer for 20 years until his eyesight failed a few years ago. Last week he died suddenly in an Oxford hospital.

Although the last scheduled run was from Risborough to Watlington, the engine and rolling stock had to return to the main line and with the largest crowd ever seen at Watlington Station, the Flyer had a wonderful send-off.

With the coaches still packed with Chinnor passengers and fog signals exploding every few feet along the track, the Flyer, whistling defiantly, pulled out of the station for the last time.

After closure, the waiting sheds were removed from the halts, the goods shed at Aston Rowant demolished and the yard layout there simplified, Kingston Crossing became unstaffed, the gates being operated by the trainmen, and the signals protecting the crossing were converted to fixed distants.

Wainhill Crossing was not considered suitable for the operation of the gates by train crews, owing to the steep gradient, so Mrs. Smith was retained as crossing keeper. Bob Williamson, former Watlington clerk, was promoted to Class 3 clerk at Chinnor, where he was assisted by a goods porter. As anticipated, the stations at Aston Rowant and Watlington were manned by a goods porter which must have been a pretty solitary job with just one goods that day and few callers. The

Under goods-only operation, the familiar Slough-based pannier tanks were displaced by Aylesbury-based interlopers like this ex-Great Eastern J15 0–6–0 No. 65390, photographed passing Lewknor Bridge Halt on 14th October 1957.

R. M. Casserley

Another view of No. 65390 on 14th October 1957, this time at Aston Rowant on its way back from Watlington with just the brake van in tow.

R. M. Casserley

The scene at Watlington in goods-only days. Compare this with the similar picture on page 82.   *C. M. Strevens*

delivery of parcels, including 'urgent/perishable traffic' between Princess Risborough and stations along the branch, was carried out daily by Messrs. Tappins, as the branch train did not run at a suitable time. However, delivery of parcels from Chinnor was carried out by the Zonal lorry from Thame.

Incidentally, instead of the J68 0–6–0T used on the trial, Aylesbury shed provided J15 0–6–0 tender engines for the goods service, and later LMS Class 2 2–6–2 tanks, which ran light engine from Aylesbury at 11.35, arriving at Risborough at 11.53 and departing with the Chinnor goods at 12.20. The engine was scheduled to shunt at Chinnor from 12.34–1.18, then return to Risborough to work a second trip to serve Chinnor, leaving Risborough at 1.50 and returning from Chinnor at 2.20.

The Watlington goods left Risborough at 2.55, arriving at Watlington at 3.42 and returning at 4.0 p.m., calling at Chinnor from 4.18–4.28 on the way back, and finally returning to Aylesbury light engine, leaving Risborough at 5.35.

In June 1958 the District Goods Manager's office at Reading began preliminary investigations into the possibility of closing the branch beyond Chinnor. The quantity of freight dealt with at Aston Rowant and Watlington for the 11 months up to May 1958 was:

	Received Wagons	Forward Wagons
Coal	396	
Other materials	218	92
General merchandise	86	69
OCS	23	3

As the accommodation at Chinnor provided for 17 wagons in position, it was felt that the traffic from Aston Rowant and Watlington could be concentrated there. Furthermore, the branch 'could be reduced in status from a one engine in steam line to that of a siding from Princes Risborough to Chinnor with the resultant economies in maintenance and renewal charges'.

A visit to the branch on Monday, 7th July 1958, revealed just two wagons of coal at Aston Rowant and one empty, whilst at Watlington there were eight wagons of coal in the yard, six of which were 16-tonners, two vans of cattle feed and four empties. Also 'a local firm has also obtained 80 sq yds of wharfage where they are dumping large quantities of scrap steel. Some comes in by rail and is sorted out but the larger quantity comes in by road. So far a small quantity has been despatched by rail'.

This was Clement Ives' son Tony who developed a scrap business in the town on the site now occupied by Watlington Fire Station, and later at How Hill. Some of their scrap may have been moved by rail before the line was closed to passengers, but apparently during 1958 there had been up to six or seven wagons in the yard at Watlington being loaded at any one time.

The scrap was largely sent to South Wales for smelting, but there was no pattern to the despatch arrangements. Some of the metal included offcuts or reject parts from Morris Motors. By this time, Ives had yards at Watlington, How Hill, Cuxham, Wapps Grove and Chalgrove, and were also sending scrap away by rail from Wallingford and Morris Cowley.

Swarf (metal shavings and filings) was also collected from another Morris Motors site at Theale and tipped by the site of

Watlington station shortly after the January 1961 closure to goods services, but before the removal of track.　　　　*Brian Morgan*

the old milk platform at Watlington station. When sufficient had accumulated, a JCB type of vehicle was taken to the station to load it into wagons positioned along the back siding, usually empties from Tappins coal deliveries.

At this time, trains are said to have been formed up in the platform and despatched about 4.0 p.m.

With piles of scrap accumulating and soiling the yard surface, vertical corrugated iron sheeting containing swarf by the site of Reg Pocock's milk platform, the goods shed in use as a sack store, the pillar tank being used to wash Ives' lorries, and the station building in use as a mess room, it must have been a very sorry sight.

Whether any of the retired staff visited the station at this time is not known, but if they did, its appearance would no doubt have filled them with dismay. In Reg Pocock's day, even the faithful porters were relegated to the goods shed for their tea breaks, the cosy interior of the pristine and well-ordered office being reserved for the station master and his clerk who presided over the neatly-kept desks, ticket rack, beautifully written accounts books and ledgers.

It was eventually realised that the 'in position' wagon accommodation at Chinnor would be inadequate for the needs of the Watlington and Aston Rowant traders in addition to those already using Chinnor yard, i.e. Messrs. Siareys timber traffic and the coal merchant. It would therefore be necessary to extend the coal yard road along the waste land adjacent to the siding, moving back the existing coal wharves for this to be done. It was

realised that some traders 'may prefer to deal with their traffic at Wallingford in preference to Chinnor'.

However, this was a minor detail when, according to a report, the annual saving for closing the line beyond Chinnor was £6,304.

When that section of line was closed on 2nd January 1961, Tappins continued to receive supplies by rail from what would more recently be termed as the new 'railhead', i.e. last surviving goods yard, at Chinnor, and the track beyond 3m 70c was recovered (later reinstated to 3m 77c in 1969). The station buildings at Aston Rowant were soon demolished but the one at Chinnor survived for a few more years before suffering the same fate. And that is where we leave the story for future historians who might find more motivation to record diesel-hauled workings over the last remnant of the old Princes Risborough and Watlington Railway, which finally closed in 1990. The line between Risborough and Chinnor has since been rescued by the Chinnor & Princes Risborough Railway Association, but that really is a separate story. If you have enjoyed this book you may understand why our interest is not sustained beyond the withdrawal of passenger services. We would rather forget the line's lingering death during the final years and remember it in happier times, fully intact, well cared for and run by as close a family of railwaymen as we have been privileged to meet anywhere, proudly serving a rural community where everyone pulled together and helped one another.

Appendix 1
SPECIFICATION OF ROLLING STOCK
FOR THE WATLINGTON & PRINCES RISBOROUGH RAILWAY

1st & 2nd Class Composite Carriage Drawing No. 1726 two 1st and two 2nd Class Compts to carry 16 1st and 20 2nd Class passengers

Length of body	26	0
Width	8	0
Height floor to roof in centre	6	8
Wheelbase	15	0

3rd Class Carriage Drawing No. 1727 to consist of 5 Compts, and to carry 50 passengers

Length	26	0
Width	8	0
Height floor to roof in centre	6	8
Wheelbase	15	0

Goods Bk Van (Passenger) Drawing 1728A to consist of one luggage and one guards compartment

Length of body	20	0
Width	7	6
" of Caboose	9	0
Height floor to roof in centre	6	8
Wheelbase	10	0

Body — The exterior framing & panels of all bodies to be of best quality Moulmein teak, the interior framing being of pitch pine, except the hoopsticks which are to be of best English Ash. The flooring (which is to be of two thicknesses of ¾in (boards) the roof (¾in thick) the partitions (in two thicknesses of ¾in boards) and the end & side linings (of ½in boards) all to be of well seasoned best Baltic Redwood.

Fittings — The handles, hinges, & other brass furniture to be of best quality and approved patterns. Each 1st & 2nd Class Compartment to have a lamp with protector and ring fitted in centre of roof.

Roofs — The roof to be covered with best quality waterproof navy canvas.

Trimming &c
First Class — The interior of 1st Class Compartments to be upholstered in blue cloth & Morocco and trimmed with lace, with spring seats and backs. The roof & the sides above the squabs to be covered with ornamental wax cloth, finished with gilt mouldings. A net to be fixed over each seat with ornamental brackets and rods. Cords for hats also to be provided. The doors to have sliding windows with Morocco & brown leather glass strings also sliding ventilators. The side light windows to be stationary & to be fitted with Merino curtains extending over them and the door lights, & meeting in the middle. The floor to be carpeted.

Second Class — The interior of second class compts to be upholstered & finished blue worsted rep, the seats & backs stuffed with horse hair, an umbrella net to be fixed over each seat with ornamental brackets & rods. The doors to have sliding windows & leather straps. The woodwork where not upholstered to be stained imitation teak & varnished.

Each compartment to be provided with a roof lamp, protector & ring.

Third Class — The 3rd Class doors to have sliding windows with leather straps & fixed ventilators. The interior woodwork of seats, sides, and partition to be stained teak colour & varnished. The roof painted white. Two roof lamps, protectors & rings & stoppers to be provided.

Brake Van — Brake Van. The guards compartment to be fitted with side lookouts furnished with seats, lockers, shelves, roof lamps & necessary fittings. Also a screw brake to the arrangement shown on drawing acting on all the four wheels.

The luggage compartment to have folding doors on each side fitted with necessary bolts & fastenings.

Underframes — The underframes to be constructed of good sound oak and Pitch pine.

The headstocks (11in x 4in) & Crossbars (10in x 4in) being oak, and the solebars (10in x 4in) centre longitudinals (10in x 3½in), end ditto (10in x 2½in) & diagonal bearers (10in x 3in) to be of Pitch Pine. The solebars to be strengthened by iron flitch plates bolted to the sides.

Ironwork — The step irons, axleguards, & general ironwork to be of iron of a quality capable of sustaining a tensile strain of 24 tons per square inch with a diminution of 20% of fractured area.

The Screw couplings & chains to be of best Cable iron.

The drawbar hooks, buffer heads and spring scroll irons to be of best hammered scrap iron. The buffer heads being turned to template.

Bearing & draw springs — The bearing springs to be of best Sheffield Spring steel consisting of 10 plates 3½in x ½in, 7ft 0in long from centre to centre of eyes. The buffing & draw springs to be of laminated steel consisting of 12 plates 3in x ½in of best Sheffield manufacture.

Axleboxes — The axleboxes to be of approved construction fitted with spring covers and brass bearings adapted for lubrication by grease.

Wheels & axles — The wheels to be 3ft 6in dia with solid wrot iron centres 8 pairs — spokes 3¼in wide, ¾in thick tapered to 5/8in at rims which are to be 7/8in thick. The nave to be of wrought iron 9in diameter & 7in thick. The tyres 5in x 2in to be of best Bessemer steel secured to rims by Mansell's patent retaining rings. The axles to be of the best selected scrap iron 6ft 7½in centres, journals 8in x 3½in.

Painting & Varnishing — The exteriors of bodies to be highly varnished, picked out & lettered in gold to order. The underframes flitch plates & headstocks to be painted & grained imitation Teak. The ironwork, wheels, & axles springs &c to be painted black. The steps, &c being bronzed. The roofs outside to be well painted with best white lead.

Generally — The material & workmanship throughout to be of the very best description & the carriages to be delivered free on the Watlington & Princes Risboro' Rly at the price of eight hundred pounds in four months from the 14th June 1878.

Per Pro Lancaster Wagon Co.
W. C. Shackleford
Manager

Lancaster June 1878

Appendix 2 – MANNING WARDLE & CO'S ACCOUNT FOR REPAIRS TO W&PRR ENGINE, August 1882

Boyne Engine Works
Hunslet, Leeds
August 15th 1882

Messrs. The Watlington & Princes Risborough Rly Co.
Watlington, Oxon.

Bot. of Manning, Wardle & Co.
Engineers, Boiler Makers &c.

Repairs to engine 'Sharp, Stewart & Co's' make in our works. – Men's time, materials, & use of tools in our works repairing engine as below –

Getting in, stripping, taking to pieces and examining engine, removing old cylinder, reboring & repairing with new patch, turning up tyres, lining eccentrics with new packings & fitting to tumblers, boring out new piston and valve spindle, glands & fitting to covers – rebushing glands of piston & valve spindle – renewing cylinder cocks – riveting new plate and angle iron to ashpan bottom, and bracket to damper – adjusting new grate bar – brazing new ends to injector & feed pipes – finishing & fitting new cotters to cross-heads, repairing steam gauge, punching & riveting new wrot iron patch to smokebox tube plate, welding new end to crossbar & fitting cylinder with new skids – adjusting liners & 8 new brasses in axle boxes, planing & finishing new box and refitting same to axles with the requisite pins – finishing and fitting new gauge & whistle cocks – fitting 3 new brass mud plugs – repairing motion with new finished and casehardened pins – welding new end to breakscrew, fitting same with nut & adjusting – repairing springs with 3 new steel back & intermediate plates, & sundry pins, cotters, & buckle & blast pipe with new clasps – renewing spring pillars – finishing & fitting new reversing trigger – refacing slide valves – drawing, filing & re-setting slide bars – repairing safety valve, & clack boxes – repairing smoke box with new plates, & buffers with new wrot iron washers – finishing jet pipe coupling – welding new ends to spring links – bolting buffer case to beam & fitting hoops to cylinder lid & boring, planing, finishing & fitting new brasses in connecting rods & securing with cotters and otherwise generally overhauling & repairing engine – re-erecting lagging, getting off old paint – repainting, lining out & varnishing engine as new – testing boiler, trying in steam & delivering on the rails in Leeds. 243 4 8

2 cast iron block pistons finished & fitting with 2 turned & finished rings as per our letter dated July 13/82 @ 5/10/- ea 11 0 0

254 4 8

Creditors

	C	qr	lb		s	£	s	d	
By cast iron scrap	3	0	7	@	3/-		9	2	
" wrot " "	2	1	8	@	3/6		8	1	
" steel " "		2	17	@	5/-		3	3	
" brass " "	1	3	18	@	6/-	5	7	0	6 7 6
									£247 17 2

Carried forward
Order dated June 6/82

Appendix 3
VALUATION OF W&PRR ENGINES, CARRIAGES AND WAGONS, 25th June 1883

4

Watlington & Princes Risborough Railway.

DESCRIPTIVE LIST OF Narrow GAUGE LOCOMOTIVE ENGINES.

25 June 1883

No. of Engine: Pass.	No. of Engine: Goods.	DATE of Starting.	DATE re-built.	MAKER.	Original COST (including Tender.)	Tender or Tank.	Weight in Working order: Tons.	Weight in Working order: Cwt.	CYLINDERS: Inside or Outside.	CYLINDERS: Dia.	CYLINDERS: Stroke.	WHEELS: Total No.	WHEELS: No. Coupled.	WHEELS: Diameter: Leading.	WHEELS: Diameter: Driving.	WHEELS: Diameter: Trailing.	WHEELS: Description of Tyre Fastening.	WHEEL BASE. L. to T.	BOILER BARREL: Length	BOILER BARREL: Outside diam.	FIREBOX: Length outside	FIREBOX: Length inside.	TUBES: No.	TUBES: Length	TUBES: Outside diam.	TUBES: Iron or Brass.	TUBES: Date.	Working PRESSURE per square inch.	MILEAGE, from date of Starting, or date of Renewal to	TANK Contents in Gallons. (if Tank Engine.)	Engine stationed at	If in working order or under repairs.	REMARKS.
No 1 Green	Mixed	1875 Sept 20		Sharp Stewart	£900	Tank	24	10	Inside	14	18	6	All	3.6	5.6	3.6	Bolt	14.6	10.3		3.6	3.1				Brass		120		650	Watlington	Working order	~~700~~ £220
No 2	Mixed	1876 Feb 1		"	£1475	"	19	11	"	12	17	6	4	2.4	4.0	4.0	"	12.5	9.3		3.0	2.6	108		2	Brass		120		400	"	"	~~750~~ £850

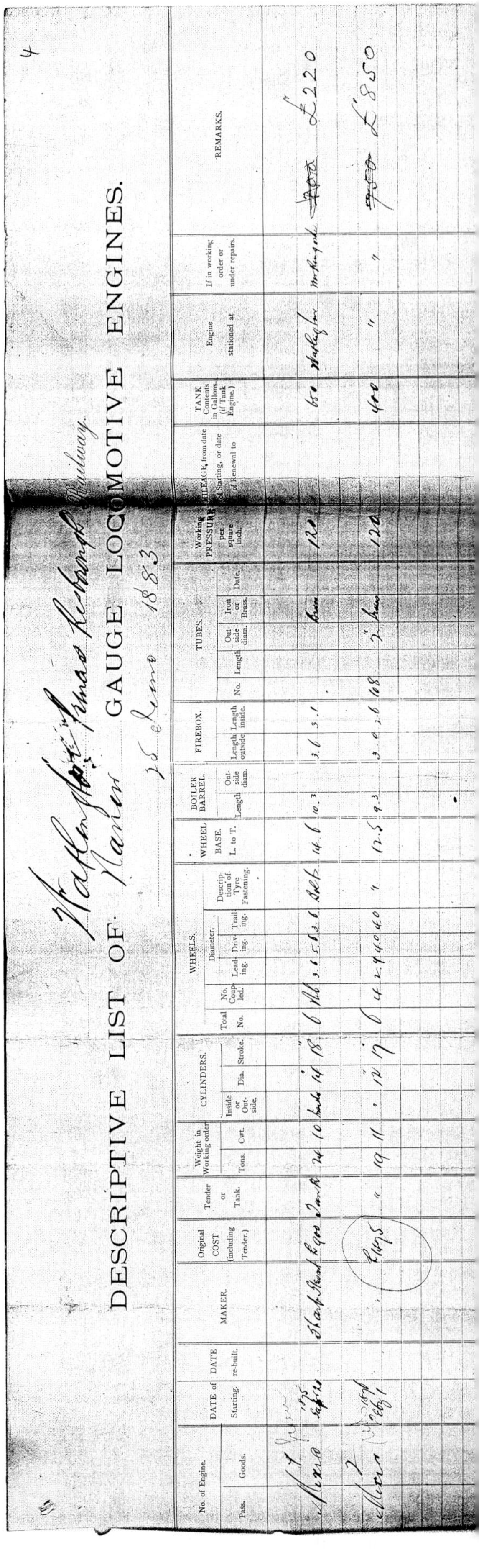

5

Watlington & Princes Risborough Railway

DESCRIPTIVE LIST OF Narrow GAUGE PASSENGER STOCK.

15 June 1883

NUMBER	Class of Vehicle.	BODY. Material	Length over Mouldings Outside.	Breadth over Mouldings Outside.	Height from Floor to Roof Inside.	FRAME. Material.	NO. OF COMPARTMENTS. 1st Class.	2nd Class.	3rd Class.	Luggage.	Guards	AXLES. Length between centres of Journals.	Size of Journals.	Diam. through Boss of Wheels.	Diam. in Middle.	WHEELS. No.	Diam.	Description of Tyre Fastening.	Wheel Base.	BUFFERS. Dead, India Rubber, Spiral Spring, or Laminated Spring	DRAW GEAR. India Rubber or Laminated Spring	BRAKE. Single or Double.	Builder.	Date of Construction.	Original Cost.	REMARKS. £
1	Composite	Pitch pine [illegible]	26.0	8.0	6.8	Pitch Pine Teak [illegible]	2	2	"	"	"	6.7½	8×3½			4	3.6	[illegible] Mansell's patent ring	15.0	Laminated Spring	Laminated Spring	~~Double~~	Lancaster Wagon Co	Jany 1879	260	~~170~~ 185
1	Third	"	26.0	8.0	6.8	"			5	"	"	6.7½	8×3½			4	3.6	"	15.0	"	"	"	"	"	~~200~~ 200	~~130~~ 145
1	Van	"	20.0	7.6	6.8	"				1	1	6.7½	8×3½			4	3.6	"	10.0	"	"	Double	"	"	180	~~120~~ 130
																									640	~~420~~ £460

3 Old Carriages & 2 pairs of Old Wheels £40

6

Watlington & Princes Risborough Railway

DESCRIPTIVE LIST OF Narrow GAUGE GOODS STOCK.

25 June 1883

Number	Class of Vehicle.	BODY. Material.	Length inside.	Breadth inside.	Height inside.	Frame Material.	AXLES. Length between centre of Journals.	Size of Journals.	Dia. through Boss of Wheels.	Dia. in middle.	WHEELS. No.	Diameter.	Description of Tyre Fastening.	Wheel base.	BUFFERS. Dead India Rubber Spiral Spring, or Laminated Spring.	DRAW GEAR. India Rubber, or Laminated Spring.	BRAKE. Single or Double.	WEIGHT. Tons.	Cwts.	Qrs.	Load to carry Tons.	Builder.	Date of Construction.	Original cost.	Remarks.
3	Open Goods Wagon	Deal	14.0	6.9	1.9	Oak & Pitch Pine					4	3.0		8.6	Dead	Indiarubber	Single				6	[illegible]	Dec 79		These wagons were purchased on deferred payments at £59 each. New to this [illegible] except wheels springs axle boxes were supplied in Dec 79 costing £102. 9. 9
2	"	"	14.0	6.9	1.9	Pitch Pine					4	3.0		8.6	"	"	"				6	"	"		
1	"	"	14.0	6.9	2.4	"					4	3.0		8.6	"	"	"				6	"	"		
4	"	"	"	"	1.9	Solebars & headstocks oak					4	3.0		8.8	"	"	"				6			~~£~~	
5	"	"	"	"	1.9	rem.					4	3.0		"	"	"	"				6				
6	"	"	"	"	1.9	Pitch Pine					4	3.0		"	"	"	"				6				

6 wagons £24 each

Appendix 4 – W&PRR TRAFFIC RECEIPTS AND EXPENSES 1872–1881

Watlington and Princes Risborough Rly.

Comparative Statement, compiled from the Government Railway Returns, for each year from 1872 to 1881.

Year ending	Length of line (single) miles	Train Miles Pass.ʳ	Train Miles Goods	Train Miles Total	Permt. Way £	Loco. Dept. £	Cars. Dept. £	Traffic £	General Charges £	Miscellaneous not in foregoing £	TOTAL £	Avg per Train Mile s. d.	Cost on Receipts %	Receipts Pass.ʳ £	Receipts Goods £	Receipts TOTAL £
1872 *		mixed		6372	165	436		86	87	15	789	2/5.11	113	329	337	666
1873	8	"		16866	447	1162		326	234	454	2623	3/1.32	142	861	980	1841
1874	8	"		16886	406	1196		263	289	524	2663	3/1.92		910	958	1868
1875	8	"		16902	714	1153	12	259	217	300	2715	3/2.55	127	954	1030	1984
1876	9	"		17638	561	761	19	254	206	291	2098	2/4.22	100	1003	1104	2107
1877	9	"		16884	694	693	21	286	216	414	2324	2/9.03	102	968	1304	2272
1878	9	"		17028	822	*329	*82	269	209	713	2402	2/9.85	109	1007	1190	2197
1879	9	"		17048	887	*330		263	216	472	2550	2/11.89	111	973	1330	2303
1880	9	"		16914	542	668	16	290	209	344	2129	2/6.10	98	976	1199	2175
1881	9	"		17082	892	668	1	284	217	348	2410	2/9.86	101	1055	1324	2379
Yearly average				13,508 / 17,056	892						21,919 / 2435	2/10.26	114	8709 / 967	1424/19 / 1158	19,126 / 2,125

Rolling Stock: Carts & Wagons — 1873: 6, 1874: 6, 1875: 3/6, 1876: 3/6, 1877: 3/6, 1878: 3/6, 1879: 3/6, 1880: +1/6, 1881: +1/2/6, yearly avg +1/2/16

* 5 months only.

* 1878 The Co. paid £404 for hire of Rolling Stock and this sum is included in Miscellaneous charges.
* 1879 " " £403

† The Rolling Stock is hired.

Appendix 5 – DESCRIPTIVE LIST OF W&PRR CARRIAGES AND WAGONS, 17th July 1883
including original carriages to be scrapped

G.W.R.—CARRIAGE DEPARTMENT.   Description of 2ft Gauge Passenger Stock.   Welshpool & Llanfair Rwy. & Railway Co.

Number.	Class of Vehicle.	Body.				No. or Compartments.					Length of Spring from Centres of Eyes.	Axles.			Wheels.		Description or			Weight.				When built.	Let.	Date taken.	REMARKS.
		Material.	Length over Mouldings outside.	Breadth over Mouldings outside.	Height from floor to roof Inside.	1st Class.	2nd Class.	3rd Class.	Luggage.	Guards.		Length between Centres of Journals.	Size of Journals.	Dia. through Boss of Wheel.	Dia. in Middle.	No.	Dia.	Buffers.	Drawgear.	Brake.	T.	c.	q.				

(handwritten ledger entries, largely illegible)

G.W.R.—CARRIAGE DEPARTMENT.   Description of 2ft Gauge Wagons.

Number.	Class of Vehicle.	Body.			Frame.		Length of Spring from Centres of Eyes.	Axles.			Wheels.		Marks on Axle boxes.	Description or			Weight.			Load to Carry. Tons.	Builder.	When built.	Let.	Date taken.	REMARKS.
		Length Inside.		Height Inside.	Material.			Length between Centres of Journals.	Size of Journals.	Dia. through Boss of Wheels.	Dia. in Middle.	No.	Dia.		Buffer.	Drawgear.	Brake.	T.	c.	q.						

(handwritten ledger entries, largely illegible)

Appendix 6 – EXTRACT FROM 1926 GWR BRANCH LINE REPORT

WATLINGTON BRANCH.

No. 47

Watlington — Lewknor Bridge Halt — Aston Rowant — Kingston Crossing Halt — Chinnor — Wainhill Halt — Bledlow Bridge Halt — Princes Risboro.

1m. 71c. — 67c. — 1m. — 8m. 75c. — 1m. 40c. — 62c. — 1m. 23c. — 1m. 52c.

EXPENDITURE.

Traffic Department Staff—Paybill Figures.

Station.	1924.	1925.	£	Percentage of Traffic Receipts.
Chinnor	£ 649	£ 657		
Aston Rowant	313	293		
Watlington	1,012	997		
	£1,974	£1,947		
TOTAL ...			1,947	7.59

Loco. Department, Engine and Train Running Expenses.

Coaching (Coal consumption 31.0 lbs. per mile) ...17,134... Total £ 2,875.
Freight (Coal consumption 31.0 lbs. per mile) ...18,894... Total £ 1,834.

	£	Percentage
TOTAL ...	4,709	18.36
Engineering Department, Maintenance and Renewal ...	2,320	9.05
Signal Department, Maintenance and Renewal ...	132	.51
Clothing ...	37	.14
Fuel, Lighting, Water and General Stores ...	81	.32
Rates ...	185	.72
TOTAL ...	£9,411	36.69

† Note.—No general charges (Abstract E. of Annual Report) nor cost of supervision, advertising, printing, etc. (Abstract D. of Annual Report) have been included in this Statement. In the 1925 Annual Report these items = 8.98% of Traffic Receipts.

The percentage of maintenance, renewal and working expenses to Traffic receipts for whole system = 83.63%.

*RECEIPTS—YEAR 1925.
* As shown on Station Traffic Statement; see note on page 2 of Report.

Station.	Passenger. £	Parcels. £	Goods. £	Total. £	1924 Total. £	Increase or Decrease. £
Chinnor	1,159	542	8,896	10,597	11,329	− 732
Aston Rowant	419	711	4,680	5,810	6,299	− 489
Watlington	1,638	2,756	4,839	9,233	9,185	+ 48
TOTAL ...	£ 3,216	£ 4,009	£18,415	£25,640	£26,813	− £ 1,173

Decrease due to :—Completion of main road improvements and less traffic at Messrs. Benton's Lime, etc., Siding.

PASSENGER TRAFFIC WORKED BY :—

Branch Train (including a Trailer for use at the Halts).
5 Trips each way and 1 Trip on Saturdays only.
Engine stabled at Watlington.

SIGNALLING ARRANGEMENTS :—

Wooden Staff : One Engine in Steam.

ALTERATIONS MADE OR PROPOSED IN WORKING ARRANGEMENTS :—

Recovery of Signals and Signalling Equipment at Watlington.

GOODS TRAFFIC WORKED BY :—

2 Trips each way and 1 Princes Risboro' to Chinnor and back.

Goods Tonnage : forwarded and received : 1925 :—

		Principal traffic consists of :
Coal and Minerals ...	31,318	Lime, Cement and Agricultural Products.
General Goods ...	16,108	

Daily average of wagons dealt with :—

	forwarded ..	received ..
Coal and Minerals ...	6	17
General Goods ...	15	8

RULING GRADIENT

1 in 69

Length .. ¼ mile.

1925
29,087 ... cans of milk.
150 ... trucks of live stock by goods train.

Estimated Annual Value of Savings £ 8

2-26 (17)

Appendix 7
WATLINGTON SIGNAL BOX DIAGRAM
following removal of signals

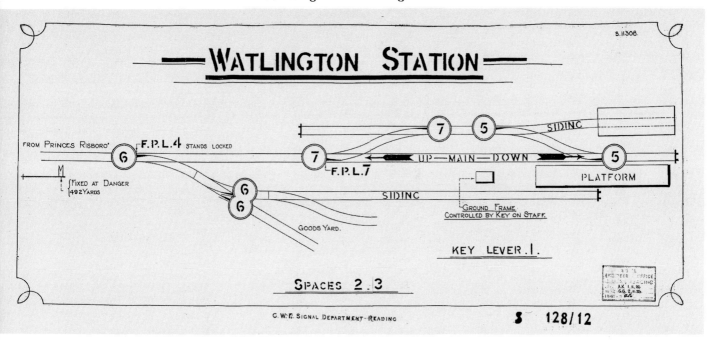

Appendix 8 – TRACK PLAN OF WATLINGTON STATION

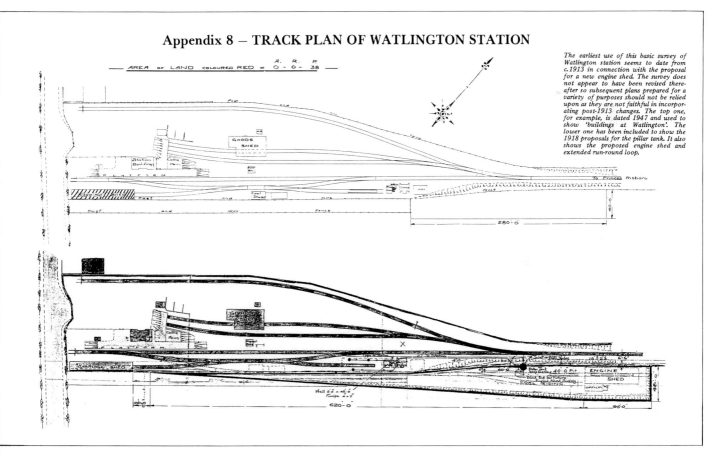

The earliest use of this basic survey of Watlington station seems to date from c.1913 in connection with the proposal for a new engine shed. The survey does not appear to have been revised thereafter so subsequent plans prepared for a variety of purposes should not be relied upon as they are not faithful in incorporating post-1913 changes. The top one, for example, is dated 1947 and used to show 'buildings at Watlington'. The lower one has been included to show the 1918 proposals for the pillar tank. It also shows the proposed engine shed and extended run-round loop.

Appendix 9 – WATLINGTON LOCOMOTIVE ALLOCATIONS 1901-1948

Year	Number	Class
1901	1465	'517' class 0–4–2T
	2081	'2021' class 0–6–0ST
1902	1465	'517' class 0–4–2T
	2081	'2021' class 0–6–0ST
1903	463	'Metro' class 2–4–0T
	1465	'517' class 0–4–2T
	2081	'2021' class 0–6–0ST
1904	4	'Metro' class 2–4–0T
	5	'Metro' class 2–4–0T
	467	'Metro' class 2–4–0T
	1465	'517' class 0–4–2T
	2081	'2021' class 0–6–0ST
	2083	'2021' class 0–6–0ST
1905	4	'Metro' class 2–4–0T
	467	'Metro' class 2–4–0T
	2083	'2021' class 0–6–0ST
1906	4	'Metro' class 2–4–0T
	981	'Metro' class 2–4–0T
	2081	'2021' class 0–6–0ST
	2083	'2021' class 0–6–0ST
	2126	'2021' class 0–6–0ST
	2132	'2021' class 0–6–0ST
	2150	'2021' class 0–6–0ST
1907	2083	'2021' class 0–6–0ST
	2126	'2021' class 0–6–0ST
	2132	'2021' class 0–6–0ST
	2150	'2021' class 0–6–0ST
1908	2126	'2021' class 0–6–0ST
	2132	'2021' class 0–6–0ST
	2150	'2021' class 0–6–0ST
	3568	'Metro' class 2–4–0T
	3599	'Metro' class 2–4–0T
1909	615	'Metro' class 2–4–0T
	2103	'2021' class 0–6–0ST
	2126	'2021' class 0–6–0ST
	2132	'2021' class 0–6–0ST
	2150	'2021' class 0–6–0ST
	2159	'2021' class 0–6–0ST
	2778	'2721' class 0–6–0ST
1910	613	'Metro' class 2–4–0T
	2103	'2021' class 0–6–0ST
	2113	'2021' class 0–6–0ST
	2159	'2021' class 0–6–0ST
1911	2103	'2021' class 0–6–0ST
	2113	'2021' class 0–6–0ST
	2159	'2021' class 0–6–0ST
1912	1172	'1076' class 0–6–0ST
	1460	'Metro' class 2–4–0T
	2103	'2021' class 0–6–0ST
	2113	'2021' class 0–6–0ST
	2159	'2021' class 0–6–0ST
1913	1172	'1076' class 0–6–0ST
	1417	'Metro' class 2–4–0T
	1460	'Metro' class 2–4–0T
	1770	'1854' class 0–6–0ST
	2113	'2021' class 0–6–0ST
	2159	'2021' class 0–6–0ST
	3500	'Metro' class 2–4–0T
	3562	'Metro' class 2–4–0T
	3595	'Metro' class 2–4–0T
1914	1172	'1076' class 0–6–0ST
	1408	'Metro' class 2–4–0T
	1770	'1854' class 0–6–0ST
	2113	'2021' class 0–6–0ST
	2159	'2021' class 0–6–0ST
	3500	'Metro' class 2–4–0T
	3563	'Metro' class 2–4–0T
	3569	'Metro' class 2–4–0T
1915	1172	'1076' class 0–6–0ST
	1408	'Metro' class 2–4–0T
	1770	'1854' class 0–6–0ST
	2113	'2021' class 0–6–0ST
	2159	'2021' class 0–6–0ST
	3584	'Metro' class 2–4–0T
1916	1172	'1076' class 0–6–0ST
	2113	'2021' class 0–6–0ST
	2121	'2021' class 0–6–0ST
	2137	'2021' class 0–6–0ST
	2159	'2021' class 0–6–0ST or PT
	3566	'Metro' class 2–4–0T
1917	2121	'2021' class 0–6–0ST
	2137	'2021' class 0–6–0ST
	2159	'2021' class 0–6–0PT
1918	2121	'2021' class 0–6–0ST
	2137	'2021' class 0–6–0ST
	2159	'2021' class 0–6–0PT
1919	2121	'2021' class 0–6–0ST
	2137	'2021' class 0–6–0ST
	2159	'2021' class 0–6–0PT
1920	2121	'2021' class 0–6–0ST
	2137	'2021' class 0–6–0ST
	2159	'2021' class 0–6–0PT
	3584	'Metro' class 2–4–0T
1921	2121	'2021' class 0–6–0ST
	2137	'2021' class 0–6–0ST
	2159	'2021' class 0–6–0PT
	3587	'Metro' class 2–4–0T
1922	2103	'2021' class 0–6–0PT
	2121	'2021' class 0–6–0ST or PT
	2137	'2021' class 0–6–0ST
	2159	'2021' class 0–6–0PT
	3563	'Metro' class 2–4–0T
	3565	'Metro' class 2–4–0T
	3566	'Metro' class 2–4–0T
1923	1953	'850' class 0–6–0PT
	2103	'2021' class 0–6–0PT
	2121	'2021' class 0–6–0PT
	2159	'2021' class 0–6–0PT
1924	2103	'2021' class 0–6–0PT
	2121	'2021' class 0–6–0PT
	2159	'2021' class 0–6–0PT
1925	2103	'2021' class 0–6–0ST
	2121	'2021' class 0–6–0ST
	2159	'2021' class 0–6–0ST
1926	616	'Metro' class 2–4–0T
	1406	'Metro' class 2–4–0T
	1969	'850' class 0–6–0PT
	2103	'2021' class 0–6–0PT
	2121	'2021' class 0–6–0PT
	2159	'2021' class 0–6–0ST
	3561	'Metro' class 2–4–0T
1927	1969	'850' class 0–6–0PT
	2072	'2021' class 0–6–0PT
	2103	'2021' class 0–6–0PT
	2121	'2021' class 0–6–0PT
1928	2026	'2021' class 0–6–0PT
	2072	'2021' class 0–6–0PT
	2087	'2021' class 0–6–0PT
	2103	'2021' class 0–6–0PT
1929	2069	'2021' class 0–6–0PT
	2074	'2021' class 0–6–0PT
	2087	'2021' class 0–6–0PT
1930	2074	'2021' class 0–6–0PT
	2112	'2021' class 0–6–0PT
1931	2026	'2021' class 0–6–0PT
	2046	'2021' class 0–6–0PT
	2069	'2021' class 0–6–0PT
	2087	'2021' class 0–6–0PT
	2112	'2021' class 0–6–0PT
1932	1427	'517' class 0–4–2T
	2046	'2021' class 0–6–0PT
	2069	'2021' class 0–6–0PT
	2081	'2021' class 0–6–0PT
	2087	'2021' class 0–6–0PT
	2112	'2021' class 0–6–0PT
1933	Not available	
1934	2081	'2021' class 0–6–0PT
	2098	'2021' class 0–6–0PT
	2112	'2021' class 0–6–0PT
1935	2046	'2021' class 0–6–0PT
	2074	'2021' class 0–6–0PT
	2098	'2021' class 0–6–0PT
1936	2046	'2021' class 0–6–0PT
	2087	'2021' class 0–6–0PT
	2112	'2021' class 0–6–0PT
1937	2026	'2021' class 0–6–0PT
	2112	'2021' class 0–6–0PT
1938	2026	'2021' class 0–6–0PT
	2087	'2021' class 0–6–0PT
1939	2055	'2021' class 0–6–0PT
	2026	'2021' class 0–6–0PT
	2087	'2021' class 0–6–0PT (renumbered 2188 the same year)
	2112	'2021' class 0–6–0PT
	4842	'48XX' class 0–4–2T (November only)
1940	2055	'2021' class 0–6–0PT
	2078	'2021' class 0–6–0PT
	2112	'2021' class 0–6–0PT
1941	2078	'2021' class 0–6–0PT
	2112	'2021' class 0–6–0PT
	5417	'54XX' class 0–6–0PT
1942	2055	'2021' class 0–6–0PT
	2078	'2021' class 0–6–0PT
	2112	'2021' class 0–6–0PT
	2747	'2721' class 0–6–0PT
1943	2055	'2021' class 0–6–0PT
	2078	'2021' class 0–6–0PT
	2112	'2021' class 0–6–0PT

'2021' class 0–6–0ST No. 2121 at Slough shed.   *J. N. Maskelyne*   'Large Metro' No. 3548 at Slough shed.

'2021' class 0–6–0PT No. 2074 at Slough shed in 1936, dwarfed by one of the '61XX' class 2–6–2Ts used for suburban work.

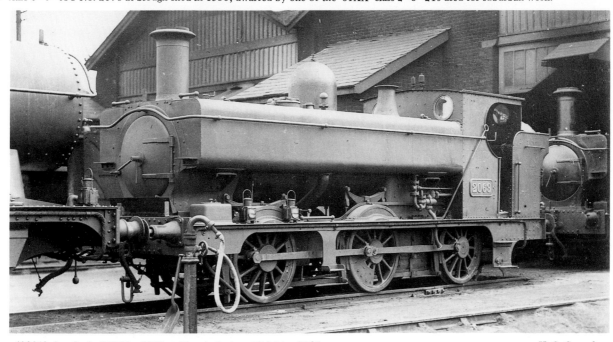

'2021' class 0–6–0PT No. 2069 at Slough shed on 17th May 1930.   *H. C. Casserley*

'2021' class 0—6—0PT No. 2078 at Tyseley on 19th May 1937.   *F. K. Davies*

'2721' class 0—6—0PT No. 2747.

Year	Number	Class
1944	2078	'2021' class 0—6—0PT
	2112	'2021' class 0—6—0PT
	2747	'2721' class 0—6—0PT
	2757	'2721' class 0—6—0PT
	3754	'57XX' class 0—6—0PT
	3769	'57XX' class 0—6—0PT
	3770	'57XX' class 0—6—0PT
	4650	'57XX' class 0—6—0PT
	5716	'57XX' class 0—6—0PT
	5783	'57XX' class 0—6—0PT
1945	2055	'2021' class 0—6—0PT
	2747	'2721' class 0—6—0PT
	2757	'2721' class 0—6—0PT
	2787	'2721' class 0—6—0PT
	5715	'57XX' class 0—6—0PT
	5737	'57XX' class 0—6—0PT
	5783	'57XX' class 0—6—0PT
1946	2055	'2021' class 0—6—0PT
	2112	'2021' class 0—6—0PT
	2787	'2721' class 0—6—0PT
	2790	'2721' class 0—6—0PT
	4650	'57XX' class 0—6—0PT
	9640	'57XX' class 0—6—0PT
1947	2112	'2021' class 0—6—0PT
	2757	'2721' class 0—6—0PT
	3677	'57XX' class 0—6—0PT
	3769	'57XX' class 0—6—0PT
	4617	'57XX' class 0—6—0PT
	5715	'57XX' class 0—6—0PT
	9640	'57XX' class 0—6—0PT
1948	3677	'57XX' class 0—6—0PT
	3766	'57XX' class 0—6—0PT
	3798	'57XX' class 0—6—0PT
	4617	'57XX' class 0—6—0PT
	5737	'57XX' class 0—6—0PT
	9653	'57XX' class 0—6—0PT

'2721' class 0—6—0PT No. 2790 at Southall.

'850' class 0—6—0PT No. 1969 at Watlington on 30th July 1949.

J. H. Meredith

'57XX' class 0—6—0PT No. 5766 at Watlington.

R. J. Buckley

Appendix 10 – STATEMENTS OF TRAFFIC DEALT WITH AT STATIONS

TRAFFIC DEALT WITH AT STATIONS.   LONDON DIVISION. (Branch Lines.)

STATION	YEAR	Staff Supervisory and Wages (all Grades) No.	Paybill Expenses £	TOTAL RECEIPTS £	Tickets Issued No.	Season Tickets No.	Passenger Receipts incl. S.P. etc. £	Parcels & Misc. Number No.	Parcels & Misc. Receipts £	Passenger Total £	Coal & Coke "Charged" Fwd. Tons	Other Minerals Fwd. Tons	General Merchandise Fwd. Tons	Coal & Coke "Charged" Recd. Tons	Other Minerals Recd. Tons	General Merchandise Recd. Tons	Coal & Coke "Not Charged" (Fwd. & Recd.) Tons	Total Goods Tonnage Tons	Total Receipts excl. "Not Charged" Coal & Coke £	Livestock Fwd. & Recd. Wagons	Total Carted Tonnage Tons
Watlington Branch.																					
Bledlow Bridge Halt } Wainhill Halt. }				Included with Watlington.																	
Chinnor	1903	4	140	2,315	6,402	*	508	4,841	221	729	—	11	1,434	4	631	1,351	1,061	4,492	1,586	—	329
	1913	4	176	3,585	6,116	*	561	6,192	371	932	—	5,947	1,037	454	650	1,901	3,332	12,481	2,653	53	363
	1923	5	626	9,682	8,533	17	1,211	4,070	463	1,674	23	2,655	9,628	3,192	2,801	1,129	3,145	22,550	8,008	24	406
	1929	5	507	12,440	6,186	46	200	7,459	560	1,460		2,322	15,484	483	1,450	973	14,070	34,810	10,980	9	275
	1930	5	552	10,633	5,873	48	844	6,645	495	1,389		3,395	12,248	565	2,591	1,166	15,888	35,794	9,224	8	331
	1931	5	528	8,021	5,752	46	726	6,611	418	1,144		2,988	9,018	500	3,876	950	14,210	31,542	6,877	5	318
	1932	5	532	7,039	5,750	38	724	6,325	392	1,116		1,152	8,275	409	3,122	675	16,913	29,646	5,923	4	530
	1933	5	436	5,107	5,533	48	716	5,139	288	1,004		2,593	5,377	539	2,025	598	14,197	23,459	4,166	5	255
	1934	5	528	5,569	5,764	48	762	5,391	224	986		2,884	6,464	578	3,963	452	12,681	26,112	4,553	5	498
	1935	5	546	5,955	5,298	38	686	5,615	125	811		2,779	9,299	567	2,691	398	13,721	29,365	5,144	16	596
	1936	5	529	6,937	5,050	40	691	5,068	137	828		1,330	10,978	561	3,964	809	15,806	33,438	6,109	8	412
	1937	5	502	9,003	4,909	36	752	5,044	125	877		516	14,761	500	5,103	760	18,830	40,470	8,191	11	525
	1938	5	562	10,583	4,550	26	793	4,487	150	853	11	488	28,652	377	7,295	380	20,706	66,779	16,130	12	232
Kingston Crossing Halt.					Included with Watlington.																
Aston Rowant (†)	1903	2	119	1,996	4,352	*	408	12,641	491	899	—	—	1,433	293	442	365	1,600	4,133	1,007	7	167
	1913	2	137	2,590	2,493	*	236	9,165	423	659	—	—	1,951	265	801	1,042	1,755	5,814	1,931	13	304
	1923	2	483	5,350	2,600	11	355	9,392	768	1,123		24	1,637	83	2,041	967	1,853	6,640	4,227	37	527
	1929	2	245	3,985	1,122	15	322	13,822	79	1,301	20		469	149	2,660	541	2,564	6,403	2,684	39	223
	1930	2	244	2,924		11	285	11,716	864	1,149	3	7	531	125	869	417	2,688	4,640	1,775	28	237
	1931	2	240	2,706	879	12	240	12,010	772	1,012	56		559	76	714	315	2,964	4,684	1,694	16	370
	1932	2	245	2,184	740	10	221	8,342	529	750		6	401	153	821	212	2,904	4,497	1,434	16	304
	1933	2	229	2,182	708	2	147	2,245	335	482	9		358	119	1,407	243	2,325	4,461	1,700	7	269
	1934	2	230	1,550	923	3	168	1,903	221	389	12		306	161	396	250	2,502	3,627	1,161	9	296
	1935	2	234	2,055	872	1	134	1,139	180	314			188	205	2,200	318	2,508	5,419	1,741	11	154
	1936	2	248	1,845	703	—	96	1,055	144	240		11	192	353	895	595	2,468	4,514	1,605	14	156
	1937	2	244	2,299	564	—	92	1,274	153	245		15	662	247	2,019	129	2,321	5,393	2,054	16	162
	1938	2	258	1,637	516	—	76	1,114	158	234	29		771	290	271	208	2,695	3,664	1,403	4	119
Lewknor Bridge Halt.					Included with Watlington.																
Watlington	1903	4	287	5,754	8,363	*	954	19,972	1,039	1,993	—	—	2,966	464	1,098	2,471	3,474	10,473	3,761	43	977
	1913	4	339	6,721	24,714	*	1,647	22,773	1,200	2,847	—	—	3,300	623	690	2,822	3,711	11,198	3,884	41	1,166
	1923	8	1,029	8,887	16,183	32	1,767	22,185	2,231	3,998	24	28	2,469	373	915	2,050	3,105	8,916	4,889	54	657
	1929	8	1,024	8,616	12,188	6	1,375	32,558	2,181	3,556	28	115	1,237	327	3,586	1,751	4,183	11,227	5,060	80	639
	1930	8	1,028	7,637	11,663	10	1,185	29,427	2,118	3,303	18	112	923	286	2,907	1,723	3,961	9,935	4,334	63	563
	1931	8	1,082	5,333	11,909	12	1,112	23,245	1,619	2,731	11	110	451	385	898	1,526	4,086	7,467	2,607	153	594
	1932	8	1,039	5,060	11,952	16	1,110	19,396	1,343	2,453	12	220	451	422	900	1,479	3,646	7,180	2,607	52	503
	1933	8	1,049	4,275	11,159	33	1,028	13,395	927	1,955	—	256	326	272	1,121	1,078	3,476	6,529	2,320	18	510
	1934	6	989	4,188	10,782	29	972	13,604	618	1,590	—	48	177	249	1,467	1,522	3,397	6,869	2,598	15	641
	1935	6	989	3,849	10,438	30	924	14,911	812	1,736	—	352	138	262	438	1,324	3,713	6,227	2,113	16	597
	1936	6	977	3,775	10,609	27	856	14,485	654	1,510	5	252	281	258	913	990	3,929	6,628	2,265	18	737
	1937	6	956	3,608	10,149	37	938	11,277	379	1,317	—	170	177	454	1,027	1,108	3,706	6,646	2,291	29	1,051
	1938	6	1,013	3,363	9,204	32	796	10,821	378	1,176	11	376	308	353	543	940	3,487	6,028	2,187	25	905
Total	1903	10	546	10,065	19,117	*	1,870	37,454	1,751	3,621	—	11	5,833	761	2,171	4,217	6,105	19,098	6,444	50	1,473
	1913	10	652	12,906	33,323	*	2,444	38,130	1,994	4,438	—	5,975	6,288	1,342	2,141	4,925	8,798	29,493	8,468	107	1,833
	1923	15	2,138	23,919	27,316	60	3,333	35,647	3,462	6,795	24	2,683	13,734	3,653	5,757	4,146	8,133	38,106	17,124	115	1,590
	1929	15	1,776	25,041	19,496	67	2,597	53,839	3,720	6,317	76	2,437	17,190	959	7,696	3,265	20,817	52,440	18,724	128	1,137
	1930	15	1,824	21,154	18,552	69	2,314	47,788	3,477	5,791	21	3,485	13,707	916	6,367	3,246	22,537	50,279	15,403	99	1,131
	1931	15	1,850	16,065	18,540	70	2,078	41,866	2,809	4,887	67	3,098	10,028	961	5,448	2,791	21,260	43,693	11,178	174	1,282
	1932	15	1,816	14,283	18,442	64	2,055	34,063	2,264	4,319	12	2,849	9,127	994	4,843	2,366	22,563	41,273	9,964	69	1,337
	1933	13	1,714	11,564	17,400	83	1,891	20,798	1,550	3,441	9	2,849	6,961	930	4,553	1,889	19,998	36,489	8,123	29	1,034
	1934	13	1,747	11,307	17,469	80	1,902	20,898	1,063	2,995	12	2,882	6,947	988	4,926	2,264	18,580	36,599	8,342	29	1,435
	1935	13	1,749	11,839	16,603	69	1,744	21,665	1,117	2,861	—	3,131	9,535	1,034	5,329	2,040	10,942	41,011	8,998	43	1,347
	1936	13	1,754	12,557	16,302	67	1,643	20,608	935	2,578	5	1,593	11,451	1,172	5,762	2,394	22,203	44,580	9,979	40	1,305
	1937	13	1,702	14,975	15,682	73	1,782	17,595	657	2,439	—	701	15,600	1,205	8,149	1,997	24,857	52,509	12,536	56	1,738
	1938	13	1,833	21,353	14,270	58	1,577	16,422	686	2,253	51	814	29,731	1,030	8,019	1,538	35,288	76,471	19,720	41	1,256

* Not available.   † Controlled by Watlington.

GREAT WESTERN RAILWAY.

STATEMENT OF TRAFFIC DEALT WITH AT STATIONS (481)

STATION (Halt or Platform): WATLINGTON
Joint with _____ Railway

DIVISION _____
SUPERVISED BY _____

Names of other Stations, etc., Traffic and Receipts from which are included below: BLEDLOW BDGE HALT, LEWKNOR BDGE HALT
or Names of Stations, Halts, Platforms, supervised: ASTON ROWANT, KINGSTON XING HALT, WAINHILL HALT

144

Item	1935 No./Fwd	1935 Rec./£	1936 No./Fwd	1936 Rec./£	1937 No./Fwd	1937 Rec./£	1938 No./Fwd	1938 Rec./£	1939 No./Fwd	1939 Rec./£	1940 No./Fwd	1940 Rec./£
No. of Authorised Staff — Clerical and Supervisory	2		2		2		2		2		3	
Wages	4		4		4		4		4		4	
Total Traffic Paybill Expenses		£ 2,990 N		£ 995 777		£ 995 964		£ 1013		£ 2735		£ 1160
COACHING TRAFFIC												
Passengers Booked by Rail, including Excess Fares Collected	104-38	836	10609	773	10149	874	9204	745	9270	808	11689	843
Season Tickets	30	88	27	85	37	63	32	52	13	20	21	92
Platform Tickets												
Seat Registration												
Cab Rents and Car Parking												
Lavatories				1		1		1		1		1
Other Receipts												
Total Passenger and Various Receipts		924		856		938		798		929		896
Parcels Forwarded	1280	166	1315	173	1454	188	1539	177	1271	184	1205	160
Parcels Received	7609	188	8040	1	8519	1	7860		7773		6531	
Miscellaneous Forwarded	5601	386	4773	444	934	165	1358	151	1438	179	1293	159
Miscellaneous Received	521	73	357	86	370	26	264	50	650	24	189	41
Total Parcels and Misc. Traffic and Receipts	14,911	812	14,485	654	11277	379	10,821	378	12041	302	9218	360
TOTAL COACHING RECEIPTS		1736		1510		1317		1176		1221		1256
GOODS TRAFFIC												
Coal and Coke, Not Charged (on "Weight" Invoices)		3713		3929		3706		3487		2813		3623
Coal and Coke, Charged		262	5	258	11	458	13	363	13	209		653
Other Minerals	352	438	252	913	170	1027	376	543	274	745	618	501
General Merchandise, Carted	151	485	105	587	131	880	69	750	103	1127	843	1488
General Merchandise, Agreed Charges Traffic				45		40		86		54		
General Merchandise, Not Carted	53	832	176	358	46	183	236	107	121	421	1461	
Total Tonnage	556	5744	538	6090	347	6299	692	5336	572	5504		6265
Total Receipts	347	1713	474	1735	364	2178	575	1504	455	2175		2175
Live Stock Forwarded and Received	Wagons 10	£ 53	Wagons 18	£ 76	Wagons 29	£ 113	Wagon 25	£ 108	Wagons 1	£ 5	Wagons 7	£
Total Goods Tonnage and Goods and Live Stock Receipts Forwarded and Received	6300	2113	6628	2285	6640	2665	6028	2187	6030	2735	4426	2735
TOTAL RECEIPTS (i.e., Coaching, Goods and Live Stock)		3849		3795		3972		3363		3720		3720
Other Coaching Traffic (Items not shown above)												
Forwarded Milk — Gallons / Cans / Tanks / No.	60761 / 5427	3610	54035	3610	Nil		Nil		Nil			
Non-Railborne		295		260								
Other Goods Traffic (Items not shown above)												
Loco. Coal and Free Hauled (Totals)	118	57	321	69	194	49	345	93	534	76	F.H. 12	
Total Other Tonnages and Receipts												
Non-Railborne												
Permitted Tonnage	1166	3819	1294	3377	1113	3225	1051	3112	1052	3712	2052	3316
Total Number of Invoices / Invoice Entries	1335	5441	1405	4745	1240	4249	1244	4263	2372	5010	2372	3730

* Also includes Receipts from Outboundary and other Cartage (excluding Non-Railborne), Weighbridge Receipts, Warehouse Rent, Siding Rent, Shunting Charges, Demurrage, and other Miscellaneous items.

24 Eks. 2025 Ivs. i: All—Est 40J—431 (25)

GREAT WESTERN RAILWAY.

STATEMENT OF TRAFFIC DEALT WITH AT STATIONS (481 A)

STATION (Halt or Platform) WHITINGTON

Joint with

_____ Railway

DIVISION

SUPERVISED BY

Names of other Stations, etc., Traffic and Receipts from which are included below BEDLOW BGE HALT, LEWKNOR BGE HALT
or Names of Stations, Halts, Platforms, supervised ASTON ROWANT, KINGSTON HALT, WAIN HILL HALT

YEAR	1941 NUMBER	1941 RECEIPTS	1942 NUMBER	1942 RECEIPTS	1943 NUMBER	1943 RECEIPTS	1944 NUMBER	1944 RECEIPTS	1945 NUMBER	1945 RECEIPTS	1946 NUMBER	1946 RECEIPTS
NUMBER OF AUTHORISED STAFF — Clerical and Supervisory	3		3		3		3		3		2	
Wages	6		6		6		7		7		6	
Total Traffic Paybill Expenses		£1474		£1612		£1152		£1845		£1751		£1902
COACHING TRAFFIC.												
Passengers Booked by Rail, including Excess Fares Collected	1877	£1430	1857	£2017	35720	£2615	37228	£2728	28140	£2441	18103	£2008
Season Tickets	48	£140	45	£127	46	£88	108	£289	56	£110	4	£11
Platform Tickets												
Seat Registration												
Cab Rents and Car Parking												
Lavatories							£1			£1		
Other Receipts		£1				£1						
Total Passenger and Various Receipts		1577		2225		2704		3018		2552		2019
Parcels Forwarded		312		351		446		261		254		290
Parcels Received		5		15		18		11		10		6
Miscellaneous Forwarded		126										
Miscellaneous Received		35		3								
Total Parcels and Misc. Traffic and Receipts		538				464		272		264		276
TOTAL COACHING RECEIPTS		2109				3168		3290		2816		2295

GOODS TRAFFIC.	1941 FWD TONS	1941 RECD TONS	1942 FWD TONS	1942 RECD TONS	1943 FWD TONS	1943 RECD TONS	1944 FWD TONS	1944 RECD TONS	1945 FWD TONS	1945 RECD TONS	1946 FWD TONS	1946 RECD TONS
Coal and Coke, Not Charged		4080		377		4241		5506		4850		3044
Coal and Coke, Charged		796		322		622		231				10
Other Minerals (Classes 1 to 6)	315	263	571	1155	929	1451	929	1100	1096	1450	914	827
General Merchandise (Classes 7 to 21)	1037	1568	925	1827	2444	4048	4169	10660	3715	1518	1962	1556
Total Tonnage	1352	6677	1514	6722	3393	10351	5098	17451	4491	9818	2882	5424
Total Goods Tonnage Forwarded and Received (TONNAGE)	8029		8236		13744		22595		12609		8313	
Live Stock Forwarded and Received (Wagons)												
Other Coaching Traffic (Items not shown above) (NUMBER)												
Forwarded Milk (Included in Miscellaneous Forwarded above) — Gallons / Cans / Tanks / No.												
Non-Railborne												
Other Goods Traffic (Items not shown above) (TONS)												
Loco. Coal and Free Hauled (Totals) (TONS F.H.)												
Total Other Tonnages (i.e., Domestic, Point to Point & Tolls)												
Non-Railborne												
Permitted Tonnage (FORWARDED / RECEIVED)	1519	3796	1454	3516	1720	3898	1509	3207	520	2657	1054	—
Total Number of Invoices	1594	3138	1512	3761	1838	4461	1664	4940	505	3741	1061	2751
Total Number of Invoice Entries												

GREAT WESTERN RAILWAY.

252 (481 A)

STATEMENT OF TRAFFIC DEALT WITH AT STATIONS

STATION (Halt or Platform). **WALLINGTON**

Joint with

Names of other Stations, etc., Traffic and Receipts from which are included below
or Names of Stations, Halts, Platforms, supervised

DIVISION _____   Railway _____

SUPERVISED BY _____

	1947			1948			19 49			1950			1951			1952		
NUMBER OF AUTHORISED STAFF		TO BE FILLED IN BY D.S.O.			TO BE FILLED IN BY D.S.O.			TO BE FILLED IN BY D.S.O.			TO BE FILLED IN BY D.S.O.			TO BE FILLED IN BY D.S.O.			TO BE FILLED IN BY D.S.O.	
Clerical and Supervisory	2			2			2			2			3					
Wages	6			5			4			4								
Total Traffic Paybill Expenses	£ 1990			£ 1929			£ 1892			£ 1837			£			£ 1818		
COACHING TRAFFIC.	NUMBER	TO BE FILLED	RECEIPTS	NUMBER	TO BE FILLED	RECEIPTS	NUMBER	TO BE FILLED	RECEIPTS	NUMBER	TO BE FILLED	RECEIPTS	NUMBER	TO BE FILLED	RECEIPTS	NUMBER	TO BE FILLED	RECEIPTS
Passengers Booked by Rail, including Excess Fares Collected	14924	2	£1676	14326	3	£1761	12795		£1490	11166		£1188	9054	3	£900	9556		£860
Season Tickets			£			£			£			£			£26	4		£32
Platform Tickets			£			£			£			£			£			£
Seat Registration			£			£			£			£			£			£
Cab Rents and Car Parking			£			£			£			£			£			£
Lavatories			£			£			£			£			£			£
Other Receipts			£ 2			£			£ 1			£			£			£
Total Passenger and Various Receipts			£ (1705)			£ 1772			£ 1491			£ 1188			£ 926			£ 892
Parcels Forwarded	5080	3	£542	4673	3	£246	4100	3	£661	8989		£1505	5141		£898	1832		£403
Parcels Received			£			£	609		£	7097		£	7228		£	3439		£
Miscellaneous Forwarded			£			£			£			£			£			£
Miscellaneous Received			£			£			£			£			£			£
Total Parcels and Misc. Traffic and Receipts	5080		£2895	4673		£2018	10102		£661	14086		£2673	12369		£1826	5271		£423
TOTAL COACHING RECEIPTS			£2895			£2018			£2142			£2673			£1826			£1375
GOODS TRAFFIC.	FORWARDED TONS.	RECEIVED TONS.		FORWARDED TONS.	RECEIVED TONS.		FORWARDED TONS.	RECEIVED TONS.		FORWARDED TONS.	RECEIVED TONS.		FORWARDED TONS.	RECEIVED TONS.		FORWARDED TONS.	RECEIVED TONS.	
Coal and Coke, Not Charged (on "Weight" Invoice—Charges dealt with by Audit Office)		3300			3235			4205			2444								
Coal and Coke, Charged (including "Weight" Invoice charges raised by Stations)	845	019		911	1078		1248	78		447	27							
Other Minerals (Classes 1 to 6)	1905	1141		1346	1342		1891	570		13	357							
General Merchandise (Classes 7 to 21)	2250	5100		2157	5652		2539	1211		369	981							
Total Tonnage									5804			424	3406					
Total Goods Tonnage Forwarded and Received	TONNAGE 4550			TONNAGE 4762			TONNAGE 8343			TONNAGE 230			TONNAGE			TONNAGE		
Live Stock Forwarded and Received	Wagons 5 £14	NUMBER		Wagons 7 £16	NUMBER		Wagons 10	NUMBER		Wagons 1	NUMBER		Wagons	NUMBER		Wagons	NUMBER	
Other Coaching Traffic (Items not shown above)	Gallons	Cases		Gallons	Cases		Gallons	Cases		Gallons	Cases		Gallons	Cases		Gallons	Cases	
Forwarded Milk (Included in Miscellaneous Forwarded above)	Cans	£		Cans	£		Cans	£		Cans	£		Cans	£		Cans	£	
Non-Railborne	Tanks No.	£		Tanks No.	£		Tanks No.	£		Tanks No.	£		Tanks No.	£		Tanks No.	£	
Other Goods Traffic (Items not shown above)	TONS. Loco.	TONS. F.H.		TONS. Loco.	TONS. F.H.		TONS. Loco.	TONS. F.H.		TONS. Loco. 640	TONS. F.H. 0		TONS. Loco.	TONS. F.H.		TONS. Loco.	TONS. F.H.	
Loco, Coal and Free Hauled (Totals)		283									£103							
Total Other Tonnages (i.e., Domestic, Point to Point & Tally)	FORWARDED.	RECEIVED.		FORWARDED.	RECEIVED.		FORWARDED.	RECEIVED.		FORWARDED.	RECEIVED.		FORWARDED.	RECEIVED.		FORWARDED.	RECEIVED.	
Non-Railborne																		
Permitted Tonnage	502	315		417	357		746	620		925								
Total Number of Invoices	513	316		421	558		763	455		915							6	
Total Number of Invoice Entries																		

BRITISH RAILWAYS
WESTERN REGION

STATEMENT OF TRAFFIC DEALT WITH AT STATIONS

481A

DISTRICT _____

SUPERVISED BY STATION MASTER AT _____

STATION (Halt or Platform) **WATLINGTON** ✓

Joint with

Names of other Stations, etc., Traffic and Receipts from which are included below or Names of Stations, Halts, Platforms, supervised

Region _____

	1953		1954		1955		19		19	
YEAR	NUMBER	RECEIPTS	NUMBER	RECEIPTS	NUMBER	RECEIPTS	NUMBER	RECEIPTS	NUMBER	RECEIPTS
Number of Staff Regularly Employed :—										
Clerical and Supervisory										
Wages										
TOTAL										
COACHING TRAFFIC										
Passengers Booked by Rail, Including Excess Fares Collected	9797	£ 928	10393	£ 932	10665	£ 956		£		£
Season Tickets	11	£ 66	8	£ 48		£		£		£
Platform Tickets		£		£		£		£		£
Seat Registration		£		£		£		£		£
Cab Rents		£		£		£		£		£
Car Parking		£		£		£		£		£
Lavatories		£		£		£		£		£
Other Receipts		£		£		£		£		£
Total Passenger and Various Receipts		£ 994		£ 480		£ 956		£		£
Parcels & Misc. Forwarded	664	£ 147	489	£ 99	354	£ 116		£		£
Parcels & Misc. Received	3264	£ 1	4196	£	3862	£		£		£
Total Parcels and Misc Traffic and Receipts	3928	£ 148	4655	£ 97	4216	£ 116		£		£
TOTAL COACHING RECEIPTS		£ 1142		£ 1099		£ 1072		£		£

GOODS TRAFFIC	FORWARDED TONS	RECEIVED TONS	FORWARDED TONS	RECEIVED TONS	FORWARDED TONS	RECEIVED TONS	FORWARDED TONS	RECEIVED TONS	FORWARDED TONS	RECEIVED TONS
Coal and Coke										
Other Minerals (Classes 1 to 6)										
General Merchandise (Classes 7 to 21)										
Total Tonnage										
Total Goods Tonnage Forwarded and Received	TONNAGE		TONNAGE		TONNAGE		TONNAGE		TONNAGE	

Live Stock Forwarded and Received	Wagons		Wagons		Wagons		Wagons		Wagons	
Other Coaching Traffic (items not shown separately above)	NUMBER		NUMBER		NUMBER		NUMBER		NUMBER	
Forwarded Milk (Included in Parcels and Misc. Forwarded above) — Gallons	Gallons		Gallons		Gallons		Gallons		Gallons	
Cans	Cans	Cases	Cans	Cases	Cans	Cases	Cans	Cases	Cans	Cases
Tanks	Tank	£	Tanks	£	Tanks	£	Tanks	£	Tanks	£
Non-Railborne (Not included above) — No.	No.	£	No.	£	No.	£	No.	£	No.	£
Other Goods Traffic (items not shown above)	TONS		TONS		TONS		TONS		TONS	
Loco, Coal and Free Hauled (Totals)	Loco.	F.H.	Loco.	F.H.	Loco.	F.H.	Loco.	F.H.	Loco.	F.H.
Total Other Tonnages (i.e., Domestic, Point to Point and Tolls)										
Non-Railborne	FORWARDED	RECEIVED	FORWARDED	RECEIVED	FORWARDED	RECEIVED	FORWARDED	RECEIVED	FORWARDED	RECEIVED
Permitted Tonnage										
Total Number of Invoices										
Total Number of Invoice Entries										

GREAT WESTERN RAILWAY.

STATEMENT OF TRAFFIC DEALT WITH AT STATIONS

(481)

DIVISION ....

SUPERVISED BY **WATLINGTON**

STATION (Halt or Platform) **ASTON ROWANT** Railway

Joint with

Names of other Stations, etc., Traffic and Receipts from which are included below
or Names of Stations, Halts, Platforms, supervised

	1935	1936	1937	1938	1939	1945
NUMBER OF AUTHORISED STAFF — Clerical and Supervisory	1				—	—
Wages	2	2	2	2	2	2
Total Traffic Paybill Expenses	£234 N	£255 248	£246 244	£258	£204	£265
COACHING TRAFFIC (NUMBER / RECEIPTS £)						
Passengers Booked by Rail, including Excess Fares Collected	872 / 131	703 / 96	564 / 92	510 / 76	434 / 61	386 / 67
Season Tickets	1 / 3			2 / 6	/ 6	13 / 23
Platform Tickets						
Seat Registration						
Cab Rents and Car Parking						
Lavatories						
Other Receipts						
Total Passenger and Various Receipts	£134	£96	£92	£76	£67	£97
Parcels Forwarded	149 / 15	249 / 22	262 / 35	152 / 16	128 / 20	212 / 31
Parcels Received	925 / 30	731 / 51	926 / 52	823 / 104	896 / 88	607 / 78
Miscellaneous Forwarded	44 / 80	51 / 62	52 / 88	104 / 114	88 / 93	242 / 98
Miscellaneous Received	21 / 55	24 / 60	34 / 30	35 / 28	17 / 36	17 / 14
Total Parcels and Misc. Traffic and Receipts	1139 / 180	1055 / 144	1274 / 153	1114 / 158	1129 / 149	1575 / 143
TOTAL COACHING RECEIPTS	£314	£240	£245	£234	£216	£240
GOODS TRAFFIC (FORWARDED TONS / RECEIVED TONS)						
Coal and Coke, Not Charged (on "Weight" Invoice—Charges dealt with by Audit Office)	2508	2468	2321	2096	2575	2532
Coal and Coke, Charged (Including "Weight" Invoice traffic — charges raised by Stations)	205	333	29 / 247	29 / 290	44 / 272	33 / 412
Other Minerals	2200	11 / 91	15 / 2019	271	21 / 275	175
General Merchandise, Carted (Collected, Delivered and Collected and Delivered)	64 / 89	45 / 100	97 / 57	41 / 68	21 / 108	107 / 120
General Merchandise, Agreed Charges Traffic	10	10	8	10	12	
General Merchandise, Not Carted	124 / 228	147 / 482	565 / 64	730 / 130	43 / 88	
Total Tonnage	188 / 5240	203 / 4311	677 / 4716	800 / 2864	108 / 3230	1319 / 3245
Total Receipts	£203 / £1506	£264 / £1271	£742 / £1205	£772 / £594	£102 / £561	£102
Live Stock Forwarded and Received (Wagons)	11 / 32	4 / 70		4 / 37	5 / 25	11
Total Goods Tonnage and Goods and Live Stock Receipts Forwarded and Received (TONNAGE / RECEIPTS £)	5428 / 1741	4514 / 1605	5393 / 2055	3664 / 1403	3358 / 688	4760
TOTAL RECEIPTS (i.e. Coaching, Goods and Live Stock)	£2055	£1845	£2300	£1637	£904	
Other Coaching Traffic (Items not shown above)						
Forwarded Milk (Included in Miscellaneous Forwarded above) — Gallons / Cans / Cases / Tanks / No.						
Non-Railborne						
Other Goods Traffic (Items not shown above) — Loco, Coal and Free Hauled (Totals) (TONS / F.H.)	715 / 85	458 / 127	12 / 54	46 / 58	124 / 62	3 / 20
Total Other Tonnages and Receipts (i.e. Domestic, Point to Point & Tolls *)						
Non-Railborne						
Permitted Tonnage						
Total Number of Invoices	804 / 1659	635 / 1375	1708 / 1359	837 / 1126	515 / 946	449 / 920
Total Number of Invoice Entries	925 / 1706	737 / 1452	1950 / 1449	912 / 1273	586 / 997	523 / 952

* Also includes Receipts from Outboundary and other Carriage (excluding Non-Railborne), Weighbridge Receipts, Warehouse Rent, Siding Rent, Shunting Charges, Demurrage, and other Miscellaneous items.

GREAT WESTERN RAILWAY.

STATEMENT OF TRAFFIC DEALT WITH AT STATIONS

(481 A)

DIVISION _____

STATION (Halt or Platform) ASTON ROWANT.

Joint with _____

_____ **Railway**

Names of other Stations, etc., Traffic and Receipts *from which are included below*

or Names of Stations, Halts, Platforms, *supervised*

SUPERVISED BY WATLINGTON

ITEM	1941	1942	1943	1944	1945	1946
NUMBER OF AUTHORISED STAFF — Clerical and Supervisory						
— Wages	2	2	2	2	2	2
Total Traffic Paybill Expenses	£ 345	£ 306	£ 392	£ 445	£ 460	£ —
COACHING TRAFFIC. (NUMBER / RECEIPTS £)						
Passengers Booked by Rail, including Excess Fares Collected	722 / 133	1977 / 216	2516 / 267	2903 / 270	2494 / 36	1292 / 175
Season Tickets	29 / 88	32 / 60	33 / 64	31 / 66	12 / 27	3 / 12
Platform Tickets						
Seat Registration						
Cab Rents and Car Parking						
Lavatories						
Other Receipts						
Total Passenger and Various Receipts	£ 221	£ 270	£ 331	£ 236	£ 283	£ 189
Parcels Forwarded	£ 153	£ 100	£ 122	£ 122	£ —	£ 216
Parcels Received	£ —	£ 2	£ 2	£ 5	£ 8	£ 4
Miscellaneous Forwarded	£ 25	£ —	£ —	£ —	£ —	£ —
Miscellaneous Received	£ 178	£ 10	£ 124	£ 127	£ 148	£ 220
Total Parcels and Misc. Traffic and Receipts	£ 399	£ 112	£ 124	£ 127	£ 148	£ 220
TOTAL COACHING RECEIPTS	£ 399	£ 348	£ 455	£ 463	£ 431	£ 407
GOODS TRAFFIC. (FORWARDED TONS / RECEIVED TONS)						
Coal and Coke, Not Charged (on "Weight" Invoices—Charges dealt with by Audit Office)	2384	2373	2042	2282	2290	2154
Coal and Coke, Charged (Including "Weight" Invoice traffic Charges raised by Stations)	532	321	208	85 / 321		
Other Minerals (Classes 1 to 6)	56 / 91	217 / 200	175 / 120	63 / 321	127 / 229	254 / 426
General Merchandise (Classes 7 to 21)	742 / 426	2538 / 257	2249 / 614	595 / 815 / 440	800 / 344 / 394	543 / 213
Total Tonnage	798 / 3439	2755 / 3151	2445 / 2984	1373 / 3128	1027 / 2913	997 / 2993
Total Goods Tonnage Forwarded and Received	4237	5906	5429	4501	28-0	3590
Live Stock Forwarded and Received — Wagons		1	1	1		1
Other Coaching Traffic (Items not shown above)						
Forwarded Milk (Included in Miscellaneous Forwarded above) — Gallons / Cans / Tanks / No.						
Non-Railborne						
Other Goods Traffic (Items not shown above) — TONS / Loco. / F.H.						
Loco. Coal and Free Hauled (Totals)						
Total Other Tonnages (i.e., Domestic, Point to Point & Tails) — FORWARDED / RECEIVED						
Non-Railborne						
Permitted Tonnage — Total Number of Invoices	358 / 383	855 / 705	586 / 633	344 / 425	344 / 372	313 / 313
— Total Number of Invoice Entries	711 / 703	812 / 891	694 / 714	177 / 700	637 / 674	411 / 433

GREAT WESTERN RAILWAY.

STATEMENT OF TRAFFIC DEALT WITH AT STATIONS.

(481 A)

DIVISION _____

STATION (Halt or Platform) ASTON ROWANT.

Joint with _____   _____ Railway

Names of other Stations, etc., Traffic and Receipts from which are included below
or Names of Stations, Halts, Platforms, supervised

16

	1947		1948		1949		1950		1951		1952	
YEAR	TO BE FILLED IN BY D.S.O.	RECEIPTS	TO BE FILLED IN BY D.S.O.	RECEIPTS	TO BE FILLED IN BY D.S.O.	RECEIPTS	TO BE FILLED IN BY D.S.O.	RECEIPTS	TO BE FILLED IN BY D.S.O.	RECEIPTS	TO BE FILLED IN BY D.S.O.	RECEIPTS
NUMBER OF AUTHORISED STAFF — Clerical and Supervisory	2		2		2							
Wages												
Total Traffic Paybill Expenses	£515		£515		£556		£645				£440	
COACHING TRAFFIC.	NUMBER	RECEIPTS	NUMBER	RECEIPTS	NUMBER	RECEIPTS	NUMBER	RECEIPTS	NUMBER	RECEIPTS	NUMBER	RECEIPTS
Passengers Booked by Rail, including Excess Fares Collected	784	109	671	108	634	97	567	91	242	56	151	39
Season Tickets	11	40	11	55	2	21						
Platform Tickets												
Seat Registration												
Cab Rents and Car Parking												
Lavatories												
Other Receipts												
Total Passenger and Various Receipts		155		163		118		91		56		39
Parcels Forwarded	1914	96	1040	131	313	128	226	139	168	122	209	263
Parcels Received					678		703		655	15	473	
Miscellaneous Forwarded												
Miscellaneous Received												
Total Parcels and Misc. Traffic and Receipts	1984	96	1040	136	991	128	927	139	723	137	682	263
TOTAL COACHING RECEIPTS	1984	251		299		246	£	230	£	193	£	302
GOODS TRAFFIC.	FORWARDED TONS	RECEIVED TONS	FORWARDED TONS	RECEIVED TONS	FORWARDED TONS	RECEIVED TONS	FORWARDED TONS	RECEIVED TONS	FORWARDED TONS	RECEIVED TONS	FORWARDED TONS	RECEIVED TONS
Coal and Coke, Not Charged		1983		2114		1764		2080		2485		2368
Coal and Coke, Charged	5	37		150	22	107		122	42	22	1	109
Other Minerals (Classes 1 to 6)										106		70
General Merchandise (Classes 7 to 21)	528	55	333	251	225	136	99	118	177	403	448	
Total Tonnage	528	2300	333	2742	225	2031	99	2417	219	2995	458	2573
Total Goods Tonnage Forwarded and Received	TONNAGE 2828		TONNAGE 2753		TONNAGE 2226		TONNAGE 2516		TONNAGE 3214		TONNAGE 2501	
Live Stock Forwarded and Received (Items not shown above)	Wagons 1		Wagons 2		Wagons —		Wagons 3		Wagons —		Wagons —	
Other Coaching Traffic (Items not shown above) — Forwarded Milk (Included in Miscellaneous Forwarded above)	Gallons	Cases	Gallons	Cases	Gallons	Cases	Gallons	Cases	Gallons	Cases	Gallons	Cases
Non-Railborne	Cans		Cans		Cans		Cans		Cans		Cans	
	Tanks		Tanks		Tanks		Tanks		Tanks		Tanks	
	No.		No.		No.		No.		No.		No.	
Other Goods Traffic (Items not shown above) — Loco. Coal and Free Hauled (Totals)	TONS Loco.	F.H. 33	TONS Loco.	F.H. 461	TONS Loco.	F.H.	TONS Loco. 12	F.H. 166	TONS Loco.	F.H.	TONS Loco.	F.H. 116
Total Other Tonnages (i.e., Domestic Point to Point & Total)	FORWARDED	RECEIVED	FORWARDED	RECEIVED	FORWARDED	RECEIVED	FORWARDED	RECEIVED	FORWARDED	RECEIVED	FORWARDED	RECEIVED
Non-Railborne			38	247			10	192	28	359	7	201
Permitted Tonnage			38	246			16	203	32	371	7	262
Total Number of Invoices	205	500	55	93								
Total Number of Invoice Entries	213	500	57	94								

BRITISH RAILWAYS
WESTERN REGION

STATEMENT OF TRAFFIC DEALT WITH AT STATIONS

481A

DISTRICT _____

STATION (Halt or Platform) **ASTON ROWANT**

Joint with _____ Region _____

SUPERVISED BY STATION MASTER AT **WATLINGTON**

Names of other Stations, etc., Traffic and Receipts from which are included below
or Names of Stations, Halts, Platforms, supervised

Number of Staff Regularly Employed :—
- Clerical and Supervisory
- Wages
- TOTAL

COACHING TRAFFIC	1953 NUMBER	1953 RECEIPTS	1954 NUMBER	1954 RECEIPTS	1955 NUMBER	1955 RECEIPTS
Passengers Booked by Rail, Including Excess Fares Collected	245	£ 72	304	£ 55	219	£ 50
Season Tickets		£		£		£
Platform Tickets		£		£		£
Seat Registration		£		£		£
Cab Rents		£		£		£
Car Parking		£		£		£
Lavatories		£		£		£
Other Receipts		£		£		£
Total Passenger and Various Receipts		£ 72		£ 65		£ 50
Parcels & Misc. Forwarded	232	£ 296	354	£ 38	235	£ 43
Parcels & Misc. Received	645	£	527	£ 8	497	£
Total Parcels and Misc Traffic and Receipts	777	£ 296	981	£ 46	732	£ 43
TOTAL COACHING RECEIPTS		£ 368		£ 111		£ 93

GOODS TRAFFIC	1953 FORWARDED TONS	1953 RECEIVED TONS	1954 FORWARDED TONS	1954 RECEIVED TONS	1955 FORWARDED TONS	1955 RECEIVED TONS
Coal and Coke		2276	13	2142	13	1969
Other Minerals (Classes 1 to 6)		137	—	144	—	149
General Merchandise (Classes 7 to 21)	62	82	52	257	24	110
Total Tonnage	62	2510	52	2513	37	2228
Total Goods Tonnage Forwarded and Received — TONNAGE	2572		2625		2265	
Live Stock Forwarded and Received — Wagons	3		5			

Other Coaching Traffic (Items not shown separately above) — NUMBER

Forwarded Milk (Included in Parcels and Misc. Forwarded above) — Gallons / Cans / Tanks / No.

Non-Railborne (Not included above) — TONS

Other Goods Traffic (Items not shown above)	1953 TONS	1954 TONS	1955 TONS
Loco. Coal and Free Hauled (Totals)	F.H. 204	F.H. 32	F.H. 3

Total Other Tonnages (i.e. Domestic Point to Point and Tolls)

Non-Railborne

Permitted Tonnage

	1953 FORWARDED	1953 RECEIVED	1954 FORWARDED	1954 RECEIVED	1955 FORWARDED	1955 RECEIVED
Total Number of Invoices	10	257	13	242	4	192
Total Number of Invoice Entries	10	257	13	242	4	192

YEAR: 19 ___   19 ___   19 ___

GREAT WESTERN RAILWAY.

STATEMENT OF TRAFFIC DEALT WITH AT STATIONS (481)

STATION (Halt or Platform) **CHINNOR**

Joint with _____ Railway

Names of other Stations, etc., Traffic and Receipts from which are included below
or Names of Stations, Halts, Platforms, supervised

VISED BY _____

(handwritten top margin: 1089)

YEAR	1935	1936	1937	1938	1939	1940
Clerical and Supervisory — TO BE FILLED IN BY D.S.O.	1 / 4	1 / 4	1 / 4	1 / 4	1 / 4	1 / 4
Wages						
Total Traffic Paybill Expenses	£ 5146 N	£ 534 / 529	£ 505 / 502	£ 562	£ 542	£ 528

COACHING TRAFFIC.
(each year: NUMBER / RECEIPTS £)

	1935	1936	1937	1938	1939	1940
Passengers Booked by Rail, including Excess Fares Collected	5293 / 629	5050 / 622	4969 / 685	4550 / 622	4513 / 625	4767 / 668
...a Tickets	38 / 57	40 / 69	32 / 67	26 / 81	33 / 88	50 / 62
...rm Tickets						
Registration						
Rents and Car Parking						
...ries						
Receipts						
Total Passenger and Various Receipts	£ 686	£ 691	£ 752	£ 703	£ 713	£ 830
...s Forwarded	812 / 60	754 / 59	553 / 50	596 / 49	665 / 52	550 / 54
...s Received	3449 / —	3216 / —	3433 / 1	2763 / 1	2821 / 1	2721 / 1
...llaneous Forwarded	1301 / 57	1058 / 6	1018 / 96	1093 / 82	963 / 48	— / 21
...llaneous Received	63 / 8	40 / 9	40 / 8	53 / 19	19 / 10	12 / 5
Total Parcels and Misc. Traffic and Receipts	5615 / 125	5068 / 137	5044 / 125	4487 / 150	4168 / 111	3304 / 60
TOTAL COACHING RECEIPTS	£ 811	£ 828	£ 877	£ 863	£ 824	£ 890

GOODS TRAFFIC
(each year: FORWARDED TONS / RECEIVED TONS)

	1935	1936	1937	1938	1939	1940
...nd Coke, Not Charged (on "Weight" Invoices Charged, dealt with by Audit Office)	— / 13721	— / 15806	— / 18830	11 / 29706	183 / 26337	290 / 23218
...nd Coke, Charged (including "Weight" Invoice traffic, charges raised by Stations)	— / 567	— / 561	— / 500	— / 377	— / 220	— / 414
Minerals	2729 / 2691	1350 / 3964	516 / 5103	438 / 7206	189 / 5055	219 / 5885
...l Merchandise, Carted (Collected, Delivered and Collected and Delivered)	392 / 304	78 / 313	205 / 318	34 / 197	29 / 218	279 / 378
...l Merchandise, Agreed Charges Traffic						
...l Merchandise, Not Carted	8817 / 104	10900 / 476	14554 / 442	28617 / 193	17242 / 154	12479 / —
Total Tonnage	11988 / 17477	12308 / 21130	15217 / 25193	29100 / 37678	17643 / 31998	13267 / 29891
Total Receipts	£ 3422 / 1690	£ 3355 / 2724	£ 4979 / 3189	£ 6458 / 3692	£ 6103 / 2739	£ 6103 / 2739
Live Stock Forwarded and Received	Wagons 16 / £ 32	Wagons 8 / £ 30	Wagons 1 / £ 25	Wagons 12 / £ 48	Wagons / £	Wagons / £
Total Goods Tonnage and Goods and Live Stock Receipts Forwarded and Received — TONNAGE / RECEIPTS £	29465 / 5144	33638 / 6109	40410 / 8191	66778 / 10150	49671 / 8845	35692 / —
TOTAL RECEIPTS (i.e., Coaching, Goods and Live Stock)	£ 5955	£ 6937	£ 9008	£ 16983	£ 9659	

Coaching Traffic (Items not shown above)

	1935	1936	1937	1938	1939	1940
...arded Milk (Included in Miscellaneous Forwarded above) — Gallons / Cans	12840 / 1266	12835 / 1093	12566 / 992	13526 / 1051	8511 / 625	
— Tanks / No.						
Railborne						

Goods Traffic (Items not shown above)

	1935	1936	1937	1938	1939	1940
...Coal and Free Hauled (Totals) — Loco / F.H.	1550 / £16 / 63	1205 / £17 / 62	320 / £24 / 92	1326 / £33 / 70	1693 / £39 / 74	1603 / £ /
...Other Tonnages and Receipts (i.e., Domestic, Point to Point & Total ✱)						
Railborne						
...itted Tonnage — Forwarded / Received	1686 / 2903	1476 / 2924	1601 / 3943	1793 / 3790	— / 3761	1622 / 1653
Number of Invoices						

GREAT WESTERN RAILWAY.

STATEMENT OF TRAFFIC DEALT WITH AT STATIONS

(481 A)

DIVISION _____ *Railway* _____

STATION (Halt or Platform) __GHINTOR__

Joint with _____

Names of other Stations, etc., Traffic and Receipts from which are included below
or Names of Stations, Halts, Platforms, supervised __WARSHILL & KINGSTON CROSSING HALTS__

SUPERVISED BY _____

	1941		1942		1943		1944		1945		1946	
YEAR	No.	Recpts	No.	Recpts	No.	Recpts	No.	Recpts	No.	Recpts	No.	Recpts
NUMBER OF AUTHORISED STAFF — Clerical and Supervisory	1		1		1		1		1		2	
Wages	5		4		4		4		5		6	
Total Traffic Paybill Expenses £		805		930		1017		1216		1225		1158
COACHING TRAFFIC												
Passengers Booked by Rail including Excess Fares Collected	14465	1449	17391	1455	22007	1824	25015	1924	19006	1603	12244	1280
Season Tickets	129	462	126	370	136	405	147	473	101	369	80	310
Platform Tickets												
Seat Registration												
Cab Rents and Car Parking												
Lavatories											1	
Other Receipts												
Total Passenger and Various Receipts £		1881		1521		2229		2397		2029		1591
Parcels Forwarded		96		96		96		112		113	601	
Parcels Received		2		2						3	659	
Miscellaneous Forwarded		3		3							2381	
Miscellaneous Received		4		4								
Total Parcels and Misc. Traffic and Receipts £		73		73		96		112		113		109
TOTAL COACHING RECEIPTS £		1954		1717		2325		2509		2142		1700
GOODS TRAFFIC	Fwd	Rcvd	Fwd	Rcvd	Fwd	Rcvd	Fwd	Rcvd	Fwd	Rcvd	Fwd	Rcvd
Coal and Coke, Not Charged		11717	-	20743		16941		16182		16113	134	54
Coal and Coke, Charged	20	559	5	1321	9	1140	6	442	5	22	730	23119
Other Minerals (Classes 1 to 6)	35	2206	1051	4021	916	3645	344	3932	577	291	5145	4129
General Merchandise (Classes 7 to 21)	3571	145	4559	952	7189	851	10569	768	323	53	16009	1000
Total Tonnage	3626	14487	5615	26713	8114	22517	10915	21324	7905	18939		28302
Total Goods Tonnage Forwarded and Received (TONNAGE)		18313		32354		30751		32243		26811		44311
Live Stock Forwarded and Received — Wagons	-		4		4		2		7			
Other Coaching Traffic (Items not shown above)												
Forwarded Milk (Included in Miscellaneous) — Gallons												
Non-Railborne — Cans / Tanks / No.												
Other Goods Traffic (Items not shown above) — TONS												
Loco, Coal and Free Hauled (Totals) — F.H.	1197		1260		1245		3658		1795		601	31
Total Other Tonnages — Forwarded / Received												
Non-Railborne												
Permitted Tonnage												
Total Number of Invoices	949	910	1044	1255	1601	1198	1119	1238	2263	1111	1531	1461
Total Number of Invoice Entries	2306	2718	3151	3454	2709	3162	2542	2998	3109	3040	1843	2146

GREAT WESTERN RAILWAY.

STATEMENT OF TRAFFIC DEALT WITH AT STATIONS (481 A)

52

DIVISION _____

STATION (Halt or Platform) **CHINNOR**

Joint with _____ Railway

SUPERVISED BY

Names of other Stations, etc., Traffic and Receipts from which are included below
or Names of Stations, Halts, Platforms, supervised

YEAR	1947		1948		19 49		19 50		1951		1952	
	TO BE FILLED IN BY D.S.O.		TO BE FILLED IN BY D.S.O.		TO BE FILLED IN BY D.S.O.		TO BE FILLED IN BY D.S.O.		TO BE FILLED IN BY D.S.O.		TO BE FILLED IN BY D.S.O.	
NUMBER OF AUTHORISED STAFF { Clerical and Supervisory	5		4		6		2		4		2	
{ Wages	5		2		2		6				10	
Total Traffic Paybill Expenses (£)	1663		1473		1296		1899		1226		1742	

COACHING TRAFFIC.

	NUMBER	RECEIPTS £	NUMBER	RECEIPTS £	NUMBER	RECEIPTS £	NUMBER	RECEIPTS £	NUMBER	RECEIPTS £	NUMBER	RECEIPTS £
Passengers Booked by Rail, including Excess Fares Collected	10063	1185	9929	1395	9778	1307	9054	1263	8926	1188	8451	1144
Season Tickets	61	221	55	197	56	212	117	340	89	254	89	194
Platform Tickets												
Seat Registration												
Cab Rents and Car Parking												
Lavatories												
Other Receipts		10		3								
Total Passenger and Various Receipts (£)		1411		1595		1519		1603		1442		1338
Parcels Forwarded	576	94	527	101	545	77	618	96	671	78	698	93
Parcels Received	1947		2123		2428		2815		2410		2647	
Miscellaneous Forwarded												
Miscellaneous Received												
Total Parcels and Misc. Traffic and Receipts (£)	2823	79	2973	110	2973	107	3403	96	3081	84	3345	93
TOTAL COACHING RECEIPTS (£)		1495		1909		1697		1699		1526		1143

GOODS TRAFFIC.

	FORWARDED TONS	RECEIVED TONS	FORWARDED TONS	RECEIVED TONS	FORWARDED TONS	RECEIVED TONS	FORWARDED TONS	RECEIVED TONS	FORWARDED TONS	RECEIVED TONS	FORWARDED TONS	RECEIVED TONS
Coal and Coke, Not Charged (on "Weight" Invoices — Charges dealt with by Audit Office)	34	25612		28362		33074		3481		34557		32852
Coal and Coke, Charged (Including "Weight" Invoice traffic charges raised by Stations)	811	4712	385	8116		7167	44	6652	49	8246	9	7338
Other Minerals (Classes 1 to 6)	2914	808	3041	819	1430	350	945	202	1001	326	1057	200
General Merchandise (Classes 7 to 21)	3759	31135	3429	34136	3430	40597	949	43915	1001	43178	1070	42595
Total Tonnage												
Total Goods Tonnage Forwarded and Received — TONNAGE	34894		60985		42022		42914		44179		41465	
Live Stock Forwarded and Received — Wagons	9		2		4		9		4		6	
Other Coaching Traffic (Items not shown above)												
Forwarded Milk (Included in Miscellaneous Forwarded above) — Gallons / Cans / Tanks / No.												
Non-Railborne												
Other Goods Traffic (Items not shown above)												
Loco. Coal and Free Hauled (Totals) — TONS / F.H.	545 / 2198		688 / 4469		694 / 971		611 / 1107		506		1108	
Total Other Tonnages (i.e., Domestic, Point to Point & Tolls) — Forwarded / Received												
Non-Railborne												
Permitted Tonnage												
Total Number of Invoices	796	1203	332	1358	305	1203	207	1185	165	1278	157	1063
Total Number of Invoice Entries	818	2092	416	2019	343	1945	212	1957	170	1401	157	1023

BRITISH RAILWAYS
WESTERN REGION

STATEMENT OF TRAFFIC DEALT WITH AT STATIONS

481A

DISTRICT _____

STATION (Halt or Platform) CHINNOR

Region _____

SUPERVISED BY STATION MASTER AT _____

Joint with _____

Names of other Stations, etc., Traffic and Receipts from which are included below
or Names of Stations, Holts, Platforms, supervised

YEAR	1953		1954		1955		195..		19..		19..	
Number of Staff Regularly Employed :—												
Clerical and Supervisory												
Wages												
TOTAL												
COACHING TRAFFIC	NUMBER	RECEIPTS	NUMBER	RECEIPTS	NUMBER	RECEIPTS	NUMBER	RECEIPTS	NUMBER	RECEIPTS	NUMBER	RECEIPTS
Passengers Booked by Rail, Including Excess Fares Collected	7552	£1039	7774	£1091	6919	£991	7380	£1185				
Season Tickets	58	£163	43	£185	27	£91	59	£159				
Platform Tickets		£		£		£		£		£		£
Seat Registration		£		£		£		£		£		£
Cab Rents		£		£		£		£		£		£
Car Parking		£		£		£		£		£		£
Lavatories		£		£		£		£		£		£
Other Receipts		£		£		£		£		£		£
Total Passenger and Various Receipts		£1202		£1276		£1082		£1344		£		£
Parcels & Misc. Forwarded	636	£86	566	£70	312	£47	297	£66		£		£
Parcels & Misc. Received	2892	£1	2584	£1	2380	£1	2044	£1		£		£
Total Parcels and Misc Traffic and Receipts	2528	£87	3150	£71	2692	£48	2335	£60		£		£
TOTAL COACHING RECEIPTS		£1289		£1347		£1130		£1440		£		£

GOODS TRAFFIC	FORWARDED TONS	RECEIVED TONS	FORWARDED TONS	RECEIVED TONS	FORWARDED TONS	RECEIVED TONS	FORWARDED TONS	RECEIVED TONS	FORWARDED TONS	RECEIVED TONS	FORWARDED TONS	RECEIVED TONS
Coal and Coke		35,793	-	37,279	10	33,595		35,529				
Other Minerals (Classes 1 to 6)		8479	9	8557	5911			6937				
General Merchandise (Classes 7 to 21)	767	231	833	214	981	152	930	843				
Total Tonnage	767	44,503	842	46,050	991	39,658	930	43,309				
Total Goods Tonnage Forwarded and Received	TONNAGE 45,270		TONNAGE 46,892		TONNAGE 40,649		TONNAGE 44,239		TONNAGE		TONNAGE	
Live Stock Traffic Forwarded and Received	Wagons 7		Wagons 10		Wagons		Wagons		Wagons		Wagons	
Other Coaching Traffic (items not shown separately above)	NUMBER		NUMBER		NUMBER		NUMBER		NUMBER		NUMBER	
Forwarded Milk (Included in Parcels and Misc. Forwarded above) — Gallons / Cans / Tanks / No.	Gallons / Cans £ / Tanks £ / No.	Cases £	Gallons / Cans £ / Tanks £ / No.	Cases £	Gallons / Cans £ / Tank £ / No.	Cases £	Gallons / Cans £ / Tanks £ / No.	Cases £	Gallons / Cans £ / Tanks £ / No.	Cases £	Gallons / Cans £ / Tanks £ / No.	Cases £
Non-Railborne (Not included above)												
Other Goods Traffic (items not shown above)	TONS		TONS		TONS		TONS		TONS		TONS	
Loco. Coal and Free Hauled (Totals)	Loco. / F.H. 929		Loco. / F.H. 861		Loco. / F.H. 482		Loco. / F.H. 328		Loco. / F.H.		Loco. / F.H.	
Total Other Tonnages (i.e., Domestic, Point to Point and Tolls)												
Non-Railborne												
Permitted Tonnage	FORWARDED	RECEIVED	FORWARDED	RECEIVED	FORWARDED	RECEIVED	FORWARDED	RECEIVED	FORWARDED	RECEIVED	FORWARDED	RECEIVED
Total Number of Invoices	151	1141	130	1133	122	914	118	1053				
Total Number of Invoice Entries	151	1141	130	1133	122	914	118	1053				

BRITISH RAILWAYS
WESTERN REGION

STATEMENT OF TRAFFIC DEALT WITH AT STATIONS 481A

STATION (Halt or Platform) **CHINNOR.**

DISTRICT _____ Joint with _____ Region

SUPERVISED BY STATION MASTER AT _____

Names of other Stations, etc., Traffic and Receipts from which are included below
or Names of Stations, Halts, Platforms, supervised

YEAR	19	1960	1961	1962	1963	19
Number of Staff Regularly Employed :—						
Clerical and Supervisory						
Wages						
TOTAL						

COACHING TRAFFIC	NUMBER	RECEIPTS	NUMBER	RECEIPTS	NUMBER	RECEIPTS	NUMBER	RECEIPTS	NUMBER	RECEIPTS	NUMBER	RECEIPTS
Passengers Booked by Rail, including Excess Fares Collected		£		£		£		£		£		£
Season Tickets		£		£		£		£		£		£
Platform Tickets		£		£		£		£		£		£
Seat Registration		£		£		£		£		£		£
Cab Rents		£		£		£		£		£		£
Car Parking		£		£		£		£		£		£
Lavatories		£		£		£		£		£		£
Other Receipts		£		£		£		£		£		£
Total Passenger and Various Receipts		£		£		£		£		£		£
Parcels & Misc. Forwarded		£	126	£ 39	208	£ 69	196	£ 49	121	£ 44		£
Parcels & Misc. Received		£	2709	£	3094	£	3394	£	1421	£		£
Total Parcels and Misc Traffic and Receipts		£	2835	£ 39	3302	£ 69	3290	£ 49	1542	£ 44		£
TOTAL COACHING RECEIPTS		£		£		£		£		£ 44		£

GOODS TRAFFIC	FORWARDED TONS	RECEIVED TONS	FORWARDED TONS	RECEIVED TONS	FORWARDED TONS	RECEIVED TONS	FORWARDED TONS	RECEIVED TONS	FORWARDED TONS	RECEIVED TONS	FORWARDED TONS	RECEIVED TONS
Coal and Coke												
Other Minerals (Classes 1 to 6)												
General Merchandise (Classes 7 to 21)												
Total Tonnage												

BRITISH RAILWAYS
WESTERN REGION

STATEMENT OF TRAFFIC DEALT WITH AT STATIONS 481A

STATION (Halt or Platform) **WATLINGTON.**

DISTRICT _____ Joint with _____ Region

SUPERVISED BY STATION MASTER AT _____

Names of other Stations, etc., Traffic and Receipts from which are included below
or Names of Stations, Halts, Platforms, supervised

YEAR	19	1960	19	19	19	19
Number of Staff Regularly Employed :—						
Clerical and Supervisory						
Wages						
TOTAL						

COACHING TRAFFIC	NUMBER	RECEIPTS	NUMBER	RECEIPTS	NUMBER	RECEIPTS	NUMBER	RECEIPTS	NUMBER	RECEIPTS	NUMBER	RECEIPTS
Passengers Booked by Rail, including Excess Fares Collected		£		£		£		£		£		£
Season Tickets		£		£		£		£		£		£
Platform Tickets		£		£		£		£		£		£
Seat Registration		£		£		£		£		£		£
Cab Rents		£		£		£		£		£		£
Car Parking		£		£		£		£		£		£
Lavatories		£		£		£		£		£		£
Other Receipts		£		£		£		£		£		£
Total Passenger and Various Receipts		£		£		£		£		£		£
Parcels & Misc. Forwarded		£	155	£ 106		£		£		£		£
Parcels & Misc. Received		£	5394	£		£		£		£		£
Total Parcels and Misc Traffic and Receipts		£	5549	£ 106		£		£		£		£
TOTAL COACHING RECEIPTS		£		£		£		£		£		£

GOODS TRAFFIC	FORWARDED TONS	RECEIVED TONS	FORWARDED TONS	RECEIVED TONS	FORWARDED TONS	RECEIVED TONS	FORWARDED TONS	RECEIVED TONS	FORWARDED TONS	RECEIVED TONS	FORWARDED TONS	RECEIVED TONS
Coal and Coke												
Other Minerals (Classes 1 to 6)												
General Merchandise (Classes 7 to 21)												
Total Tonnage												
Total Goods Tonnage Forwarded and Received	TONNAGE		TONNAGE		TONNAGE		TONNAGE		TONNAGE		TONNAGE	
Live Stock Forwarded and Received	Wagons		Wagons		Wagons		Wagons		Wagons		Wagons	
Other Coaching Traffic (Items not shown separately above)	NUMBER		NUMBER		NUMBER		NUMBER		NUMBER		NUMBER	
Forwarded Milk (Included in Parcels and Misc. Forwarded above)	Gallons		Gallons		Gallons		Gallons		Gallons		Gallons	
	Cans	Cases	Cans	Cases	Cans	Cases	Cans	Cases	Cans	Cases	Cans	Cases
	Tanks	£	Tanks	£	Tanks	£	Tank	£	Tanks	£	Tanks	£
Non-Railborne (Not Included above)	No.	£	No.	£	No.	£	No.	£	No.	£	No.	£
Other Goods Traffic (Items not shown above)	TONS	TONS	TONS	TONS	TONS	TONS	TONS	TONS	TONS	TONS	TONS	TONS
Loco, Coal and Free Hauled (Totals)	Loco.	F.H.	Loco.	F.H.	Loco.	F.H.	Loco.	F.H.	Loco.	F.H.	Loco.	F.H.
Total Other Tonnages (i.e., Domestic, Point to Point and Tolls)												
Non-Railborne												
Permitted Tonnage	FORWARDED	RECEIVED	FORWARDED	RECEIVED	FORWARDED	RECEIVED	FORWARDED	RECEIVED	FORWARDED	RECEIVED	FORWARDED	RECEIVED
Total Number of Invoices												
Total Number of Invoice Entries												

Two views of the derelict waiting room at Watlington station, showing (top) the little ticket window and (below) more of the interior and the doorway leading into the ladies waiting room. Both pictures were taken looking towards the platform, the doorway to the office being off the right of the top view and behind the photographer in the bottom view. It seems doubtful that any of Pocock's staff would have imagined their proudly maintained headquarters ending up like this. *J. E. Cussen*

Appendix 11 – A SELECTION OF TICKETS

Four types of rail motor car tickets. Although these are undated, the Bledlow Bridge and Lewknor Bridge examples are believed to date from around the period of the Great War.

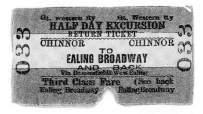

A selection of GWR tickets from the mid-1930s. The Oxford one probably dates from the 1920s.
Cty. John Strange

Appendix 12 — LIST OF STATION MASTERS

WATLINGTON STATION MASTERS
Robert Lett
    'Booking Porter'   October 1872 — June 1900
    'Station Inspector'   June — September 1900
Mr. Fay (or Fry?)   1900
Walter Colbourne   May 1900 — 1903
Ernest William Harry Sexton   October 1903 — May 1911
William Thomas Yeates   1911 — 1924
Reginald Henry Pocock   1924 — 1946
S. F. Jarvis   1946 — 1949
Post then combined with Chinnor.

ASTON ROWANT STATION MASTERS
Unknown   1872 — 1877
Martin Day
    'Booking Porter'   January 1877 — 1886?
Unknown   1886 — 1894
Ernest Henry James
    'Station Inspector'   February 1894 — April 1896
Walter King
    'Station Inspector'   April 1896 — February 1899
Rowland Henry Hillier   February 1899 — April 1900
Unknown   1900 — 1904
Frank Harvey Jacques   October 1904 — May 1907
Lawrence Forsey   May 1907 — January 1910
William Charles Williams   February 1910 — October 1913
George Thomas Eggleton   October 1913 — 1915
Francis Henry John Sexton   1915 — 1919
F. Boulter   1919 — ?
Reginald Henry Pocock   1922 — 1924
Post combined with Watlington.

CHINNOR STATION MASTERS
J. Reynolds
    'Booking Porter'   August 1872 — 1883?
Joseph Parker
    'Booking Porter'   June 1884 — August 1888
John Owen Lawrence
    'Booking Porter'   September 1888 — July 1890
William Kitson
    'Station Inspector'   July 1890 — September 1892
Daniel Foster
    'Station Inspector'   September 1892 — June 1893
Edwin Passmore
    'Station Inspector'   June 1893 — August 1897
Albert William Widdicombe
    'Station Inspector'   July 1897 — September 1900
    (regraded Station Master   November 1897)
William Pearce   July 1900 — August 1902
Alfred John May   August 1903 — February 1908
Wilfred George Humphrey   February 1908 — January 1911
Thomas Burden Chesterman   January — December 1911
Ernest Edward Wilkins   November 1911 — August 1912
Wilfred George Humphrey   August 1912 — September 1913
William Charles Williams   October 1913 — ?
Ernest Edward Hunt   There in 1919 — other years unclear.
Arthur George Harmsworth   1921 — 1933
Sydney Pratley   1933 — 1941
E. Davies   1941 — 1946
James Pearce   1946 — 1947
Eric Humphrey   1947 — c.1951
Mr. Barrett   ? mid 1950s
G. Williams   ? — 1956
(Ron Cox and Keith Lewis, both Relief Station Masters, covered for several years in the 1950s)

This picture of station master Buckland and his staff at Risborough c.1910 shows from left to right. *Back row —* Owen Gurney (signalman), Frank Rutland (foreman), Bill Hiscock (lampman), Fred White (signalman), Harry 'Buz' Rutland (P.Way), 'Pip' Turner (foreman), Unknown, S. Tubb (signalman), Unknown, Frank Stephens (shunter), ? Fred Eales, Bill Wells (shunter), Bill Swatton (? foreman). *Front row —* Bill Mead (parcel porter), Wally Harvey (goods porter), Unknown, Unknown, station master Buckland, Unknown, Unknown, Unknown, Jack Walker (signalman).

PRINCES RISBOROUGH STATION MASTERS
Christopher Frederick Hensley   August 1862
Evan Albert Leyshan   August 1862 — January 1863
Frederick Edwin Godwin
    'Booking Porter'   January — October 1863
Thomas J. Pritchard   October 1863 — December 1864
Unknown   1864/5
Alfred Gray   August 1865 — December 1866
William Paul   December 1866 — March 1868
James B. Seddon   April 1868 — January 1869
John Owen   January 1869 — ?
John Templeton Nicholl   January 1874 — October 1875
Walter Cottman   October 1875 — August 1876
Henry Newman   August 1876 — February 1878

Edward Allen   March — October 1878
Frederick Herbert Fraser   December 1878 — November 1879
Alexander Robinson   November 1879 — September 1881
Henry Arthur Yeo   September 1881 — June 1882
Henry William Mason   June 1882 — June 1885
Henry Mark Terry   May 1885 — May 1886
Henry Watkins   May 1886 — June 1888
James Page   July 1888 — November 1897
Frederick John Buckland   November 1897 — 1915
    (transferred to GW/GC 31.7.99)
Arthur Gozney   1915 — 1942
Samuel Rudd   1942 — 1946
Charles Day   1946 — 1960
John Ellwood   1960 — mid-1960s

Appendix 13 – GRADIENT PROFILE

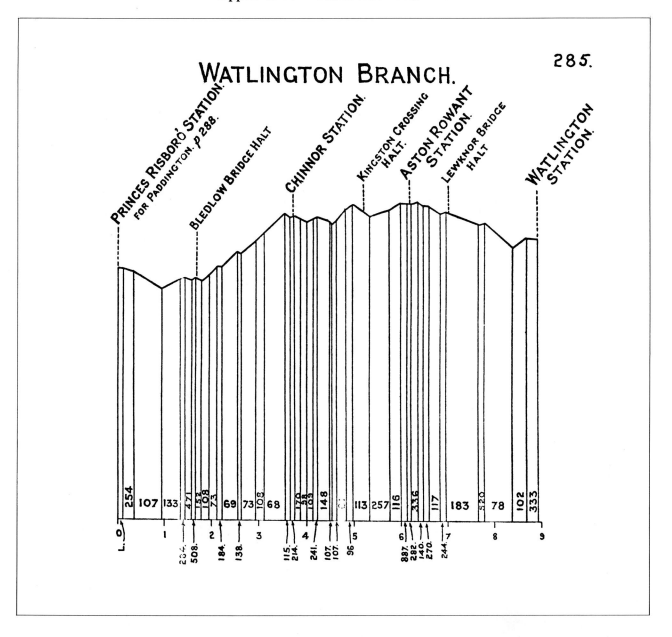

Appendix 14 – WATLINGTON BRANCH PERMANENT WAY STAFF

Details of the Watlington branch permanent way staff are sparse and often sketchy, but it would appear that at least since the First World War there were separate gangs at Watlington and Chinnor. The Watlington gang (officially based at Aston Rowant) looked after the line from the terminus to the Kingston Crossing down distant, and the Chinnor gang were responsible for the rest of the line from there to Risborough. There were permanent way huts at Watlington, Lewknor, Aston Rowant, Kingston, Chinnor and Bledlow Bridge.

The Chinnor-based gangers were H. Wagerfield 1913, W. J. Drummond 1914-17, and possibly Fred Price from 1917 to the 1930s. The 1920s picture on page 114 of Volume 2, shows Fred Price with Fred Seymour, who is believed to have been Chinnor sub-ganger, Bob Johnson, and Reg Gibbons. The Watlington staff group for 1924 on page 72 shows Albert Brown, 'Darkie' Sowden and Tommy Johnson who were presumably members of the Watlington gang. T. G. (Tommy) Johnson, who was born in Wheatley in 1885, is believed to have been at Watlington since the Great War and remained in the branch PW Department until his retirement about 1950. Jim Lambourn, who lived at Kingston Crossing, is said to have been the Watlington ganger from about 1918-27, but this has not been confirmed.

Around the time Charlie Adby joined the Watlington gang in 1929, the Watlington ganger, Ike Green, died, his place apparently being taken by Fred Seymour, who transferred from Chinnor to take charge at Aston Rowant. The c.1930 picture on page 59 of Volume 2 shows Walter Hopkins, Paddy Darmody, Tommy Johnson, his brother Bob Johnson, Charlie Adby and Chinnor ganger Fred Price, whilst official records for 1930 mention F. Gibbs in the Aston Rowant gang.

Charlie Adby recalled that as part of the 1930s economies, he was laid off in 1932 and remained out of work until re-employed on the branch in 1934. By this time, the two gangs had been amalgamated and were based at Chinnor (Gang 132). Walter Hopkins is said to have been ganger at this time yet he is described as patrolman when he retired in 1946, with Tommy Johnson becoming sub-ganger in 1935.

Walter's daughter Maude remembers him starting each day at Chinnor where the gang assembled at 7.0 a.m. and enjoyed a good breakfast in the hut before gathering up their tools and starting out on their day's work.

Walter usually caught the first train down to Watlington and walked back along the track, carrying out his inspection and replacing any keys that had dropped out. Anything that required attention was noted and assigned to the gang when he got back to Chinnor. Afterwards he would either walk out to Risborough or, depending on the time, catch a train there and walk back.

Aubrey Woodward's employment in the PW Department for three months in 1948 provides a clear picture of a specific time, with the ganger and four men based at Watlington and two at Chinnor working from 7.0 a.m. until 4.0 or 5.0 p.m. on weekdays and 7.0 a.m. to midday on Saturdays.

By this time, the ganger was Bill Kendall, who travelled in from Lewknor to Watlington

The Chinnor PW hut seen from the branch train in the mid 1950s. *A. Attewell*

The post-1948 replacement PW hut at Watlington. Its predecessor features in Volume 2 on pages 29 and 32. *C. M. Strevens*

on a motorbike which he left in the yard. Tommy Johnson was the patrolman and the three lengthmen were Tommy Carter, Tommy Appleby and Aubrey Woodward, each of whom lived in Watlington. The sub-ganger, E. G. Hopkins (Walter's son), often referred to as 'Chip' or 'Tom', was based at Chinnor along with R. W. Gibbons (known as both 'Reg' and 'Cecil'), who guard Don Gray recalls as a "typical cockney with a very dry sense of humour". Both men lived at Chinnor.

Of the daily routine, Aubrey recalls "We didn't sign on but usually met at the cabin, from where we worked to the orders of Bill Kendall. Tommy Johnson checked the length as far as Chinnor and reported back to Bill. We had a pump trolley but I don't remember it being used much . . . I took in sandwiches and cold tea."

Other members of the Chinnor PW gang and who may have served only for a short time included D. J. Morgan (1941), William North (1946/47) and Walter Crowby who is believed

to have been there around 1949-50. Tom Hopkins died in 1951. There were probably many others but, perhaps less predictably, a report of a minor accident on 28th January 1948 records that a Polish refugee, Pilzeck Roman, from St. John's camp, High Wycombe, had been employed as a 'relayer' for about two months and was working on a 7.15 a.m. to 4.45 p.m. duty.

Arrangements varied over the years and fireman Tony Benham recalls that in the late 1940s, patrolman Tommy Johnson walked half the line on one day, i.e. Watlington to Chinnor, and travelled back on the 1.55 Risborough and covered the rest of the line the next day by travelling out to Risborough on the 8.42, walking back to Chinnor, then catching the 1.55 Risborough back to Watlington.

Reg Gibbons and Bill Kendall remained on the branch, Reg becoming patrolman at Chinnor in 1955 and ganger in 1962 when Bill Kendall was appointed PW inspector/timekeeper at Chinnor.

ACKNOWLEDGEMENTS

Compiling a book of this nature provides an excuse to contact both former staff and older inhabitants of Watlington and the surrounding villages, to find out all about the railway. We are pleased to say that a fluctuating succession of interviews over many years, frequently with the warmest reception, has resulted in some lovely friendships and what has at times seemed like unlimited access to the past.

One of my earliest approaches was to driver Harry Humphreys who, wearing his railway overalls, was working in the garden of his home in Spring Lane when I called some time around 1972. He had retired in 1947 and sadly, by the time I met him, he was a widower. He listened to the request of what probably seemed an anxious young man, then took me around the side of the house and in through the back door. As I crossed the threshold I entered another world — a timelock. The interior probably differed little from how it had been in the 1930s and quite unspoiled by any tacky 'improvements'. As I walked through the scullery, I passed a small table covered with an old oilcloth and noticed a stove enamel dish with the remains of a home-made steak and kidney pie left over from lunch. Miss Nelms, the daughter of guard Jimmy Nelms had made it for him. She kept an eye on him, Harry quietly commenting "She's a good sort". As we sat in the living room, the steady tick of the clock seemed to make me aware of the stillness. He instantly won my respect and while I poured out no end of questions about the routines and operation of the Watlington branch, he showed patience and kindness. I was thrilled to be able to find out something of the life, and found myself puzzling why I could not find any books or magazine articles which conveyed the everyday things that I was now uncovering.

Towards the end of the interview, I racked my brains, desperately trying to think of all the things I'd forgotten to ask and, of course, I've kicked myself ever since over the host of things I'd like to have known for this account. Nevertheless, it was a valuable and treasured experience.

Unfortunately, Harry died before my first book, *Great Western Branch Line Termini* was published in 1977, but I did manage to present a copy to driver George Nicholson who lived across the road from Harry and had also been very helpful. When I handed him the book, he glanced through the pictures of Watlington station and was so moved that tears literally poured down his face. It was an unforgettable moment which even now brings a huge lump to my throat. The line meant so much to him.

I have done so many more interviews since that time and learned so much more, particularly since enlisting the help of my co-author Chris Turner. It's not easy tracking people down so many years after the line closed and there were many blind alleys. However, before we try and list the names of all those who have helped, I would like to record my own special thanks to the late Tony Smith, my woodwork teacher, who in 1965 brought into school some pictures he had taken of the derelict station at Watlington. These rekindled memories of my earlier encounter with the line while helping out with my Uncle Bill's Sunday paper round which began at Risborough station and ended in Chinnor. Tony was more than instrumental in making me realize what I could achieve and indirectly giving me the confidence to tackle all sorts of things which I used to think only other people could do.

Joe Cussen also became a pen friend around this time and generously guided me through early sources of information and pictures which he'd secured for his own interest. Thank you, Joe. I hope you think these volumes repay your kindness to a young enthusiast all those years ago. Waiting to see what the postman would bring could be very exciting then.

Chris and I would both like to record our thanks to the following: Charlie Adby, Mrs. Ahern, Dr. I. C. Allen, A. Attewell, Robin Ball, Bill Bass, Mrs. M. Bass, Millie Batten, Charles Bayes, Gerry Beale, Doris Beech, Tony and Janet Benham for warm welcomes and kind hospitality through numerous visits, Peter Billson for invaluable help with the Chinnor Cement Works history in Vol. 2, Sheila Bingham, Bob and Sylvia Bird, Bryan Bowler, Colin Bowler, Grace Bracey, Len Breadmore, Ted Buckle, R. J. Buckley, Peter Burton, W. Burton for use of the Mowat photographs, Mrs. M. L. Bush, Mary Cadle, Ralph Cann, W. A. Camwell, Gerry Carpenter, R. S. Carpenter, Rev. Ralph Cartmill, R. M. and H. C. Casserley, Victor Chamberlain, Joe Christie, Gwen Clarke for so much help and information about her father, Jim Clarke, Derek Clayton, Col. Clerke-Brown, Wally Coles, Connie and Wally Collins, 'Bacca' Collins, Tony Cooke, Brian Copcutt, John Copsey for so much help with the main line traffic through Princes Risborough, Mrs. Cory, Ian Coulson, Mrs. D. Crickmer, F. K. Davies, Colin Dawson, M. E. J. Dean, N. De Courtais, Daniel Digweed, Jim Digweed for explaining all about Chinnor cement but in particular the old Chinnor lime works, lime burning process, etc., Ian and James Donaldson, David East for help with the history of Timothy East Ltd (in Vol. 2) and other coal merchants, Howard East, Roye England, M. J. Esau, Francis Evitts, John Faulkner, Mike Fenton for so willingly trying to find out more about the elusive Bluebell Specials, Ernie Forte, P. J. Garland, Ron Gilbey, R. E. Gilbert, Eddie Glidden, Max Goodearl, Ronald Goodearl, Jan Gooders, Leslie Graham, Ron Grantham, Don Gray, Doug Green, Bernard Griffiths, Audrey Griffiths, Sylvia Guntripp, Barbara Hall, Betty Hall, Tom Harding, Hugh Harman for his memories and wonderful photos of Risborough, Eric Harmsworth, Gerald Harris, Brian Hart for generously giving up his own time at postcard fairs to help find Watlington views, Bill Hawthorn, Joan Heyward, Joe Hill, Gerald Hoar, Doreen Hobbs, Mr. & Mrs. F. Holmes, Arthur Hopkins, Cyril Hopkins, Katherine Hopkins, Arthur House, Henry House, Ben Howell, George Howlett, Mabel Howlett, Len Howse, Jill Hudson for the loan of photos from Lewknor School, Eric Humphrey, Geoffrey Hyde, Mr. Ives, Alan A. Jackson, Laurie Johnson, Joan Jones, J. E Kite, Sally Kirk, Brian Lacey, Lucy Lacey, Harvey Lambourne, David Leggett, Lens of Sutton, Basil Lewis, Margaret Lockwood, Mrs. D. Mackie, Trevor Mackie, David Madley, John Mann, Barbara Maydom, Brian Maynard, Connie McCulla, Ken McQueen, Mrs. F. Mead, J. H. Meredith, George Messenger, Joan Miller, Roy Miller, Wally Mitchell, Crystal Mitchum, Brian Morgan, J. Scott Morgan, Mrs. W. Morris, Eric Mountford, Joe Nicholson, L. Nicholson, Henry Nixey, Olive Nixey, Peter Norman, Percy Palmer, Mark Pardoe, Hon. J. Parker, Brian Paxton, Mrs. J. Pearce, Percy Peyman, Dave Pinfold, Billy Pitkin, Mrs. A. E. Plumridge, Bernard Pocock, Cecil Pocock, Gerald Pratley, Clifford Price, Brian Pugh, Mary Read, Bryan Rich, R. C. Riley, Daphne Roadnight, Peggy Rockall, E. S. Russell, Mrs. G. Russell, J. H. Russell, J. F. Russell-Smith, Jack Rutland, Mrs. Rust, Cyril and Jean Saunders, Frank Saunders, Tom Saunders, Ken and 'Girlie' Saw, Peter Schwier, Max Seymour, Arthur Sherwood, Fred Shirley, Sid Shirley, Phyllis Shorter, Mrs. C. M. Siarey, R. H. G. Simpson, Gerald Smith, Mrs. H. E. Smith, Jessie Smith, Les Smith, Tom Snow, 'Bimbo' Spicer, Mrs. M. R. Stanmore, Wilf Stevens, John Strange, Norman Stratford, Alan Strathdee, C. Strevens, Vic Stroud, Molly Suckling, Ernie Tappin, Janet and Les Tappin, Eileen Taylor, Mr. and Mrs. J. Thompson, Ted Thompson, Jim Tidmarsh, Joyce Tidmarsh, Frank Tredwell, T. Tunnicliffe, Vera Tunnicliffe, Cyril Tutty, James Venn for reading the results of our efforts with such enthusiasm, Daisy Walker, David Walker, Pat Walker, Stewart Wallace, Beatrice Wallen, Mervyn Wallen, John Walton, Mrs. Watts, Michael Webb, Peter Webber, John Whitehead, Ron Williams, Doris Wilson, Arthur Witcher, Audrey and Henry Witney, Aubrey Woodward, Ron Woolford, Jack Wright, Nick Wright for reading the text and coming up with some very useful suggestions, Richard Wright, M. F. Yarwood, and Bob Young.

We would also like to thank the following institutions for their co-operation: Hunting Aerofilms; Public Record Office, Kew, House of Lords Record Office; British Library; British Railways; the Railway Club; Westgate Library, Oxford; Bodleian Library, Oxford; Oxford County Record Office; National Monuments Record, and the Guildhall Library.

Finally, but by no means least, we should like to thank June Judge for typing everything up from a frequently illegible manuscript and for putting up with all the subsequent changes in our attempts to get things right.

If you have enjoyed this book you may be interested in Volume Two which presents a detailed portrait of each of the stations and halts along the line, including staff, daily routines and details of traffic and traders.